THE ISLAND
BROKEN IN
TWO HALVES

HERMENEUTICS: STUDIES IN THE HISTORY OF RELIGIONS

Kees W. Bolle, Editor

Advisory Board

Jean Bottéro, Jaan Puhvel,
William R. Schoedel, Eric J. Sharpe,
Margaret Washington, Guy R. Welbon

RICHARD G. MARKS

The Image of Bar Kokhba in
Traditional Jewish Literature:
False Messiah and National Hero

JOANNE PUNZO WAGHORNE

The Raja's Magic Clothes:
Re-visioning Kingship and Divinity
in England's India

DEVIN DEWEESE

Islamization and Native Religion
in the Golden Horde: Baba Tükles
and Conversion to Islam in
Historical and Epic Tradition

GREGORY D. ALLES

The *Iliad*, the *Rāmāyana*, and the
Work of Religion: Failed Persuasion
and Religious Mystification

ARVIND SHARMA

The Philosophy of Religion and
Advaita Vedānta: A Comparative Study
in Religion and Reason

GREGORY SHAW

Theurgy and the Soul:
The Neoplatonism of Iamblichus

JESS BYRON HOLLENBACK

Mysticism: Experience, Response,
and Empowerment

CHARLES D. ORZECH

Politics and Transcendent Wisdom:
The *Scripture for Humane Kings*
in the Creation of Chinese Buddhism

JEAN E. ROSENFELD

The Island Broken in Two Halves:
Land and Renewal Movements
among the Maori of New Zealand

Jean E. Rosenfeld

THE ISLAND
BROKEN IN
TWO HALVES

Land and Renewal Movements
Among the Maori of New Zealand

The Pennsylvania State University Press
University Park, Pennsylvania

Library of Congress Cataloging-in-Publication Data

Rosenfeld, Jean Elizabeth, 1940–
    The island broken in two halves : land and
renewal movements among the Māori of New Zealand
/ Jean E. Rosenfeld.
        p.   cm. — (Hermeneutics, studies in the
    history of religions (University Park, Pa.)
    Includes bibliographical references and index.
    ISBN 0-271-01852-6
    1. Maori (New Zealand people)—Religion.
    2. Maori (New Zealand people)—Land tenure.
    3. Maori (New Zealand people)—Government
    relations.   4. Nativistic movements—New
    Zealand.   5. Millennialism—New Zealand.
    I. Title.   II. Series.
        BL2615 .R67 1999
        299′.92442093—dc21   98-023951
                                               CIP

It is the policy of The Pennsylvania State University
Press to use acid-free paper for the first printing of all
clothbound books. Publications on uncoated stock
satisfy the minimum requirements of American National
Standard for Information Sciences—Permanence of
Paper for Printed Library Materials,
ANSI Z39.48-1992.

CONTENTS

To my parents,
Maxwell and Bernice Risvold

ACKNOWLEDGMENTS

The writing of the history of religions may be the most controversial task one can undertake. Religion is a matter of ultimate concern. It asserts a claim to a truth that transcends all other forms of knowledge. The academic pursuit of historiography is, after all, the callow child of a venerable art, the oral recitation of communal myth.

Well before I began this book, the study of Ringatu had occasioned much conflict. I was advised to step carefully through the minefield of Maori prophet movements. Thus, I was not surprised when my Fulbright travel grant was not approved in New Zealand and my nomination to the University of Auckland by the University of California was denied. However, what all this stir demonstrated was that I was on the right track in hypothesizing that the King Movement, Pai Marire, and Ringatu were intrinsically and primarily religious phenomena.

A grant from my parents made research in New Zealand possible. Upon our arrival my husband and I were graciously welcomed by Brian Davis of the University of Auckland's student exchange program and his lovely wife, Ann. I am deeply indebted to Ranginui and Deirdre Walker for their spontaneous hospitality and valuable orientation to Maori ideas and customs.

Without the guidance and inspiration I received from Peter Webster's work this book would not have been possible. It was his fine study of Rua Kenana that whetted my appetite for understanding modern new religious movements. Peter and Jane Webster welcomed us most warmly at their home. Nancy Pollack gave us her indispensable support at Victoria University and other Wellington libraries.

The Curator of Art Collections at Te Whare Taonga o Waikato, Linda Tylor, invited me to learn from those who were working on the Rua exhibit. Librarian Gloria Edward and Professor Wharehuia Milroy of Waikato University helped me understand how to treat sensitive matters in researching and writing about Ringatu.

David Retter of the Alexander Turnbull Library assisted my study of

Te Kooti's Chatham Islands notebook, and I was able to peruse Te Ua's Gospel with the help of Helen Renwick of Auckland's Public Library. The staff of the University of Auckland Library and the National Archives of New Zealand made research in special collections efficient and productive.

Two schoolteachers whom we met, Tungia Kaihau of Kohanga Reo in Otaki and Genevieve McManus of Te Whaiti, instilled in me a better grasp of *mana* and *tapu* as they were and are experienced. Last, but not least, our friends David and Sue Lane and Jack and Joan Skurr provided us with respite and a warm hearth during a rainy winter.

The indispensable mentorship of Kees W. Bolle prepared me for this research with his disciplined and informed approach to the conundrum of religion past and present. He taught me to listen carefully to the voices to religious texts. I am deeply grateful to my teacher, S. Scott Bartchy, for his unwavering support and exceptional understanding of Christianity.

To Birger Pearson, the late Robert Benson, and William Worger, I am humbly indebted for their patient and thoughtful readings of this manuscript in its early, very rough stages. I owe G. W. Trompf, F. Allan Hanson, and Jorunn Buckley my sincere thanks for providing the critical suggestions that guided my work of revision. Many thanks also to my shepherd, Philip Winsor, and to Andrew Lewis and Cherene Holland, for their deft touch in matters editorial.

My husband, Howard, journeyed to the "end of the earth" to support and assist my work. After years of living with this engrossing project, I believe we can truly appreciate the plaintive and triumphal words of Paora of Otaki, "New Zealand is ours, I love it."

GLOSSARY

Macrons are indicated above vowels in Maori words only in the glossary but not in the text.

ahi-kā-roa	to keep the fires burning, ancestral claim to land
anahera	angel
ariki	chief
aroha	love, charity
atua	god
aukati	line which one may not pass
autaia	troublemaker
hahunga	ritual reinterment of the bones of the dead
haka	ritual dance
hākari	great feast
hapū	"subtribe," section of a large tribe
hau	wind, breath, spirit
Hawaiki	mythical homeland, destination of the dead
heke	migration
hine	woman, girl
Hinenuitepō	Great Woman of the Night, goddess of the underworld
hoko whenua	land sellers
hui	ritual of meeting
hūrai	Jew
Iharaira	Israelite
inoi	prayer (Ringatū)
iwi	tribe, people, bone
kāinga	village, settlement
kaitiaki	guardian
kai whakawā	magistrate
karakia	prayer, incantation, ritual
kenana	Canaan
kīngitanga	kingship
kokiro	set free from *tapu*
kōrero	dialogue at the hui, conversation
kōrero whenua	peace making
kotahitanga	unity, oneness
kūmara	sweet potato
kūpapa	Maori loyalist
kupu	prophecy

kupu whakaari	prediction or oracle
kura	sacred feathers, sacred knowledge, angel(s)
mana	efficacious power, authority
mana o te whenua	power over the land
mana motuhake	sovereignty
māngai	mouthpiece of the god
māoritanga	Maori-ness
marae	plaza in front of the meeting house
matakite	foresight, visionary, seer
mate māori	Maori sickness, a punishment for not observing *tapu*
mauri	life force
mere	war club
mīhaia	messiah
moko	tattoo
motu	island
ngā	the (plural)
ngā mōrehu	the remnant, the survivors, the chosen ones
niu	a Pai Marire sacred post, sacred stick
noa	the female complement of *tapu*, not *tapu*
Nuku Tawhiti	the mythical First State, earth personified
orangitanga	salvation
pā	fortified village
paepae	horizon, line between *te ao mārama* and *te pō*
pākehā	European, white person, stranger
Papatuanuku	Earth Mother, Primal Mother
pōrewarewa	stupefied
poti (pooti)	Pai Marire ritual, boat
pōtiki	youngest child
poropiti	prophet
pou	pole, stick, pillar
poutikanga	head of the Ringatu church
pupuri whenua	land holders, those who hold fast to the land
rā	day, holy day
rangatira	chief
rangatiratanga	chiefly authority
Ranginui	Sky Father, primal Father
raupatu	land confiscation, conquer
riri	anger
rohe pōtae	demarcated tribal territory
rūnanga	council, assembly
tangata	man
tāngata whenua	the people of the land
taonga	treasure, treasured possessions
Tāne	creator of the human realm
tapu	prohibited, the male complement of *noa*, demarcation between two cosmic realms
taua muru	raiding party, plunder party
te ao hou	the new world, the time after the coming of the Europeans

te ao mārama	the world of light, the realm inhabited by human beings
te ao tawhito	the old world, the time before the coming of the Europeans
te ika a Maui	"the great fish of Maui," the North Island
te maungarongo	the long abiding peace, everlasting peace
te maunga	the mountain
te moana	the sea
te pō	sacred realm of night, death, and the underworld; darkness; night
te rangi	sky, realm of sky deities and multiple heavens
te riri pākehā	"the white man's anger," i.e., the Land Wars
te ture	"Torah," biblical law; civil British law
te whakapono	religion, Christianity
tino rangatiratanga	full chieftainship (Treaty of Waitangi)
tipuna (var. *tupuna*)	ancestor
tiu	Jew
tohi	rite to dedicate a child or prepare one for a dangerous undertaking
tohu	sign
tohunga	expert (old); prophet, healer (new)
tohunga ariki	expert in sacred matters
tū, Tū	stand upright, warrior god
tūāhu	sacred precinct
tūrangawaewae	a place to stand
tūwareware	forsaken, forgetful of God
urua	seized by the god, trance
utu	redress an imbalance, avenge an insult
wāhi tapu	sacred place, burial place
waiata	song
wairua tapu	the Holy Spirit, name of the Holy Spirit movement
Whaitiri	goddess who guards *tapu* boundaries
whaikōrero	make a formal speech
whakakotahitanga	making unity, uniting
whakanoa	neutralize *tapu*, make *noa*
whakapapa	genealogy, myth-history
whānau	"extended family"
whare puni, *whare whakairo*	meeting house
whare wānanga	school of learning
whatu	sacred stone
whenua	land, placenta

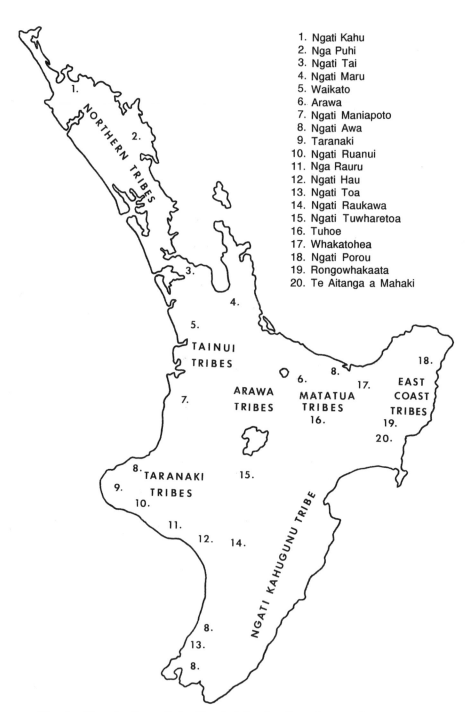

1. Ngati Kahu
2. Nga Puhi
3. Ngati Tai
4. Ngati Maru
5. Waikato
6. Arawa
7. Ngati Maniapoto
8. Ngati Awa
9. Taranaki
10. Ngati Ruanui
11. Nga Rauru
12. Ngati Hau
13. Ngati Toa
14. Ngati Raukawa
15. Ngati Tuwharetoa
16. Tuhoe
17. Whakatohea
18. Ngati Porou
19. Rongowhakaata
20. Te Aitanga a Mahaki

Fig. 1 Maori tribes of the North Island referred to in the text

INTRODUCTION:
RENEWAL MOVEMENTS

*A part of space . . . is not a "part" at all
but a place, and the place becomes a
"position" when man occupies it and
stands on it. . . . Sacred space may . . . be
defined as that locality that becomes a
position by the effects of power repeating
themselves there, or being repeated by man.*

Gerardus van der Leeuw

Revitalization movements have arisen in the wake of Christian evangelism wherever contact between Europeans and non-Western peoples has taken place. These movements are religious, political, and social; and they occur when a people has been dislocated from its position in its cosmos.[1] In the nineteenth century a series of Maori prophets initiated new religious movements to safeguard their land and to heal "a people, standing naked in the Island in two halves."[2]

Aotearoa, "land of the long white cloud," is the Maori name for New Zealand. The people of the island speak of *turangawaewae*, "a place to stand," in the sense that van der Leeuw speaks of sacred space or position. The Maori word for land, *whenua*, also means "placenta." The

---

1. Throughout this book, I employ the word "people(s)" in the sense of *ethnos* (*oi*), from which our term "ethnic" is derived.

2. From Te Ua Haumene's gospel, *Te Ua Rongopai*. Cf. W. L. Williams's translation, "for the people who are stripped naked, and for the islands reduced by half," in *East Coast Historical Records*, p. 37.

relationship between a people and its land is binding like that of a fetus to its mother. According to myth, in the beginning the god Tane separated Father Sky from Mother Earth, who were locked in a primal embrace, by standing on his head and pushing them apart with his legs. This maneuver created *te ao marama*, the "world of light," for human habitation.

A tribe's place to stand is on its plaza (*marae*) in front of the meeting house. There, the people of the land welcome visitors and engage in *whaikorero*, "speech-making," in order to resolve issues of vital importance. It is recognized that those who are qualified to speak for their people possess *mana*, the numinous gift that ensures the success of their endeavors on behalf of their community. Three formal features of religion are sacred place, sacred word, and sacred act. In the central ritual of meeting, the *hui*, these three features are symbolically present. For example, the act of peacemaking is called *korero whenua*, an expression that unites "speech" with "land" (place) in the ultimate act of ending conflict. When the British arrived, they knew nothing of sacred place, sacred word, or sacred act in Maori tradition, but erroneously assumed that they were barbaric and in need of the Christian gospel.

As it happened, *whaikorero* and the *mana* of the chiefs did not suffice to ward off the threat to the Maori world posed by European settlers, who introduced muskets, new diseases, Christianity, and commercialism to an island people long isolated from the rest of the world. Most significantly, the gods of the *tangata whenua* ("people of the land") were not able to thwart the sustained purpose of the invaders to alienate the Maori from the land—that greatest of treasures without which the people could not survive.

PERSPECTIVES ON RELIGION

To the Maori the land, the community, and the ancestors are inextricably interwoven. Earth and sky, female and male, night and day, *noa* and *tapu*, have been complementary aspects of the world since the time of Creation. As complements, they are inseparable. The *mauri*, the "life force" of the community, derives from the power of special stones, places, words, and rituals. In the nineteenth century when the space in which these were located or expressed was removed from the community through the alien economic transaction of landselling, the life force of the people waned. From 1850 until the early 1900s the Maori expected to become extinct. Neither printed currency, nor the plow, nor sheep, nor pigs, nor potatoes—all of which they eagerly adopted from the Pakeha,[3] could save them from what seemed inevitable.

As it gradually became apparent that the Europeans intended to separate the people permanently from their land, Maori protest against colonialism took the form of setting boundaries beyond which foreigners were not permitted to pass. This was an intrinsically religious act. Boundaries were safeguarded by *tapu*, a prohibition against touching that which possesses *mana*. Anyone who crossed a *tapu* barrier was liable to a lethal sickness. Maori prophets rose up to call upon god(s) to recreate their world by reestablishing the boundaries between the human and the sacred realms, and between the tribe and the stranger.[4]

Pakeha scholars have produced excellent studies of the imperial conquest of New Zealand and its struggle to become a nation-state. Maori experts have composed oral histories of the colonial period. Ranginui Walker, Buddy Mikaere, and Hugh Kawaru have published significant work on Maori history, culture, religion, and law. In addition, a new generation of Maori scholars is reclaiming the contested ground of indigenous knowledge and history, and their contributions to the chronicle of Maori-Pakeha relations is expected to revise existing scholarship significantly.

Social scientists have tended to fix upon the social, economic, political, and psychological expressions, causes, and consequences of historic contact between Europeans and aboriginal peoples—to the exclusion of religious factors.[5] Pronounced secular bias is peculiar to the intellectual tradition of the modern West, blinding many to the irreducible role of religion in history. As a result, very few studies of the response of the Maori to British settlement have given priority to the formal features of religion, such as myth, rite, and sacred space. Too often, religion is discounted or subsumed under the psychological rubric of aberrant data, because it is not regarded as amenable to analysis. Prophets and visions, hermeneutical constructions, miracles, in-

---

3. "Pakeha" is a term for non-Maori strangers, in particular, Europeans. See Herbert Meade, *A Ride through the Disturbed Districts of New Zealand*, p. 131.

4. Although I use the word "tribe," it would be more correct to speak of *whanau* (extended family), *hapu* (subtribe), or *iwi* (tribe). For the readers' ease of understanding, I use the general term "tribe" to refer to a group that identifies itself as a social unit upon a specific territory.

5. Cf. Peter Webster's review of theory in *Rua and the Maori Millennium*, pp. 43–68; Theda Perdue, "Native American Revitalization Movements in the Early Nineteenth Century," in Jock Phillips, ed., *New Worlds? The Comparative History of New Zealand and the U.S.*; and David Aberle, "A Note on Relative Deprivation Theory as Applied to Millenarian and Other Cult Movements."

dwelling powers, invocations, syncretism, ultimate concerns, and non-rational symbols of transcendent, inbreaking, divine forces are not easily acknowledged or understood. And that which does not easily fit our dominant methods of analysis tends to be discounted as epiphenomenal.

In the West we can use the word "myth" to denote "falsehood." In psychology, myth is sometimes associated with delusional behavior, and religion has been confused with an undifferentiated "oceanic" feeling. However, many non-Western peoples still understand myth as a claim to truth, not the provisional truth of science or academic discourse, but the foundational truth of the social, material, and mysterious cosmos they inhabit.[6] Even secularized states seem to need a national myth as a pole star to locate their "position" in the universe, else the sight of a nation's flag would not bring tears to the eyes of its citizens. Paradoxically, as Westerners have moved away from the sacred at home, they have spread their biblical myths to other nations throughout the world. Wherever the Bible has accompanied colonization, aboriginal peoples have selected some of its archetypes and paradigms to heal the potentially mortal consequences of the invaders' trespass.

NEW SYMBOLIC CREATIONS

The dislocation of the Maori from their position on the land fueled new formations of symbol, myth, and ritual in the guise of "heresy cults,"[7] which attempted to renew the mythical "world of light" at a time when population decline and alienation from the land threatened the life force of the people. Each new formation sought to regain power over *te whenua*, "the land"—the paramount sacred symbol of Maori religion. By safeguarding the land, the Maori prophets created a place where the *iwi* could live according to divinely sanctioned mandates.

This study is limited to three sequential and related renewal movements—the King Movement, Pai Marire, and Ringatu[8]—that profoundly influenced the history of New Zealand from the time of its transition to "responsible rule" (self-governance) in the 1850s until the

6. For an extended discussion, see Mircea Eliade, *Myth and Reality* (New York: Harper & Row, 1966).

7. The term is employed by Judith Binney in her essay, "Christianity and the Maoris to 1840, A Comment," pp. 143–65.

8. I regard Rua Kenana's Wairua Tapu movement as a branch of Ringatu.

eve of World War I. These three movements offered new means of redemption to redress the grievances of the North Island tribes against missionaries and settlers, but few Pakeha scholars have appreciated their religious foundations.[9]

COMPARATIVE VIEWS

Myths that describe the creation of the world are found among all peoples; myths that foretell the destruction and re-creation of the world are likewise widespread. Religions commonly mark the New Year with rites that renew the cosmos. Because the nations who invaded and settled "new" continents and islands during the last five hundred years were European and Christian, the biblical renewal myths of paradise gained and lost and regained again at the end of historical time were often blended with indigenous myths of return.[10] This syncretism marries two conceptualizations of time: the Western model of time as linear and of events happening only once, and the "archaic" conceptualization of time as cyclical and of ancestors returning to heal and renew the cosmos.[11] Both biblical and non-Western myths speak of the creation and of the re-creation of the world by the god(s). Maori prophets discerned correspondences between, for example, Jesus as the Word of God in the Gospel of John and Revelation and the demiurges Tane and Maui, or between the Holy Spirit or Gabriel and Rupe,[12] but their new religious creations were repudiated by orthodox Christians. In the preface to his book, *Polynesian Mythology*, ethnologist-statesman George Grey could not properly appreciate Maori religion, much less the King Movement that sprang up under his eyes:

> That their [the Maori] traditions are puerile is true; that the religious faith of the races who trust in them is absurd is a melancholy fact; but all my experience leads me to believe that the Saxon, Celtic, and Scandinavian systems of mythology, could we

9. Paul Clark, Bronwyn Elsmore, Evelyn Stokes, Judith Binney, and Peter Webster are notable exceptions.

10. See Mircea Eliade, *The Myth of the Eternal Return, or Cosmos and History*.

11. Ibid. Eliade used the word "archaic" to describe time and ontology in the nonbiblical religions.

12. Jesus as the preexistent *logos* was present at Creation, and Jesus as the "new Adam" signifies a new creation of the world; Tane created the world by his heroic act; Maui fished the North Island out of the sea and divided time into night and day; Rupe ascended to the heavens which Tane pierced and is sometimes identified with Tane. Like Rupe, the Holy Spirit in the form of a dove and Gabriel as messenger, ascend to and descend from heaven.

have become intimately acquainted with them, would be found in no respects to surpass that one which the European reader may now thoroughly understand. I believe that the ignorance which has prevailed regarding the mythological systems of barbarous or semi-barbarous races has too generally led to their being considered far grander and more reasonable than they really were.

Governor Grey's assessment represents the most enlightened view of indigenous religions in the nineteenth century held by educated Britons. While erudite Victorians overlooked the power of biblical paradigms and archetypes to inspire new religious movements, untutored Maori charismatics constructed an alternative hermeneutics to bridge the abyss between the intact world of the past and the broken one of the present. Missionaries demonized any Maori rite or belief that departed from orthodox liturgies and doctrines. There were, of course, some rare exceptions, such as Thomas Kendall and the Reverend Thomas Grace, whose curiosity and tolerance subjected them to accusations from their fellows of immorality or disloyalty.

Most peoples interweave what Westerners compartmentalize as the sacred or the profane. A word, a place, or an act may be numinous all or part of the time. Among the Maori, even the latrine has religious significance.[13] Unless scholars engage in an impartial and comparative study of religions, the achievements of Maori renewal movements will remain only partially understood. Since religion concerns ultimate matters of life and death and mystery and freedom, any reluctance to examine religious phenomena at face value "as they appear" will impede efforts to account for the impact of colonization and Christianization on the people of the land.

IDENTIFICATION OF THE MAORI AS JEWS

A significant feature of the renewal movements was their adoption of Israelite ancestors and Jewish paradigms. Thomas Kendall wrote about the similarities between biblical and Maori myths in 1824. Maori prophets identified their people as *Iharaira, hurai,* and *tiu,* "Israelites"

---

13. Mircea Eliade, ed., *Encyclopedia of Religion,* "Sacred Space," p. 526; J. Prytz Johansen, "Studies in Maori Rites and Myths"; F. Allan Hanson and Louise Hanson, *Counterpoint in Maori Culture,* pp. 77–86.

and "Jews."[14] They were keenly aware of the parallel positions of Jews in Greco-Roman Palestine and the *iwi* in British-dominated Aotearoa. The story of the Exodus from Egypt to Canaan resonated with their oral chronicles of migration and inspired their *heke* to reclaim sacred sites in Aotearoa.

The vastly separated traditions of the ancient Israelites and the nineteenth-century Maori became historically identified after Anglican and Wesleyan missionaries began to translate parts of the Bible into the Maori language in the 1840s.[15] Converts absorbed the scriptures, astounding the clergy with their prodigious feats of memorization, to which Polynesian tradition with its extensive oral histories had accustomed them. They also incorporated biblical symbols, paradigms, similes, and analogic thought into *whakapapa*, their oral literature or "genealogies."

RENEWAL

One of the powerful symbols carried by the missionaries around the world was the myth of Eden, which was lost at the beginning of time, but will be found at the end of the world in the reign of God's kingdom on earth. Biblical apocalyptic is a corpus[16] of symbolic literature about the Eschaton that transmitted a myth of ultimate consolation and renewal to colonized peoples. In the first and last books of the Christian Bible, Genesis and the Revelation of John, the Tree of Life and the River of Life are paramount symbols of renewal. Ezekiel 47:1–12 envisions the renewal of the Dead Sea by the River of Life flowing from the Throne of God on the Temple Mount to the desert, where it makes the water fresh, fish thrive, and the land bear fruit. This edenic promise of fertility and life may have inspired the first-century Essenes to wait near the Dead Sea for God's miracle of renewal. Eighteen-hundred years later an Anglican missionary referred to the same symbols as a foundation for the evangelization of the Maori: "But the Water of Life flows to give life. 'And it shall come to pass, that every thing that

14. See Bronwyn Elsmore, *Like Them that Dream: The Maori and the Old Testament* and *Mana from Heaven: A Century of Maori Prophets in New Zealand*.

15. Elsmore, *Mana from Heaven*, pp. 27–29.

16. It includes the books of Daniel and Revelation, as well as passages from the synoptic Gospels and the Hebrew prophets. The Christian Apocalypse is only one myth of the destruction and re-creation of a world beyond repair found in the scriptures. Although Yahweh is the Lord of history, which had a beginning and will come to an end, the Bible preserves archaic myths of the death and rebirth of the world: including the Flood and the Incarnation.

liveth, which moveth, whithersoever the rivers shall come, shall live.'
[Ezek. 47:9] And this prophecy has indeed been remarkably fulfilled;
the leaves of God's Word have indeed been given for the healing of the
nations."[17]

The theme of renewal is inextricable from the understanding of religion as *the means of salvation through symbolic word, act, and place that gives orientation and meaning to life according to the sacred and efficacious knowledge imparted from a transcendent source to human beings.*

THE CENTRALITY OF LAND

One cannot grasp the Maori history of struggle without acknowledging and examining the relationship of the people to their land. From the first years of European settlement, Maori voices lamented the loss of the land. Nearly all geography in New Zealand is invested with religious meaning. In addition to sacred mountains and specified *wahi tapu*, "sacred places," guarded by the *kaitiaki*,[18] each Maori *hapu* claims an inalienable territory wherein gods, ancestors, and the living give potency and definition to space. Gerardus van der Leeuw explains that a place is not just any segment of space, but one which has a special value because powerful things have happened and continue to happen there. Establishing a "position" or "a place to stand" is a way of orienting oneself to space and of orienting a community to its social world and to the unseen world, from which sacred power comes. At the *hui* the visitors identify themselves by giving the names of their sacred places[19] and the hosts recite the myth-history of their ancestors, their deeds, and the places where these sacred things happened. John Rangihau of the Tuhoe tribe contrasted Maori *whakapapa* with Pakeha history as follows: "This is not the history of the historian which must be couched in fact. But, nevertheless, it is history because it is part and parcel of our living."[20] His words distinguish myth-history from the academic discipline of history.

17. Richard Taylor, *The Past and Present of New Zealand*, p. 18. Taylor remarks that the words for "book" in Latin, Greek, Egyptian, and Maori all derive from local words for the tree or plant from which paper is made or which resembles paper.

18. *Kaitiaki* are the guardians of the sacred places; the word also denotes the policemen on the sacred plazas of the meeting houses in the Ringatu religion; see Michael King, ed., *Tihe Mauri Ora*, p. 64.

19. Ranginui Walker, *Ka Whawhai Tonu Matou: Struggle without End*, p. 71.

20. Evelyn Stokes, J. Wharehuia Milroy, and Hirini Melbourne, *Te Urewera Nga Iwi Te Whenua Te Ngahere, People, Land and Forests of Te Urewera*, p. 11.

REVITALIZATION MOVEMENTS / MILLENARIANISM

The Maori prophet movements fall into a type of worldwide phenomena that anthropologist A. F. C. Wallace termed revitalization movements, which he defined as the "deliberate, organized, conscious effort by members of a society to construct a more satisfying culture."[21] Utilizing comparative data from over five hundred historical cases, Wallace differentiated among "nativist," "millenarian," and "messianic" movements. His definition falls short of his intention to demonstrate that such movements seek to change the "total gestalt" of society. Michael Barkun's definition of millenarianism as "those instances in which human beings band together and actually act upon a belief in imminent and total transformation" fits Wallace's data better.[22] Wallace postulated various subtypes of revitalization movements but acknowledged that many movements are obvious mixtures and do not conform to any one theoretical category. As yet, there is no necessary and sufficient explanation of revitalization phenomena in academic literature.[23]

Our earliest records of revitalization movements date from about 200 B.C.E. in Palestine, although they must have occurred earlier. Palestinian examples include the Maccabees and the Hasidim, the Pharisees, the Essenes, the Zealots and Sicarii, the movements of John the Baptist and Jesus of Nazareth, and the Bar Kochba rebellion. Millenarian expectations have accompanied the spread of the Bible by Christian evangelists throughout the world since late antiquity. However, it is important to acknowledge that millenarianism is an archaic form of myth-history and has existed for as long or longer in many other parts of the world.

THEORIES CONCERNING REVITALIZATION

Wallace's article on revitalization movements came out in 1956, but there is still no consensus on what exactly they should be called, why

21. A. F. C. Wallace, "Revitalization Movements," p. 265.
22. Michael Barkun, *Disaster and the Millennium*, p. 2.
23. Among the general studies are Vittorio Lanternari, *The Religions of the Oppressed*; Paolo Freire, *Pedagogy of the Oppressed*; Sylvia Thrupp, ed., *Millennial Dreams in Action*; John Gager, *Kingdom and Community*; Kenelm Burridge, *New Heaven, New Earth*; G. W. Trompf, ed., *Cargo Cults and Millenarian Movements*; and Peter Worsley, *The Trumpet Shall Sound*. For an explanation of the theory of cognitive dissonance, see Leon Festinger, Henry W. Riecken, and Stanley Schachter, *When Prophecy Fails*. Of particular theoretical interest are Wallace, "Revitalization Movements"; Mircea Eliade, *Myth of the Eternal Return*; Aberle, "Relative Deprivation Theory"; and Mary Douglas, *Purity and Danger*. Individual studies include Euclides da Cunha, *Os Sertoes* (*Rebellion in the Backlands*), Bengt Sundkler, *Zulu Zion*, and Webster, *Rua and the Maori Millennium*. Bernard McGinn's selected apocalyptic texts in *Apocalyptic Spirituality* document revitalization movements in medieval Europe.

they arise, and what they have in common. David Aberle's theory of relative deprivation and Leon Festinger's theory of cognitive dissonance have been employed to explain revitalization phenomena.[24] Anthropologists F. Allan Hanson and Roger Keesing have argued that sovereignty movements in Oceania have appropriated academic reconstructions of their past as authentic story.[25] New Zealand scholars have debated whether or not the Maori actively accepted or passively received British cultural artifacts and institutions.[26] Still others have proposed that the prophet movements arose as alternatives to missionary doctrines through the prophets' own interpretations of the Bible in translation.[27] Paul Clark regarded the Pai Marire movement as one of several "adjustment cults," by means of which the Maori sought "to regulate the processes of cultural change for the benefit of Maoris," an approach that Bronwyn Elsmore and Evelyn Stokes have likewise taken.[28] Unfortunately, the current hypotheses, findings, and nomenclatures remain less satisfying than the more comparative body of inquiry stimulated by Wallace, Festinger, Aberle, and others over thirty years ago.

EPOCHÉ, THE PHENOMENOLOGICAL METHOD

Recently, some postmodern scholars have voiced doubt that rituals have any meaning and that symbolism can be interpreted at all.[29] Although a rational investigation of religious phenomena may seem like an exercise in futility, a phenomenological[30] approach to religious data can produce a more satisfying understanding of nonrational events in history. The phenomenological approach assumes the reality and primacy of religious experience. It is very difficult for a stranger to pene-

24. Aberle, "Relative Deprivation Theory," studied the religion of the Navajo; and Festinger, Riecken, and Schachter, investigated a midwestern sect of UFO worshipers. Aberle hypothesized that individuals who felt "relatively" deprived in their society tended to join movements, while Festinger, Riecken, and Schachter found that after a date-setting prophecy failed, a core of adherents would redouble their faith and their efforts to convert others.

25. Roger Keesing, "Creating the Past: Custom and Identity in the Contemporary Pacific," pp. 19–42; F. Allan Hanson, "The Making of the Maori: Culture Invention and Its Logic," pp. 890–97.

26. Ann S. Parsonson, "The Pursuit of Mana," pp. 140–67; M. P. K. Sorrenson, "Land Purchase Methods and Their Effect on Maori Population 1865–1901," pp. 183–99.

27. Binney, "Christianity and the Maoris"; Elsmore, *Mana from Heaven.*

28. Paul Clark, *"Hauhau": The Pai Marire Search for Maori Identity*, p. x; Elsmore, *Mana from Heaven*; Evelyn Stokes, *Pai Marire, the Niu Pole at Kuranui*, and *Te Raupatu o Tauranga: Land Transactions and Race Relations at Tauranga 1864–1886.*

29. Frits Staal, "The Meaninglessness of Ritual"; Dan Sperber, *Rethinking Symbolism.*

30. See *Religion in Essence and Manifestation* by Gerardus van der Leeuw, as well as the works of Raffaele Pettazzoni, Joachim Wach, and Mircea Eliade.

trate to the meaning of that experience by studying documents, whether oral, written, visual, or tangible.[31] Nevertheless, hearkening to the various forms of symbolic expression and examining the scholarly debate about them provoke questions and hypotheses that, if confirmed by further data, can yield a relatively clear picture; data can speak and a trained ear can hear a coherent story. If investigators routinely dismiss what a prophet says as gibberish or nonsense or limit their focus to a specific academic framework, they may miss an important finding. It is useful to assume that a prophet's utterance is coherent and his or her hermeneutics are systematic, instead of inscrutable or meaningless. If one can empathize with any given community's sense of grievance, one may grasp the ultimate concern that motivates people to join new religious formations. The ability to empathize with or to imagine the experience of the object of one's study is not equivalent to the subjective error of sympathizing with the subject matter. One needs to stretch beyond one's own limited experience, in order to comprehend data that, at first appearance, are so radically other. The discipline of approximating van der Leeuw's ideal of "pure description systematically pursued" requires "adopting the attitude of intellectual suspense, or of abstention from all judgment"—*epochē*—with respect to controversial topics.[32] Often there is a tension between this self-imposed discipline and the attitude of one's mind and heart, but it is possible to achieve a requisite detachment if one is superordinately passionate about understanding a phenomenon. As van der Leeuw observed, "Understanding, in fact, itself presupposes intellectual restraint."[33]

UNDERSTANDING RELIGION

David Aberle was admittedly uncomfortable with religious phenomena, possibly because he found it unsettling to "assume randomness of social behavior or an indefinite plurality of causes."[34] While sociologists look for patterns in data from which they can extract models or formulas, historians are trained to respect the differences and particularities of each case they study. Both efforts are conscientious and useful. However, patterns do occur in history and events have their

31. A document is any positive datum and can encompass oral conversation, the performance of symbolic acts, and artifacts, as well as written texts.

32. Van der Leeuw, *Religion in Essence and Manifestation*, p. 646 n. 1.

33. Ibid., p. 684.

34. Aberle, "Relative Deprivation Theory," p. 213.

speciation. Religious traditions are extremely varied, yet they still may
be characterized by core paradigms. It is selective memory that guides
the redaction and transmission of the paradigmatic stories that people
reenact in times of humiliation and crisis. Most peoples possess a body
of knowledge-from-beyond that bestows efficacious or saving power.
Myth, genealogy, and history are intermingled in rituals and liturgies,
in the creations of schools of poets and priests, in stone texts, papyri,
codices, tapes, and other kinds of databases, including spatial formations. These constitute inestimable resources when a community experiences dislocation and consequent disorientation. It is usually from its
religious traditions that a community learns some means of redemption
authorized by the god(s) that promises to extricate it from despair. No
matter how heterodox a prophet's message may seem, on closer examination one sees that it has roots in orthodox, "parent" religions.

Prophets and poets stand in the place of *demiurgoi,* and the stuff
they create with is given to them in revelations or insights from the
religious body of knowledge. Their idiom is symbol, and using symbols,
they plot the coordinates of a renewed social world. The world-creating
activity of prophets, shamans, and saviors impacts history with mag-
num force sometimes, and it is impossible to understand their influence without taking symbolic data into account.

In order to understand religious experience, ideally one must employ both the particularism of the historian and the search for general
patterns that characterizes the social scientist. The phenomenological
method enables one to maintain a critical distance from the subject
matter while examining religion on its own terms *as it appears in the
messiness of the data.* Religious experience is the phenomenon to be
investigated, and myth and symbol are its language.

David Aberle has postulated that people rise up in protest movements when they feel blocked. However, he acknowledged that "blockage," namely, the "insufficiency of ordinary action" to save the community from a threat to its continuance, is not a sufficient explanation.[35]
A renewal movement does not rely on "ordinary action" to effect a total
transformation of a run-down world. It fulfills divine mandates and
magically or efficaciously reenacts paradigms of freedom, such as
Jehovah's[36] liberation of the Israelites from Egypt. A blockage in com-

---

35. Ibid., pp. 212, 214.
36. The Hebrew word for the Lord, "Yahweh," was vocalized as "Jehovah" in Christian bibles,
and the Maori adopted the latter name from the English translators.

munication between people and the god(s) is a significant finding, but it is not likely to be discovered if an investigation is limited to non-religious factors.

Some questions we have failed to ask include: What happens when a people's access to the traditional means of maintaining and renewing the world is blocked? What happens when the rituals are lost and the elders who carry them in their memories die out and cannot pass them on to their novices? What happens when the boundaries of purity and pollution are transgressed and a community is blocked from differentiating one place or act or office or role from any other? Time and again, the history of this type of blockage reveals that something more than an abstract idea or formal institution dies; too often it is people who die.[37] When a community foresees its own extinction, prophets may arise to speak for it and proclaim a means of salvation.

Widespread misconceptions about revitalization movements persist. Revitalization movements are not benign efforts to adjust to a changed set of conditions, nor do their members seek political representation or power alone. They do not appear everywhere people are oppressed or blocked. Generally, they are not led by schizophrenics or the feeble-minded, but by gifted visionaries of strong character. Wallace's sub-types—"messianic," "nativistic," "millennial"—do not help us understand such cases as the Maori renewal movements that exhibit features of all three types. Furthermore, typological features do not describe in detail a given movement's mode of transforming its world according to the revelations of the god(s).

Prophets renew their communities through divinely instituted means of salvation: sacred myths, laws, acts, and prayers. They may proclaim a peaceful message or resort to violence to attain their ends, and any particular movement may alternate between peaceful and violent phases. Their messages are nonrational, but coherent and mythological. They dispense divine knowledge, sometimes in language only the adherents can fully understand, and they transform time and place by reestablishing boundaries between that which is sacred and inviolable and that which is ordinary and ephemeral. Most of all, they labor to transform the tired and hopeless present world by calling forth the transcendent power that created the world at the beginning of time.

---

37. On this phenomenon, see Anastasia M. Shkilnyk, *A Poison Stronger Than Love*.

NEW ZEALAND SCHOLARLY SOURCES

In my study of the religious aspects of the King Movement, Pai Marire, and Ringatu I am particularly indebted to the work of Bronwyn Elsmore, Buddy Mikaere, Judith Binney, Peter Webster, and Evelyn Stokes, J. Wharehuia Milroy, and Hirini Melbourne, who have patiently gathered together much important data in their insightful accounts of New Zealand prophets and messiahs of the nineteenth and twentieth centuries.

Elsmore's *Mana from Heaven* is a compendium of the prophet movements that contains snippets of information on very early evidences of syncretism and satisfying chapters on the major innovations of King Tawhiao, Te Ua, Te Kooti Arikirangi Te Turuki, Rua Kenana, and Ratana. Their historical sequence, elaboration of a shared symbolism, and common goals make it clear that these heterodox movements influenced one another and were rooted in a precolonial religion, despite their borrowings and novelties. Prophets from the North Island, for example, influenced messianism on the South Island.[38] Those who proposed a Maori King were well aware of the rebellion of Hone Heke against the British fifteen years earlier. Sacred migrations characterized Arowhenua, the King Movement, and Ringatu, among different tribes.[39] Various sectarians identified themselves as Jews, which Elsmore believes indicated their disillusionment with Christianity and its missionaries.

Buddy Mikaere tells the story of the Kai Tahu messiah of the South Island with aching clarity in *Te Maiharoa and the Promised Land*. Governor George Grey conspired to remove the Kai Tahu permanently from their food-gathering places, many of which became incorporated into large sheep runs for colonial estates.[40] To save his people, Te Maiharoa led them on an exodus to the sacred center of their ancestral territory and founded a new world of light on disputed land.

Judith Binney has produced the largest body of articles and books

---

38. Cf. Buddy Mikaere, *Te Maiharoa and the Promised Land*, pp. 39–46.

39. Arowhenua was the movement of the Kai Tahu of the South Island, who founded a settlement called Omarama at a sacred place. A capital laid out according to British methods of surveying, but never completed, was established at Ngaruawahia, the center of the Waikato tribes who formed the nucleus of the King Movement. The messiah of Ringatu, Rua Kenana, founded *Hiruharama Hou*, "New Jerusalem," in the East Coast region of the North Island.

40. Extract from "Instructions from the Colonial Office to Captain Hobson Regarding Land in New Zealand," in John Ward, Esq., *Information Relative to New Zealand (compiled for the use of colonists)*, pp. 165–68; Walker, *Ka Whawhai Tonu Matou*, pp. 105–10.

on the Ringatu religion and its offshoot, Wairua Tapu. Her biography of lay missionary Thomas Kendall, *The Legacy of Guilt*, includes his valuable letter on Maori mythology.[41] Binney has collected and published oral histories and photographs of those who knew Te Kooti and Rua Kenana in *Nga Morehu: The Survivors*; and with Gillian Chapman and Craig Wallace, she produced *Mihaia: The Prophet Rua Kenana and the Community at Maungapohatu*. Her most recent and ambitious chronicle is *Redemption Songs*, a comprehensive biography of Te Kooti, the founder of Ringatu.

Peter Webster's *Rua and the Maori Millennium* was inspired by Euclides da Cunha's *Os Sertoes*, the great study of the Brazilian backlands and its people. Webster took into account the effect of Tuhoe land, specifically the haunting Urewera forest and mountains, upon Rua's people, and emphasized their mythic, as well as ecological, importance to the last people in New Zealand to be dislocated from their ancestral space. Webster focused upon millennial myth as an indispensable framework for understanding how and why Rua consolidated a block of land around the tribal sacred mountain in order to build his "New Jerusalem."

Together with J. Wharehuia Milroy and Hirini Melbourne, geographer Evelyn Stokes has produced a painstaking account of the Tuhoe people and Rua's movement in *Te Urewera Nga Iwi Te Whenua Te Ngahere: People, Land and Forests of Te Urewera*. Their work details the incremental alienation of the Tuhoe people from their land through the rulings of the Land Court and the legislation of successive New Zealand governments between 1870 and 1920. The authors candidly discuss the ongoing conflict over the uses of the Urewera between the Pakeha, who have established a national park that excludes the Maori from their traditional uses of the forest, and the Tuhoe, who demand access to their ancestral territory.[42] Stokes has also written clear and valuable expositions on land confiscation and the millenarian fervor of Pai Marire.

In addition significant studies by Alan Ward, Keith Sinclair, Ranginui Walker, James Belich, Paul Clark and many others have educated this stranger in the general and fine points of an incredible "history of struggle"[43] between the two peoples of New Zealand. To all these schol-

41. Judith Binney, *The Legacy of Guilt: A Life of Thomas Kendall*, appendix 1, pp. 171–76.

42. Stokes, Milroy, and Melbourne, *Te Urewera*, pp. 109–11, 149–54.

43. This is Steven Webster's phrase in "Postmodernist Theory and the Sublimation of Maori Culture," *Oceania* 63, no. 3 (March 1993): 224.

ars I owe far more than this small book can give back. And there is a
new generation of Maori historians on the horizon who promise to re-
fine and challenge many of the premises of existing scholarship.

RELIGION AND REBELLION

Among the Maori, the sacredness of land and space is the central
feature of community, culture, and religion. Sacred place signifies both
location and position relative to all other things and peoples, realms
and gods. Removal from the land created a breach between *te ao tawhito*, "the old world," and *te ao hou*, "the new world." Whereas "culture" is an abstraction and "community" can have a variety of refer-
ents, "religion" is omnipresent among human beings, and its symbolic
expressions pervade and give form to both community and culture.

It is a great misfortune that renewal movements are frequently denounced as heretical or seditious by civil authorities. Paramilitary police raided Rua Kenana's peaceful settlement in 1916. The prophet
was arrested, and imprisoned after the second longest trial in New
Zealand's history. Maori dissidents and their Jewish analogues in late
antiquity struggled against the determined policies of imperialists to
amalgamate them into "civilized" empires. The Romans and their clients also regarded Jewish sects as heresies.[44]

Religion gives rise to the most intense feelings of which human beings are capable.[45] Theologian Paul Tillich observed that religion always involves ultimate concern.[46] Western civilization is marked by life
and death struggles over religious expression, beginning with the Jewish wars of 66–70 and 132–35. In the sixteenth and seventeenth centuries the Reformation and the rivalries of civil states with standing
armies set off a century of war in Europe that caused humanists and
intellectuals to blame religion for fomenting endless bloodshed, because it was the state sponsorship of religious factions that made the
carnage possible. The rise of science and its new method of inquiry
provided reflective persons with a compelling alternative to the Bible
and the Catholic church as the only conduits of authoritative knowledge. The secular challenge to Christianity freed the laity from depen-

44. See especially, Jacob Neusner, *From Politics to Piety*, and Richard A. Horsley and John S.
Hanson, *Bandits, Prophets, and Messiahs*. Our word "heresy" derives from Josephus's use of *haeresis*,
"school" or "sect."

45. Joachim Wach, *Types of Religious Experience*, p. 32.

46. Paul Tillich, *Dynamics of Faith*, passim.

dence upon the clergy by providing direct access to new sources of knowledge and power: telescopes, microscopes, inductive logic, and mathematics. Anticlericalism, positivism, utilitarianism, atheism, and objectivism are only some of the new philosophies that grew out of an internal critique of Christianity in a dawning age of commerce. In the twentieth century the union of German state fascism and a quiescent state church in the 1930s and the passivity of the Vatican in the 1940s demonstrated how feeble the churches had become in relation to the dominance of politics. The state attained a murderous apogee of power in the mid-twentieth century. In Nazi Germany and the Soviet Union all churches were completely subordinated to secular authorities.

It is possible that the twentieth-century complicity of church and state began with four centuries of European imperialism, which joined colonialism and evangelism in a marriage of convenience. Increasingly, civil courts have granted "positive" law precedence over natural law (and the *jus gentium*), undermining legal recognition of aboriginal title to land appropriated by imperial regimes in both hemispheres.[47]

THE CASE OF NEW ZEALAND

New Zealand's struggle to become a modern state under the catch-phrase "one law for both peoples" began in 1840 with the signing of the Treaty of Waitangi by representatives of the Crown and the indigenous tribes. The sheer size of the Maori population today—approximately 13 percent and growing—innoculates them against the invisibility of Australian and American aboriginal peoples in their respective homelands. The Maori prophet movements challenged the British drive to bring the light of civilization to the dark races and to carry the Christian gospel to the end of the earth. Pioneer missionaries founded small utopias governed by biblical law among Maori Christians, only to have their converts later denounce them for stealing their land.

Because of a special history that has dissociated religion from science and allocated the study of religious phenomena to theological schools, Western academic disciplines tend to avoid, discount, or misconstrue religious phenomena. David Aberle largely ignored "millenarian movements," protesting that "I grant nothing to the utility of theories which are based on supposedly pan-human experiences, since

---

47. See Frederika Hackshaw, "Nineteenth Century Notions of Aboriginal Title and Their Influence on the Interpretation of the Treaty of Waitangi," pp. 92–110.

constants cannot be used to explain variables."[48] The problem is that when human beings declare themselves willing to live by or die for an ultimate concern at all costs, they act in a manner that defies rational prediction or logical analysis. The conviction of the followers of Handsome Lake or the Ghost Dance or Pai Marire that bullets could not harm them is a nonrational datum that randomly appeared on two different continents among three independent groups, confounding any explanation but a "pan-human" one. Repeatedly, the intense encounters of human beings with "the holy" through visions, revelations, calls, and commands to go forth and enact the will of the god(s), have, indeed, changed history. Conventional wisdom construes renewal movements as "bizarre" examples of aberrant behavior and delusional thinking. However, these bracketed heterodoxies have also produced political parties, created churches, and inaugurated new epochs: Islam united continents under *sharia* and the caliphate and contributed to the Renaissance in Europe; Pauline Christianity altered the Roman empire; both of these world religions began as prophet-led renewal movements. Muhammad doubted his own sanity for a time, and Paul was declared "mad" by the Roman procurator Festus, according to Acts 26:24. How do we distinguish between prophets and madmen? What differentiates ephemeral from world-shattering new religious movements? Why is religion such a potent force for change?

After he had compared a body of extensive cross-cultural data collected by ethnologists, philologists, sociologists, archaeologists, and historians, Mircea Eliade concluded that the human being is *homo religiosus*.[49] That humanity is set apart as a species by its symbolic expressions in word, act, and place is a "pan-human" assumption that became the basis of Eliade's investigation of religious phenomena throughout the world and history. That *homo sapiens* is *homo religiosus* is a philosophical first principle, just as Aristotle's statement in his *Politics* that it is evident that man is more of a political animal than the bee is a first principle—which he concluded from his acquaintance with the experience of Greeks who lived in city-states. The positive discipline of social science has accepted Aristotle's dictum. Similarly, in order to understand renewal movements we must first acknowledge that religion is intrinsic to human nature. I speak here of the formal features of religion that are expressed in hierophanies, patterns, and

48. Aberle, "Relative Deprivation Theory," p. 213.

49. Eliade's sources are dated and have been subjected to revision. However, his extrapolations from this corpus continue to yield testable hypotheses.

symbols—not of the conventional American view that religion is a kind of morality or priestcraft or alternative "worldview," such as "creationism."

In the *Politics* Aristotle noted that man is the only animal that nature has endowed with speech. All speech is symbolic, but not all speech is religious. Religious symbolism points to something "Wholly Other" than everyday, visible verities. Religious speech evokes, enacts, wards off; it is magical and efficacious. In religion, speech and act are rarely differentiated. The Maori word *karakia* means "incantation" or "prayer" and also "ritual." A *korero* is, at one and the same time, an exchange of words and an invisible contest. In recitations of cosmogonic myths, everything is religious and symbolic. By venturing halfway across the globe to convert "barbarians" in obedience to Christ's command in Acts 1:8, missionaries believed they were fulfilling God's plan of salvation for all humanity and hastening the advent of the Millennium.

The prophecies, rites, and myths of the Maori renewal movements attempted to ward off the disorienting impact of colonialism and Christian evangelism. Most movements flamed up briefly and died, but all of them contributed to the emergence of *kotahitanga*, "overarching unity," and *mana motuhake*, "sovereign power," the rallying cries of Maori activists, who continue a political and cultural struggle for the position and location of the *iwi* in contemporary New Zealand. New Zealand provides the investigator with ample data about a continuous tradition of nativist, millenarian, messianic, guerrilla, pacifist, pentecostal, and democratic movements of renewal. I regret that I can only focus on three of the most intriguing ones.

The Maori language has changed since Captain James Cook circumnavigated Aotearoa in 1769. The meanings of many ancient Maori *karakia* have been lost.[50] Whalers and traders from Australia arrived in the 1790s, and the first missionaries set foot in Northland in 1814. As stranger and native interacted with one another, a layer of "missionary Maori" and other neologisms were added to the language. Williams's Maori dictionary, now in its seventh edition, continues to ignore them, which is a great pity. These new linguistic creations throw light on the historic encounter between Europeans and the people of the land.

The study of the pre-contact history and religion of the Maori has suffered from ethnocentric bias. Early Pakeha scholars looked for a

---

50. H. W. Williams, *Dictionary of the Maori Language*, p. xxviii.

Supreme Being (and found one), posited one great canoe migration from eastern Polynesia, instead of many lesser ones, and discounted the new religious movements of the nineteenth- and twentieth-century Maori charismatics.[51] Self-taught ethnologist Elsdon Best studied ancient Tuhoe myths and rituals at the same time that he derided and opposed the Ringatu movement unfolding before his very eyes. As a result of the infatuation of scholars with ancient origins and putatively untainted traditions, we are left with an incomplete and somewhat distorted record of *te ao tawhito*. It seemed necessary for the Polynesian Society of Johannes Andersen, Percy Smith and Elsdon Best to create a virtual Maori past, in order to set an idealized standard against which the actual Maori experience of their day could be judged—and found lacking.

Usually, phenomena characterized as political or sociological, upon closer examination, prove to be intensely religious also. Renewal movements are political in that their ultimate expectation is that a disordered world will be reordered by divine law. In Christian tradition, law and morality have roots in the Mosaic code, and Moses was a judge among his people as well as a prophet. In the Maori world, law is expressed as a set of prohibitions that maintains order in the cosmos by setting boundaries between two gendered complements that characterize all that exists: *tapu* expresses what is cosmically male, and *noa* what is cosmically female.[52] The newcomers to Aotearoa did not tolerate Maori customs, and Christian converts petitioned the imperial government for civil institutions to curb disorder.[53] Because the government did not respond, the Maori King Movement proposed to set up a Maori polity side by side with Queen Victoria's rule over Pakeha settlements under the higher rule of the Christian God. Civil law and religious codes, enforcement techniques and ethical rules substantiate one another. Religion and politics are the warp and woof of the social fabric.

HONE HEKE'S REBELLION

Maori nationalism began with Hone Heke's flagstaff rebellion of 1844–45. Heke was an entrepreneurial chief who had imbibed American

---

51. See *The Lore of the Whare-wananga* by S. Percy Smith and its rebuttal by D. R. Simmons, *The Great New Zealand Myth*.

52. Ann Salmond, "'Te Ao Tawhito': A Semantic Approach to the Traditional Maori Cosmos," pp. 5–28.

53. *Appendices to the Journal of the House of Representatives (AJHR)*, 1860, F-No. 3, pp. 59–67, 70, 74, 122, 134.

political ideals from Yankee traders.[54] The target of Heke's wrath was the British flagstaff, which he regarded as a claim to Maori territory. Traditionally, the Maori had claimed unoccupied land by planting a pole on it and kindling fires. By erecting a flagstaff near a customs facility the British had unwittingly laid claim to Heke's territory. Accordingly, he cut the staff down several times.

Nationalism is an expression of self-determination by a community that shares a language, history, ancestry, territory, and religion.[55] A nation's power is expressed in myth, namely, the story of how this particular people—often distinguishing themselves from others as "the people" from "the strangers"—has created a social world by the power of the god(s). When a nation is overpowered by a rival power, defeat is often interpreted as a sign that the god(s) have withdrawn their protection.[56] To reestablish their world, the people must regain their access to the transcendent power that created the world in the beginning.

After cutting down the British flagstaff, Hone Heke reasserted the claim of the Nga Puhi[57] to the Bay of Islands. The British had assumed the Maori would accept the imposition of British rules regarding land and commerce. Since land selling was an alien concept, the Nga Puhi did not comprehend that once they had sold their land, it was no longer theirs. Heke's effort to strike down British control over Nga Puhi land failed, but his nationalism took widespread root fifteen years later when the King Movement installed their monarch and planted their own flagstaff in the central section of the North Island.

The British symbol of the flagstaff resonated with the traditional symbolism of the *pou* or *taki*, "sacred pole." The *pou* became prominent in subsequent Maori renewal movements, signifying a center, both geographical and sacred, around which a disenfranchised people could claim a position relative to their rivals. The revival of the sacred pole in the *niu* ritual of Pai Marire gave dislocated people access to divine powers. The *niu* poles of Pai Marire, a few of which still survive, incorporated certain symbols of British domination—the flag, the flagstaff, and the ship's mast. What Pai Marire claimed to regain through the *niu* pole rite was the power of life the British occupation had taken from the people.

54. Keith Sinclair, *The Origins of the Maori Wars*, p. 66. See also J. Rutherford's earlier exposition of the American influence thesis in *Hone Heke's Rebellion 1844–1846*.

55. In multiethnic or heterogeneous polities it is the collective experience of building or settling a nation that provides people of separate origins with a common history marked by the adoption of symbols that transcend differences and unite the body politic.

56. Perdue, "Native American Revitalization Movements," pp. 60–65.

57. Use of "the" before *nga*, "the" (pl.), is redundant, but sounds better in English.

Movements to renew a broken social world have occurred elsewhere. Cognizant of parallels between indigenous New Zealanders and Native Americans, Theda Perdue reexamined Seneca and Cherokee attempts to reestablish their social worlds after disruption by European conquest.[58]

> I suggest that the social survival of native peoples stems from the spiritual basis of their aboriginal cultures, a base that has been far more difficult for Europeans, obsessed with economic and political domination, to assault. European disease, techno-logical superiority, economic power, and political sophistication certainly wreaked havoc with these peoples, yet they periodically revitalized their cultures by spiritually rejuvenating themselves. . . . In the scholarly accounts of these revitalization movements, the spiritual basis often has been lost in the recounting of political confederacies, military campaigns and acculturative responses.[59]

For the Maori, the "spiritual basis" of society is the land, the body of the primal Mother, who nourishes the people. The word for "land" in Maori is *whenua*, which also means "placenta." Specific sacred places are still memorialized in Maori recitation on the *marae*. Much as the portable Torah became for diaspora Jews a symbolic substitute for the Temple, so the Maori meeting house with its *marae* has come to represent the nurturing earth to the displaced people of Aotearoa. In the ensuing pages, I hope to demonstrate that the King, Pai Marire, and Ringatu renewal movements were fundamentally religious phenomena and that the Maori endure today as did the Jews during their great dispersion, as eloquent, if disparaged, witnesses to the power of an undying religious tradition.

58. Perdue analyzes the source material of A. F. C. Wallace on the Handsome Lake movement, among others. Wallace did not regard religion as a fundamental human imperative, but his comparative work lends support to that finding.

59. Perdue, "Native American Revitalization Movements," p. 72.

1

CHRISTIANITY AND COLONIZATION: THE PAKEHA MYTH

> We have to speak of the introduction of the
> race of Japhet and their religion into this
> country, and to give some notices of the
> effects of Christianity and colonization
> upon the Maoris.
>
> Thomas Buddle

THE SONS OF JAPHET

Reverend Thomas Buddle spoke on a winter's day, August 20, 1873, in the Wesleyan church of Nelson, New Zealand, to a dispirited audience eager to hear the distinguished missionary affirm that their forebears had not suffered and struggled in vain.[1] From 1860 to 1872, New Zealand had been wracked by the Land Wars, during which the distant British colony had become both self-governing and responsible for its own defense. The Constitution was brought home to New Zealand in 1852, but the imperial governor, Sir George Grey, set it aside until the fledgling House of Representatives could devise a practical structure for "responsible rule."[2] Fearing that a

---

1. Thomas Buddle, "Christianity and Colonisation among the Maoris."
2. "Responsible rule" refers to the self-rule that London granted to the colonists during the Land Wars; see volume 2 of G. W. Rusden's three-volume *History of New Zealand*.

settler-controlled government would terminate London's Humanitarian[3] policies and alienate aboriginal lands, dissident Maori chiefs also experimented in self-government with a visionary boldness that the Pakeha found both intolerable and seditious. After choosing a king, "rebel" tribes declared their intention to prevent any further sales of land to the Crown. In response Governor Grey invaded the Waikato heartland of the North Island in 1863, but as the fighting progressed, the War Office in London withdrew British troops and left the colony to face the Maori alone. Maori loyalists and a settler militia confronted guerrilla leaders in Taranaki and the East Coast, where the Ngati Ruanui and the Tuhoe tribes had set inviolable boundaries between themselves and the Pakeha. The separatists also proclaimed a new identity for themselves as *Iharaira*, "Israelites," the Jewish descendants of Shem, the son of Noah.[4] As God's chosen people, they confronted the European "sons of Japhet," who sought to amalgamate them into a "new Albion."[5]

However, by 1872 and after twelve years of war, British pioneers had failed to turn Maori dissidents into docile Protestants, and many of the missionaries' hard-won converts had left the church to join one of several related prophet movements. The Land Wars marked the birth of New Zealand as an independent state, but they also inaugurated a religious and political struggle for power over the land within the context of the biracial society that had been suggested by the language of the Treaty of Waitangi.[6]

Buddle's 1860 report, *The Maori King Movement in New Zealand*, assesses the temper of the Waikato chiefs who met at Ngaruawahia to

3. The Humanitarians were members of or sympathized with the Aborigines Protection Society in London and lobbied for safeguarding the Maori from the "pressures of settlement." Alan Ward, *A Show of Justice, Racial "Amalgamation" in Nineteenth-Century New Zealand*, p. 33.

4. In Genesis 10:1–32, Noah's three sons, Japhet, Ham, and Shem, are identified with the Hittite territories and their peoples, Egypt and the people under its rule, and the Semites, respectively. This ancient classification is based upon Genesis 5:1, the "book of generations." From the beginning of Western contact, the missionaries identified the Maori as descendants of Shem or, alternatively, as Egyptians who had been influenced by the Jews in Egypt. See Judith Binney, "The Heritage of Isaiah," pp. 124–39.

5. The reference to New Zealand as the "new Albion" is found in the debates of the National Assembly in the 1860s during the Land Wars. See Ward, "Book Review," Alan Ward's review of Miles Fairburn's *The Ideal Society and Its Enemies: The Foundations of Modern New Zealand Society 1850–1900*.

6. An abundant body of excellent literature exists on this controversial founding document, beginning with translator William Colenso's eyewitness account, *The Authentic and Genuine History of the Signing of the Treaty of Waitangi*. See also I. H. Kawharu, *Waitangi: Maori & Pakeha Perspectives of the Treaty of Waitangi*, and Claudia Orange, *Treaty of Waitangi*.

debate the question of war. This interesting and unjustly neglected document records the speeches at Kingite assemblies and makes the following commonsense recommendations as redress for their grievances:

First—The status of the chiefs should be secured by giving them a position in connection with the Government, in the administration of justice and all other matters affecting the interests of their respective tribes. Second—Native interests would be represented in the councils of the country, either by some of the chiefs or by Europeans in whom they have confidence. Third—The system of purchasing land should be revised. If some division of tribal property could be made so that each family could possess as *bona fide* personal property their own portion with power to alienate some, while other portions were made inalienable, the case might be met.[7]

Buddle promulgated these offers on the eve of war in an attempt to win back the disaffected younger chiefs. A paternalist, he believed in the Humanitarian policy of "racial amalgamation," which sought "to effect that great desideratum (if the native race is to be preserved and the peace of the Country maintained) the elevation of the mere Maori into a reasoning citizen."[8] From the first years of British national interest in New Zealand concern for the protection of indigenous peoples became part of imperial policy, which devised the office of Protector of the Aborigines (later the Native Minister) to meet this need. Through subsidies, loans, and limited education, the purpose of amalgamation was to detribalize the Maori and assimilate them into the economic life of the British crown colony by converting them into Christians, farmers, and laborers—thereby "civilizing" them. The most likely source of Buddle's proposed reforms was Donald McLean,[9] who held a dual portfolio as Native Minister and Chief Land Commissioner.

In his address to the Nelson church after the wars, Buddle sought to justify the amalgamation policies of church and government against the

7. Thomas Buddle, *The Maori King Movement in New Zealand*, pp. 69–70.

8. E. W. Stafford in *AJHR*, 1860, F-No. 3, p. 1. For a historical account of the Humanitarian movement, see Sinclair, *The Origins of the Maori Wars*, pp. 19–26.

9. James Cowan gives the family's preferred spelling as "Maclean" in *Sir Donald Maclean, The Story of a New Zealand Statesman*, p. *viii*, but the common spelling of Sir Donald's name is "McLean."

chill perception that they had failed to civilize the Maori. He began with a gloss on Genesis 9:27, one of the Bible's creation myths.

There is a remarkable prophecy in Genesis concerning the descendants of Japhet now in course of fulfillment."God shall enlarge Japhet and he shall dwell in the tents of Shem." This prediction was uttered when the world was just emerging from the waters of the Deluge, and the Rainbow—beautiful symbol of peace—appeared in the clouds. What meant these words of the Most High on that auspicious moment? When the robe of beams was first woven in the sky, and these words of peace spoken by God to man—"God shall multiply Japhet, and he shall dwell in the tents of Shem." It obviously meant that the race of Japhet should become the dominant race and spread over the world.

How marvellously is the promise being fulfilled. The whole of the European races are allowed to be descendants of Japhet and God has caused them to multiply and is giving them possession of the earth. . . .

Now Christianity has been committed especially to the race of Japhet. . . . This is the great, the dominant race, the most powerful race in existence. To it Divine Providence has clearly assigned the rule of the world, and deposited with it the blessings of the Christian religion, which it is commissioned to carry abreast of its commerce and its colonies. . . . I heard a New Zealand chief once refer to it in a similar manner, it was at one of the largest gatherings of Natives I ever attended, when all the tribes of Waikato and many representatives from other and distant tribes were met at Ngaruawahi [sic], in the days of old Potatau, to inaugurate their Maori kingdom and declare themselves an independent people. William Naylor, Te Awhaitaia, an influential chief, second only to Potatau[10] and who had formerly been his fighting General, but for many years a consistent Christian, opposed the King movement, and did his utmost to dissuade his countrymen from taking such a step, affirming it as his conviction that Providence had ordained that the Pakehas, who are the descendants of Japhet, should dwell in the tents of the Maoris, who are descendants of Shem.[11]

10. Potatau (Te Wherowhero) was the first Maori king.
11. Buddle, "Christianity and Colonisation," p. 5.

Te Awhaitaia, also known as William Naylor, was Reverend Buddle's most illustrious convert, a paramount chief who had exchanged Uenuku, the rainbow god of war and cannibalism, for Noah's rainbow covenant of peace. In the great meeting at Ngaruawahia in 1860, William Naylor spoke in favor of allegiance to the queen and of selling land to the Pakeha.[12] Buddle invoked Naylor to buttress his argument for white racial dominance in 1872 and to validate the Pakeha myth of conquest and conversion. Buddle's ringing affirmation of the British imperium[13] must have cheered his Methodist audience at a time when their labors in the vineyard of the Lord seemed to have yielded the bitter fruit of Maori apostasy and rebellion. His narrative served to confirm their fervent belief—in the face of evident failure—that their pioneering mission had fulfilled God's redemptive plan for all the nations.

HOMO RELIGIOSUS

Buddle's address supports the view that British colonists were no exception to Eliade's designation of the human race as *homo religiosus;* they relied upon the authoritative truth of myth to give meaning to their mission. Myth binds and delineates the social world, orienting human beings and investing their deeds with a transcendent significance. The opening statements of Reverend Richard Taylor's memoir, *The Past and the Present in New Zealand* (1868), illustrates the divine imperative that inspired pioneering missionaries in New Zealand:

> The last great command given by our Lord to His followers previous to His Ascension was, "Go ye into all the world and preach the gospel to every creature." (Mark xvi: 15). . . .
>   . . . The advance of the Gospel in Heathen lands in this day is evident, and fully establishes the fact that it is the Lord's doing. The wonderful way the Word of God is multiplied and dispersed throughout the world, can only be regarded as a miracle, far greater than that wrought at Jerusalem on the Day of Pentecost.

12. Te Awaitaia was baptized as Wiremu Nera, "William Naylor," in 1833 or 1834, according to the *Dictionary of New Zealand Biography (DNZB)*, 1:441. He remained a government loyalist and *hoko whenua*, "proponent of land-selling," until he died in 1866.
13. In ancient Rome the *imperium*, a power bestowed by the gods upon civil rulers, signified ultimate, sacred authority.

The preparing of the way of the Gentiles is also to be observed,—
a highway for the Heathen.[14]

Like Buddle, Taylor incorporated colonialism into his myth of evangelization, regarding the settlement of "new" lands as the divine extension
of God's timely and miraculous intervention in human history.

The increase of commerce; the bringing of the most distant ends
of the world together; the facilities of intercourse with nations,
scarcely known even by name some few years ago; the breaking
down of the barriers which opposed the entrance of the Gospel, as
in China and Japan; clearly prove a work is going on, and on such
a scale of magnitude as far exceeds that of past experience.[15]

Taylor found evidence of God's intervention in the population explo-
sion of the nineteenth century, when Malthusian threats of starvation,
civil disorder, and crime hung over the mother country. In a section
labeled "Our Surplus Population," he wrote: "It seems from the wonderful increase of our race in the old populated parts of the earth, that
it is now necessary for them to move off to those fair regions which,
though equally fitted and intended for man's abode, are now desolate
and uninhabited. God appears to have wrought a miracle to compel
them to depart."[16]

Pressure to resettle the "wonderful increase" in offshore colonies
derived from the inability of Britain to feed her population, the increase in destabilizing Fenianism, and the alarming rise in crime, according to Taylor. Clearly, God's remedy was obvious, for "God bestowed upon Britain the vast Australian continent, with its fair sunny
fertile plains, all but destitute of inhabitants," and he furnished the
enterprising English with the technological means to transport their
impoverished masses to the antipodes, in giant ships, such as the
"Great Eastern," a "huge leviathan" that could carry "10,000 at a
time."[17]

Taylor and Buddle and most of the of Humanitarian missionary-pi-
oneers bound Christian evangelism to British colonization policies in a
special hermeneutical construct, a Pakeha myth with millenarian over-
tones that imbued colonists with "an ethos of acadianism—the belief

14. Taylor, *The Past and Present of New Zealand*, pp. 1–2.
15. Ibid., p. 2.
16. Ibid., p. 176.
17. Ibid., p. 177.

in a land of natural abundance where immigrants (provided they worked hard) could pursue their individual self-fulfillment without the barriers of entrenched social hierarchy or class division."[18] Concerning the Church of England's evangelical fervor in the nineteenth century, Bronwyn Elsmore has observed: "One of the signs preceding the end was that the gospel would be preached around the world, and the missionaries were well aware of their own part in the fulfillment of prophecy as they were obeying scriptural command to teach all nations."[19] Evangelists truly believed that their mission, linked with the Crown in its colonial enterprise, would hasten the establishment of God's kingdom on earth. Without this life-sustaining myth, it is doubtful that the Church Missionary Society's Anglican mission could have endured its initial dry years of domination and harassment by the Maori chiefs.[20] Taylor reports that the first Christian converts in New Zealand were Maori slaves; however, the second wave included the high-born, members of the *ariki* class, the families of hereditary chiefs.

Buddle cited Chief Ruatara (Duaterra), as "one of the principal instruments in preparing the way for the introduction of Christianity and the arts of civilization into his native country."[21] Samuel Marsden, the Anglican chaplain of New South Wales, met Ruatara on a voyage from London to New Zealand, where Marsden intended to establish the first Anglican mission station. The trip was postponed after reports of the massacre of a ship's Pakeha crewmen reached the colonists,[22] and it wasn't until 1814 that Marsden and three lay missionaries, a schoolteacher and two artisans, were welcomed by Ruatara's people at the Bay of Islands. The sabbath following their arrival happened to be Christmas. Ruatara prepared an enclosure with a pulpit and seats where, in Buddle's words, "A flagstaff was erected, and *the flag of old England, the flag that has braved a thousand years*, the battle and the breeze, was hoisted, an expressive symbol of the dawn of religion and civilization on these savage lands" (my emphasis).[23]

18. See Ward, "Book Review," pp. 74–76.

19. Elsmore, *Mana from Heaven*, p. 31.

20. Binney, "Christianity and the Maoris," p. 39 n. 104; Ward, *A Show of Justice*, p. 22.

21. Buddle, "Christianity and Colonisation," p. 3.

22. The Maori attack on the *Boyd* was one of the earliest instances of redress for the mistreatment of a chief.

23. Buddle, "Christianity and Colonisation. Cf. Marsden's own account in J. B. Marsden, *Life and Work of Samuel Marsden*, p. 82. The Church Missionary Society had a flag that was adopted by an assembly of chiefs in 1834. Hone Heke attacked the Union Jack as a symbol of *imperium* in 1844, and later Maori renewal movements featured their own unique banners and flagstaffs. During the Land Wars each dissident group created its own ensigns. In 1902 the New Zealand Parliament adopted a national flag.

Samuel Marsden initiated the Christian mission in New Zealand with a ceremony in which religious symbolism and imperial sovereignty, Protestantism and capitalism, Christianity and colonization, were inextricably interwoven. Reciting the 100th Psalm and a sermon on the text, "Behold, I bring you tidings of great joy," Marsden inaugurated a new Albion that was to become "a home for thousands of the surplus population of other lands, and [to present] an attractive field for the profitable employment of both capital and labour."[24]

Christianity claimed few converts in the first twenty-five years of evangelization, although muskets were much in demand. While warring chiefs in the North Island slaughtered thousands of their tribal enemies in the ensuing decades, the most effective role filled by the early missionaries was that of peacemaker.

"What did Christianity accomplish among the Maoris?" Buddle asked his Nelson audience sixty years after Marsden's landing; "We are told the New Zealand Mission has been a failure. . . . I believe not." With Hobbesian certitude, he catalogued the evils of the Maori's "old system. . . . Their social condition was degraded, savage, barbarous, wretched in the extreme." He derided the romantic view of "savage life—its freedom, simplicity, innocence, and generosity . . . these pictures only exist in poems, romances, and fiction." "The liberty enjoyed by the savage," he concluded, "consists in a freedom to oppress and plunder those weaker than himself; and an exposure to the same treatment from those who are stronger than he." He noted in passing that "a great part of the land" was held sacred and bound by *tapu,* which he defined as "a powerful system of religious despotism."[25]

LAND AND *TAPU*

From their first years in New Zealand, missionaries had observed the connection between land and *tapu* without truly understanding that in their zeal to abolish native customs they would usher in an era of intense social disorientation. Land and *tapu* comprised the religious foundation of the ancient Maori social world of the privileged class, the commoners, and the enslaved. The sacred prohibition of *tapu*[26] guarded

24. Buddle, *The Maori King Movement,* p. 72. Cf. account in A. T. Yarwood, *Samuel Marsden,* pp. 174–75.

25. Buddle, "Christianity and Colonisation."

26. *Tapu* prohibits trespass over sacred space on pain of divine punishment mediated by lizard deities or the goddess Whaitiri.

the boundaries between dangerous and neutral spaces and actions. Violating a designated *tapu* barrier, such as crossing the threshold of the sweet potato storehouse or touching the head of a chief, would bring sickness or death upon the transgressor. The Maori world was a complex, integrated system of pervasive complementarities that had no counterpart in the European world.[27] By attacking, denouncing, and destroying the system of *tapu*, the missionaries undermined the integrity of Maori society. Viewing the lives of the "savages" in Hobbesian terms as "solitary, poore, nasty, brutish, and short," the Pakeha prescribed the benevolent rule of British law to ameliorate the natives' allegedly wretched state. There were no police or prisons in Aotearoa, because *tapu* rules regulated one's actions and indicated one's social position. The British introduced the novel institution of gaol, which the Maori equated with enslavement, namely, loss of power and standing as a human being. Missionaries crafted the language in the Treaty of Waitangi that subordinated the mere "governance" of the chiefs to the superordinate "sovereignty" of the Queen. Buddle catalogued the sins of the "old system" in the local newspaper: "War was their principal employment, their greatest delight; they loved its excitement. . . . Cannibalism was the constant companion of war. . . . Infanticide was common. Female children were frequently destroyed. . . . Polygamy was general. . . . Woman was degraded, except in the case of rank. . . . Slavery, too, was practised."[28]

In his fervid view, only the British "children of Japhet" who came to dwell in the "tents of Shem" could dispel the evils of native society with the light of the gospel. In fact, Maori converts displayed greater piety in their sabbath observance and daily worship than did most British settlers, erecting churches where "the tribes [went] up to the House of God with deep emotion."[29]

HUMANITARIANISM

Evangelists labored to transform the barbarians into Englishmen. Early nineteenth-century religious fervor flowed from the Humanitarian movement in London, which extolled country life and the romantic

27. See Anne Salmond, "Te Ao Tawhito: A Semantic Approach to the Traditional Maori Cosmos." Symbolic expression in myths, cults, gods, ancestors, etc., may vary from tribe to tribe in emphasis and detail.

28. Buddle, "Christianity and Colonisation."

29. Ibid.

vision of "each family with their neat boarded cottage, surrounded by their orchards and wheatfields."[30] By the middle of the century many Maori converts had dissociated themselves from their traditional villages and founded Christian communities that resembled English hamlets, where they could abide by *ture*, "biblical law."[31]

As Thomas Buddle stirred his audience with his recitation of the Pakeha myth against the backdrop of the "sad declension" of the mission during and after the Land Wars, he concluded with a triumphal affirmation of their utopian achievements:

Need I add that Christianity prepared the way for Colonisation. Would this land ever have been occupied by foreigners if Christianity had not first tamed the savage? Would these thriving British Settlements have existed at this day? Would the trade and commerce now carried on have been opened? and the fortunes that have been made amassed? and steamers carried our travellers from one end of the colony to the other—or the telegraph wires brought the extremes of the Island within a few minutes of each other—Would a Constitutional Parliament have been sitting in Wellington, legislating for both races? I believe not. . . . I am bold to say, that if New Zealand become a gem in the British Crown, Christianity will be entitled to the credit of having placed it there.[32]

30. *DNZB*, 1:299.
31. A neologism derived from the word "Torah," *ture* first referred to the law of the Bible and eventually to British civil law.
32. Buddle, "Christianity and Colonisation," p. 12.

2

MYTH AND LAND

The "sacred" is what has been placed within boundaries, the exceptional (Latin sanctus*); its powerfulness creates for it a place of its own.*

Gerardus van der Leeuw

Myth is the stuff that worlds are made of. The essential difference between apes and humans, according to Mircea Eliade, is neither toolmaking, nor the opposable thumb, nor even the ability to communicate through language. Rather, it is that language, like other products of human thought and action, symbolizes something beyond the limits of our understanding. For Eliade, humans must express themselves in symbols. He views the pollen grains from flowers in a Neanderthal tomb site on Mt. Carmel as prehistorical documentation of *homo religiosus;* the artifacts of burial attest to a myth of a world beyond the known one.[1] The most rudimentary myth human beings recite reveals the original world at the time of creation as the perfect model for establishing and renewing human society.

1. Mircea Eliade, *A History of Religious Ideas*, vol. 1, *From the Stone Age to the Eleusinian Mysteries*, pp. 8–11.

RELEGERE

It is the myth-world that guides our most notable endeavors and repetitive social acts. Without myth there can be no orientation in space or time, no meaning, no boundaries, no ordering of the cosmos. Sacred symbols resonate throughout history and permeate human experience, transforming consciousness and motivating action. Social customs and laws have their origin in the rules of *religio*, from *relegere* "to observe or pay attention."[2] According to Joachim Wach, "religious experience is a response to what is experienced as ultimate reality. . . . as [that which] we realize as undergirding and conditioning all that constitutes our world of experiences."[3] We recite and reenact our myths in public and in private, consciously and unconsciously, overtly and covertly, because they reveal to us the ultimate reality that is the foundation for all that exists.

To reinvigorate his fellow Methodists, Buddle reminded them of the covenant of peace between God and Noah in the wake of destruction. Especially in times of disappointment, humiliation, or despair, *homo religiosus* turns to myth for guidance and consolation. Nations have recorded and continue to recite their sacred stories at holy, fateful, and triumphal times, memorializing and transmitting the history of their people and their world. Recitation of sacred story is a ritual that invokes the power of the god(s) and makes it accessible to a human community as a means of salvation that is overwhelmingly efficacious after all other, merely human, means have failed. In the most dire times, a communal invocation of the power that created the world facilitates a process of transformation: word becomes act that proceeds from the realm of the god(s). Sacred word, sacred act, and sacred space call forth the transcendent power(s) to requite and punish, reorder and redeem, redress and assuage, and finally, to set the people free from humiliation, bondage, and that most terrible of deaths—the loss of their particular, created, ancestral world. These myths, rites, boundaries, powers, symbols, and appeals constitute that encompassing cosmic orientation we refer to as "religion" in all societies and times.

2. Van der Leeuw, *Religion in Essence and Manifestation*, p. 50.
3. Wach, *Types of Religious Experience*, p. 32.

CHRISTIAN AND MAORI LAND MYTHS

Christian myths and Maori myths regard the land quite differently. Embedded in Maori myths is the inviolable principle that the land and the people are inseparable. Like the bond between *eretz yisrael* and the Jews, so the attachment between a Maori tribe and its land is sacred and is expressed in the designation, *tangata whenua*, "people of the land." In Maori myth the land is the primal Mother, Papatuanuku, and the sky is the Primal Father, Ranginui. In the beginning, their son, Tane, stood on his head and pushed them apart, creating *te ao marama*, "the world of light," where human beings live. According to Jewish creation myth, God commanded Adam to till the soil by the sweat of his brow. In ancient Near Eastern oral and written texts, traces of which undergird the book of Genesis, wilderness symbolized disorder, chaos, or the void. The European treats land as a commodity that can be owned, leased, or sold, because God gave him dominion over it. It must be made productive, or it is "empty" and "waste"—*terra incognita*—unknown; it is without definition, boundaries, and signs of human activity. However, to the Maori land is inalienable, because it is both Mother and "placenta," the repository of the *mauri*, "life-force," of the people. The Christian and the Maori relationships to the land are mutually exclusive. It is in their respective mythologies that one first encounters adumbrations of the Land Wars.

Witi Ihimaera's autobiographical novel, *The Matriarch*, evokes the mythological connections between human beings and the earth when the protagonist reminisces:

> It was my custom, whenever I was home in Gisborne, and no matter whether I had the time or not, to go out to Waituhi. This was the one ritual that could never be broken. . . . I would walk the boundaries of the land, or criss-cross it at least once a year for, oh how we walked this land, the matriarch and I, and how fearful I was that I might forget some small yet significant detail of what had been told me as a child.
>
> You see, in the old days, the boundaries between the neighbouring canoe areas or tribal grounds were mutually arranged and decided upon. Natural features like the hill of Ramaroa Pa, or the Waipaoa River, or sea coasts, cliff escarpments, and the like, were taken to define boundaries. Where natural features were absent,

definite marks, like the mound at Pa Whakarau, would be struck
on the ground. Sometimes a cairn of stones or a post or a pole or a
hole dug into the ground would be used. These boundaries, and
the stories attached to their making, would be memorised. In this
way the entire land was like a living geography text and history
book in one. The minutiae of life, ah yes, all imprinted and still
living inscribed on the land. And to ensure the continuity of the
tribal memory, the people would traverse the land from time to
time and from generation to generation.[4]

The "boundaries [marked by posts and poles] and the stories attached to their making" are religious symbols of the community. Tribal
memory depended not only upon oral record and recitation, but also
upon the performance of the ritual of walking the land "from time to
time." "The minutiae of life" is "imprinted and still living inscribed"
on the "living geography text and history book" of the land for as long
as the people perform the ritual and observe the boundaries: in this
text we see *religio* as *relegere*. Ihimaera illustrates how a people creates
and maintains its wholeness, and his memoir demonstrates the obverse
of Mary Douglas's theory that without boundaries human communities
are at sea, disoriented, and anxious.[5] Specific, named places touched
by sacred power marked where and under what conditions one could
trespass. These indicated *wahi tapu*, "sacred place." A proverb states,
Whatu ngarongaro te tangata / Toitu te whenua! "People perish / But
the land is permanent!"[6]

TE AO TAWHITO

Among the Polynesian peoples expert orators composed tribal history
by taking full advantage of the multiple meanings of Polynesian words
and phrases and of a shared cultural literacy among the members of
the social unit.[7] The recitation of *whakapapa*, "genealogy," memorial-
izes and makes present again what has happened here, at this particular place to ancestors, tricksters, and gods. Humorous,[8] fearsome, di-

---

4. Witi Ihimaera, *The Matriarch*, pp. 102–3.
5. Douglas, *Purity and Danger*, pp. 120–28.
6. George Asher and David Naulls, *Maori Land*, p. 3.
7. Michael Kioni Dudley, *Man, Gods, and Nature*, pp. 5–8, reviews the *kaakaa oolelo* tradition
of scholars in Hawaii, and D. R. Simmons discusses the institution of the *whare wananga* from New
Zealand sources in *Iconography of New Zealand Maori Religion*, p. 24.
8. The humor of myth is not necessarily funny; see Kees W. Bolle, *The Freedom of Man in Myth*.

dactic, *whakapapa* instructs and entertains the listeners. It is both high drama and higher education.

The removal of the Maori tribes from their land during the one and a half centuries of Christianization and colonization created a lasting breach in the ancestral world. Money, status, even political participation in the institutions of the modern state of New Zealand, were not enough to repair the rupture between *te ao tawhito* "the ancient world," and *te ao hou*, "the new world," after the Pakeha alienated the people from their lands. All of the religious renewal movements of the Maori prophets were, in a fundamental sense, attempts to reestablish the vigorous "world of light," *te ao marama*, by bridging the discontinuity between *te ao tawhito*, when land and people were connected, and *te ao hou*, when the people became alienated from the land.[9]

UTOPIANISM

The architects of colonization used New Zealand as a safety valve for Britain's surplus population. Governor George Grey sympathized with British soldiers and the urban poor, who had little opportunity to acquire land or capitalize a business in England.[10] However, unlike America and Australia, New Zealand was not colonized by huddled masses or exiled convicts. It became instead a proving ground for the millenarian hopes of a relatively educated and genteel class, typified by Samuel Butler, who composed his utopia, *Erewhon*, in New Zealand (although Butler returned to England after his "ethos of acadianism" was somewhat dashed by the realities of colonial life). The brilliant Richmond-Atkinson "mob"—English liberals who read Swinburne, cleared the land, served in government, studied the Maori and fought them during the Land Wars—instituted the amalgamation policy of the *imperium*. Those immigrants who stayed the course founded a new state by gradually assuming control over the North Island during the war-wracked 1860s. In the essentially Christian, religious act of transforming a "waste land" into a new Albion flowing with milk and honey,

9. Land was permanently alienated by any of several means unknown before the British arrived and unrecognized by Maori custom. Among such means were sale, change of licit tenure, confiscation, appropriation, and special legislation.

10. Grey settled soldiers on the confiscated lands of dissident Maori *hapu* during the Land Wars, but even before the wars he established "200 military pensioners & families" in a new village in Taranaki, according to J. C. Richmond, in Guy Scholefield, ed., *The Richmond-Atkinson Papers*, pp. 102–3.

it was the pioneer's resourcefulness, not his social class, that won for him a position in the new world. Some of the leading Pakeha, such as Donald McLean, were Scots from proud, but impoverished families, whose talents were rewarded in the less crowded isles at the antipodes.

The initial engine of colonial settlement was the Wakefield Company, an enterprise set in motion by Edward Gibbon Wakefield, who fraudulently advertised the new colony as a mild and empty place with gentle, welcoming natives.[11] Wakefield's propaganda was tested and found wanting in the first major conflict between Maori and Pakeha, the Wairau Affray on June 17, 1843, a battle that flared up when local chiefs defended land they claimed under their customary authority. Twenty armed settlers died, and the fledgling imperial government proved too weak to prevent determined chiefs from protecting their interests by force. Fifteen years later, it was a similar confrontation between the land-thirsty Wakefield colony at Taranaki and the resident Ngati Awa tribe that sparked the outbreak of the Land Wars.

CHRISTIAN AND MAORI MILLENARIANISM

Given the millennial fervor of the Church of England in its colonial enterprise, it is not surprising that Maori prophets appropriated Christian apocalyptic myth for their own purposes. Te Ua, founder of Pai Marire, the "good and peaceful" movement, compared himself to John of Patmos and wrote his own gospel, *Te Ua Rongopai,* which unleashed a dynamic and volatile new creed. The Christian text that inspired Te Ua, the Revelation of John, had originated in a time of tribulation. Early Christians read it aloud in their house churches in Asia Minor to assuage their sufferings by invoking the return of the Risen Christ as the eschatological judge who would establish a reign of justice after the destruction of Rome.[12]

Christian apocalyptic may have appealed to those who foresaw the end of their ancestral world, because through it they were able to place their hopes in a "more perfect age to come"[13] that would replace a

11. Wakefield conceived of a "science of colonization" that would ease "the threat of revolution in the unemployment, low wages and grim living conditions which afflicted the poor. . . . Wakefield believed that England could ease her discontents by exporting large numbers of the discontented." Sinclair, *History of New Zealand,* p. 58.

12. Gager, *Kingdom and Community,* p. 56. See also Steven Friesen's "Ephesus—Key to a Vision in Revelation."

13. Thrupp, *Millennial Dreams in Action,* p. 12.

world that had fallen into desuetude and despair. Millenarian communities expect god(s) to rescue them by reversing cosmic injustice and
requiting the elect. Apocalyptic myth fosters a fevered optimism that
divine agents[14] will save a righteous people who have been overpowered by a superior, but evil, force. Te Ua and his disciples read into
Israelite texts their own particular predicament and took out of them
what resonated most with their own antecedent tradition.

In Polynesian story *Hawaiki* refers to an ancestral homeland and
also to the place where the dead return; it is a mythical place that
symbolizes both the origin of the tribes and the end of life. Maori
prophets syncretized Christian and Polynesian religion in an new oral
tradition that chronicled their struggle against European hegemony and
promised the ultimate return of their land. This post-Christian hermeneutics is an extension of the age-old tradition of *whakapapa*. As
British evangelists introduced a new material culture, muskets, and
plagues into Aotearoa, the old ways fell into disuse. People neglected
to perform the rites that protected the land and the community. Prophets fell ill, dreamed, and revealed divine messages that instructed
them to graft biblical history onto the ancient tree of Polynesian religion[15] and to enact the roles of archetypal forbears. Te Ua counseled,

> Look to the ways of your ancestors when men grew to great age to
> such an extent that their knees projected beyond the back of their
> necks, so old and decrepit did they grow. . . . turn to and encour-
> age and preserve such worthwhile things as the quiet *waiata*
> [song] and *haka* [ritual dance], the lullabies, the *moko* [tattoo] of
> the chin and lip.[16]

Although Te Ua's religion was syncretistic, it renewed older forms
and practices. In the renewal movements, biblical gods became Maori
divinities. Te Ua worshiped Jehovah as the god of Maori Jews, but he
appealed as well to Rura and Riki, syncretisms of the Holy Spirit with
Maori sky deities. His *niu* ritual, performed around a sacred pole, gave
ordinary people access to *hau*, "breath," "wind," "spirit"—a wide-

14. In Christianity the agent is Jesus the Messiah; among the Essenes two or more messiahs are
mentioned; and in both Christianity and intertestamental Judaism the archangels, Michael and Gabriel, are also active agents. Non-Western prophets may expound a hermeneutics that reinterprets
biblical material in terms of their own religious traditions and particular histories.

15. Austronesian (Malayo-Polynesian) languages span the distance from Madagascar to Easter
Island. Early migrations from South Asia brought Polynesian peoples to Tonga at least three thousand
years ago.

16. Clark, *Hauhau*, p. 124.

spread expression of the numinous in Judaism, Christianity, and Brah-
manism. Pai Marire was a democratizing cult that enabled the disenfranchised Maori to assume the identity of a saved community, whom
God had designated as Jews, His chosen ones from time immemorial.
Thus did Te Ua revive old customs and proclaim new laws based upon
the transcendent authority of celestial gods, in whom the power to create and order human society originates.[17]

Within the framework of Christian eschatology the missionaries also
perceived their call from God as an inbreaking revelation. They were
able to establish twenty mission stations in the North Island within
twenty-five years, an achievement they regarded as evidence of the
Holy Spirit working in human history. Their millenarian myth combined the imperial imperative to establish a "superior" civilization in
the waste lands of an alien place with a Christian evangelism that
transmitted the "Water of Life" and the "Tree of Life" in the form of
the Bible to a barbaric people. It had never occurred to the missionaries that the scriptures might become authoritative (and millenarian)
for the converts in a different way—as a foundation for a Maori "kingdom come" in their native "Canaan," that was occupied by British
"Samaritans." The Maori made use of Pakeha religion to expound a
new interpretation of God's word that made sense out of their circumstances. In F. Allan Hanson's words, their renewal movements had
"Maori roots" and "Christian branches."[18]

The King Movement, Pai Marire, and Ringatu were millenarian;
their adherents expected the return of the land to the *tangata whenua*,
the exodus of the Pakeha in their great ships back to their homeland
across the sea, and the dawn of a new age of peace and plenty in
"Canaan." Nourished by revelation, the movements were dynamic, exciting fear among the Pakeha; and when imminent expectation of a
cosmic reversal was delayed by defeat or oppression, the promise of
the return of the land became the durable sustenance of new sects and
churches. Sectarian dissidents called themselves variously, *Iharaira,
tiu, hurai*—Maori neologisms for "Jew"—and "the children of Shem,"
in their rediscovered identity as the righteous remnant over and against
Anglicans and Methodists. Te Ua exhorted his people, "Do not return

17. Eliade's comparative study, *Myth of the Eternal Return*, is a comprehensive essay on religious
renewal among premodern peoples. For an incisive comparison of Christianity and Pacific Island
cults, see Peter Lawrence, "The Fugitive Years: Cosmic Space and Time in Melanesian Cargoism and
Mediaeval European Chiliasm."

18. F. Allan Hanson, "Christian Branches, Maori Roots: The Cult of Rua."

to the House of Japheth, but return to the House of Shem."[19] So effective was Pai Marire in attracting Maori Christians between 1862 and 1872 that the Wesleyan and Anglican societies abandoned their missions and sought sanctuary in the Pakeha settlements.[20]

The government heard only the rumble of a secular rebellion against the Crown, and Buddle lamented the King Movement's "large gatherings for political purposes."[21] Governor Gore Browne issued the "Declaration by the Governor to the Natives assembled at Ngaruawahia," in May 1861, warning the Kingites that their movement was illegal. The symbolic expression of new sects is frequently regarded as illicit, bizarre, and seditious. Whether millenarians are first-century Jews or twentieth-century Kanak liberationists, whether they expect the return of their lands imminently or gradually, their movements are usually characterized as purely political threats to civil authority. Occasionally, their religious aspect may be acknowledged in a negative sense by labeling them pejoratively as "heresies" or "cults." Renewal movements select and transform particular sacred symbols within an existing tradition. They are not creations *ex nihilo*, but re-creations of certain myths or rites, such as the annual reburial of bones or celebration of the new year. Prophets reenact archetypal roles of messiahs, divinities, and messengers. Thus, their words carry the transcendent authority of *muthos*—sacred utterance. In Judaism and Christianity the Word of God is synonymous with Creation. "And God said . . ." is the phrase that brings the world into being in Genesis. In Maori, *karakia* means what is said and the act of saying it, "incantation" and "ritual," both of which are intrinsically religious. Unlike academic discourse, incantation and ritual reveal the ultimate truths of sacred knowledge in the garb of symbol. It is incorrect to regard myth and secular discourse as occupying the same level of analysis.

SACRED SPACE

Human beings are at sea until they know their position or location in geo-religious space. In the fictional story of an apocryphal shaman, *The Teachings of Don Juan*, we are told about an initiate who is taken to a remote shack in the desert and ordered by his Yaqui teacher to "find a

19. Lyndsay Head, "The Gospel of Te Ua Haumene," p. 29.

20. See Allan K. Davidson and Peter J. Lineham, *Transplanted Christianity*, pp. 142–65, on the missionaries' retreat.

21. Buddle, *The Maori King Movement*, p. 65.

spot."[22] He spends hours testing first one site in the confined space and then another until he locates a place for himself that seems both natural and right. The ancient epic *Gilgamesh* extols a king who built a walled city that organized a civil world for his subjects apart from of the fearful chaos of wilderness. These metaphors of finding a spot and founding a settlement convey sacred space as an ultimate concern among human tribes. Locating coordinates and marking boundaries is simultaneously a geographical, social, and religious imperative for *homo religiosus*.

For the Pakeha in the strange land at the antipodes neither animal nor tree nor landscape resembled counterparts in British landscape, myth, or story. *U-topia* means "no place." The word-play in the title of Samuel Butler's book *Erewhon* conveys (1) the antithesis of a familiar someplace and (2) *terra incognita*, the Pakeha word for undomesticated territories. Colonists regarded the landscape as alternatively unwelcoming and alien or romantic and sublime,[23] but never as the orienting text of their myth-history or the sustaining body of their primal mother. Only after the missionaries had obtained land from paramount chiefs and established their first agricultural mission in 1827, did the Pakeha became independent, at-home, and increasingly effective in making Maori converts. Not only did they find their position in the strange land, but the overall efficacy of their mission increased.

A homesick Charles Darwin limned the miniature Albion of Waimate Mission Station at Christmas time in 1835:

> At length we reached Waimate; after having passed over so many miles of an uninhabited useless country, the sudden appearance of an English farm house and its well dressed fields, placed there as if by an enchanter's wand, was exceedingly pleasing. . . . At Waimate there are three large houses, where the missionary gentlemen, Messrs [Henry] Williams, Davies, and Clarke, reside; and near them are the huts of the native labourers. . . . There were large gardens, with every fruit and vegetable which England produces, and many belonging to a warmer clime. . . . asparagus, kidney beans, cucumbers, rhubarb, apples, pears, figs, peaches, apricots, grapes, olives, gooseberries, currants, hops, gorse for fences [later to become a rampant botanical pest], and English oaks; also many kinds of flowers. Around the farm-yard there

22. Carlos Castenada, *The Teachings of Don Juan*, pp. 29–34.
23. Trudie McNaughton, *Countless Signs: The New Zealand Landscape in Literature*, pp. 3–7.

were stables, a threshing-barn with its winnowing machine, a blacksmith's forge, and on the ground ploughshares and other tools: in the middle was that happy mixture of pigs and poultry, lying comfortably together, as in every English farm-yard. . . .

All this is very surprising, when it is considered that five years ago nothing but the fern flourished here. Moreover, native workmanship, taught by the missionaries, has effected this change;— the lesson of the missionary is the enchanter's wand. The house had been built, the windows framed, the fields ploughed, and even the trees grafted, by the New Zealander [Maori]. At the mill, a New Zealander was seen powdered white with flour, like his brother miller in England. When I looked at this whole scene, I thought it admirable. It was not merely that England was brought vividly before my mind; yet, as the evening drew to a close, the domestic sounds, the fields of corn, the distant undulating country with its trees, might well have been mistaken for our father land; nor was it the triumphant feeling at seeing what Englishmen could effect; but rather the high hopes thus inspired for the future progress of this fine island.[24]

Darwin's nostalgic prose bears witness to the longing for a place where each thing and person is bounded and defined in completely familiar terms. He saw a "whole scene," an "admirable" cosmos that conveyed a "triumphant feeling" and "high hopes" for the future progress of the island. However, his description is most striking for its failure to notice the loss of identity and power of the Maori laborers who were transformed by the "enchanter's wand" into a subservient class, with faces "powdered white with flour."

Colonization and Christianization were inseparable processes. To create an Albion at the antipodes, the missionaries believed they would first have to transform the heathen into a subordinate class of Christians, and the "civilising" of the landscape was a duty "inextricably bound up with" converting them to Christianity.[25] A settler wrote, "New Zealand is much in the state that Britain was when Caesar landed; and if Caesar's Britain could now be shown us, many a bright champaign country which we call beautiful, would vanish, to reveal the gloomy forest and repulsive rugged waste"; he advised that in New Zealand

24. From Charles Darwin, *The Voyage of the Beagle*, pp. 423–24.
25. McNaughton, *Countless Signs*, p. 8.

"plough sickle and mill would singularly enrich and brighten the land-scape."[26]

THE POLICY OF AMALGAMATION

The purpose of settlement in the words of colonial entrepreneur, Edward Gibbon Wakefield, was to re-create England's rural past in the "good old days before industrialism and new ideas had upset the rural harmony."[27] He envisioned a scientific colony that would "invigorate" imperial expansion and "encourage" new settlements by relieving England of the urban poor, although his colonies were supposed to include a cross-section of social classes.[28] While advising that the Maori would be better left alone "to remain forever the savages that they are," he planned to make New Zealand a caste-based society of laborers and landowners by acquiring nearly all the land from the natives and re-selling it at a "sufficient price" to support the enterprise of colonization.[29] This naive capitalization scheme was adopted as policy by the Crown. From the outset, the *imperium* committed itself to a policy of acquiring "waste" lands and "amalgamating" the Maori into British economic and social institutions, while denying them equal representation in the political institutions of the colony. The Treaty gave the chiefs a "guarantee" of governance over their own lands and treasures, but reserved ultimate sovereignty for the Crown alone.

The policy of amalgamation fostered by the imperial governors meshed neatly with the Anglican doctrine that it would be necessary to civilize as well as Christianize the Maori in order to save them from the fate of the Australian aborigines or the Yahgan tribes of Tierra del Fuego. Even though the Humanitarian lobby in London deplored Wakefield's disregard of the Maori, they shared his goal of colonizing New Zealand. The amalgamation policy salved the Pakeha conscience by promising to free the Maori from the sin and idolatry of their "natural" state while surplus Europeans would colonize Aotearoa. The Treaty of Waitangi gave to the British monarch the exclusive right to acquire land from chiefs willing to sell. By the end of his first administration in

---

26. Ibid., p. 7.
27. Sinclair, History of New Zealand, pp. 60, 66.
28. Ibid., pp. 58, 60.
29. Ibid., pp. 60, 64.

1853, Governor George Grey had purchased thirty-two million acres from the chiefs for only fifty thousand pounds.[30]

Thirty years later, Donald McLean's advice to the Waikato Committee proved that the policy of amalgamation had not changed since Darwin's time: "[Maori] attention should always be directed to habits of industry, to have their farms improved and fenced. I believe that annual prizes, to be given to those who had their best land cultivated, would cause emulation and have a very good effect."[31]

McLean's dual portfolio as Minister of Maori Affairs and Chief Land Commissioner empowered him to devise strategies for alienating Maori land at the same time he was charged to protect their interests. The Crown policy of aboriginal protection was instituted in the words of the Treaty of Waitangi, "to avert the evil consequences which must result from the absence of the necessary Laws and Institutions" under private colonization schemes like Wakefield's, but this Humanitarian objective was vitiated from the beginning by an insoluble conflict between capitalizing a new colony, on the one hand, and safeguarding the treasured possession of the indigenous people, on the other.

The noble objective of the imperial amalgamation policy was, in the words of James Armitage, "to bring them [the Maori] into subservience to and connection with the English law; in fact to make them good and loyal subjects; or, . . . to do away with the distinction of 'Pakeha' and 'Maori,' and introduce the word *'Tangata'* [people] instead. This would be a real fusion of the two races, a very desirable object in my opinion."[32] In real terms this meant that a "civilised" Maori was to become a farmer or laborer, give up his world for that of the European, trade the power and influence of his chiefs for the law of the Crown, and to sell his "waste land" to the Pakeha, who would put it to productive use in the colonial enterprise.

In truth, the Pakeha myth incorporated the *tangata whenua* into the Christian cosmos by displacing them from their own world. This ethnocentric purpose propelled the government's unremitting land-acquisition policies. Eventually, it provoked the series of renewal movements before, during, and after the Land Wars of the 1860s. In order to establish their own position in the land, the Pakeha needed to amalgamate the indigenous people into a European, Christian state. The Maori countered this strategy with powerful religious resources—the rituals,

30. Asher and Naulls, *Maori Land*, p. 18.
31. *AJHR*, 1860, F-No. 3, p. 10.
32. *AJHR*, 1860, p. 5; the testimony of James Armitage.

visions, and mandates of the Maori *poropiti* and *mangai*, "prophets" and "mouthpieces." Their nativist, millenarian formations promised to safeguard the land and treasures of the *iwi*.

LAMENT FOR THE LAND

Between 1843 and 1860 the Pakeha population increased sevenfold— from 11,489 to 79,000.[33] The overall Maori population had declined in the same period, and in 1860 was only slightly greater than that of the Pakeha. In the North Island where the wars took place, the Maori numbered slightly fewer than the colonists. The great meetings in Waikato to establish a Maori kingship were punctuated with traditional laments, such as the following:

> *Ka Ngapu te whenua*
> *Ka haere nga tangata Kihea?*
> *E Ruaimoko*
> *Purutia tawhia, Ki aita.*

> Like a creeping thing
> The land is moving
> When gone, where shall man
> Find a dwelling?
> Oh, Ruaimoko!
> Hold it fast
> Retain it firmly
> In thy grasp
> And bid it stay.[34]

In Taranaki, Chief Wiremu Kingi warned,

These lands will not be given by us into the Governor's and your hands, lest we resemble the sea-birds which perch upon a rock: when the tide flows the rock is covered by the sea, and the birds take flight, for they have no resting place.[35]

The major grievance of the Land Wars is summed up by Werahiko Panipoaka in a letter of 1869 to a sympathetic Pakeha:

33. Asher and Naulls, *Maori Land*, p. 14.
34. Free translation published in Buddle, *The Maori King Movement*, pp. 39–40.
35. Caselberg, *Maori Is My Name*, p. 75.

You first brought us guns and powder . . . you gave these things to us to destroy each other with. Then you sent us missionaries, and we became religious. You told us to look up to heaven, and we turned our eyes upwards towards the heaven. While we were engaged in that way—in looking up to heaven—you looked down to earth with a covetous eye to grasp the land.[36]

Panipoaka's lament became a familiar refrain. At the end of the wars in 1873 Wi Tako spoke before the House of Representatives:

You say our lands should be taken for the benefit of the natives; and our lands are taken, and our children are to be taught the English language. And after they come out of the schools what land are they to live upon? Are they to live upon the earth, or fly like the pigeon? . . . My people have seen this bill, and they say it will be like the time of Pharaoh when the yoke was placed upon the necks of the children of Israel.[37]

The conviction that his people were Jews in bondage motivated Te Kooti to lead his fellow captives out of prison in the Chatham Islands, take revenge upon his pursuers, and to found the Ringatu church. In a prayer composed while he was under indefinite sentence Te Kooti identified the Maori with the people of Moses:

O God, if our hearts arise from the land in which we now dwell as slaves, and repent and pray to Thee to confess our sins in Thy presence, then, O Jehovah, do Thou blot out the sins of Thy own people, who have sinned against Thee. Do not Thou, O God, cause us to be wholly destroyed. Wherefore it is that we glorify Thy Holy Name.

Amen.[38]

36. Ibid., p. 117.
37. Ibid.
38. Ibid., p. 110.

3

FATAL IMPACT VERSUS
POSITIVE ADAPTATION

> *. . . the lesson of the missionary is the
> enchanter's wand.*
>
> Charles Darwin

overnor George Grey[1] instituted Humanitarian-inspired pro-
grams to educate the Maori in Western traditions, employ
them in an agricultural economy, and subject them to British
laws in a deliberate attempt to avoid the bloody confrontations similar
to those which had characterized the Australian frontier. He initiated a
"flour and sugar" policy that subsidized the mills and farms of paramount chiefs, who in return gave their support to his imperial policies.[2]
Grey cultivated close relationships with the Maori *ariki,* "chiefly families," and a reputation for fostering "One law for both races,"[3] a slogan

---

1. Grey's first imperial governorship, 1845–53, succeeded that of Robert Fitzroy, former captain of the *Beagle.* His second term as governor, 1861–68, followed the administration of Gore
Browne.

2. Ward, *A Show of Justice,* pp. 86–87.

3. The phrase may have come from an ad hoc comment made by the Crown's representative,
Captain Hobson, after the chiefs signed the Treaty of Waitangi in 1840. As they departed, Hobson
shook each by the hand, "saying (in Maori), *'He iwi tahi tatou'* ('We are [now] one people'), at which

that has been invoked by Pakeha and Maori at different times in history to advance their own respective interests.[4]

CONVERSION RITES

An inadequate appreciation of the Maori way of organizing and maintaining their world undermined the Humanitarian intentions of missionaries and imperial officers. British ideas about native religions were smug and naive. Philosopher Thomas Hobbes argued that "naturall" religion invented gods from one's dreams or reflections. He based this theory on what he had read about Native Americans and later applied it to the austral peoples. *Tapu*, regarded by missionaries as a melange of satanic rules that impeded the conversion of the natives, was actually an indispensable system of governance and law, but at baptism a convert was required to renounce not only Satan but Maori customs as well. Attempting to mitigate the Church Missionary Society's harsh rejection of Maori identity, Chief William Naylor devised a rite called *kokiro*, which assured the new convert that the old gods would not punish him for breaking *tapu*, but Henry Williams denounced it as a perversion. The notion that people could utterly abandon their old ways and embrace "civilisation" with eager hearts was a persistent misperception on the part of missionaries, governors, and settlers. Perhaps this is why fewer than half the Maori population were converted by 1840.[5] Most Protestant missionaries forbade any departure from orthodoxy that might have eased the transition from Maori practices to Christianity,[6] although rites such as *kokiro* might have swelled the numbers in their congregations. Even after meeting the test of baptism, the converts' faith was viewed as fickle by many Pakeha: "However readily the gospel was received and eagerly as this sagacious and inquisitive people learned to read and write, it may be feared that only a rather small proportion of nominal converts became really Christian."[7]

---

the Natives were greatly pleased": from the notes of William Colenso, *The Authentic and Genuine History*, p. 35.

4. The Ringatu messiah, Rua Kenana, defended his right to a liquor license by appealing to the slogan that there should be "one law for both people," which was emblazoned on one of his flags at Maungapohatu, according to Webster, *Rua and the Maori Millennium*, p. 237.

5. J. M. R. Owens, "Christianity and the Maoris to 1840," p. 23.

6. Elsmore, quoting from the New Plymouth Wesleyan Circuit Report of 1857, *Mana from Heaven*, p. 138.

7. Governor Robert Fitzroy, *Remarks on New Zealand*, p. 8.

APORIA, "WITHOUT A BRIDGE"

In addition to baptism, the Crown's drive to acquire "waste lands"—all Maori land apart from villages and fields—greatly impacted traditional society before 1860, and land legislation passed by the New Zealand House of Representatives after 1860 imposed European rules of inheritance and land tenure upon the *iwi*. Under the onslaught of Christianization and colonization, significant numbers of people began to exhibit a new malaise, characterized by,

> First, a general loss of morale and a lack of confidence in themselves as a group, or in their leaders as well as an aimlessness. Second, an increase in behaviour patterns associated with anxiety/frustration and depression, such as heavy drinking, alcoholism, and an increase in certain types of diseases and even crime. Third, the type of lethargy, both mental and physical, which is linked with a reactive depression in clinical psychology, and reflected in conversation, dress, habits, and attitudes to improvement. . . . To an outside observer they often seem like people walking in a dream.[8]

Te Ua Haumene called this condition *tuwareware*, which means "forsaken by" or "forgetful of" God.[9]

In the old world, *te ao tawhito*, one who trespassed on prohibited sites or touched a *tapu* person incurred *mate maori*, a sickness that caused severe abdominal pain (from the lizard that ate one's vitals) and could be fatal. After a shrinking populace abandoned their sacred thresholds and precincts, including burial grounds, latrines, potato storehouses, and food-gathering sites, any chance contact with them could bring on the sickness, but there was a shortage of the religious experts who could perform the *whakanoa* rites that removed *tapu* sickness. Te Ua blamed the increased morbidity of his people on their inattentiveness to Jehovah's wishes, but the manner in which he ascribed illness to the violation of divine mandates was the same in 1862 as it had been before his people had converted to Christianity.

Anomie, a condition of increased social pathologies, does not adequately describe the specific and intense consequences of violating

---

8. Webster, *Rua and the Maori Millennium*, p. 151.
9. Lyndsay Head gives the latter translation in "The Gospel of Te Ua Haumene," pp. 7–44; whereas Clark, *Hauhau*, p. 116, gives the former translation.

tapu. If one must borrow from the Greek, the word *aporia*, "without a bridge," better describes the profound dislocation from the ancestral world that they were suffering. *Anomie* describes a set of symptoms without identifying the causes that give rise to them. *Aporia* locates the cause in a rupture between the counterposed worlds of *te ao tawhito* and *te ao hou*. It was this rupture that the prophets of renewal were called by divine beings to bridge.

When the Crown set about acquiring land from willing chiefs, it cut the umbilicus between land and people. Separated from a world in which time, place, act, role, past, future, the dead, and the living all cohere, the affected tribes lost their vital access to rites of renewal, which left them disoriented and literally out-of-place. The alien imperatives of colonial occupation, imperial government, conversion, and amalgamation wrenched them from their cosmos.[10] Historical data from the postcolonial era reveal an invariable association between the unprecedented experience of permanent alienation from the land and the condition of forsakenness addressed by Te Ua.

LAND LOSS AND POPULATION DECLINE

M. P. K. Sorrenson uncovered a significant correlation between the increase in Maori land sales and the decline of the Maori population after settler-dominated administrations accelerated the rate of land acquisition in the mid-1860s.[11] In a deliberate effort to detribalize the Maori, the 1862 Native Land Act nullified aboriginal title[12] to land by legalizing direct land transactions between individual Maori and private parties of settlers for the first time. As a consequence, the 1870s saw "a sordid trafficking in land."[13] The intent of the postwar land legislation was to "destroy . . . the principle of communism, which ran through the whole of [Maori] institutions . . . which stood as a barrier in the way of all attempts to amalgamate the Native race into our own social and political system."[14] This so-called principle of communism referred to the ancestral system of usufruct, which had no standing in law after 1862. "The authority of chiefs was undermined when British

10. Taylor, *The Past and Present of New Zealand*, pp. 115–17, 125, 163–64.
11. Sorrenson, "Land Purchase Methods," pp. 183–99.
12. "Aboriginal title" is a British phrase that has no analogue in Maori custom, but it was employed to subsume tribal claims under European civil law.
13. Ward, *A Show of Justice*, p. 257.
14. Sorrenson, "Land Purchase Methods," p. 185; quotation from Henry Sewell in 1870.

law awarded full rights to individuals to sell 'their' shares of land. The Native Lands Act of 1865 intensified intratribal conflict, as the struggles of competing owners were carried to the new *marae* of the Native Land Court."[15] The latter institution busied itself for the rest of the century in applying increasingly cynical land legislation to Maori tribal lands, which were no longer conceived of as inalienable, but as privately owned. The Land Court's procedures sparked internecine feuds among families and *hapu*, which further undermined Maori social cohesion. Sorrenson's finding that there was a significant correlation between the selling off of tribal lands and the decline of the Maori population, supports the thesis that a social world coheres only when a people locate themselves in space and time according to their own myths, rituals, and traditions.

Sorrenson also found that as land sales increased, there was a corresponding rise in the people's conviction that they had no future. Between 1850 and 1900, Pakeha and Maori alike assumed the Maori were a doomed race. This tragic concern facilitated the rise of the millenarian movements that also happened to correlate with the transition to "responsible rule" and the imposition of alien land-tenure laws.

The loss of the land, the decline in population and fertility, the phenomenon of *aporia*, and the renewal movements were intimately associated. A communal belief that the future holds only further humiliation induces both anxiety and despair. Paradoxically, despair may engender dreams and visions that promise a return of power, orderliness, peace, and lost treasure. What stands out in the copious data on the prophet movements is that the *land is an ultimate concern, namely, a religious commitment that a group lives by and will die for.* One hears this ultimate concern in the retort of the messiah, Rua Kenana, to a divine voice, "If your wish is for me to save only people, I won't help, but if it is to save the land, then I shall carry out this task. . . . I shall save the land, for if I save only people, there will soon be no land on which they can live."[16]

Rua spoke as a *Tuhoe* tribesman and guardian of the sacred mountain where the Tuhoe's ancestors are buried. Rua's genealogy positioned him within the borders of the Urewera region. So close is the bond between oneself and a place that "the turangawaewae, the stand-

---

15. Ibid., p. 191. A *marae* is the outside courtyard of the meeting house where issues of conflict are debated.

16. Webster, *Rua and the Maori Millennium*, p. 158.

ing and identity of a people, was defined by their territory."[17] When
visitors announced themselves at a ceremonial gathering on their
neighbors' sacred plaza, the chief would utter a formulaic greeting that
expressed his tribe's bond with its territory, such as: "Tongariro is the
mountain, Taupo is the sea, and Te Heuheu is the man."[18] Thus it is no
wonder that Sorrenson perceived a "close connection between land
purchase, the drink traffic, and the occurrence of European diseases."[19]
Loss of the land made sacred places inaccessible to the people. The
specific, traditional, and vital connection between ancestral territory
and a people is a religious one. Its severance produced nothing less
than the phenomenon of diaspora, a condition of disconnection from
the "Promised Land."

MAORI HERMENEUTICS

Maori renewal movements restored the boundaries that had delineated
the realms of sky deities, earth deities, and human beings since the
beginning of the world: *te rangi* is the realm of sky gods and multiple
heavens; *te po*, the realm of night, death, and underworld and the goddess, Hinenuitepo; *te ao marama* is the world between, "the realm of
light," given to human beings. The prophets reestablished communication with the divine sources of power and life, *mana* and *mauri*, which
flowed as nourishment from the realms of Sky and Earth to the world of
human beings. They reinstated the complements of male and female,
tapu and *noa*, that established and maintained society. They also borrowed selectively from biblical religion in order to establish a new
world that was, once again, wholly Maori and regulated by divine mandates.

Te Ua's movement fostered a new hermeneutics that promised ultimate justice for the "people standing naked in the Island in two
halves."[20] It may have been necessary for the complex process of syncretism to accelerate before widespread conversion to Christianity became possible. The visionary prophets wove Maori and biblical myths
and symbols into a unique genealogical and liturgical tapestry that was
fashioned from the historical experience of those who followed them.
The renewal movements were integral transformations of Maori reli-

17. Walker, *Ka Whawhai Tonu Matou*, p. 70.
18. Ibid., p. 71.
19. Sorrenson, "Land Purchase Methods," p. 192.
20. Refrain, *Te Ua Rongopai*, January 1863, Grey Collection. Maori MSS: GNZ, MMS1, APL.

gion; they were not just Christian heresy cults. The *tangata whenua* adopted new symbols—flags, Jewish ancestors, sacred numbers, Israelite law and paradigms—to bridge the past and the present. Only particular biblical stories and figures resonated with Maori traditions and were assimilated as resources for repairing a world that had been disturbed by alien forces.

Only a year after Buddle's Nelson address, Roman Catholic missionary Sister Mary Joseph Aubert acknowledged the new hermeneutics in a remarkable statement.

Hauhauism [Te Ua's religion] reflects the independent religious convictions of the people, though of course greatly distorted by passion. The hostile feeling which provoked its development led to the rejection of many things . . . because it was thought their rejection would make the Maori protest stronger against the Pakeha Christian's inconsistencies. It is not to be wondered at, that when they broke away from their European guides and tried to conceive of God for themselves, that the result of their independent study of Holy Writ was to convince them, that Jehovah was the God of the sons of Shem, the family to which they believed themselves to belong, and the Lord Jesus the God of the sons of Japhet, the family to which the English belong.[21]

Sister Mary recognized Maori hermeneutics as a legitimate response to Pakeha "inconsistencies." In her 1874 analysis we see how Maori and Pakeha myths began to engage in a dialectic of competing orthodoxies. As disillusionment with Christianity grew, unconventional movements offered alternatives to Pakeha-dominated churches.

Te Ua claimed Jacob's twelve sons as ancestors and worshiped Jehovah as Lawgiver.[22] He set in motion a series of renewal movements, whose disciples claimed Jewish identity as *tiu* and *Iharaira*.[23] Jewish scriptures became one source of their myths of the return of land, power, peace, and plenty. Te Ua's successor, Te Kooti, led an exodus of captives back to the "Promised Land" in imitation of Moses and Joshua. Maori messiahs founded settlements on disputed sacred sites. Given their disillusionment with Pakeha Christianity, one can under-

21. Davidson and Lineham, *Transplanted Christianity*, p. 160.

22. Christ played a lesser role in Pai Marire; see Lindsay Head, *DNZB* 1 (1990): 512.

23. A parallel myth that the Anglo-Saxons were the true Israelites was simultaneously developing among British-Israelites in England; see Michael Barkun, *Religion and the Racist Right: The Origins of the Christian Identity Movement.*

stand how the followers of the prophets felt a kinship with the Jews of
the New Testament who contended with the Christians in their midst.[24]

BRITISH MILLENARIANISM

The Pakeha were not inclined to recognize the impact of so radical a
document as the Bible on a people they were seriously engaged in
dominating. Erudite missionaries regarded biblically inspired dissidents as backsliding barbarians or fools. British social philosophy classified nations as savage, barbarian, or civilized—typified by Australian
aborigines, Maori, and Europeans respectively.[25] God commissioned
Japhet to rule over the sons of Shem until they could be brought into
the fold of civilization. The biblically inspired Pakeha myth sanctioned
conquest, conversion, and assimilation. In the early nineteenth century
the Anglican church sent missionaries abroad to civilize the heathen to
ensure that Jesus would return to usher in the Christian millennial
kingdom. The Jesus of the missionaries was the eschatological Lamb;
the Jesus of the British imperium was Christ with a Sword. British
Christian imperialism was fundamentally the enactment of a violent
millenarian myth.

HISTORICAL DEBATE

The effects of Christianity upon the Maori sparked a debate among
New Zealand historians. J. M. R. Owens[26] argues that the Christian
mission had a delayed impact between 1814 and the signing of the
Treaty of Waitangi in 1840. Samuel Marsden had expected the planting
of the Union Jack to herald a "signal for the dawn of civilization," but
it was eleven years before the first Anglican convert, Christian Rangi,
was baptized in the Bay of Islands. Similarly, in 1830, after seven
years of evangelizing, the Wesleyan-Methodist Missionary Society had
not made a single convert.

According to Owens, the process of Christianization was gradual and
varied. Citing statistical information from 1841 that Maori converts

24. Elsmore, *Mana from Heaven*, pp. 64–68.
25. See Tony Swain, "The Aborigines in European Mythology," in *Interpreting Aboriginal Religion*, pp. 1–21; Sinclair in *The Origins of the Maori Wars*, pp. 19–26. Maori chiefs also divided the
Pakeha population into superior and inferior categories of beings; see Ward, *A Show of Justice*, p. 22.
26. Owens, "Christianity and the Maoris to 1840."

comprised no more than 3 percent of the indigenous population, he concluded that "nowhere does one find a pagan religion suddenly yielding to the impact of the white man or supinely accepting his doctrines."[27]

Challenging Owen's gradualist thesis, Judith Binney argues for a two-part "common pattern" in the history of the South Pacific missions: a long initial period of little impact on the native culture, followed by a "relatively sudden breakthrough . . . during which church attendance rises sharply." She noted that around the mid-1830s in New Zealand, "simultaneous with the beginning of conversion," the first of the "heresy cults" arose, in which "a Maori prophet set up his own quasi-Christian sect in opposition to the Europeans."[28] Binney relates the "historic shift" from the initial "little impact" of Christianity to its "sudden breakthrough," to the arrival of the Anglican minister (later bishop) Henry Williams in 1823.

Samuel Marsden had sent laymen to Ruatara's people to teach them the "civilizing arts" of European crafts and agriculture before they heard the gospel, but his approach failed to promote conversions. Henry Williams reversed Marsden's policy, arguing that "only Christianity would supply the motive for initiation into the new way of life."[29] By 1828 Williams and his fellow evangelists had became famed as peacemakers[30] among the tribes during the sanguinary Musket Wars, and their diplomatic skills enhanced the reputation of the new faith among the people.

Owens, on the other hand, argues that conversion tended to occur as the Maori learned to read and write and as the missions trained native evangelists. The employment of native missionaries invigorated the spread of Christianity in New Caledonia.[31] In New Zealand the literacy factor merits special consideration. Although a prevailing assumption that the Maori learned to read and write with remarkable alacrity has

27. A quotation from Vittorio Lanternari in Owens, "Christianity and the Maoris to 1840," p. 22.

28. Binney, "Christianity and the Maoris," pp. 143–44.

29. Ibid., p. 148. It is unclear in the text whether the words were Williams's or Binney's précis of his words.

30. Ibid., p. 150, refers to Janet Ross's unpublished thesis to argue that Christianity became accepted when the Maori associated the new religion with peacemaking. Ward, *A Show of Justice*, p. 20, notes that Ernest Dieffenbach wrote in 1843 that some Maori accepted Christianity to end cycles of feuding. However, the Maori did have their own institutions of peacemaking, and there is no compelling evidence that Christian skill in mediating disputes was the only variable that accounted for the more numerous conversions that began to occur in the 1830s and 1840s.

31. French missionary Maurice Leenhardt said, it is the "young churches in pagan lands which will provide us with the fresh blood needed for the revitalization of our tired milieu." *Do Kamo*, p. *ix*.

been challenged, there is no reason to question the numerous reports in primary data that they absorbed the scriptures within a surprisingly short time.[32] A people with a prodigious oral tradition, the Maori impressed contemporaries with their ability to memorize long texts. The translation of the Bible into the native language and its dissemination corresponded with a "great leap forward in missionary influence." Moreover, "the enthusiasm for literacy spilled over into enthusiasm for the ideas conveyed by this means."[33]

Notwithstanding the debate over what factors facilitated conversion, European religion had penetrated Maori culture even before Marsden preached his first sermon. Owens notes in passing that "Christian concepts were being blended with Maori religious concepts . . . and from the first contact of [Capt. James] Cook[,] Maoris had the chance to pick up European ideas of religion . . . the idea of the Sabbath as a holy day [began] to creep in before 1814."[34] As early as 1805 certain northern tribes "had the idea of rewards and punishments in a future state."[35] S. Percy Smith of the Polynesian Society reported that a prophet from Waikato, Te Toroa, spread his knowledge of a foreign god, Wheawheau, [Jehovah?] and a new ritual to the East Coast in the 1820s. Nearly a hundred years later ethnologist Elsdon Best recorded the god Wheawheau in a list of Tuhoe *atua*, "gods," and described a ritual associated with what had come to be a local god of war.[36]

In addition to denouncing Maori customs, Thomas Buddle likewise noted the deleterious effects of colonization. In May 1849, the Ngati Ruanui met to decide whether all land sales should be prohibited or whether individuals should exercise their "right to do as they pleased with their own [land]."[37] Buddle reported that

> some of the thoughtful men spoke of the invariable results of colonization, and argued that a pakeha's town would bring immorality and disorganization among them; that their young women would be debauched and their young men be tempted to drunkenness. How much it is to be regretted that our European settlements,

32. D. F. McKenzie, *Oral Culture, Literacy, & Print in Early New Zealand*. Whether the Maori memorized whole passages or read the Bible does not alter the fact that they absorbed it.

33. Owens, "Christianity and the Maoris to 1840," pp. 34–35.

34. Ibid., pp. 26–27.

35. Ibid.

36. Elsmore, *Mana from Heaven*, pp. 17–18.

37. Buddle, *The Maori King Movement*, p. 4.

composed as they are of professedly christian people, should furnish savage tribes with such arguments as these![38]

This awareness was disturbingly at odds with the Pakeha myth, which extolled civilizing the savages. Buddle was capable of admitting that there were "thoughtful men" who could draw their own conclusions about the "invariable results" of Pakeha innovations, but he and his associates failed to realize that Maori leaders who forbade land sales were also devising thoughtful religious responses to "immorality and disorganization."

The debate between Binney and Owens reveals that Christianization was a complex and interactive process. Their competing views of the Maori "response" to the "stimulus" of Christianization and colonization do not fully account for the tribes' nuanced experience of contact and displacement. Other scholars have fostered a "fatal impact" view of cultural contact, namely, that an initial, brief period of Maori dominance over the missionaries gave way to the tribes' descent into a cultural disorganization marked by war, disease, and alcoholism, a state of affairs from which they have never completely recovered.[39] Owens has dubbed this the "decline and response" theory.[40] More recently, revisionist scholars have objected that the "fatal impact" view ignores data that support a more positive view of adaptation to European ways. However, those who espouse either view would agree that with the advent of Christianization and colonization, the Maori world began a process of irreversible historic change.

PARSONSON AND POSITIVE IMPACT

In her revisionist essay, "The Pursuit of Mana," Ann Parsonson argues that the "fatal impact" theory wrongly assumes that the Maori were passive victims of colonization; she contends that the traditionally assertive Maori were eager to learn new ways and turn them to their own advantage. Agreeing that major social and economic dislocations resulted from the progressive loss of Maori land after 1865, she proposed

38. Ibid., pp. 4–5.

39. Proponents of this thesis include Harrison Wright, author of *New Zealand, 1769–1840: Early Years of Western Contact*; Keith Sinclair, author of *A History of New Zealand* and *The Origins of the Maori Wars*; I.L.G. Sutherland, *The Maori Situation*; and Sorrenson, "Land Purchase Methods." The recent popularity of Maori writer Alan Duff and his novel *Once Were Warriors* attests to the broad acceptance of this theory.

40. Owens, "Christianity and the Maoris to 1840," p. 26.

the idea that it was a Polynesian ethos of competitiveness that was responsible for Maori social and economic misfortunes. In spite of abundant evidence that tribes regularly engaged in a collective redistribution of resources,[41] she depicts the Maori as a "race of individualists."[42] Unfortunately, her thesis relies heavily upon the missionary stereotype of Maori society as bellicose and schismatic, which has been perpetuated by questionable Western scholarship.[43] She has ignored a large body of contradictory data and assumed a rather romantic European view of the Maori as a warrior nation.

While there is ample evidence that imperial policies enabled privileged loyalist chiefs to enjoy a temporary increase of wealth and prestige, they became impoverished after the settlers became self-governing and discontinued Maori-friendly policies. Withdrawal of government subsidies happened to coincide with increased market competition from Australian agriculture, which caused a farm depression in New Zealand. Postwar land confiscations and the imposition of unfair land legislation contributed to a decline in Maori population and capital. The failure of native New Zealanders to prosper under a European economic system should be attributed to the transfer of their primary capital assets in the form of land to the Pakeha over a broad period of time. Unlike their settler counterparts, enterprising Maori had neither capital reserves nor political representation.

In *Native Custom and Law Affecting Native Land*, Norman Smith documents the tenacious purpose of successive administrations to convert all Maori land to individual title and, thereby, to assimilate it into government capitalization schemes for national development.[44] It was these intentional policies that instigated intratribal conflicts, not Parsonson's putative, intrinsic ethos of competitiveness. Government land agents actively fostered factions within tribes. The passage in 1870 of

41. Two quite different methods of redistribution were the annual *hakari* festival and the punitive *taua muru*.

42. Parsonson, "The Pursuit of Mana," pp. 140–42, 149, 153.

43. Edward Tregear in *The Maori Race* used faulty data to assert that the Maori were descended from the Aryans who invaded the early Indus Valley civilization. M. P. K. Sorrenson refutes Tregear in *Maori Origins and Migrations*. Andrew Vayda and other Western scholars have characterized the tribes as violent, cannibalistic, and driven to feuding and schism. For an insider's view of early Maori history, see Walker, *Ka Whawhai Tonu Matou*, pp. 7–62. Other historical revisions include Tipene O'Regan, "Old Myths and New Politics," *NZJH* 26, no. 1 (April 1992): 5–27, and the Waikato University report of Evelyn Stokes, *Mokau: Maori Cultural and Historical Perspectives*, pp. 1–64.

44. The collective land legislation after 1860 is complex, but its general intent is clear—to convert the Maori from alleged "communist" to capitalist modes of ownership while denying them the means to invest in new enterprises.

the first Native Lands Frauds Prevention Act is an indicator of the prevalence of unscrupulous transactions around that time. Parsonson's essentialist concept of Maori rivalry does not take into account the politics of land acquisition.

"A SHOW OF JUSTICE"

Alan Ward presents a more compelling argument for the positive adaptation viewpoint in his study of racial amalgamation in nineteenth-century New Zealand, *A Show of Justice*. The title is taken from a mordant, but prescient statement by Reverend Montagu Hawtrey, a Humanitarian: *"Where one of two parties was unsophisticated in the forms of Western civilization, 'the only consequence of establishing the same rights and the same obligations for both will be to destroy the weaker under a show of justice.'"*[45]

This is precisely what the settlers instituted fifty years later when "responsible rule" replaced the imperial administration and instituted "one law for both races." The new government abandoned Humanitarian policies under the guise of equality and conveniently ignored the economically, politically, and socially disadvantaged position of the Maori. It was the postwar settler administrations, time and again, that failed to acknowledge the Maori people as full partners in a parliamentary state, and that instituted policies that led to the failure of Maori enterprise in order to secure title to tribal lands. Although Ward disparages the "myth" that the Maori entered a dark period of apathy after the Land Wars, even his most positive data on the postwar era led him to conclude that "it was the sordid and demoralising system of land-purchasing, not war and confiscation, which really brought the Maori people low."[46] Ranginui Walker has also chronicled the British land expropriation policies that forced the *tangata whenua* out of a traditional economy without repositioning them in a capitalist system.[47] The old "fatal impact" thesis may have been flawed, and Parsonson's instinct that it had little explanatory value was keen. However, Ward's rigorous historiography unveils a far more complex picture of Pakeha "conquest" and Maori "response" than does Parsonson's narrow focus on an alleged ethos of Maori competitiveness. Both Ward and Walker

45. Ward, *A Show of Justice*, p. 34.
46. Ibid., pp. 264, 267.
47. Walker, *Ka Whawhai Tonu Matou*, p. 108.

consider racism the potentiating factor in the marginalization of the
Maori, without denying the failure of Maori efforts to adapt to a capitalist system.

AN ALTERNATIVE THESIS

As early as 1839, when the Crown gave its written "Instructions" to
Captain Hobson, the acquisition of Maori land was an explicit imperial
objective. One of the chief motivations behind the Crown's purpose in
signing the Treaty of Waitangi with the cooperative chiefs was to acquire their land cheaply.[48] Under Article Two of the Treaty, the chiefs'
authority over Maori *taonga*, "treasured possessions,"[49] was extended,
with one hand and, with the other, cleverly and effectively withdrawn
by the Treaty's proclamation of the queen's sovereignty and "her exclusive right of Preemption over such lands as the proprietors thereof may
be disposed to alienate."[50] The enduring issue of competing chiefly and
royal sovereignties that continues to bedevil New Zealand today is embedded in the ambiguous language of its founding document.[51]

For the next twenty years, the Crown hatched schemes to induce the
chiefs to sell their "waste lands." On the cusp of the Land Wars, Buddle assuaged the imperial conscience by mouthing the polite fiction
that "amalgamating the races, and . . . the colonization of a barbarous
country is possible without the extermination of its aboriginal race."[52]
The paternalistic Mr. Buddle's sense of guilt was far stronger than that
of his contemporaries, officials and entrepreneurs such as C. W. and
J. C. Richmond, Frederick Whitaker, and J. C. Firth. He promulgated
Donald McLean's proposals for Maori participation in New Zealand's
parliament, a fairer system of land purchase, and safeguarding the
chiefs' power of adjudication over their respective tribes just as settler
fury against Maori sympathizers was reaching a crescendo.[53] McLean
and Buddle thought that a Humanitarian policy would achieve amalgamation, and that unused tribal territories would then be more available for sale and settlement.

48. Ward, *A Show of Justice*, p. 43.

49. *Taonga*, "treasure(s)," included sacred places, food-gathering sites, greenstone, and other
resources of the land.

50. Orange, *Treaty of Waitangi*, p. 258.

51. See R. J. Walker, "The Treaty of Waitangi as the Focus of Maori Protest," in Kawharu, ed.,
Waitangi, pp. 263–79.

52. Buddle, *The Maori King Movement*, p. 72.

53. Ibid., pp. 69–70.

From the very beginning of British colonization, a truly human-itarian policy was vitiated by British ignorance of what would consti-tute sufficient safeguards for the well-being of the indigenous people. How could empire-builders from Britain's industrializing society accu-rately compute the amount of land an indigenous people required in order to maintain their numbers and their position in the world?

SUMMARY

It was the separation of the Maori from their land that led to the de-cline of their ancestral world, and to the rejection of the missions by the Maori prophets. Although positive factors, such as economic adap-tation, and negative factors, such as political (and racial) oppression, did indeed influence the experience of the Maori people under coloni-zation and Christianization, it was the incompatible myths of Pakeha and Maori concerning the *meaning* of the land that made it impossible for both peoples to inhabit the same space without a collision of views, values, and ultimately, armies. The fatal impact theory is arid, because it describes only the deleterious effects of contact on the Maori world without accounting for them and without acknowledging the dynamic interaction between the two peoples thereafter. Even though it restores some balance to European historiography, Parsonson's positive adapta-tion thesis does not take into account the divisive impact of Chris-tianity and colonization upon the basic social units of Maori culture, and upon the entire religious framework of their society.

Beginning in 1823 with the first "heresy cult" on record, innovative Maori leaders fashioned new religious movements that sought to bridge their old and new worlds in a time of unprecedented change. From the time that Hone Heke repeatedly chopped down the British flagstaff and replaced it with his own standard, until the Ringatu messiah proclaimed a Maori millennium, the inseparability of *mana* and *te whenua*, "power" and "the land"—the twin pillars of the Maori world—has been the ultimate concern of the renewal movements that flared up and spread among the children of Shem as alternatives to the Pakeha myth.

4

HOLDING FAST TO THE LAND

*The New Zealanders, though remarkably
superstitious, have no gods that they
worship; or have they any thing to
represent a being which they call god.*

William Yate, 1835

*Religion pervaded the life of the Maoris;
yet they do not seem to have been what we
should regard as a religious people.*

Keith Sinclair, 1957

If religion "pervades" the life of a people, how can they not be religious? Sinclair unwittingly reveals a secular bias against acknowledging religion on its own terms "as it appears" in documents, histories, and even before our eyes. We often discount symbolic, nonrational, *meaningful* behavior as the epiphenomena of politics, sociology, psychology, or economics. The primary features of religion—sacred word, sacred act, and sacred place—are quite tangible, compared to the favored abstractions of "culture" and "society." Religion, like life and raw data, can be messy stuff and highly controversial, not very amenable to those who like to tie up loose ends.

The preference for monotheism exerts a more subtle and pernicious influence upon the reporting of religious phenomena. William Yate looked upon the great annual *hakari* festival as a pagan feast where false stories were recited. His assessment of Maori religion as "superstition" is only a little less pejorative than Sinclair's denial that the

Maori were what we "should regard" as a religious people. As out-siders, Western missionaries and scholars are bound to misunderstand Maori religion and to be regarded at best as sincere novices in the subject matter. Yate and Sinclair are two of the best reporters/histo-rians in New Zealand letters and their level of misunderstanding about Maori rituals and ultimate concern should caution all who study non-Western cultures.

PROPHETS

The opinions of Reverend Yate and Professor Sinclair bracket more than one hundred years of Pakeha historiography in New Zealand. In 1860 a parliamentary committee of inquiry concluded that the King Movement was a political response to government neglect. Gore Brown considered it an unlawful "combination." Sinclair preferred John Eldon Gorst's report, *The Maori King* (1864), not Buddle, as a primary source for his major study, *The Origins of the Maori Wars*.[1] Like Yate, Gorst observed human behavior without discerning its religious significance. Only recently has a New Zealand scholar included the King Movement in the quasi-religious category of "adjustment cult."[2]

The highborn founder of the King Movement, Tamihana Te Waharoa, has been called *take*, "kingmaker," but not *matakite*, "seer," or *po-ropiti*, "prophet," titles usually reserved for charismatics such as Te Ua and Te Kooti. Yet the biblical prophets did not conform to any single type: Ezekiel was a visionary; Jonah, an ordinary bumbler; Moses, a political firebrand; and Nathan, a privileged court official. Jews, Chris-tians, and Muslims regard a true prophet as a messenger sent by God to diagnose and heal social ills. Conversely, we may call shamans false prophets because we associate them with "uncivilized" peoples and their "superstitions," but both prophets and shamans are called by their god(s), who endow them with divine power and knowledge, which they must use to deliver their people. Among Northwest Coast Indians, for example, a community without a shaman risked defeat and enslave-ment by enemies. Shamans and prophets may be fully human, but they serve as warners and saviors.

1. Gorst, a Cambridge graduate, was a Resident Magistrate in the Waikato when the King Move-ment arose, and he chronicled its progress, calling it "the revolt of the most intelligent and patriotic Natives' against the policy of *laissez faire* adopted by the Government in Maori districts." Sinclair, *The Origins of the Maori Wars*, p. *xii*.

2. Elsmore, *Mana from Heaven*.

TAMIHANA TE WAHAROA

Wiremu Tamihana [William Thompson] Te Waharoa sought to restore the order of God's law to the North Island tribes by establishing a kingdom on land enclosed within an *aukati*, or *tapu* boundary. He was the first prophet of Maori nationhood. The Christian son of a militant chief who had expanded his control over neighboring tribes through conquest, Tamihana received the *mana ariki*, "mantle of leadership," that enabled him to bring together independent chiefs by means of his peaceful charisma.

A "commonly related" story in Maori circles affirmed that Tamihana reached a crisis in his relationship with Pakeha officials in 1857 after a friend criticized his praise for British institutions with the aphorism, *E tomo koe i raro i aku huha*, "Your path is through underneath my thighs," meaning that he was in danger of losing his *mana* to the government.[3] Tamihana had just visited Auckland to ask Governor Browne[4] to institute a code of laws the chief had drawn up for the disordered Waikato tribes, but Browne refused to see him.[5] Then Tamihana tried to speak to Donald McLean about a loan for a new flour mill, but his petition was rejected. Finally, he endured a personal insult on his way home. The master of a coastal vessel addressed him as "nigger," demanding that he go ashore and bring water back to the ship.[6] Abandoning all efforts to adjust to British rule, Tamihana resolved to bring law to his people by anointing a Maori king who would guard the fertile Waikato heartland from Pakeha encroachment. The same year that Tamihana became a dissident, an article in Auckland's newspaper, the *Southern Cross*, took note of a growing desire for a king among disaffected North Island chiefs.

> The movement still goes on; while the propriety, the thoughtfulness, and the caution with which it is conducted render it all the more serious by nature. . . . it is clear that a great change is approaching, either for good or for evil, in the relations between the races. The natives thoroughly understand what they want, and it is not a play-thing that they seek. They are resolved on making an effort to preserve their existence, not only as a race, but, as

3. Buddle, *The Maori King Movement*, p. 7.

4. Browne was governor from 1855 to 1861 between George Grey's two terms.

5. Walker, *Ka Whawhai Tonu Motou*, pp. 111–12; John Eldon Gorst, *The Maori King*, pp. 54–55.

6. L. S. Rickard, *Tamihana the Kingmaker*, pp. 62–64.

they understand it, a nation, before they shall be over-numbered, and therefore out-mastered by the whites.[7]

"TWO SUNS"

Waikato Kingites addressed the government on June 25, 1857, announcing that the establishment of a Maori kingdom was the fulfillment of God's will and challenging the imperial officials that "if you disapprove of this (act) of God's take back the Gospel also."[8] Governor Browne responded with indignation: "Are there two suns in the heavens? Can there be two sovereigns in New Zealand?"

The power of the monarch emanates from heaven and cannot be divided, responded the British, first in 1857, and again in March 1908, when Prime Minister Joseph Ward confronted the Ringatu messiah, Rua Kenana, on the beach in Whakatane and reiterated Browne's imperial metaphor: "In New Zealand King Edward is King, and is represented here by his Government. There can be no other Government or King . . . there cannot be two suns shining in the sky at one time."[9]

The British missed a historic opportunity to grant the Waikato tribes a measure of self-governance in the 1850s, after London decided to promote colonial self-rule. In 1864 Henry Sewell, former attorney general of New Zealand, lamented that "a wise and vigilant government would have turned the King Movement to good purpose; but the Government of the colony has been neither wise nor vigilant."[10] In 1857, a feeble attempt was made to introduce civil institutions into the Waikato district and abandoned.[11] After Browne and McLean rebuffed Tamihana, he unified the central chiefs under their own separate flag and carved out a kingdom in the heartland of the North Island.

METAPHORS OF NATIONHOOD

The King Movement set out to build a new *pa*, or "house,"[12] that would shelter the unsold tribal lands under the overarching *mana* of the

---

7. Angus J. Harrop, *England and the Maori Wars*, p. 47.

8. Ibid.

9. Webster, *Rua and the Maori Millennium*, p. 227.

10. Sewell, *The New Zealand Native Rebellion*.

11. In 1857 the Waikato chiefs demanded that Governor Browne set up British civil law and local ruling councils of chiefs in their district, but Browne sent only a token magistrate.

12. See Rickard, *Tamihana the Kingmaker*, and Gorst, *The Maori King*. Normally *pa* referred to a

Maori monarch. Tamihana illustrated his vision in a circle metaphor as well:

> He illustrated his conception of the king by pushing two sticks into the ground. "One is the Maori king, the other is the Governor." He laid a third stick on top of the other two. "This is the law of God and the Queen." He then traced on the ground a circle around the sticks. "That circle is the Queen, the fence to protect all."[13]

The "fence" around the Waikato kingdom calls to mind the Pharisaic "fence" of the Law and the Prophets that buffered first-century Jews from assimilation into Greco-Roman culture. Circles symbolize discrete worlds in many traditions. A Kingite song during the wars included the following line, "The King shall encircle the whole island. / So be it, so be it, so be it. Amen."[14] Adopting Tamihana's metaphor a few years later, Te Ua renamed the second Maori king Tawhiao, which means, "hold back the world," "encircle the world," or "hold the people together"[15]—all of which signified holding the Maori world intact from penetration by the Pakeha.

SYNCRETISM

The ultimate concerns of renewal movements do not necessarily correspond to academic theories about adaptation, adjustment, response, or rebellion. Archaic myths of "eternal return" signify that the world of *our* people may wear out or be destroyed, but it will rise up anew, usually through the extraordinary intervention of a savior or ancestor whose return signals the inauguration of a new age. The inclusion of the Mesopotamian myth of the Flood into the book of Genesis indicates that archaic myths of cyclical renewal were not wholly replaced even in the Bible by Jewish linear salvation history. God, through one just man, Noah, created a better, more peaceful world from the ashes of Babel. The King Movement offered the *iwi* an inviolable place to stand within a biracial New Zealand state-in-the-making.

---

fortified village, but in the language of the King Movement, it meant the kingdom or union expressed metaphorically as a safeguarded house.

13. Rickard, *Tamihana the Kingmaker*, p. 74.

14. Ibid., pp. 73–74.

15. Clark, *Hauhau*, pp. 57, 154, from the translated *Te Ua Rongopai* and from P. Te Hirini Jones.

The Old Testament stories of Israel's first kings, Saul and David, were published in Maori translation in 1855 at the same time that the new idea of a Maori king was circulating around the North Island. Maori prophets tried to bridge the gap between the past and the troublesome present by identifying with the Jews of Exodus. In the songs of the dispossessed we hear an emerging Maori hermeneutics: "We have left Egypt the place of bondage, we seek another land, a land of rest."[16] The King was addressed as "bone [iwi] of our bone . . . a saviour for us."[17]

Between 1833 and 1918, myriad movements struggled to establish a position on the land in the modern state of New Zealand. Bronwyn Elsmore has properly treated them as transformations from within Maori tradition, not as foreign constructs that fraudulently replaced some "pure" ancient tradition. J. M. R. Owens distinguishes between movements that advocated a return to traditional practices and those that "adjusted" to European influences,[18] but he overlooks the fact that their salient feature is not the precise mix of the old and the new; rather, it is how they attempted to restore that which they considered sacred by retaining power over the land. In any given prophet movement, old and new are intermingled.

The continuous tradition of Maori revitalization movements constitutes a discrete era in Maori history that is reflected in the oral history of Pai Marire and Ringatu. Elements of Jewish identity and the Promised Land, the sabbath, Jehovah, apocalyptic, angels, and the Decalogue were woven into Maori religion in such a manner that biblical religion was reinterpreted as a true and direct revelation of Jehovah to the *tangata whenua*. The ultimate concern of all the renewal movements was to hold fast to the land.

TE KEREMA OF THE KAI TAHU

The dependence of people upon their land is powerfully and poignantly revealed in the history of *Te Kerema*, "the claim" of the Kai Tahu people to the large territory they lost. This South Island tribe supplemented their marginal horticulture in a climate difficult for yam cultivation with seasonal hunting and gathering. In 1848 they were tricked

16. Buddle, *The Maori King Movement*, p. 29; from a lament sung by Wiremu Kingi's deputation to Waikato.

17. Ibid., p. 28.

18. Owens, "Christianity and the Maoris to 1840," pp. 25, 37.

and threatened by the governor's agent into selling their land to New Zealand Company speculators, who removed them from their *mahika kai*, the wide-ranging locales where they gathered food, leaving each person with less than two and a half hectares to cultivate. As Buddy Mikaere observed, "For a people whose kai [food] was gathered from the Southern Alps to the sea and its islands, their impending confinement to reserves consisting of fixed farming plots spelled the end of a way of life."[19]

In an attempt to win back Kai Tahu land by consent of the New Zealand parliament in 1878, Horomona Pohio, stood and recited to John Sheehan, the Minister of Native Affairs, the history of Kai Tahu's relationship with the land, which was based upon the most effective Maori claim, *ahi-ka-roa*, the act of "keeping the fires burning" over a period of generations.

> The certainty of ownership was enshrined in the remembrance of acts which had been performed upon the land: here a chief's umbilical cord might be buried; there the eel weir of the family was erected; somewhere else an ancestor had fought or died. If he was the founding ancestor of the group, then even the places where he stopped to rest or relieve himself might be remembered in place names or as boundary markers for the land which made up the territory of the tribe.[20]

Wahi tapu are particular places made sacred because something significant happened there, transforming the land into a "book" or a "text." However, Pohio's oral document had no standing in British law. It is true that that throughout their own history Europeans had held certain places sacred, in the Holy Land for example, and had even fought wars to regain them; however, the European regard for sacred places has long since been superseded by the secular priority of private ownership and the right of the owner to decide what to do with his or her space. It is therefore little wonder that Parliament did not return their *wahi tapu* to the Kai Tahu.

After Horomona Pohio recited the history of *Te Kerama* in front of the government's representatives, John Sheehan asked him to "state his case" for the claim to the land. Pohio replied, "I have nothing to say. As for my words [argument], they are in the submission which has been

19. Mikaere, *Te Mahairoa and the Promised Land*, p. 22.
20. Ibid., pp. 89–90.

read out." Sheehan replied, "The speeches within that document are just traditional sayings."[21]

Sheehan's deaf response recapitulated the precipitating cause of the Land Wars almost twenty years earlier: the Taranaki chief, Wiremu Kingi, refused to debate his claim to the Waitara Block before the governor of the colony. Teira, a rival with a grudge against his chief, claimed the Block was his to sell, although individual landholding was unknown in Maori society. The governor angrily noted Kingi's "want of courtesy to myself" and later argued that because the chief had not defended his right to the land when they met, he had forfeited it.[22] However, the perspicacious Donald McLean declared that "the actual owner . . . seldom makes a noisy or boasting demonstration of what his claims really are; it may therefore be inferred, from his silent and uncompromising demeanour, that his rights are not to be trifled with, and that without his acquiescence it will be impossible to make a valid purchase."[23]

If McLean knew of this custom, then his superior, Browne, likewise knew; and we must conclude that the governor's accusation of Kingi was a sham, blown out of proportion to hide his real intent, which was the abolishing of aboriginal claims in favor of the establishment of individual ownership. When Browne publicized Kingi's "silent and uncompromising demeanour" as an affront and accepted Teira's offer to sell the land, Kingi's people tore down the surveyor's chains at Waitara, and the First Taranaki War broke out.[24]

Almost twenty years later in 1878, Te Maiharoa, the "messiah," led more than a hundred Kai Tahu men, women, and children to their mythical place of origin in a *heke*, "migration," that reenacted the Israelite Exodus.[25] The site was owned by three titled Pakeha who used it for sheep runs. The messiah's followers built a settlement and called it Omarama, "world of light," the name of the world in the creation myths.

The ritual of *heke* to a sacred retreat in order to found a new world was replicated at various times by Maori prophets and messiahs. The migrations began with peaceful occupations of disputed land, but in each instance civil authorities regarded resettlement as politically an-

---

21. Ibid., p. 90. See Thomas McDonnell, "Maori Titles to Land, and Native Land Courts," pp. 490–91.

22. See Harrop, *England and the Maori Wars*, p. 57, for Browne's account of the meeting.

23. Thomas Gilbert, *New Zealand Settlers and Soldiers or, The War in Taranaki; Being Incidents in the Life of a Settler*, p. 210.

24. Harrop, *England and the Maori Wars*, p. 57, writes, "Possibly no other single act in all the long and controversial history of New Zealand has led to more conflict in deeds or in words."

25. Mikaere, *Te Maiharoa and the Promised Land*, p. 69.

tagonistic. Comparable phenomena of exodus, pilgrimage, diaspora, and migration, whether forced or voluntary, have been communally remembered as paradigmatic events in the histories of Israelites, Americans of African descent, Amerindians, Muslims, Chinese communists, and the early Essenes. Among the Polynesian peoples, migrations are celebrated in ritual, story, song, and myth.

In August 1879, Inspector Andrew Thompson and a few dozen volunteers forcefully evicted Te Maiharoa and his disciples from Omarama. In 1945 the government paid 300,000 pounds to the Kai Tahu to settle their longstanding claim to the "Promised Land." The New Zealand government agreed to resettle the claim and to apologize for the land loss in 1996.

LAND HOLDERS AND LAND SELLERS

The rise of pan-Maori nationalism in the King Movement exacerbated the polarization of the people into two warring factions: *pupuri whenua*, "land holders," and *hoko whenua*, "land sellers." Maori loyalists who supported amalgamation fought beside government troops against the Kingites, who forbade land-selling.

During the 1850s and 1860s the placing of inviolable boundaries around disputed land revived the institution of *tapu* as a prohibition against trespass. The *pupuri whenua*, "land holders," demarcated the King Country with the *aukati*, a boundary line that no one dared cross on pain of death. Establishing a geo-religious boundary purifies a people by warding off assimilation into a polluted, alien world. Guarded by the *aukati*, the Waikato kingdom endured for many years after the Land Wars ended.[26]

REJECTION OF THE MISSIONS

Anglicans and Methodists who had devoted their lives to converting the heathen were aggrieved by the rise of the King Movement.[27] Despite the settlers' general perception that missionaries were Maori sympa-

26. James Belich claims that "not all historians have noticed it," but that "an independent Maori state nearly two-thirds the size of Belgium existed in the middle of the North Island" until at least 1884. *The New Zealand Wars and the Victorian Interpretation of Racial Conflict*, p. 306. See Walker, *Ka Whawhai Tonu Matou*, pp. 136–37.

27. Davidson and Lineham, *Transplanted Christianity*, pp. 119–20, point out that the Methodist Mission was particularly aligned with the settlers, while the Anglican Mission had ministered primarily to the Maori.

thizers, several of them served as informants for the government.[28] Thomas Buddle and Richard Taylor supplied intelligence to Governor George Grey. A Hauhau apostle murdered the Reverend Carl Volkner of Opotiki for his alleged spying.[29] Before his death in 1865, he wrote to the Reverend William L. Williams that Maori scholars were leaving missionary schools as a result of "the war," and that the clergy feared "that all Waikato is in that state that the slightest thing would put all in a blaze."[30] Shortly thereafter, Williams was forced to abandon his mission station because of civil war between loyalists and Hauhau on the East Coast of the North Island.

At Waimate, some thirty years after Darwin thought he had stumbled upon the perfect image of an English country manse, a Maori "doctor" conducted rites to heal *tapu* sickness by combining the traditional practice of placing cooked food on a sacred site with biblical recitations and Christian prayers. Insofar as he utilized church liturgy, he affirmed Christianity, but he also proclaimed a new god—"a brother of Christ," who exerted superior power over the traditional gods. The adoption of an "alternative" Christ expressed a rejection of the missionaries' authority over religious matters and signaled a growing Maori disaffection with orthodox Christianity.[31] He was only one of many local charismatics who conducted innovative nullification-of-*tapu* services during the "decade of the healers" in the 1850s.

Maori dissidents took the initiative in breaking from the church. By 1868, they distrusted the missionaries for turning a profit on lands granted to the church by the tribes, and, most damning of all, for supporting military trespass on Maori land, contrary to their early roles as teachers of peace.[32] A spokesmen for the tribes who were implicated in Reverend Volkner's death declared in a letter to the government four days after the fact that Volkner had been "crucified according to the laws of New Canaan, in the same manner as has been ordained by the Parliament of England, that the guilty man be crucified," and that the

28. See Belich, *The New Zealand Wars*, p. 102; Walker, *Ka Whawhai Tonu Matou*, p. 131; Clark, *Hauhau*, pp. 13–14, 69.

29. The charges against Volkner are listed by his fellow hostage, T. S. Grace, in his edited papers in S. J. Brittan et al., eds., *A Pioneer Missionary among the Maoris, 1850–1879*, pp. 142–43.

30. Williams Family Papers, MS Papers 69, Letters 74a, Alexander Turnbull Library (ATL), New Zealand National Library (NZNL), Wellington.

31. Elsmore, *Mana from Heaven*, pp. 131–32. Similarly, a "sister of Christ" manifested herself to Rua Kenana fifty years later on the sacred mountain of the Tuhoe people. Webster, *Rua and the Maori Millennium*, p. 189.

32. Brittan et al., *Pioneer Missionary*, pp. 154–55, 202, 257; Davidson and Lineham, *Transplanted Christianity*, pp. 118–19.

reasons for his execution included the killing of women noncombatants by General Cameron's army at Rangiriri and Rangiaowhia.[33]

"Maori ministers and laity experienced acute tension, torn as they were between tribal loyalties and their commitment to the church."[34] Maori Anglicans were not represented on any diocesan synods until 1898; it was half a century after the wars before a Maori bishop was consecrated. In 1866, the Secretary of the Church Missionary Society observed that "the painful fact that the great majority of the Natives have entirely put aside Christianity as taught them from the Scriptures and have either embraced Hauhauism or are living without any religious service whatever, was one that no member of the [CMS] Conference wished to discuss."[35]

The personal feeling of betrayal on both sides was expressed in the following statements by the Reverend T. S. Grace, who was taken hostage with Carl Volkner in 1865. He wrote, "They [the people of Opotiki] have returned him [Volkner] evil for good. their wickedness is too horrible to relate, it makes one feel that it is a righteous thing in God to take vengeance."[36] However, true to his surname, Grace soon overcame his rage and rededicated himself to listening without rancor to the grievances of the North Island people:

> They say, that at the commencement of the war without any sufficient cause we all forsook them in the time of their trouble. . . . They say "that we came to this country and taught them to lift up their eyes to heaven while we ourselves kept our own turned down to the land." A very important chief said to me on my late journey "The people will never come back to you because you have obtained lands from them for the use of the Church and have given them to the Europeans."[37]

The fearful conviction that the Maori had abandoned Christianity for barbarism gripped many Pakeha, and it gravely influenced the punitive manner in which even the most pacific "independent religious convictions" of the subsequent Maori movements were dealt with by the government. On the other hand, the Maori grievance that colonizers and

33. Davidson and Lineham, *Transplanted Christianity*, p. 141.
34. Ibid., p. 143.
35. Ibid., p. 142.
36. Williams Family Papers, MS Papers 69, Letters 74a, Alexander Turnbull Library (ATL), New Zealand National Library (NZNL), Wellington.
37. Davidson and Lineham, *Transplanted Christianity*, p. 148.

missionaries had stolen their land from them while deceiving them with talk of peace and brotherhood, compelled them to rely upon their own religious leaders and salvific movements. Thus, as each people, Pakeha and Maori, moved toward creating, on the one hand, a constitutional state and, on the other, a confederated kingdom, they began to regard each other with deep distrust.

Judith Binney posits two phases of the Christianization process up to 1840: the period of few or no converts (which corresponded to the dependence of the missionaries upon the chiefs) and a "breakthrough" period of significant converts in the 1830s after the missions had acquired their own land. The 1850s inaugurated a third phase that culminated in the rejection of the missionaries and the formation of intertribal movements that inspired a Maori interpretation of Jewish experience as a story that applied to their present conditions. As Jews, new prophets claimed *mana* from a new source, their Israelite ancestors.

The first of the Land Wars began in Taranaki after British troops fired on Wiremu Kingi's defenders of the Waitara Block on March 16, 1860. The initial act of war was the end result of a process that had begun with contact between the Ngati Awa tribe and a Pakeha colony at New Plymouth twenty years earlier. Given the sequence of events that characterized their uneasy interactions, perhaps war was, as Keith Sinclair has argued, inevitable.

5

"IT ALL STARTED AT WAITARA"

> It is not to be wondered at that an
> imaginative and poetic race like the New
> Zealanders, whose memories live so much
> in the past, should have a strong
> attachment to the land of their
> forefathers. . . . Almost every mountain,
> hillock, forest, river, or stream has its
> particular history of wars, defeats,
> conquests, or secret repositories of their
> dead . . . and while the Europeans are too
> apt to believe that the land is a mere
> article of commercial exchange, of little
> consideration beyond its monetary value,
> the natives on the other hand, from motives
> not easily understood or appreciated, deem
> the alienation of certain spots, which they
> regard with romantic veneration, as a
> species of desecration.
>
> William Rusden

In the Bay of Islands where colonization began, the chiefs sold land to the British Crown, which in turn sold it at a profit to settlers seeking a new Eden, but the relative ease with which the settlers obtained land in the North gave way to resistance and conflict when the New Zealand Company[1] attempted to found a colony on the West Coast of the North Island at Taranaki. Sir William Martin, Chief Justice of the New Zealand Supreme Court and a lifelong defender of aboriginal rights, chronicled what went wrong in *The Taranaki Ques-*

---

1. The New Zealand Company was a private enterprise modeled after the companies that had initiated North American settlements. Its first venture at New Plymouth was led by Colonel William Wakefield, brother of the activist utopian, Edward Gibbon Wakefield.

tion, his 1860 report to the imperial Parliament in London and the members of the General Assembly of New Zealand.

A FATEFUL BARGAIN

Before 1827 the Waitara Valley and surrounding territory in the Taranaki region were held "by unbroken descent from remote ancestors" by the Ngati Awa people.[2] Part of the tribe, led by Chief Wiremu Kingi's father, left the land for Waikanae on the southern coast, in order to trade with European vessels there. A few years later, the rest of the Waitara people were overrun by their northern neighbors from Waikato, who, in turn, were being menaced by their northern neighbors led by Hongi Hika after he had obtained arms from Europeans and initiated the destabilizing Musket Wars.[3] Some of the Ngati Awa fled south to safety, some were enslaved by the Waikato invaders, and a remnant took refuge in the nearby Sugar Loaf Rocks near the future Wakefield colony of New Plymouth. Because the Waikato aggressors did not remain in the conquered territory, they could not claim it by conquest; but the weakened Ngati Awa could not return to it as long as the Waikato threatened to overrun them again. Thus, the Taranaki people struck a fateful bargain with the English. Colonel William Wakefield wrote in 1839: "The Natives here, some of the ancient possessors of Taranaki, are very desirous that I should become the purchaser of that district, in order that they may return to their native place without fear of the Waikato tribes."[4]

His surveyor, F. A. Carrington, selected Taranaki for the colony of New Plymouth in 1840, after Wakefield's agents paid "the resident aboriginal inhabitants—the only people then occupying the country" an agreed upon price for the land.[5] In response, the Waikato tribes threatened a second invasion, until their chief, Te Wherowhero, was

---

2. Sir William Martin, *The Taranaki Question*, p. 11.

3. Whereas early observers such as Richard Taylor assumed that the Maori suffered a state of chronic warfare with high casualties, Keith Sinclair speaks for most historians in acknowledging that this state was almost certainly a consequence of contact and European weapons. Ranginui Walker argues from archaeological evidence that the Maori experienced at least one prehistorical increase in the intensity of warfare, but Alexander Vayda recognizes their effective peacemaking institutions. As an insular people, they had to maintain a steady population state, but there is no convincing evidence that the large-scale violence witnessed by the Europeans in the 1830s was the norm. Indeed, Polynesian oral histories suggest they found a nonviolent solution to overpopulation: canoe migrations.

4. Martin, *The Taranaki Question*, p. 12.

5. Ibid., pp. 12–13.

paid 500 pounds for the same territory by Governor William Hobson in December 1841.[6] His payment had no standing under Maori custom, but it reveals how the chiefs had learned to negotiate for power with the Pakeha on terms the strangers would accept. Governor Hobson revealed his knowledge of Maori custom when he observed at the time: "Tewherowhero certainly has a claim on the land, but not a primary one; as the received rule is, that those who occupy the land must first be satisfied. But he is the most powerful Chief in New Zealand, and I fear will not be governed by abstract rights, but will rather take the law in his own hands."[7]

In 1844 this cynical bargain was overruled and the rightful claim to the land by the Ngati Awa was upheld by Governor Fitzroy, the former associate of Darwin and captain of *The Beagle*. The ill-fated Waitara Block remained the property of Wiremu Kingi's people, and as high chief, Kingi had the *tino rangatiratanga,* "full chieftainship," and final say in its ultimate disposition.[8]

THE "NEW POLICY" OF GORE BROWNE

In 1858 New Plymouth settlers were agitating for the Waitara Block, upon which sat two fortified villages of Wiremu Kingi and his deter-mined people. Governor Gore Browne announced a "new policy" in 1859: first, Browne reversed Fitzroy's ruling and recognized the sale of the land by Te Wherowhero to Governor Hobson as binding. Then he applied the European principle of individual land tenure to the Maori for the first time, asserting that "the Governor's rule is, for each man to have the word (or say) as regards his own land"[9]

Gore Browne overturned twenty years of British recognition of Maori custom in order to satisfy the land hunger of the New Plymouth settle-ment. A colonial surveyor insisted that to remain economically viable, New Plymouth must have Waitara as a seaport and as fertile and un-forested farmland. Moreover, an influential Auckland group wanted the governor to cancel the Crown preemption policy that permitted only

6. Sinclair reports the story of the sale with some variations on Martin in *The Origins of the Maori Wars*, pp. 111–16.

7. Martin, *The Taranaki Question*, p. 20.

8. Ibid., pp. 12–13.

9. Ibid., p. 23. See Gilbert, *New Zealand Settlers and Soldiers*, pp. 1–25, appendix B, pp. 208–12, for a Pakeha dissenter's account of Browne's treatment of the Waitara offer and his new land policy.

chiefs to sell tribal land exclusively to the Crown, in order that the
evolving settler administration might buy land directly from individual
Maori.[10] In capitulating to Pakeha interests, Brown reversed imperial
land acquisition practices.

The "Instructions from the Colonial Office to Captain Hobson, Regarding Land in New Zealand" (1839) had established "that henceforth
no lands shall be ceded either gratuitously or otherwise except to the
Crown of Great Britain."[11] Codified in the Treaty of Waitangi, the
"Crown preemption" had assured government control over the enterprise of colonization. The "Instructions" sanguinely asserted that "the
resales of the first purchases that may be made will provide the funds
necessary for future acquisition, and beyond the original investment of
a comparatively small sum of money, no other resource will be necessary for this purpose [capitalization of the colony]."[12] Discouraging
"large land-holders, whose possessions must long remain an unprofita-
ble, or rather a pernicious, waste,"[13] the "Instructions" attempted to
avert the land grabs that had occurred elsewhere in the British empire.
In London the Colonial Office and the Aborigines Protection Society
feared that the New Zealand Company would dispossess the aboriginal
people. Hoping to regulate the purchase of Maori "waste lands" by
judiciously prohibiting all transactions except those between chiefs and
the government, the "Instructions" also affirmed that the Crown would
not tolerate abuses.

> All dealings with the aborigines for their lands must be conducted
> on the same principles of sincerity, justice, and good faith as
> must govern your transactions with them for the recognition of her
> Majesty's sovereignty in the islands. Nor is this all: they must not
> be permitted to enter into any contracts in which they might be
> the ignorant and unintentional authors of injuries to themselves;
> you will not, for example, purchase from them any territory the
> retention of which by them would be essential or highly condu-
> cive to their own comfort, safety, or subsistence.[14]

Unfortunately, their Humanitarian intent was coupled with the tragic
misperception that "to the natives or their chiefs much of the land of

---

10. A. G. Bagnall, "No Known Copy? T. S. Grace's suppressed Circular, W264," pp. 78, 84.
11. "Instructions" (August, 1839), in Ward, *Information Relative to New-Zealand*, appendix no.
xi, p. 165. The spirit of this document is reflected in the Treaty of Waitangi.
12. Ward, *Information Relative to New Zealand*, p. 167.
13. Ibid., p. 166.
14. Ibid., p. 168.

the country is of no actual use, and in their hands it possesses scarcely any exchangeable value."[15] The British erroneously believed that the Maori also considered land a commodity. Consequently, the pervasive conflict of interest between "protecting" the aborigines and securing their "waste lands" was instituted at the outset through a cultural misunderstanding. In the imperial administration of the new colony the designated "Protector of the Aborigines" was the same individual who conducted land sales for the Crown! Since the Crown did not understand that land was sacred, it reasoned that to pay the Maori little for it and to resell it at a large profit was no "real injustice."[16]

Crown policy was founded upon the Eurocentric myth of untilled land as "waste." The Crown-mediated sale of the ancestral land of the Kai Tahu to a body of Wakefield investors nine years after the "Instructions" were issued exposed London's humanitarianism as only a "show of justice." For two thousand pounds the government gained eight million hectares of the South Island, and the Kai Tahu lost access to their food-gathering places. Because food-gathering, their calendar, and rituals were interwoven in Kai Tahu life, the community lost the means of maintaining their *mana* and *mauri*.[17] Moreover, they were not granted enough reserve land to insure their self-sufficiency. Although an enterprising chief, Matiaha Tiramorehu, petitioned the government for additional space to cultivate wheat and potatoes and to run cattle and sheep—changes that were smiled upon—his pleas were ignored.[18]

Gore Browne's reversal of Crown policy at Waitara sent a shudder through the North Island tribes. Despite its serious flaws, the Treaty's Crown preemption had recognized the right of chiefs alone to conduct land sales. In New Plymouth the Ngati Awa chief unalterably opposed the sale of the Waitara Block. Browne justified his assault upon the *tino rangatiratanga* of the chiefs as an extension of the amalgamation policy: "The individualisation of property and the exchange of a communal title to a Crown grant are most desirable and will contribute more than any one thing to the amalgamation of the two races."[19] (His incredible misjudgment of the reaction to the new edict may have been promoted by his success on the very day he announced the policy in acquiring a vast tract of land near Wellington for the Crown.)[20] Less

15. Ibid., p. 167.
16. Ibid.
17. Mikaere, *Te Maiharoa and the Promised Land*, pp. 29–31.
18. Ibid., pp. 22–23.
19. Dispatch to the Colonial Office on June 13, 1858, in Harrop, *England and the Maori Wars*, pp. 59–60.
20. Ibid., p. 58.

than a year later, Browne acknowledged the serious effects of his new policy: "The natives have seen the land they alienated for farthings sold for pounds; they feel that dominion or power, or as they term it 'Substance,' went from them with the territories they alienated, and they look with apprehension to the annihilation of their nationality."[21]

PRELUDE TO THE WARS

In fact, Browne was well aware of Maori concerns before he decided to accept an illegitimate offer of the Waitara Block by Teira. The determination of the New Plymouth settlement to extend its boundaries and the equal determination of the Ngati Awa to resist that extension had fueled hostilities between rival Maori factions even before Browne's fateful intervention. In the same dispatch Browne dispassionately spelled out the genocidal threat posed by land feuds between Maori rivals, which were stimulated by government land schemes: "The immediate consequence of any attempt to acquire Maori lands without previously extinguishing the native title to the satisfaction of all having interest in them would be a universal outbreak in which many innocent Europeans would perish, and colonization would be definitely retarded, but the native race would be eventually extirpated."[22]

Under Browne an "extirpation" agenda supplanted the Crown's amalgamation policy, as war over disposition of the land broke out, pitting loyalists against dissidents and colonists against the indigenous people. It was Browne's underestimation of the broader impact his new land policy would have upon the chiefs of the North Island that set the stage for the Land Wars. In 1859 Britain faced a war in India and the threat of war with France. On the one hand, Britain wished to inaugurate responsible rule in New Zealand and shift the cost of government and defense onto the settler population. On the other hand, the War and Colonial Offices sagaciously feared that a settler-run government would abolish all Humanitarian policies and provoke Maori hostility by concocting land-grabbing schemes. The last two imperial governors[23] strongly recommended that the Crown retain control over Maori affairs until the settlers could defend themselves.[24] The process of transition from imperial to responsible rule spanned the first half of the period of

21. Ibid., p. 64.
22. Ibid.
23. Gore Brown and George Grey.
24. Harrop, *England and the Maori Wars*, pp. 64–65.

war between 1860 and 1872. The King Movement was a preemptive assertion of Maori sovereignty over lands that the chiefs expected to be contested and appropriated by a truculent, emerging, settler-dominated state.

Browne's Machiavellian blunder at Waitara precipitated the very hostilities London wished to avoid. He was posted to Tasmania in 1861 and replaced by George Grey, whose self-cultivated reputation for resolving disputes with the chiefs would, London hoped, avoid looming conflict.

As Browne fumbled, the Maori watched astutely. Fearing "extirpation," the Waikato chiefs under the leadership of Wiremu Tamihana united their *mana* under a king. The governor denounced their confederation as a tactic to halt Pakeha expansion, charging, "The consequence of this feeling [the annihilation of their nationality] has been the formation of a league to prevent the alienation of land, commenced by the tribes in the Waikato before my arrival in the colony and which has since been combined with the so-called King Movement."[25] Browne treated the King Movement as a rebellion against the queen. The wars were fueled by mutually discordant positions on "sovereignty" that were expressed in terms of control over land. According to James Belich,

The boundaries between Maori and British spheres of control were generally defined by the area of land "sold" by the former to the latter. "Sale" is rather a deceptive term for the most common type of alienation. By the 1860s, both races tacitly recognized that the sale of large blocks of land contiguous to British settlements involved the transfer of political and magisterial control as well as of property rights. This process had more in common with the Louisiana Purchase than the sale of a farm in England. Thus the expansion of the area of real British control was inextricably interwoven with the purchase of Maori land. Conversely, to oppose land sales was to oppose the extension of British sovereignty and to defend Maori autonomy.[26]

Donald McLean reported to the Colonial Office in July 1860 that "indeed it may be safely assumed that the King Movement is not supported so much with a view to the regaining of national independence,

25. Ibid.
26. Belich, *The New Zealand Wars*, p. 78.

but as a means of exacting such a recognition of their rights as may ensure the preservation of the declining influence and power of their chieftainship."[27] As usual, McLean's assessment was correct. Between 1852—when the Maori population was double that of the settlers— and 1860, the European population surpassed that of the indigenous people for the first time. While the Maori declined in number and the tide of European immigration swelled, Pakeha settlement became a clear and present threat to Maori survival. The consequence was war. In the words of Wiremu Kingi, whose followers tore out the surveyor's pegs from the disputed Waitara Block on February 20, 1860, and incurred the violent response of government soldiers on March 17, 1860, "It all started at Waitara."

27. Harrop, *England and the Maori Wars*, p. 86.

6

KOTAHITANGA AND THE KING
MOVEMENT

*The Queen of England agrees to protect
the chiefs, the subtribes and all the people
of New Zealand in the unqualified exercise
of their chieftainship [tino rangatiratanga]
over their lands, villages and all their
treasures [taonga].*

Treaty of Waitangi, Article Two

MANA

Ann Parsonson translates *mana* as "prestige."[1] *Mana* also has a religious aspect.[2] Maharaia Winiata compares it to Max Weber's concept of charisma,[3] which derives from the New Testament Greek word, *charis*, "grace," and *charismata*, referring to "gifts of the [Holy] Spirit" (1 Cor. 12:1–11). Specific uses of the term in Aotearoa include *mana ariki* (the traditional mantle of leadership passed from a chief to his successor), *mana o te whenua* (authority over the land), and *mana motuhake* (sovereignty).[4] *Mana* is imparted by the

1. See also Raymond Firth's "The Analysis of Mana: An Empirical Approach."
2. Hanson and Hanson, *Counterpoint in Maori Culture*, p. 61, and James Irwin, *Introduction to Maori Religion*, pp. 21–23.
3. Maharaia Winiata, *The Changing Role of the Leader in Maori Society*, p. 30.
4. See Walker, *Ka Whawhai Tonu Matou*, pp. 227–28, 244.

gods to the ancestors, who bequeath it to worthy leaders of the current generation. *Mana* can be diminished by an insult or extinguished by enslavement. A contemporary woman who is studying her language for the first time explained simply that "mana is like a light. When someone insults you, the light weakens."[5] Her simile conveys how one's *mana* can wax or wane in response to triumph or insult, allowing us to understand better how humiliating treatment provoked Tamihana to commit himself to Maori nationhood.

DIVIDE AND CONQUER

Parsonson assumed that the Maori lost their land because of their essential divisiveness. Providing evidence to the contrary in his detailed analysis of the Waitara dispute, Keith Sinclair argues that the *tangata whenua* of Taranaki were victims of government strategies to divide and conquer, noting that "when an [government] agent was negotiating for land, a whole district would be agitated for months," and that land purchasing was often "carried out by the same officials who were responsible for the administration of native policy."[6] Donald McLean had negotiated with Taranaki tribes for 12,000 to 14,000 acres of fertile land next to New Plymouth as early as 1854, and his activity had heightened tensions within and between the tribes.

Te Teira Manuka, "a minor chief of Waitara," offered to sell the government 600 acres of the Waitara Block, which was under the authority of the paramount chief, Wiremu Kingi, with whom Teira had quarreled.[7] He was prompted by McLean and his local deputy, Robert Parris, who had conceived a long-term strategy to foster the individual sale of land in the New Plymouth area.[8] Teira's co-conspirator was Ihaia, who had been first enslaved and then converted by the landselling loyalist, William Naylor. Teira and Ihaia were indulging in *whakahe*, "bringing trouble upon one's own people."[9] Even McLean's sym-

---

5. Conversation with Tungia Kaihau in August 1990.

6. Sinclair, *The Origins of the Maori Wars*, pp. 53, 136–57.

7. James Cowan, *Sir Donald Maclean*, pp. 67–70.

8. Sinclair, *The Origins of the Maori Wars*, p. 143, quotes part of a letter from McLean to a Taranaki land agent, Robert Parris, in August 1858, which suggests that the former had conceived a plan to acquire "a more general purchase of land in that Province . . . which it may take some little time to unfold." See also Alan Ward's discussion of McLean and his methods in *A Show of Justice*, passim.

9. Gilbert, *New Zealand Settlers and Soldiers*, pp. 6–11; and Cowan, *The New Zealand Wars*, 2:157, quotation from Edward Shortland.

pathetic biographer deplored the transaction, observing that "Teira was a land-owner, it was true, but the native title was so intricate, and the hostile feeling between sellers and non-sellers so great, that Waitara was the very last place the Government should have attempted to buy at that moment."[10]

The land alienation methods of McLean and Browne often relied upon fomenting divisions between *hoko whenua* and *pupuri whenua* within the same tribe. The former occupant of McLean's office, George Clarke, resigned after he realized that he could not broker land sales and protect the aborigines without a conflict of interest.[11] McLean was a far more pragmatic man.

The Second Article of the Treaty of Waitangi, guaranteed the chiefs' authority over tribal possessions: *Ko te Kuini o Ingarani Ka wakarite ka wakaae ki nga Rangatira ki nga hapu—ki nga tangata katoa o Nu Tirani te tino rangatiratanga o ratou wenua o ratou kainga me o ratou taonga katoa,* "The Queen of England arranges [and] agrees to the Chiefs to the subtribes to people all of New Zealand the unqualified exercise of their chieftainship over their lands over their villages and over their treasures all."[12] *Taonga,* "treasures," "refers to all dimensions of a tribal group's estate, material and nonmaterial—heirlooms and *wahi tapu,* ancestral lore, and whakapapa, etc."[13] The Treaty of Waitangi is the *de facto* founding compact of the biracial state of New Zealand, and from 1858 until the present, Maori leaders have brandished Article Two as evidence of the Crown's recognition of Maori sovereignty. New Zealanders remain uncertain of their nation's title and status; some consider it a Dominion in the Commonwealth; others simply prefer to refer to themselves by their country's name.[14] With respect to its unfolding history as a biracial polity, New Zealand resembles Azania and Palestine more than it does its neighbor, Australia. In 1860 New Zealand was no longer a colony and not yet a nation-state.

10. Cowan, *Sir Donald Maclean,* p. 70; Maori custom recognized a chief's authority over tribal land, but did not conceive of private ownership of the land. McLean and Browne were engaged in strategies that would split tribal claims and effect individual tenure without basing the latter on legislation. This only heightened the feuds between land sellers and land holders.

11. George Clarke Jr. was a participant in and witness to conflicts and trials over land in the years between the signing of the Treaty of Waitangi and Grey's aggressive treatment of the Kai Tahu people; see *Notes on Early Life in New Zealand,* passim.

12. A literal translation by I. H. Kawharu, ed., *Waitangi: Maori and Pakeha Perspectives of the Treaty of Waitangi,* pp. 319–20.

13. Ibid., p. 317.

14. Keith Sinclair, *A Destiny Apart: New Zealand's Search for National Identity,* pp. 178–79.

KOTAHITANGA, EXPRESSIONS OF UNITY

Parsonson ignored the significant *kotahitanga* movements from the 1850s to the present. *Kotahitanga* denotes "oneness" and connotes "wholeness." Buddle blamed a south Taranaki people, the Ngati Ruanui, for initiating Maori resistance to land sales well before the Waitara dispute. The europhobic Ngati Ruanui began to feel accelerating pressure to sell land in 1849, when their neighbors, the Ngatiapa, sold a vast tract of land to the Crown for twenty-five hundred pounds. After some Ngati Ruanui tribesmen proposed the sale of a block within their territory, the elders met and proposed that henceforth "no person, or family should sell land within the boundary of the Ngati Ruanui territory without the consent of the tribe."[15] This was only a formal declaration of long-standing custom, but the Pakeha regarded it as a "Land League," a "new combination" formed for the express purpose of halting colonial expansion.

In 1853 the Ngati Ruanui raised a very large meeting house, 120 by 35 feet, and named it Taiporohenui, or "the finishing of the work." Like many Maori names, this one is metonymical and invokes an archetypal *Taiporohenui*, "house of instruction," in Hawaiki.[16] At its dedication the people sang, "Taranaki shall not be lost, shall not be abandoned to the stranger."[17] The next year the Ngati Ruanui invited neighboring tribes, including Ngati Awa, to meet in this house at Manawa-pou and to agree not to sell any more land to the Pakeha. A thousand people came. The Taiporohenui meeting in 1854 inaugurated a movement toward *kotahitanga* among the Taranaki people in response to the divisive methods of the land commissioners.

Attendees included two young chiefs from south of Taranaki, Matene Te Whiwhi and Tamihana Te Rauparaha, relatives of warriors who had defeated armed settlers at Wairau in 1843. Taking as their motto, *whakakotahitanga*, "making unity," they had just returned from the East Coast, where they had proposed that the North Island tribes unite under a king. Declining their invitation, the eastern tribes nevertheless formulated a historic schematization of Aotearoa–New Zealand that symbolized the unity of the Maori together with the unity of the Pakeha under the overarching governance of God,

15. Buddle, *The Maori King Movement*, p. 4.
16. Cowan, *The New Zealand Wars*, 2:15; Keith Sinclair, *A History of New Zealand*, p. 112.
17. Cowan, *The New Zealand Wars*, 1:147.

We salute you all. This is our word to you, New Zealand is the house, the Europeans are the rafters on one side, the Maories are the rafters on the other side, God is the ridgepole against which all lean, and the house is one.[18]

This metaphor of the house singularly expresses the chiefs' interpretation of the Treaty of Waitangi before the Land Wars. The traditional *whare puni*, "meeting house," is an architectonic representation of a sacred ancestor, and it incorporates the stories of the people, living and dead, who comprise the *iwi*.[19] By including the Europeans in its construct of Aotearoa–New Zealand, this striking metaphor demonstrated that the visionary goal of *kotahitanga* was to make Pakeha and Maori equal partners in the new nation. The British never fully understood and consequently repudiated this invitation to partnership under the ridgepole of the Lord.

MAORI INITIATIVE

The Taiporohenui meeting enunciated three principles that were embraced by the King Movement: *mana o te whenua*, "power over the land"; the *aukati*, "boundary"; and the *runanga*, "traditional council":

1st. That from this time forward no more land shall be alienated to Europeans without the general consent of this confederation.
2nd. That in reference to the Ngati Ruanui and Taranaki tribes, the boundaries of the Pakeha shall be Kai Iwi on the South side, and a place within a short distance of New Plymouth on the North.
3rd. That no European Magistrate shall have jurisdiction within native boundaries, but all disputes shall be settled by the runanga [chief's council].[20]

Almost immediately, *kotahitanga* caught fire as well in the interior at Taupo and Waikato. Many of the inland chiefs had refused to sign

18. Maori original in Sinclair, *The Origins of the Maori Wars*, p. 69; English translation from Buddle, *The Maori King Movement*, p. 4.
19. See *Tane-nui-a-Rangi, the Symbolism of the Meeting House*, published by the University of Auckland, and *Hui, a Study of Maori Ceremonial Gatherings*, by Anne Salmond.
20. Buddle, *The Maori King Movement*, pp. 5–6.

the Treaty of Waitangi in 1840 and did not consider themselves subordinate to the British; they viewed the increasing penetration of European migrants with great alarm.

Wiremu Tamihana adopted the idea of setting up a Maori king from Matene and Tamihana Te Rauparaha. He proposed that the Kingites set up their own councils to administer law and order within the *aukati* that separated Pakeha settlements from the Waikato. Tamihana believed that biblical law, *ture*, provided a model for the regulation of the affairs of men. He conceived of a peaceful resolution of the conflict in the Treaty between the queen's protection of "the unqualified exercise of [Maori] chieftainship over their lands, villages and all their treasures" in Article Two and the queen's "governance" (*kawanatanga*) in Article One. The English version of the Treaty translated *kawanatanga* as "sovereignty," which the Pakeha interpreted to mean that the Crown not only protected but superseded the chiefs' authority. The Kingites asserted that each tribe should exercise sovereignty over its respective territory and forbade any further land sales.[21]

A meeting to unite the North Island tribes was convened in 1856[22] by Te Heuheu Iwikau, a fiercely independent critic of British colonization, at Taupo [Pukawa]. It extended the king's "mana-tapu" over the soil—despite the fact that the king had not yet been formally installed. Te Heu Heu Tukino, son of Iwikau, told the story of the "union of the tribes" to historian, James Cowan.

> Te Heuheu Iwikau . . . caused a high flagstaff to be erected on the *marae*, the meeting-ground, at Pukawa. At the masthead he hoisted a national flag; the pattern was that of the flag given by King William IV of England to the northern Maori tribes at the Bay of Islands some years before the signing of the Treaty of Waitangi.[23] Beneath this flag at intervals down the mast he had long ropes of plaited flax attached. The flagstaff symbolized Tongariro, the sacred mountain of our tribe. The Maoris were assembled in divisions grouped around the foot. Te Heuheu arose and said, indicating a rope, "This is Ngongotaha" (the mountain near Rotorua Lake)."Where is the chief of Ngongotaha who shall attach this mountain to Tongariro?" The leading chief of the Ar-

---

21. The geographical boundaries of the safeguarded territory are detailed by J. H. Kerry-Nicholls, *The King Country, or, Explorations in New Zealand*, pp. 1–2.

22. Cowan's date for the meeting is 1857, but Buddle's date is 1856.

23. A "Declaration of the Independence of New Zealand" was signed by His Majesty's Resident and thirty-five chiefs on October 28, 1835. See Orange, *Treaty of Waitangi*, pp. 255–56.

awa Tribe, of Rotorua, rose from his place in the assemblage, and taking the end of the rope fastened it to a *manuka* peg, which he drove into the ground in front of his company. The next rope indicated by the Taupo head chief symbolized Pu-tauaki . . . the sacred mountain of Ngati-Awa, of the Bay of Plenty. The next was Tawhiuau, the mountain belonging to Ngati-Manawa, on the western border of the Urewera country. Each tribe giving its adherence to the king movement had its rope allotted to it, representative of a mountain dear to the people. Hikurangi, near the East Cape, was for the Ngati-Porou Tribe, Maunga-pohatu for the Tuhoe (Urewera), Titi-o-kura fro the Ngati-Kahungunu Tribe, Kapiti Island for the Ngati-Toa, and Otairi for the Ngati-Apa.

The great mountains of the South Island also were named. Each had its symbolic rope—Tapuae-nuku and Kaikoura, and the greatest of all, Aorangi. Those were for the Ngai-Tahu tribe, whose representative at the meeting was Taiaroa. Returning to the North Island mountains, our *ariki* took in turn the ropes emblematic of the west coast and the Waikato, and called upon the chiefs from those parts to secure them to the soil. These mountains were Para-te-taitonga, . . . for the Whanganui tribes; Taranaki, . . . for Taranaki, Te Atiawa, and Ngati-Ruanui tribes; Pirongia and Taupiri, for the Waikato clans; Kakepuku, for the Ngati-Maniapoto; Rangitoto, for Ngati-Matakore and Ngati-Whakatere; Wharepuhunga, for Ngati-Raukawa; Maunga-tautari, for Ngati-Haua and Ngati-Koroki; Maunganui, . . . for Ngai-te-Rangi; Te Aroha, for Ngati-Tama-te-ra; and finally Moehau, . . . for the Ngati-Maru Tribe.

Each of the ropes representing these sacred mountains of the tribes was hauled taut and staked down. So in the middle stood Tongariro, the central mountain, supported and stayed by all these tribal cords, which joined the soil of New Zealand to the central authority. Above floated the flag, emblem of Maori nationality. Thus was the union of the tribes demonstrated so that all might see, and then did Te Heuheu and his fellow-chiefs transfer to Potatau all the mana-tapu of the soil and acclaim him as the king of the native tribes of New Zealand.[24]

---

24. Cowan, *The New Zealand Wars*, 1:152–53. Regarding the sacredness of specific mountains, early pioneer, William Yate, *An Account of New Zealand and of the Formation and Progress of the Church Missionary Society's Mission*, pp. 4, 6, memorialized their awesome aspect in his description of the North Island landscape before it was tamed by roads and clearcutting. J. H. Kerry-Nicholls, *King Country*, pp. 7, 49, emphasized the sacredness of Tongariro.

To symbolize *kotahitanga* each chief grasped the rope that tied his tribe and its mountain to the paramount mountain, Tongariro, and himself to the paramount chief, King Potatau, who was the old warrior, Te Wherowhero. The ritual signified the binding together of all Aotearoa, not only the Waikato. Despite their rivalries, the tribes stood together on this day, although not all participants could sustain their allegiance.[25]

Western symbols: king, flagstaff, musket volleys, "honor guards," and the flag—and Maori symbols: chiefs, sacred mountains, *mana*, and the sacred pole—were employed. Hohepa, a converted chief, compared King Potatau to Melchizedek, the high priest of Jerusalem and the New Covenant.[26] Because King Potatau had left his government-provided residence to return to his Waikato homeland, some likened him to the gods who returned to the people when the priests called them forth.[27] Paora gave voice to Kingite hermeneutics that linked the Maori ancestral world to the Jews of the New Testament who converted to, and then rejected, the Jesus movement:[28] "But we are like Jews who, after they had received the Gospel, returned to the law of their fathers. We are looking toward the customs of our ancestors."[29]

The Pukawa participants treated the flagstaff with the solemnity they attached to the *pou* or *toko*, "sacred stick," in the ancient religion. They raised a flag patterned after the one King William IV gave to the chiefs in 1835, five years before Waitangi, to legitimize their confederation. After the meeting, Kingite chiefs drafted a letter to Governor Browne that reiterated their allegiance to a bi-national state under the overarching power of God: "Perhaps you think that the Maori King will be separated from the Queen. Not so. . . . Let us work together . . . lest there be strife between them. . . . It is now ten years since the Maori chiefs first talked about a King for themselves."[30]

The ceremony of union at Pukawa was followed by meetings at Rangiriri and Ihumatao that same year. On June 2, 1858, Wiremu Tamihana ritually installed King Potatau I at Ngaruawahia, his Waikato capital, and he was acclaimed again on June 18 and 19 at Rangiaowhia.[31] The Kingmaker compared the inauguration of Potatau to the

25. Tuhoe and Ngati Porou fought bitterly a few years later during an East Coast civil war.
26. Buddle, *The Maori King Movement*, p. 36.
27. Gorst, *The Maori King*, p. 272.
28. Biblical scholars believe that Jewish-Christian apostates were the intended audience of the Epistle to the Hebrews. See Hebrews 7:15, in which Jesus is compared to Melchizedek.
29. Buddle, *The Maori King Movement*, p. 37.
30. Harrop, *England and the Maori Wars*, p. 47.
31. Keith Sinclair resolved the confusion over the date of the king's installation from a letter of

anointing of Saul, the first Israelite king, by Samuel, the judge, in the
face of a Philistine invasion.[32] At Ngaruawahia in May 1860, Potatau
asserted his authority over the land by planting his flagstaff at the foot
of Taupiri, the sacred mountain, while an elder proclaimed, "The top of
this Flag-staff signifies the King, the centre is for the Chiefs, these four
ropes represent the tribes, east, west, north, and south. The name of
this Flag-staff is Pane—(Potatau's ancestor)."[33]

THE PAKEHA RESPONSE

James Busby, the colonial official who had drafted the English-lan-
guage version of the Treaty of Waitangi, presented the Pakeha case
against aboriginal rights in his response to Sir William Martin. Until
the Maori came under British legal institutions, he argued, they had no
natural right to their own land. He asserted that the only "natural right
of a man to land" was over land "which he had subdued from the
forest, to the uses of man." This right "approaches to that instinctive
sense of right which a man possesses in his own children,"[34] he insisted
in paternalistic Victorian fashion.

A polity is established in geopolitical space by setting boundaries,
which exclude "matter out of place."[35] It is noteworthy that the Ngati
Ruanui and the Kingites extended the meaning of *tino rangatiratanga*
from its limited reference to a single chief's *mana* to that of the king's
sovereignty over the unsettled areas. Wiremu Tamihana argued with
some sophistication that the Israelites, as well as the English, Rus-
sians, French, and Tahitians, had exercised their legitimate right to a
king from among their own people, adding,

> Is it on account of the Treaty of Waitangi that you are angry with
> us? Was it then that we were taken possession of by you? If so, it
> is wrong. . . . What harm is there in this name [King] that you are
> angry about. The great thing has been given to us, even the sa-

Tamihana's to Auckland's newspaper that he unearthed in 1958; see *The Maori King*, p. *xxv*. The letter
confirms Buddle's date.

32. Davidson and Lineham, *Transplanted Christianity*, p. 130, letter of Tamihana to Governor
Grey, June 7, 1861.

33. Buddle, *The Maori King Movement*, p. 59; Honana addressed these words to the assembly.

34. James Busby, "Remarks upon a Pamphlet Entitled 'The Taranaki Question,' by Sir William
Martin, D.C.L., Late Chief Justice of New Zealand," p. 10.

35. Douglas, *Purity and Danger*, pp. 164, 122–28.

cred things of God. . . . My friends, why have you grudged us a
king, as if it were a name greater than that of God?[36]

Sidestepping the Kingite invitation to engage in a mutual debate
over what kind of state New Zealand would become, the Pakeha regarded the King Movement as a rude, unidimensional opposition movement, an aggressive outgrowth of the Ngati Ruanui land league. Buddle
remembered that when Taiporohenui was built,

> To give solemnity to the proceedings, and confirm the bond into
> which they entered with each other, they buried a New Testament
> in the earth and raised a cairn of stones on the spot; and to re-
> assert and perpetuate their determination, parties have been ap-
> pointed to beat the boundaries at certain periods.
> This was the origin of the notorious Taranaki land league,
> which evidently contains the elements of the present King move-
> ment.[37]

Taiporohenui stood for the unpartitioned Maori cosmos; burying a
New Testament took the place of the old human sacrificial rites, and
the cairn stood for the ancient *whatu*, or "sacred stone."[38] Beating the
boundaries is a land-based ritual. Buddle voiced Christians' fears that
Maori converts were reverting to barbarism, and settlers viewed the
"land league" as a direct challenge to their new Albion. As Sinclair
observed:

> Speculation in land proved the quickest road to wealth in the
> early years. . . . the acquisition of land was the aim of most new
> arrivals, and to the settlers as a body it was the symbol of the
> progress of their colony. Nothing else aroused such passionate
> interest. As one settler said for the rest, they had the Biblical
> mandate, "Be fruitful, and multiply, and replenish the earth, and
> subdue it." This blessing, first pronounced on man, would seem
> indeed to have been peculiarly inherited by the British people.[39]

Buddle believed he was one of the sons of Japhet who were destined
to dominate the islands, but the Crown opposed any private party, in-

36. From a letter to Gore Browne quoted in Rickard, *Tamihana the Kingmaker*, pp. 109–11.
37. Buddle, *The Maori King Movement*, p. 6.
38. Cowan, *The New Zealand Wars*, 2:15.
39. Sinclair, *The Origins of the Maori Wars*, p. 4.

cluding the churches, that would establish its own fiefdom. As early as 1846, Governor Grey complained to William Gladstone that the members of the Church Missionary Society had laid claim to tracts of land that would require an expenditure of "blood and money" to annex. Reverend Henry Williams heatedly denied Grey's charge, but their dispute was monitored by the Kingites, who bitterly accused the missionaries of land-stealing.[40] Adding to missionary woes, disaffected settlers began to accuse them of philo-Maori sentiments, and Buddle was obliged to defend the clergy against charges of disloyalty.[41]

GENERAL CAMERON CROSSES THE *AUKATI*

On July 12, 1863, after rumors of an incipient Maori uprising, Governor George Grey ordered Lieutenant-General Duncan Cameron to lead his troops across the Mangatawhiri Stream, which marked the border between Auckland settlement and the Waikato. The Kingites had anticipated the invasion, knowing Grey was planning to build a road across the line to encourage Pakeha settlements in their territory.[42] Surveyors followed the troops, establishing their trig stations upon the mountains of *terra incognita*, the Pakeha term for uncolonized regions. In fact, the War Office in London objected to the colonials' requests for imperial troops, complaining that what they really intended to obtain were not soldiers, but surveyors.[43] The army routed even loyalist chiefs in its path along the Waikato River, dislocating Tamati Ngapora and Ihaka from their villages. After winning a pitched battle with Waikato warriors at Rangiriri, Cameron sneaked by a Maori fortification at Paterangi to attack and burn homes and fields at Rangiaowhia, killing noncombatants.[44] Grey's preemptive initiation of war commenced a "struggle without end" between colonizers and colonized over the ultimate return of tribal lands and fishing rights that persists to this day.[45]

The British victory in the Waikato war of 1863–64 was equivocal.[46] King Potatau's successor refused to relinquish the title of king,[47] a name that perpetuated the authority of subsequent monarchs. The wars

40. Davidson and Lineham, *Transplanted Christianity*, pp. 53–54, 62–64.
41. Buddle, *The Maori King Movement*, p. 22.
42. Rickard, *Tamihana the Kingmaker*, p. 132.
43. Harrop, *England and the Maori Wars*, pp. 56–57.
44. Ranginui Walker, *Ka Whawhai Tonu Matou*, p. 124.
45. Ibid., 129.
46. Belich, *The New Zealand Wars*, p. 197.
47. Kerry-Nicholls, *King Country*, p. 11.

fed the dream of *kotahitanga*. The Kingmaker had soldered traditional enemies together for the first time in a pan-tribal union that was both religious and political.

Maori loyalists who served in government militias were every bit as determined to retain their land as the dissident movements they bitterly fought.[48] As the great scythe of punitive land confiscation—over three million acres—began to sweep over loyalists, noncombatants, and dissidents without distinction in the 1860s, charismatic messengers of Jehovah prophesied that Maori Jews, the *tiu* and the *Iharaira*, would regain their Promised Land in a coming time of the long peace.

"ADJUSTMENT CULTS"

New Zealand scholars sometimes refer to the prophet movements as "adjustment cults," a misnomer that suggests that they sought to accommodate themselves to British hegemony. In actuality, the prophets asserted Maori identity, chosenness, and self-sufficiency as their alternatives to amalgamation. From the outset, *kotahitanga* movements pressed for equality of Maori and Pakeha under the ridgepole of a common God. The creative political imagination of Maori leaders, whether they were pious and educated or charismatic and illiterate, envisioned the Maori "sun" shining in the same sky as the Union Jack. Their dreams were cosmic and millenarian—alternatives to the "show of justice" preached by the Pakeha. By no means did Maori prophets counsel adjustment to what they perceived as virtual enslavement.

---

48. Karen Neal, "Maori Participation in the East Coast Wars, 1865–1872," pp. 14, 121.

7

MANA O TE WHENUA:
POWER OVER THE LAND

> *The Land—always the land, from the*
> *days of Wakefield onward—that was the*
> putake o te riri, *the grand root of all the*
> *trouble.*
>
> James Cowan
>
> *New Zealand is ours; I love it.*
>
> Paora of Otaki

When in May 1860, at Ngaruawahia, the Waikato chiefs debated how the people should respond to the March 17 outbreak of the First Taranaki War at Waitara, the king's *mana o te whenua* was challenged by a loyalist chief, "You speak of mana, what is the mana? Where is the mana? There is no such thing as putting mana on the land."[1]

Buddle quoted him to prove that *mana o te whenua* was "altogether a new application of the term. . . . this Maori King Movement originated it," and speculated that "it has been adopted in consequence of the Queen's Sovereignty over the Island having been translated as the Queen's mana."[2] He argued that it was a neologism adopted by the Kingites from a free translation of *mana*.

---

1. Paora of Orakei, not to be confused with Paora of Otaki; Buddle, *The Maori King Movement*, p. 51.
2. Ibid., p. 18.

"MANA TO THIS LAND"

According to Thomas Lambert, a similar term is found in traditional genealogies in such statements as "Parau was a man who had mana to this land."[3] In 1835, thirty-four northern chiefs, at James Busby's behest, signed an "article of confederation" that established their "mana i te whenua" or "sovereignty of the land."[4] The King Movement appears to have employed *mana o te whenua* in the novel historical context of pan-tribal unification and expanded its older meaning. New religious movements usually produce semantic transformations that resonate with the collective experience of their followers.

In 1860, Wiremu Kingi sent a deputation to Ngaruawahia to plead for Kingite support in his struggle to hold Waitara. The assembly split between those who wished to study the question further and an activist contingent who set off to aid the Ngati Awa. The new confederation needed a peaceful breathing space to "build its house" and broaden its reach, but the immediacy of the Waitara dispute intruded, threatening its tenuous achievement.

RELIGIOUS FOUNDATIONS OF
THE KING MOVEMENT

From the outset the King Movement asserted itself as a separate, but equal, authority in Aotearoa-New Zealand, and Buddle noted with distaste that the Kingites did not pray for the queen in their meetings. Three years earlier at Pukawa,

> it was decided that "Tongariro" (the burning mountain of Taupo) should be the centre of a district in which no land was to be sold to the Government, and that Hauraki, Waikato, Kawhia, Mokau, Taranaki, Wanganui, Rangitiki, and Titi Okura, the circumference; that no prayers should be offered for the Queen, no roads be made within this district, and that a king should be elected to rule over the New Zealanders, as the Queen and Governor do over the settlers.[5]

3. Thomas Lambert, in *The Story of Old Wairoa*, p. 183, elaborated, "The chiefs, of course, represented the whole of the land of the tribes and they exacted tribute from the various hapus, or rather, it was freely rendered, and the chiefs jealously guarded this custom."

4. R. J. Walker, "The Treaty of Waitangi as a Focus of Maori Protest," p. 263.

5. Buddle, *The Maori King Movement*, p. 8.

Tamihana inscribed a circle to symbolize the inviolate King Country in front of the assembled chiefs at Ngaruawahia: "Here is our territory, this is ours (pointing to the circle made by Wetini). Let us retain this. Let not the Pakeha cross to us. Let not the Maori cross to the Pakeha. I say let both labour for things of eternity."[6]

According to Cowan, "The land, always the land, was the theme of [Tamihana's] earnest argument."[7] Just as Tamihana set the geographical boundaries that held the line against new Pakeha roads or settlements,[8] so the king defined its ethical boundaries: *"Heoiano taku, ko te whaka-pono, te aroha, te ture* [I have nothing, or mean nothing, or wish nothing but religion, love, and law]."[9] In an *apologia* to Governor Browne, Tamihana disclosed his early commitment to spreading the gospel as a Maori minister and his sense of vocation:

My "karakia" ["mission"] commenced after the departure of my minister, and I stood in his place. —the [Maori] war at Rotorua still being carried on. I urged that the feud should cease, and that feud was ended. . . .

At that time my name was Tarapipipi. I had no minister to strengthen me in that work which God sent into New Zealand, to every part, and to every Island. I was given this work to do by the stewards of Christ. . . . I worked at quarrels about land, and through my exertions these troubles were with difficulty ended. . . .

I thought about building a large house as a house of meeting for the tribes who were living at variance in New Zealand, and who would not become united. . . .

I then sent my thoughts to seek some plan by which the Maori tribes should become united. . . . However, they merely assembled together; evil still manifested itself; the river of blood was not yet stopped. . . . and I therefore sought for some thought to cause it to cease. . . . I considered how this blood could be made to diminish in this Island. I looked into your books, where Israel cried to have a king for themselves to be a judge over them, and I looked at the word of Moses in Deuteronomy xvii. 15; and in Revelations [i.e. Proverbs] xxix. 4; and I kept these words in my memory through all the years . . . I was still meditating upon the

6. Ibid., p. 46.
7. Cowan, *The New Zealand Wars,* 1:154.
8. Buddle, *The Maori King Movement,* p. 23.
9. Ibid.

matter. When we arrived at the year 1857 Te Heuheu called a
meeting at [Pukawa]. . . .

When the news of that meeting reached me . . . I commenced
at those words in the Book of Samuel viii. 5, "Give us a King to
judge us." This is why I set up Potatau in the year 1857.[10] On his
being set up the blood ceased . . .

That, O friend, was why I set him up, to put down my troubles,
to hold the land of the slave, and to judge the offences of the
Chiefs. The King was set up, the runangas were set up, the Kai-
whakawas [magistrates] were set up, and religion was set up. . . . I
do not desire to cast the Queen from this island, but, from my
piece [of land] I am to be the person to overlook my piece.[11]

Deaf to the religious imperatives of the King Movement, Browne denounced it as a land league that agitated for the allegiance of the
younger chiefs in order to set them against the government.

Tamihana incorporated the ideas proposed earlier by the Ngati
Ruanui and the young chiefs, Matene and Tamihana Te Rauparaha—
holding fast to the land, sovereignty, unification, and the king's overarching *mana*—into a well-crafted movement. The Kingite confederation was forged by a leader whom a contemporary characterized as
"one of the most able debaters and keenest thinkers he had ever met."[12]

Maori Christians believed that Jehovah sanctioned kings. At Paetai
in May 1857, Paora of Otaki identified the Maori monarch with the
ancient Israelite kingship.

God is good: Israel were his people, they had a king. I see no
reason why any nation should not have a king if it likes. The
Gospel does not say we are not to have a king. It says, "Honor the
King, love the brotherhood." Why should the Queen be angry?
We shall be in alliance with her, and friendship will be preserved.
The Governor does not stop murders and fights among us. A King
will be able to do that. Let us have order. So that we may grow as
the Pakeha grows. Why should we disappear from the country?
New Zealand is ours, I love it.[13]

10. Tamihana formally installed King Potatau in 1858.
11. Davidson and Lineham, *Transplanted Christianity*, pp. 129–30.
12. Cowan, *The New Zealand Wars*, 1:153–54, from a conversation with Sir John Gorst in 1906.
13. Buddle, *The Maori King Movement*, p. 9.

"Let us have order. So that we may grow as the Pakeha grows": Paora linked social stability with increase in population. Social order and demographic expansion depended upon retaining the land. The colonists regarded the sparse Maori population of Taranaki as dogs in the manger snapping at Europeans who wished only to turn their unused lands into farms and pastures, much as Waimate station had been transformed into a miniature England.

INSTALLATION OF THE KING

The transformed concept of chiefly authority—*mana o te whenua*—signified the transcendental power of the king to safeguard a Maori cosmos. It is invoked in the liturgy of the king's installation rite on June 2, 1858:

> The parties . . . met at nine a. m. , the flag was hoisted, and a party comprising Ngatihaua, Ngati Maniapoto, and part of Ngatimahuta [the king's *hapu*] proceeded to Potatau's tent. William Thompson [Tamihana's English name] entered to ask Potatau if he would become their King. When he returned these tribes were asked by Paul Te Ahuru "Will you have this man for a King?" The reply was "*Ae.*" He asked again "Will you give all the power (mana) and all the land to the King? They replied "*Ae*" again.
>
> The Manukau and Lower Waikato tribes headed by Ihaka and Katipa then faced the other party, and Katipa addressing Potatau said, " Will you be a father to us?" He answered in an audible voice "*Ae,*" when a salute of blank cartridge and three hearty cheers followed.[14]

According to Tamihana's personal account of the installation ritual, he approached Potatau with the Old Testament, the Psalms, and the New Testament in his hand and, after pointing out several scriptural verses, he asked the old chief if he preferred the title, "Chieftain" or "King."[15] Potatau responded that he preferred the title of king and that his protectors would be Jehovah and Jesus Christ. Tamihana recited the "words of David, 'The Lord is my shepherd,' and the words of Christ 'I am the good Shepherd' &c."[16] Just as Samuel Marsden saluted the

14. Ibid., p. 13.
15. Gorst, *The Maori King*, pp. 265–66.
16. In the ancient Near East a common metaphor for king was shepherd.

Union Jack and preached a sermon in 1814, so the Kingites hoisted their own flag and Tamihana delivered the following invocation.[17]

> Listen to our words, as the south, east, and west winds are too weak to carry out the law of God and man amongst us, as evils are still existing amongst us, as God says, "Come to me ye that are heavy laden and I will lighten your burden," we have united this day to give the power into the hands of one man, so as to give force to the laws of God and man amongst us. The birds of heaven are uniting and warbling their thoughts, the fishes in the sea are doing the like, the rivers and rivulets are running into one body, and so we are uniting to give hands and feet to this man, that he may assist the oppressed and wrench the sword out of the hands of those who are dark [i.e., "angry"].[18]

Tamihana invoked the law of God as a divine template for the law of the kingdom. The river of power relayed to the "one body" who is the king is *mana*, which will "give force" to law, namely render it effective. Divinely instituted *mana* will ensure the triumph of justice over oppression and conflict. *Mana*, like the Roman *imperium* that was adopted by European states, is an ancient religious manifestation of the power of the god(s) in the lives of human beings.[19] The men who took part in the installation rite were chiefs; all had inherited *mana* from their illustrious ancestors. *Mana* legitimates civil authority and is a gift from the gods to select men, whose deeds validate their roles as leaders and saviors of their people. In asserting his "mission," Tamihana imitated the biblical prophets, those "fathers" who, like the Creator of the cosmos, brought order, law, and stability out of the void. Thus did the Kingmaker transform Maori religion by invoking the creative force of Jehovah to establish the Kingite *pa* in the sacred center of Waikato.

DISSENT

Putting the *mana* of the king over all the land claimed by the *iwi* was a revolutionary idea, and not all chiefs were ready to accept it. The Nga

---

17. From this time forward the flags of various movements were raised over redoubts and during rites that sanctioned the return of the land. Hardly any of these standards and poles survive today.

18. Buddle, *The Maori King Movement*, pp. 13–14.

19. Van der Leeuw, *Religion in Essence and Manifestation*, pp. 43–51, 116; Mircea Eliade, *Patterns in Comparative Religion*, pp. 19–23.

Puhi of Northland had already relinquished their territory and depended upon government largesse. Other *ariki* did not wish to subordinate their *mana* to the king's. Finally, Christian clients like William
Naylor had irrevocably cast their lots with the British. Those who
spoke in the numerous Kingite meetings of the time expressed many
points of view.

The King Movement held the line against European settlement in
the interior of the North Island along the Waikato River and Lake
Taupo and rejected amalgamation in favor of a nonbelligerent separatism. Ever since, the *iwi* have pursued the goal of "full exclusive and
undisturbed possession of their Lands Forest Fisheries and other properties which they may collectively or individually possess so long as it
is their wish and their desire to retain the same in their possession,"
which is guaranteed in Article Two of the Treaty of Waitangi.[20]

"MANA I TE WHENUA"

Today, Maori sovereigntists argue that power over the land was ratified
by the Crown itself in the language of an agreement that preceded the
Treaty of Waitangi. In 1835, James Busby, called a conference of
thirty-four northern chiefs to sign "A Declaration of the Independence
of New Zealand," in order to thwart a challenge to British interests
posed by Frenchmen, adventurers, and utopians. This document includes references to kingship and *mana*, such as "*Ko te kingitanga ko
te mana i te whenua.*" The "Declaration" alludes to the *kingitanga,*
"sovereignty," and the *mana i te whenua*, "power of the land," of the
Maori chiefs.[21] This prior contract furnished the Waikato tribes with an
alternative tradition of the meaning of sovereignty—a trenchant fact
that was either discounted by or unknown to Thomas Buddle, Donald
McLean, and Gore Browne. The phrase *te mana i te whenua* resembles
the *te mana o te whenua* later employed by the Kingites. It appears
that the King Movement founded its claim to political legitimacy on the
1835 precedent. The earlier "Declaration" tended to identify the meaning of "sovereignty" (*mana*) and "kingship" (*kingitanga*), whereas the
Treaty of Waitangi used a missionary term for sovereignty (*kawanatanga*) that tended to subordinate the chiefs' authority (*tino rangatiratanga*) to that of the Crown. To the Kingite leaders, the words *king-*

20. I. H. Kawharu, *Waitangi*, p. 317.
21. R. J. Walker, "The Treaty of Waitangi as a Focus of Maori Protest," pp. 263–64.

itanga, tino rangatiratanga, and *mana* all guaranteed the sovereign power of the chiefs over their lands and people in the 1835 "Declaration" and the 1840 Treaty of Waitangi. The Pakeha refused to recognize the chiefs' astute interpretation of *mana* over the land as political sovereignty.

In his history of the Maori people, *Ka Whawhai Tonu Matou* (1990), Ranginui Walker argues that the 1852 Constitution Act, under which the New Zealand General Assembly was set up in 1854, contained an article, Number 71, which gave to the chiefs the right to advise the Pakeha executive.[22] In 1855 Tamihana tried and failed to secure Maori membership in the lower house of the Assembly.[23] From this, Walker concluded the following: "This institutionalisation of racism at the inception of democracy in New Zealand was the root cause of the conflict between Maori and Pakeha in the North Island and the colonial spoliation which followed."[24] Racism in itself was not a sufficient cause for the Land Wars, for there were Maori on *both* sides of the conflict. Insult may have been a precipitating cause, but the unresolved conflict over the "waste lands" was the fundamental cause of a war between Maori dissenters, who defended the independence of the chiefs (which had never been directly challenged until the Waitara dispute),[25] and Maori loyalists, who supported the imperial policy of amalgamation. In some districts, Donald McLean observed, where "Europeans are much intermixed with Natives. . . . there is a very great desire to conform to English law and usages."[26] The root cause of the wars was the Pakeha commitment to displace the Maori from their geographical, social, and religious cosmos by any means possible, first by stratagem and then by force, if necessary. The Kingites countered by building a Maori *pa*, fortified by laws and institutions that would defend their world against dismantlement without inciting war.

Tamihana's admitted goal was to stop Maori feuding and establish order in the Waikato. Before the advent of colonization and Christianization, *tapu* "had the force of law among [the Maori] as a people."[27] The King Movement relied upon *ture*, biblical law, to organize society much

---

22. Ibid., p. 112.

23. The right to vote for and serve as a representative was dependent upon a property qualification that most Maori could not meet.

24. Walker, *Ka Whawhai Tonu Matou*, p. 111.

25. Belich, *The New Zealand Wars*, p. 78.

26. *AJHR*, 1860, p. 91.

27. *AJHR*, 1860, p. 90, testimony of Donald McLean.

as *tapu* rules had maintained order under the old system, and it revived *tapu* by prohibiting trespass across the *aukati*.

ANTECEDENTS OF THE WARS

Decades of imperial schemes to acquire Maori land in order to accommodate the increasing tide of European immigrants set the stage for the midcentury wars. During Grey's first administration (1845–53), he secured the entire South Island from the weak Kai Tahu people by threat and manipulation. George Clarke Jr., Protector of the Aborigines, protested: "I was vexed by some things which the Governor had lately done in the South, and I thought they were not as straight-forward as in our dealings with the Maoris we should have been. I was very unwilling to be an agent in a policy against which my private conscience revolted, or to be entangled in a business that I could not stomach in the way of morality."[28]

Clarke moved to Tasmania. Donald McLean took his place in 1854 and vowed that he would secure the North Island from the Maori within eight years. A protégé of George Grey, McLean had worked with him to consolidate relations with client chiefs who wanted to assimilate. Takerei Te Rau declared that he was "tired of poverty" and wished to "put down all Maori ways and become like the white people."[29] He received loans from the government to establish agriculture and flour milling on his land.[30] Paikea, the chief of a small and weak tribe, sought shelter from his enemies under the queen's protection. Waka Nene, paramount chief, and mediator in two major violent disputes between whites and natives, preferred European technology to Maori traditional arts.[31] The motives of the loyalists were legion, but they were carefully fostered by a government that realized that a system of rewards was a means of pacifying a proud people who might successfully challenge the mythical invincibility of British arms. Initially, in the Bay of Islands and the Auckland area, Maori enterprise flourished, but with the midcentury upsurge in European immigration and the vicissitudes of international commerce, the northern tribes became marginalized and impoverished for lack of capital and representation in the civil institutions of the imperial government.

28. Clarke, *Notes on Early Life in New Zealand*, p. 97.
29. Ward, *A Show of Justice*, p. 106.
30. *AJHR*, 1860, pp. 149–50.
31. Ward, *A Show of Justice*, p. 116.

After Browne's "new policy" provoked Maori resistance, London returned Grey to the governorship in hopes that he could assuage the
chiefs. However, because of their mutual distrust, George Grey and
Tamihana failed to meet and negotiate a political agreement that would
establish an equal position for the two races during the transition to
responsible rule.[32] The Maori hope of sovereignty was thwarted by the
increasing hostility of the settlers after 1852 and the great demographic
reversal that by 1858 saw the Maori outnumbered by whites. Pakeha
advances provoked a great rift between the Maori dissidents and loyalists in the 1850s that presaged the Land Wars of the 1860s.

---

32. William Fox, no friend to Grey or Tamihana, recounts the fateful inability of the two ablest
New Zealand leaders to avert impending crisis, in his memoir, *The War in New Zealand*, pp. 88–91.

8

THE DESCENT INTO WAR

I believe a severe struggle would ensue,
before they would allow any force to take
possession of their soil. . . . The rights of
possession are held most sacred in New
Zealand; and everyone knows the exact
boundaries of his own land.

William Yate

One of the earliest reports on New Zealand was penned in 1835 by William Yate, a careful observer of this "new" land.[1] English Romantic sensibilities permeate his first chapter, which nostalgically depicts the landscape as "all nature—untouched by art" before roads and industry had reduced its sublime aspect.[2] The North Island's *kauri* forests and splendid mountains excited the young pioneer's sense of awe, and he especially noted the singular peak that figured in the ceremony at Pukawa two decades later.

There is a large volcano, called the Tongariro, in active operation, midway between the Mahia or Table Cape and the opposite coast. The mountain is very lofty; and is visible, in some parts of Wai-kato, at an immense distance. That there are, in the bowels of the

1. Yate, *An Account of New Zealand.*
2. Ibid., p. 13.

earth, abundant materials for producing heat, is evident from the
numerous hot springs, and springs impregnated with sulfuric acid,
which here and there bubble up within a few miles from the base
of these hills. . . .

In the neighbourhood of these sulfuric springs is one remarkably cold: the water appears very clear, but of a red colour, as
though slightly tinged with alkali root. When quiescent, it soon
precipitates a red earth; with which the natives paint their bodies,
and dye their garments; and which to them is very valuable.[3]

Red is the color of the sacred in Maori tradition, and Yate has sensed
the numinous bond that united Tongariro, the land, and the *iwi*.
Twenty-three years later the King Movement was established in the
shadow of Tongariro at the sacred center of the North Island.

TE RIRI PAKEHA

Thomas Buddle and John Gorst recorded the rise of the King Movement, which heralded the great conflict of the ensuing decade, called
by the Pakeha the Maori Wars, and by the Maori, *te riri pakeha*, "the
white man's anger." In 1863–64, Cameron's troops swept over the
Waikato. Keith Sinclair's conscientious history of the events leading up
to Cameron's invasion noted that the British fought more wars in the
1900s than any other nation and attributed *te riri pakeha* to colonial
bellicosity.[4] Maori warfare had been sporadic until the Musket Wars of
the 1820s.[5] Hongi's aggression lent credence to the British belief that
the natural state of the Maori was a war of all against all. In fact, they
had effective traditions of peacemaking before colonization, and the
taua muru or "plunder party," their customary means of redress, also
served to distribute material goods among the population.[6] In his recon-
struction of Maori prehistory, Ranginui Walker notes evidences of eras
of peace and periods of intertribal hostilities. It seems the *iwi* were not

3. Ibid., p. 6.
4. Sinclair, *The Origins of the Maori Wars*, p. 18. English bloodletting took place in Britain's far-
flung colonies.
5. The introduction of firearms into Maori culture led to the death of approximately one-fifth of
the involved population. See Binney, "Christianity and the Maoris," p. 149 n. 30.
6. See Vayda, "Peacemaking," in *Maori Warfare*, pp. 119–24, and Ward, *A Show of Justice*, pp.
8–10. The *taua muru* was levied against victims of injury as well as perpetrators. It was a means of
restoring a spiritual balance. Yate observed villagers storing their provisions high in trees to protect
them from raiding parties, and F. E. Maning, in *Old New Zealand*, p. 119–20, recorded that the
custom died out as the Maori began to acquire more precious goods, such as blankets and cash.

very different from most peoples in the world. Maori periods of terri-
torial expansion, like those of the Europeans, were evidently marked
by warfare also.

IMPERIAL DESIGNS

The Victorians took pride in civilizing alien tribes, enforcing their laws
with an army they considered gallant and invincible, but by the 1860s
the Colonial and War Offices in London sought to reduce the heavy
taxation that financed their overextended military forces. London was
reluctant to underwrite New Zealand's defense. Most of all Britain
feared that an intemperate settler-run administration would provoke a
war that would exacerbate the burdens of empire.[7] On the other hand,
the Crown could not abide sedition; and London emphatically objected
to a Maori king. In 1856 Donald McLean warned London that the
Maori were fearful of the Pakeha "taking possession of their country
and subjugating themselves."[8] McLean's agents informed him of an alleged conspiracy to make all land under the chiefs' authority unavail-
able for sale to the Crown,[9] and from this time forward Governor
Browne cautioned London that a land league was spreading over the
North Island. In May 1861 he issued his "Declaration by the Governor
to the Natives assembled at Ngaruawahia," which denied the legitimacy of the King Movement and forbade any other "unlawful combi-
nations."[10]

Between 1860 and 1868, the transition from imperial to responsible
rule in New Zealand was marked by the failure of the last two imperial
governors, Browne and Grey, to moderate the settlers' abandonment of
Humanitarian policies. Justice William Martin debated the question of
Waitara with Busby and the government, but the gravity of his opinion
did not alter the course of events, which were driven more by the
historic transition to responsible rule. Grey ordered Cameron's invasion, and William Fox, as New Zealand's first settler premier, tangled
with Grey over the conduct of the war.[11]

Fox was a former agent of the New Zealand Company, known for his
anti-Maori views, who served as acting Native Secretary in 1862 and as

7. Harrop, *England and the Maori Wars*, pp. 14–15, pp. 289–311.
8. Ibid., p. 42.
9. Sinclair, *The Origins of the Maori Wars*, pp. 61–62.
10. Rickard, *Tamihana the Kingmaker*, pp. 103–6.
11. For a history of the transition to responsible rule, see Rusden, *History of New Zealand*, vol. 2.

both Colonial Secretary and Native Minister in 1863–64 during the transition to government by ministers and a General Assembly. Supported by rising anti-Maori sentiment, Fox pressured Grey to enforce punitive measures against dissident tribes, while London fidgeted about fomenting a wider war that could be put down only at great expense.[12] London entrusted Grey with the impossible mission of dampening hostilities and reducing the budget, while Fox excoriated him for delaying land confiscations that, in turn, provoked the prophet movements.[13] Under the Fox-Whitaker administration, the General Assembly enacted the 1863 New Zealand Settlements Act, authorizing the taking of rebels' land, and in 1864 the Public Works Land Act gave the government the power to take land from dissidents without payment. These initiatives sowed lasting seeds of discord between Pakeha and Maori.[14] Maori land became the capital that paid for militia campaigns against those who rose up to defend themselves against the taking of their land!

DEFENDING THE VINEYARD

The Duke of Newcastle, Colonial Secretary in London, had drawn up a gameplan for confronting a possible Maori uprising well before war broke out.[15] At the same time, the Kingites were attempting to allay government concern about their intentions. In a conciliatory letter dated June 10, 1857, the Waikato chiefs disclosed these intentions.

We are now assembled for the purpose of appointing an Assembly for each and every tribe in New Zealand, for the purpose of examining into the good and the evil, with their Magistrates appointed for each, to carry out the principles of Christianity, that we may be one flesh. Perhaps you think that the Maori King will be sepa-

12. Fox wished to borrow three million pounds from London in order to prosecute the war with militias instead of imperial soldiers; he intended to pay back this sum by confiscating rebel lands that would be purchased by Pakeha and transformed from waste land to productive farms; see Fox, *The War in New Zealand*, pp. 239–54.

13. Ibid., pp. 146–54. Grey's mandate was constrained by power struggles and his recall to London in 1868 effectively ended imperial rule. See Harrop, *England and the Maori Wars*, pp. 289–311, and Fox's memoir, *The War in New Zealand*.

14. Rickard, *Tamihana the Kingmaker*, p. 176, quotes from a Royal Commission in 1928, which stated that the Maori deserved compensation for being branded as rebels and suffering confiscation of their lands. As the Land Wars also constituted a civil war among Maori tribes and even among members of the same family, it was impossible to restrict confiscation to the alleged guilty parties.

15. Harrop, *England and the Maori Wars*, p. 62.

rated from the Queen; not so, but it will be better for them to be friendly. . . . let the law of God govern both, that is, (the law of) love.[16]

On May 21, 1860, Tamihana counseled the chiefs to examine the merits of Wiremu Kingi's Waitara claim in terms of righteous versus unrighteous causes, citing 1 Kings 21:2–3 as a case study in the latter.

But let us not take up arms in an unrighteous cause. Ahab coveted Naboth's vineyard, and because Naboth would not give up the inheritance of his fathers, Ahab was greatly disturbed. Jezebel his wife saw his trouble and said, I will give it thee. She brought Naboth to death by falsehood, and took it, but God avenged the deed. I do not forget some of the Kings of Judah who engaged in unrighteous war, how they perished for their sin. Therefore I hesitate, and say let us see our way. Wm. King says the land is his; Taylor [Teira] says it is his. I say let us find out the owner . . . I do not condemn the Governor for I am not informed. As for the Queen she is the minister of God, and the minister of God is not supposed to do wrong. . . . I also remember the words of Paul, "Let every soul be subject unto the higher powers, for there is no power but of God; the powers that be are ordained of God." . . . let me have a just cause [to go to war].[17]

Six years earlier the Reverend T. S. Grace of Taupo had also cited 1 Kings 21:2–3 in an anonymous pamphlet that supported those who refused to sell land to the Crown[18] It circulated among the Waikato chiefs, but all 250 copies eventually were destroyed or disappeared. Bishop Selwyn reportedly used the same passage in a sermon of rebuke to the settlers of Taranaki for coveting Maori land in 1855. By 1860 the story was well known as a subtext for land disputes, particularly Waitara. Grace had framed the question in 1854, "Is it just for you to sell the food that is their ground [namely, the ancestral land], for [to] the children of the strange people?"[19] The matter was conveyed in symbolic

16. *AJHR*, 1860, p. 122.

17. Buddle, *The Maori King Movement*, pp. 37–38.

18. "Some Questions to the Maori People about the Selling of Land"; see Bagnall, "No Known Copy?" p. 80; see also Buddle, *The Maori King Movement*, pp. 23 and 37.

19. Bagnall, "No Known Copy?" In 1854 Grace was in Auckland when the members of the New Zealand Parliament met for the first time. He heard them propose that a loan be raised to buy up eleven or twelve million acres in the next few years, and he hastily wrote his circular against land-

terms by invoking a biblical story that was common knowledge, just as in the tradition of *whaikorero* important arguments were expressed in the symbolic language of Maori myth and history.

Tamihana's reminder that "the powers that be are ordained of God" affirmed the legitimacy of the house with two sets of rafters, signaling that Maori and Pakeha should divide the land, respecting one another's boundaries. The landholding Maori movements did not advocate that the Pakeha should be "driven into the sea," as the settlers believed and historians have claimed.[20]

THE FIRST TARANAKI WAR

Contrary to conventional wisdom in the Victorian age, Thomas Hobbes's "war of all against all" is not the "naturall" state of primitives, but the unfortunate consequence of a descent from civil order into anarchy, which happens when traditional rules and customs are violated with impunity. The press in Taranaki waged a propaganda campaign to convince settlers to side with the landselling Maori.[21] Gore Browne considered invading the Waikato in 1861, but London was not yet convinced that the Kingites posed a threat.[22] The settlers wished to teach the Maori a lesson by force of arms.

British pride provoked the First Taranaki War of 1860–61.[23] Governor Browne felt publicly humiliated when Wiremu Kingi "and all his people marched off without any salutation" at a meeting intended to transact the sale of Waitara.[24]

When His Excellency the Governor visited New Plymouth in March 1859, a block of land situated on the south bank of Waitara was offered for sale by a Chief named "Teira," supported by his friends who were joint claimants. The Governor accepted the

---

selling. Although the CMS distanced itself from Grace's position, the missionaries were branded as land league sympathizers, leading Buddle and others to disavow Grace.

20. Cowan commented in *The New Zealand Wars*, p. 241: "It was a racial war; the Maori aim was to sweep the *Pakeha* to the sea, as the *Pakeha* Government's object was to teach the Maori his subjection to British authority."

21. Sinclair, *The Origins of the Maori Wars*, pp. 202–3.

22. Ibid., p. 234; Ward, *A Show of Justice*, p. 124.

23. See Harrop, *England and the Maori Wars*, passim, and Sinclair, *The Origins of the Maori Wars*, passim. Sinclair's data support the view that Browne provoked a confrontation at Waitara that could have been avoided.

24. Quoted in Sinclair, *The Origins of the Maori Wars*, p. 137.

offer, provided that the ownership of the land was undisputed, and Teira laid at His Excellency's feet a *Parawai* (a Taranaki Mat) as a symbol that the offer was accepted. William King was present, but did not . . . condescend to assert in a becoming manner any claims on his own behalf, but in an insulting and defiant tone arose and left the room saying, "I will not permit the Sale of Waitara to the Pakeha. Waitara is in my hands, I will not give it up; *Ekore, Ekore, Ekore.* (I will not, I will not, I will not) I have spoken."[25]

After Kingi upstaged him, the governor sent surveyors to Waitara under the protection of troops. The Ngati Awa retreated behind their fortifications, joined by their neighbors, the recalcitrant Ngati Ruanui. Kingi appealed for King Potatau's support. Settlers left their farms to the mercy of the tribes and sought protection from the army in New Plymouth. After a year marked by pitched battles, the army prevailed over the Taranaki land holders, and Wiremu Tamihana brokered a truce at Pukarangiora *pa*. The government punished the Taranaki hostiles by confiscating their lands, a harsh measure advocated by Fox's party that created a perpetual grievance and exacerbated resistance and violence. Meanwhile, Grey's attempts to avoid an outbreak was vitiated by political battles with colonial leaders and military officers that weakened his command of events between 1861 and 1868.[26] It appears that Pakeha leaders were as sensitive to insult as their Maori counterparts and that the wars were ignited by pique as well as the conflict over land.

On behalf of New Plymouth settlers, the *Taranaki Herald* complained that the Land Purchase Department was procrastinating in its acquisition of the vast tracts of forest needed by the struggling settlement. It suited Browne's political purpose, as well as his slighted feelings, to take aggressive action against Kingi's people, even though he anticipated that it might lead to a genocidal war.[27] He believed that New Plymouth colonists were on the verge of vigilantism, and he ordered troops to attack the Waitara survey protesters before the "vigilantes" did:

At the beginning of March, 1860, Governor Browne arrived at New Plymouth and instructed Colonel Gold to enforce the survey

25. Buddle, *The Maori King Movement*, p. 29.
26. Ward, *A Show of Justice*, p. 251; Harrop, *England and the Maori Wars*, pp. 289–311.
27. Harrop, *England and the Maori Wars*, pp. 65–66.

of Waitara. This amounted in practice to the occupation of the block. On 17 March, Kingi and seventy or eighty of his warriors threw up a pa, Te Kohia or the L-pa, at Waitara, and refused to evacuate it. Shots were exchanged, and the Taranaki War had begun.[28]

POLARIZATION

In the early 1860s, another dangerous polarization—between Auckland, then the seat of government, and the separatist Waikato chiefs—was intensified on both sides by widespread rumors of imminent attack.[29] Grey prepared to send troops across the border after receiving unauthenticated reports that the Kingites were planning to attack first.[30] In a series of letters that constituted a "misinformation campaign," he advised London that the Maori were bent on hostilities.[31] No mediation could have dispelled the sense of grievance and suspicion that had grown up between the two populations by mid-1863. The Maori feared that they would "be eaten up and cease to be" as the English incrementally obtained their lands.[32] War historian James Belich cautiously asserts, "Perhaps the Taranaki and Waikato conflicts were more akin to classic wars of conquest than we would like to believe."[33]

When Grey offered to meet Wiremu Tamihana face-to-face, the Kingites were certain that the invitation was a plot to capture him.[34] It was too late for peace, despite the best efforts of New Zealand's two storied statesmen. The sons of Japhet were unable to coexist with Maori *mana*; it was essential to their pride to prevail over the sons of Shem. Sensing this, Maori leaders spoke often of their fears of virtual enslavement, their metaphor for cultural and spiritual death.

28. Belich, *The New Zealand Wars*, p. 82. Belich's use of the passive is meticulous, but the stage had been set for offensive action by the British.

29. John Featon, in *The Waikato War*, pp. 15–31, gives an Aucklander's view of the months of unease before Grey notified the Waikato chiefs of his intent to establish military posts along the river on July 11, 1863. Featon attests that the settlers did not want war, that the "Waikatos hated the settlers with an exceedingly great hate," and that the causes of the war were the threats and violence of the Maori against law-abiding settlers.

30. Ibid., pp. 15, 18, averred that "the settlers as a body did not want war," but he reported that the Waikatos had assembled in 1863 to "march on and burn Auckland."

31. Belich, *The New Zealand Wars*, p. 124.

32. Harrop, *England and the Maori Wars*, p. 45.

33. Belich, *The New Zealand Wars*, p. 80.

34. Rickard, *Tamihana the Kingmaker*, p. 124.

As tensions increased, the missionaries were ready targets of settler innuendo. In 1860 Buddle wrote, "It may be also proper to place on record a denial of the allegations that have lately been made in some of the journals of this country against the Missionaries, and to protest against the injustice done to them as a body, by insinuations of disloyalty and selfishness. If any solitary members of the body have acted foolishly, let them bear their own burdens."[35] The church removed T. S. Grace[36] from his mission in Taupo after Donald McLean objected to his anti-land-selling tract.[37] Buddle complained that Grace helped "to stigmatise [missionaries] as opponents of colonization and enemies to the country's progress." Promoting the more acceptable view that the "small and rapidly declining" Maori tribes did not deserve to claim "extensive tracts of country" which "can never be cultivated by them," Buddle agreed with James Busby's dominionist view:

The questions very naturally arise, does Divine Providence intend these vast tracts of county to remain a wilderness, or are these parts of the earth, like other parts, to be subdued and made to yield food for man and beast? Would it not be greatly to the advantage of the owner to dispose of such portions are not likely to be required for himself or children, and thereby obtain the means of improving his property, and of securing the instruction and example of civilized neighbours to aid him in the improvement of his circumstances?[38]

Ironically, it was Thomas Grace who was held hostage by the Hauhau extremist, Kereopa, in 1865. The misadventures of the resilient reverend, who kept refreshingly unbiased accounts of his life as a missionary, serve to illustrate the temper of a time when any errant settler's respect for Maori aboriginal rights to the land was equated with sedition.

35. Buddle, *The Maori King Movement*, p. 22.

36. T. S. Grace had served as locum tenens for Bishop William Williams in Poverty Bay before securing his own mission at Taupo. No two missionaries presented a greater contrast in temperament and purpose. Grace was a former businessman who taught Maori converts how to develop and manage their own commercial projects, while Williams preferred to limit their practical education to homemaking and farming skills. Grace never ceased ministering to the Maori. Even after he was driven from Taupo he became a circuit rider among disaffected tribes.

37. Harrop, *England and the Maori Wars*, pp. 32–33, 42. The benighted pamphlet was not even identified on Bishop H. W. Williams's 1924 bibliography of works printed in the Maori language.

38. Buddle, *The Maori King Movement*, p. 22.

9

WHY THE PROPHETS ROSE UP

> *The teaching of Christianity had destroyed
> the old barbarous customs of* tapu, *and all
> the superstitious reverence for priests and
> chiefs, which had supplied the place of law
> and government, but neither the
> missionaries nor the Government had been
> able to substitute a better system in the
> place of that which had been pulled down:
> thus the natives were left in a state of
> absolute anarchy.*
>
> John Gorst

An atmosphere of impending catastrophe suffused native and settler populations before each outbreak of war between 1860 and
1868, when a series of regional conflicts in Taranaki, Waikato,
and the East Coast were associated with the rise of prophets and saviors
that included Wiremu Tamihana; Te Ua Haumene, the founder of Pai
Marire; Te Kooti Arikirangi Te Turuki, the leader of Ringatu; and Rua
Kenana, the messiah of Wairua Tapu, a branch of Ringatu.[1] The latter
three movements constitute a sequential "Spirit tradition."[2]

1. There were various additional movements in this renewal tradition. See Karen Sinclair's dis-
sertation, *Maramatanga: Ideology and Social Process Among the Maori of New Zealand*; James Belich,
"I Shall Not Die": Titokawaru's War; and Hazel Riseborough, *Days of Darkness* (Wellington: Allen &
Unwin, 1989).
2. Jean E. Rosenfeld, "Pai Marire: Peace and Violence in a New Zealand Millenarian Tradition,"
in Michael Barkun, ed., *Millennialism and Violence*, pp. 83–103. In a slightly different vein, Judith
Binney refers to a continuous "wairua tapu tradition" in Ringatu that links the prophecies of a series
of nineteenth- and twentieth-century seers.

PAI MARIRE

Te Ua's Pai Marire, "good and peaceful," movement sprang up among the landholding Ngati Ruanui tribe in 1862. Fueled by land confiscation during and after the 1863 Waikato invasion, the enthusiastic new religion spread like "a fire in dry fern" across the North Island.[3] Its energetic proselytizing ignited a civil war between Maori loyalists and dissidents on the East Coast.

Instructed by Jehovah's messenger, Gabriel Rura ("ruler"), Te Ua produced a written gospel, *Te Ua Rongopai*, and instituted a mesmerizing new ritual, the *niu* rite, that recast the ancient sacred sticks called *pou* or *toko*[4] as a tall pole connecting sky spirits with worshipers. This rite was ordained by Jehovah through Gabriel and gave direct access to the divine winds called *hau*, which led others to call the new sect and its members, Hauhau.

By the 1850s the loss of land and *tapu* rules produced a condition that Te Ua called *tuwareware*, "forsakenness," similar to that which Buddle lamented among tribes in contact with European traders. Charismatic movements are open to all who flock to them, and their rituals of spirit-possession extend access to the sacred to all participants. Pai Marire was open to all who marched around the *niu* pole chanting Te Ua's *karakia*. The wind spirits descended from the sky down the pole and entered the worshipers, filling them with power and knowledge. Spiritual authority invested in Christian bishops or priests was democratized in the *niu* cult, and local leaders, called *tiu*, "Jew," followed their own inspirations. This "pentecostalism" appealed to its numerous converts, but Te Ua soon lost control over his "good and peaceful" sect; it inspired Titokowaru's guerrilla campaign in Taranaki and repressive countermeasures on the East Coast. Local leaders were pursued and jailed in the Bay of Plenty region. Neighboring tribes battled each other. Punitive confiscations increased. A remnant of men, women, and children were sent into exile on the remote Chatham Islands. By 1868 both Te Ua and Pai Marire appeared to have died, but the hope of reclaiming "Canaan" was resurrected by Te Kooti, one of the jailed exiles.

3. Cowan, *The New Zealand Wars*, 2:3.

4. Taylor, *Te Ika a Maui*, p. 91, states, "The natives had a way of divination by means of sticks; this was called Niu." Shirres, in "An Introduction to Karakia," states that rods were used in all major and minor rituals. Johanson "Studies in Maori Rites and Myths," p. 82, distinguishes the ancient *niu* rite as "taking auguries for a warlike undertaking from small sticks," while other rites using poles may enact cosmic complementarities of Day and Night.

ETHICAL NORMS AND SOCIAL ORDER

The gospel of Te Ua refers to New Zealand as *Kenana*, the "land of Canaan";[5] and Ringatu tradition refers to Donald McLean, the man who imprisoned Te Kooti, as "pharaoh."[6] Prophets, messiahs, and disciples sought to restore the people's access to celestial sources of power and knowledge through new rituals, prayers, and observances. They created a hermeneutical body of myth-history that linked Maori followers to the Israelites, as well as to their Polynesian ancestors. Te Kooti reinvigorated the oral tradition and instituted new holy days, or *ra*, that memorialized the dramatic experiences of his community of dispossessed survivors.

In her study of ethics in non-Western societies, *Purity and Danger*, Mary Douglas concluded that when ethical norms, such as the prohibition against adultery, are routinely ignored by members of a community, religion may compel their observance. For example, among the Ashanti, only a wife can conduct the rite that protects a husband who commits adultery from divine punishment; thus a man who deceives his wife has good reason to fear a god's retaliation. A sincere conviction that the violation of rules will incur divine wrath tends to reinforce normative behavior. The intricate network of *tapu* maintained sanctioned behavior in Maori society until it was undermined by Christians or supplanted by civil courts and gaol. When a chief accepted baptism he not only renounced Maori custom, but he relinquished his obligation to maintain *tapu* rules governing purity, pollution, and trespass. There were no police or prisons in Aotearoa, because tapu regulated the proper relationship of one person to another and punished the transgressor with *mate maori*. One of the purposes that an *aukati* served in the nineteenth century was to mark off a place of refuge for Maori who feared imprisonment for breaking British statutes. Gaol was regarded as enslavement, which effectively canceled a person's *mana*. Nevertheless, by the 1850s the system of *tapu* had fallen into such disuse that chiefs appealed to Governor Browne to set up British magistrates in the Waikato to help restore social order. Had he responded in a timely fashion, he might have blunted the King Movement.[7]

5. Clark, *Hauhau*, p. 118.
6. Ward, *DNZB*, p. 257.
7. *AJHR*, 1860, F-No. 3, pp. 2–5.

TURE, BIBLICAL AND CIVIL LAW

When a chief converted he often founded a separate Christian village, because the two different ethical systems could not operate in the same community without strife. In 1839 the Reverend B. Y. Ashwell, led a Waikato Christian contingent away from their relatives, who were enjoying a banquet of human flesh, crying, "Come, let us leave this pa, and build a pa for Christ." At the request of his flock he drew up for them biblical laws and regulations called *ture* (from "torah").[8] Wiremu Tamihana instituted *ture* in the King Movement, just as he had replaced *tapu* with *ture* at Peria, a new village he had founded as a Christian chief.[9] Those who considered biblical law too harsh would sometimes petition secular authorities for civil law, which also came to be called *ture*. Gore Browne promised the Waikato leaders in 1857 that he would set up a system of self-governing local councils under civil magistrates, but by 1860 he had not sufficiently followed through, and the King Movement intensified. Alarmed, the House of Representatives convened a Select Committee to inquire into the obvious failure of Browne's administration to ward off the "disturbances," which were regarded as a consequence of his lethargic response to the chiefs' appeals for magistrates and courts.[10] The period of confusion between a society regulated by *tapu* and a state regulated by *ture* characterized the decade before the wars. The king was set up, said Wiremu Tamihana, to bring law and order to the people.

The chiefs' request for civil institutions was accompanied by their desire to establish an equal position alongside the Pakeha in the emerging political structure of a constitutional state. Infatuated with new technologies, such as the plow and the mill, many chiefs had become dependent upon the British. During his tenure as imperial governor, George Grey had maintained peace while expanding settlement by striking up alliances with landselling chiefs, who became a bulwark against Maori dissent against government policies.

Ironically, one of the chiefs who had aided Grey's suppression of rebellion by the Hutt Valley people in the 1840s was Wiremu Kingi of Waitara. Gore Browne alienated clients like Kingi, forcing them to make a difficult choice between supporting their government benefactors or joining the King Movement. Some chiefs were unable to

---

8. Featon, *The Waikato War*, p. 15, quoting from "Recollections of a Waikato Missionary."
9. Elsmore, *Mana from Heaven*, pp. 59–64; Rickard, *Tamihana the Kingmaker*, pp. 51–53.
10. *AJHR*, 1860, F-No. 3, p. 1.

reconcile their dual allegiances in an era of uncompromising polarization. Others, like William Naylor, one of the candidates for Maori
kingship, tried to persuade the Waikato tribes to return to the queen's
fold.

F. D. FENTON'S CENSUS

F. D. Fenton, destined to become the chief judge of the postwar Land
Court, was the only civil magistrate Browne ever appointed to the
Waikato.[11] When he conducted a census of the North Island tribes in
1856, he noticed the dilemma of assimilated Maori. He called them
"isolated beings," who had neither changed their own people nor found
a place in Pakeha society.[12] In notable contrast to Parsonson, Fenton
reported that Maori educated in government-supported schools were
unprepared for the "amount of competition which first astonishes and
ultimately disheartens [them]."[13]

He also criticized government for undertaking "improvements," such
as road building, to serve only the "white interest . . . for the convenience of which the roads would serve," despite the fact that Maori enterprise also contributed to the advancement of the colony.[14] Land selling
and road building were hotly debated issues on the *marae*, as well.
People were divided over accepting roads that provided infrastructure
for agricultural commerce, but also encouraged further Pakeha incur-
sion. Because it generated revenue without relinquishing control over
their resources, land-leasing was a popular source of revenue for the
tribes, and Pakeha tenants complained bitterly of their treatment at the
hands of Maori landlords.[15] The 1856 census revealed that the Maori
had adopted European ways at great cost to themselves. Ironically, it
was Fenton, a Pakeha bureaucrat, who reported to his superiors that
the Humanitarian policy was not working: "The observation has been
general amongst the flour producing tribes that though they have followed the precepts of the European authorities, and have obtained
ploughs and horses, and engaged industriously in the cultivation of

11. Fenton's analyses of Maori conditions proved more skillful than his brief tenure as a magistrate and more enlightened than his powerful career as head of the Land Court.

12. *AJHR*, 1860, p. 136.

13. Ibid.

14. Ibid.

15. Ward, *A Show of Justice*, pp. 119–20.

wheat, still the advancement they have made is slight, and the increase of their personal comforts imperceptible."[16]

Fenton's data revealed that both population and fertility were in decline: "The almost entire destruction of the old Maori law has been caused by the contact with the superior race, and the void left has not been supplied." Because of the loss of *tapu* and their amalgamation into Pakeha society as "hewers of wood and drawers of water," the subjects of his census reported feelings of humiliation and the "deep-rooted conviction that the Maori is gradually disappearing before the white man."[17]

Alan Ward's thorough account of racial amalgamation in nineteenth-century New Zealand relates that from the beginning British institutions had fostered the subordination of the Maori in the New Zealand economy. The Nga Puhi testified in 1860 that they had sold their land and spent themselves into poverty.[18] Maori agriculturalists incurred indebtedness from loans before the wars; and, afterward, economic depression and increasing competition from Australia deprived them of the capital needed to reinvest in pastoralism or manufacturing. During and after the wars, land confiscation left many tribes impoverished. Given Fenton's census data, and his critique of the amalgamation policy,[19] Parsonson's thesis that inherent competitiveness was responsible for Maori troubles is unconvincing.

THE "NEW INSTITUTIONS"

The "responsible Ministers" who conducted the Select Committee's series of hearings in 1860 reported that Governor Browne was guilty of "neglect and indifference" in not restoring law and order in the Waikato. They regarded the King Movement as a benign attempt to provide self-governance.[20] Fenton tried to craft a British solution for the Maori dilemma. He favored bringing "new institutions"[21] to the Waikato

16. *AJHR*, 1860, p. 134.

17. Ibid.

18. Buddle, *The Maori King Movement*, p. 49.

19. See "Minute by Mr. Fenton in Reference to Native Affairs (13 October 1856)," *AJHR*, 1860, Appendix B, No. 1, pp. 133–40.

20. *AJHR*, 1860, p. 2.

21. "The scheme was simply a variation of the *runanga* (councils) scheme suggested by Waikato Maori, elaborated by Fenton and revived in recent memoranda by Browne. Village Runanga under the direction of Resident Magistrates, and District Runanga under new officers called Civil Commissioners would make by-laws; the Pakeha officers, commissioned as Circuit Court Judges, and Maori

before war over Waitara broke out, but his political rival, Donald McLean, succeeded in delaying their implementation until 1861, despite the fact that he had proposed similar reforms himself. They were the last, best hope of finding "a way through conflicting interests without war."[22] Had William Fox, George Grey, and the Waikato Kingites succeeded in establishing this compromise between amalgamation and Maori governance before 1860, the history of New Zealand might have taken a very different course. Social order would have been reestablished by a combination of civil magistrates and tribal councils. The settlers would have grudgingly accepted the principle of *mana o te whenua*, but chiefs would have been encouraged to consider land sales in the future. However, Fenton's efforts proved to be "too little, too late," according to Attorney-General Henry Sewell, who published a sober analysis of what went wrong with Maori policy for the British Colonial Secretary in 1864.[23] Polarization, distrust, and the inevitable political struggle over power in a new state had vitiated any viable context for mutual trust. Fear of the Waikato Kingites led to Cameron's invasion in 1863. Suspicion that Grey intended to subjugate them by offering the "new institutions" as a subterfuge undermined Maori cooperation. Finally, the colonists never accepted the plan and consistently opposed any brake on the expansion of settlements.

The truth is that neither Grey's "flour and sugar" subsidies nor Fenton's proposals furnished a viable framework for the renewal of the Maori world. They were secular, rational, European approaches to a problem that cried out for a religious response. It was Te Ua who diagnosed the Maori dilemma as a turning away from God, and it was the *poropiti*, "prophets," who proposed revelatory new means of salvation from "eventual extirpation."

SETTLER BIAS

The Pakeha resembled other colonial populations who had forged resilient national characters out of pioneer experiences; they were intolerant of London's Humanitarianism. A French observer compared their frontier "insolence" to that of their counterparts in Australia and

---

Assessors would enforce the laws, the Assessors having independent jurisdiction. . . . [I]t was planned to appoint paid Maori police." Ward, *A Show of Justice*, p. 125.

22. Ibid., p. 126.

23. Sewell, *New Zealand Native Rebellion*.

America.[24] The antagonism between settlers and natives developed out of a competition for land in all three colonies. To the Pakeha it was the native who was the stranger, the savage, and the enemy: "It is plain from the tone of the letters, diaries, and pamphlets written by the semi-educated or the opinions of the magazines and newspapers written for the barely-literate, that the generality of immigrants regarded the Maori with strong antagonism."[25] Settler hostility was not limited to the "semi-educated"; J. C. Richmond, stellar member of the brilliant Richmond-Atkinson "mob," described the stereotypical Maori as an "ignorant, arrogant strong schoolboy with a spice of the jew in him."[26]

CONFLICT AND HERMENEUTICS

The pioneers found themselves in fundamental conflict with a people bound to forests, watercourses, mountains, birds, and sacred places. Remove the tribe from the land in order to exploit its resources, and the power of religion to bind a people together is severely weakened. Without their text of the land, remembering the past became possible only on the portable "ground" of meeting house and *marae*, where history and identity were evoked in song and *whakapapa*. Harold W. Turner reminds us that "we have forgotten that history always has a geography, and that each is essential to the other."[27]

Listening to the Bible, Maori prophets absorbed the "millennial dream"[28] of a Promised Land that had been given in the beginning, was lost, and that finally will be returned in the Eschaton. In Genesis Adam and Eve are forcibly expelled from Eden, and Abraham follows God's call to go forth to Canaan. Exodus tells how the Israelites were led by God from the land of bondage to a land flowing with milk and honey. The book of Daniel and the Revelation of John console those who are persecuted for their faith with a promise that God will reward the just and punish their adversaries at the end of history. "Thy kingdom come," may have been formulaic to an Englishman, but it was received by the Maori as God's imminent promise to restore justice and renew the world.

24. Sinclair, *The Origins of the Maori Wars*, p. 3.
25. Ibid., p. 9.
26. Scholefield, *The Richmond-Atkinson Papers*, p. 103.
27. Harold W. Turner, *From Temple to Meeting House: The Phenomenology and Theology of Places of Worship*, p. 6.
28. Webster, *Rua and the Maori Millennium*, pp. 68–73.

Early Christian millennialists identified Rome with "Babylon," a place of exile where the saints suffered while they awaited the return of their divine champion, the Messiah. Millennial dreams seem to be myths of consolation for those who feel overpowered by the symbolic "beasts" of empire.[29] Maori prophets also believed the eschatological kingdom was close at hand, and their people were a righteous remnant, but because Pai Marire and Ringatu did not preach the Lord's resurrection and salvation by faith, Protestant missionaries regarded them as non-Christian cults that worshiped an Old Testament God.[30]

The prophets embraced Jehovah and his angels as liberators, weaving Maori identity as children of Shem into a sectarian *whakapapa*. Referring to the same texts, Anglicans and Methodists constructed a rival hermeneutics that justified their hegemonizing roles as children of Japhet. Samuel Marsden spoke of Britain in terms that identified it with God's "thousand-year reign," while Rua Kenana founded a New Jerusalem near the burial caves of his Tuhoe ancestors. Both peoples invoked God's millennial kingdom on earth. Both consoled themselves with millennial dreams in action, the Pakeha by converting a strange land into a homeland, the Maori by reclaiming their homeland from a strange people.

WHY THE GOVERNORS FAILED

New Zealand's early governors, Robert Fitzroy and George Grey, had seen the demise of aboriginal peoples after contact with Europeans in South America and Australia, and their imperialism was tempered by paternal concern. As captain of the *Beagle*, Fitzroy had witnessed the decimation of the Yahgan people of Tierra del Fuego, and while serving in Australia, Grey had become an ethnologist. After bungling the Waitara affair, Gore Browne became governor of Tasmania, where the aboriginal people were eventually exterminated. All three statesmen attempted to avoid racial warfare in New Zealand. Why, then, did their efforts fail?

According to Keith Sinclair, well-meaning imperial officials did not know enough about anthropology to save New Zealand from the violent clash of cultures; but in the context of present-day unease between

29. Revelation 13:1, 11–12; Friesen, "Ephesus."

30. William L. Williams, "Notes on the Ringa-Tu Religion," MS Papers, 134U, ATL, NLNZ; A. P. Godber, "Papers on Ringatu Religion and the Ratana Church," MS Papers, 78, Folder 43, ATL, NLNZ.

indigenous people and ethnologists, his faith in anthropology seems a bit naïve. Sinclair's impressive history of what he calls the "Maori Wars" mainly addresses the political and economic causes of *te riri pakeha*, but overlooks the religious and psychological factors.

UTU, INSULT, AND RESTORING THE BALANCE

Insult was a proximate cause of the wars. To the extent that insult diminished or extinguished *mana*, it weakened the power of the chiefs over their adversaries. As early as 1840 a Maori leader predicted the decline of chiefly *mana*: "What is the Governor come for? . . . He to be high, very high, like *Maungataniwha*, and we low on the ground; nothing but little hills."[31] The disdain the British demonstrated for Kingi's authority and the insults that Tamihana endured undermined their confidence in and allegiance to the Pakeha state, motivating them to seek *utu*, "redress through action."

Much has been written about the Maori custom of *utu*, retaliatory "redress." Within, as well as between, tribes any accidental or deliberate insult was likely to provoke retaliation by *taua muru*, a posse whose object was to settle the score. Intended or not, insult upset communal equilibrium and threatened the life force of a person, and it had to be neutralized by response in kind. An early pioneer, Judge Frederick Maning, reported that the Pakeha were also subject to the *taua*, and it could be deadly. A careless missionary who consigned a chief to hellfire for breaking the sabbath, was roasted and eaten by the outraged *ariki*.[32] The *taua muru* died out after the Maori acquired a taste for precious material objects they could not easily replace, and because it was incompatible with English law. But its loss meant that an important means of neutralizing the damage wrought by insult was no longer available. William Naylor found that even after baptism, Maori converts feared the impact of inadvertent *tapu* violations, upon their lives and spirits. Christianization and Pakeha law combined to weaken the traditional roles of chiefs and priests. Insult accumulated, *mana* declined, the people fell sick, and charismatic prophets rose up to restore the balance.

31. Caselberg, *Maori Is My Name*, p. 47.
32. Ibid., pp. 30–31.

REPRESENTATIONS OF THE SACRED

The collective is symbolically expressed by various peoples as a human body, whose orifices constitute openings in the protective shield of the human form and can therefore issue forth or admit polluting substances. Pollution is dangerous and must be contained by rules and barriers.[33] *Tapu* in Maori culture and purity in Judaism segregated the cosmos into that which was ritually prohibited or "pure" and that which was fundamentally impure. These binary complements are variously designated as "sacred" and "profane," or "clean" and "unclean," or in the Maori case, as *tapu* and *noa*. The rules that order a people are set forth in its creation myths; order is created by deities out of chaos by their establishment, once and for all time,[34] of divinely ordained boundaries and proscriptions. Sky was separated from earth by Tane, the cosmic tree; hence *Po*, "darkness," and *Papa*, "earth," were eternally associated as one part of the great complementarity of opposites in the Maori cosmos, along with *Hine*, "woman." In the myth of Hinenuitepo, "great woman of the darkness," death, woman, and night are associated as one feminine complex. Woman, specifically woman's genitals, contains the power to neutralize *tapu*, and to render it *noa*, "without power to harm." The masculine complement associates the heavens, *Rangi*, with the Primal Father, and with light or *marama*, and with that which reaches toward the sky, such as the head of the person and the sacred mountain. In Maori myth the boundaries between the all-pervading complements are scrupulously maintained. That which is associated with earth and woman, e.g., food, must be kept separate from the largely male enterprises of war and sacred learning. However, each complex is sacred; each has power; women conduct or participate in some of the nullification (*whakanoa*) rites.

Maori myth conveys the creation of sacred space in the *whare whakairo*, "meeting house." Its sculpted pillars physically sustain the structure of the house and, by extension, provide the foundation of the tribe and of the universe. The architecture of the *whare whakairo* represents the body of a revered ancestor,[35] and both represent the *iwi*. The "eye" of the building, *matapihi*, is the window. The "ribs" of the

---

33. Douglas, *Purity and Danger*, passim.

34. In fact, the rules change through a variety of sanctioned methods of reinterpretation, but are still regarded as constant.

35. See *Tane-Nui-a-Rangi*, published by the University of Auckland in 1988.

ancestor, *heke*, are the rafters. The *tahuhu* is both "ridgepole" and "backbone." Fractious debate must take place outside the house on a demarcated grassy area (*marae*) in front of it. *Hui*, "gathering(s)," are hosted by the resident tribe (*tangata whenua*) for visitors and feature *whaikorero*, "speech-making," by designated orators—usually high-born males over forty years of age—who speak for the respective groups. Songs, *waiata*, and dances, *haka*, are also part of the ritual. People must sit in designated places; they must enter and exit in pre-scribed ways, and no one may raise his head higher than the speaker. Visitors to the *marae* are treated to an elaborate hospitality that is not without its solemn purpose. The Reverend James Irwin once found himself perplexed by an embrace in which an elder touched him on the shoulder with a biscuit. He afterward learned that this *whakanoa* gesture dispelled the evil spirits he unwittingly was about to carry with him into a communal feast after a *hui*.[36] In the mythic architecture and art, the formal speeches, the songs and dances, and the prescribed behavior of the meeting house, one witnesses the striking holism of Maori words, acts, places, and communal life.

The central support pillars, or *poutokomanawa*, symbolize the "heart" of the tribe and establish its sacred center. The *whare whakairo* stands on the land of the tribe. When this land was lost, the house became a portable *whenua* of the people. Where the house is set up, there the community flourishes.[37]

Nearly all peoples acknowledge the power of place. The British use of land for commercial purposes does not sufficiently account for the response of the homesick Darwin to the Waimate Station. "Homeland" is more than an economic resource. Home is a sanctified space. The planting of orchards, flowers, and hedgerows produces a mythic land-scape and orders the cosmos. In prehistoric times homes were blessed and sometimes sacrifices were laid at the base of a supporting pillar of a house, a temple, or a city wall. In modern times, the secular celebra-tion of "housewarming" inaugurates the home as a special place. Euro-peans still celebrate the remnants of religious observance in the man-ner in which they become attached to a habitation where significant events—births, weddings, deaths—have taken place."Homesickness"

---

36. Irwin, *Introduction to Maori Religion*, pp. 23–24.

37. The movement of the Maori to urban centers in the twentieth century has been accompanied by establishing *whare whakairo* in the cities; see Ranginui Walker, "Marae: A Place to Stand, and John Rangihau, "Being Maori" and "The Politics of Voluntary Association," in I. H. Kawharu, ed., *Conflict and Compromise*.

occurs when one is removed from the land where one feels "at home." The sanctification of place is one of many persistent "pan-human" behaviors. Contemporary tensions between environmentalists and developers in Western societies are based upon disagreements about what constitutes the proper stewardship over the land. Land is an ultimate concern, and space is still the subject of religious imperatives even in the most secularized societies.

We have seen that the Kingites envisioned the kind of society New Zealand should become in terms of the metaphor of the meeting house. In Kingite meetings that took place between 1856 to 1860, the metaphor of the house stood for the Waikato heartland in the center of the North Island and the position of the Maori in an emerging state.

THE GREAT MEETING AT NGARUAWAHIA

Between February and April of 1890, Kingi sought allies among neighboring tribes. After government troops fired on Waitara protesters, Kingi erected an L-shaped fortification (*pa*). The first "battle" was virtually bloodless, but indecisive. Both Kingi and the government presented their views to the Kingites. Kingi hoped to enlist their support, while government tried to ensure their neutrality. Kingi and sixty supporters traveled to Waikato to discuss the issue, while the war heated up. Tamihana urged his followers to study the issue before offering help, but the Kingites were divided. One leader counseled patience while the King Movement consolidated its gains:

> Our Pa stands broken . . . I consider that our pa for our wives and children is not yet complete, let us finish it, dig the trenches, throw up the breast-work and bind the fences. Look at his (the Pakeha's) work in other lands, never too late, never behind time. . . . therefore I say quickly build our Pa.[38]

A Kingi supporter responded:

> What pa is that you are building? we have built our pa, and it is broken down and stained with blood. The wealth we had collected into our bag is scattered, it is thrown out into the fern, who shall

38. Buddle, *The Maori King Movement*, p. 31.

gather it up again? (alluding to the men who had already fallen at
Taranaki).[39]

During the *whaikorero* some leaders referred to the deaths at Waitara
as wounds upon themselves, that is, upon the body politic. Others complained that the hostilities had "broken" the house they were building
at Waikato and that Waikato had to "repair" it by aiding Kingi against
the governor's troops.[40] Hari of Ngati Maniapoto, added:

> We were made one by Christianity. Our union commenced when
> we heard the name of Christ— but I am looking at what Tapihana
> [of the war faction] said—it is right. Yours is blood that was shed
> in one day, . . . Let us arise and go.[41]

A sizable group of Ngati Maniapoto warriors decided to return with the
Taranaki deputation to defend Waitara, splitting the Kingites into neu-
trals and belligerents and undermining the foundation of a peaceable
kingdom dedicated to religion, law, and love before it had completed
the building of its own *pa*.

39. Ibid.
40. Ibid., p. 32.
41. Ibid., pp. 32–33.

10

KORERO

*I looked at your books, where Israel cried
to have a king to themselves . . . and I
looked at the word of Moses in
Deuteronomy xxix. 4, and I kept these
words in my memory through all the years;
the land feuds continuing all the time,
blood still being spilt, and I still [am]
meditating upon the matter.*

Wiremu Tamihana

Donald McLean succeeded in alienating more Maori land during his tenure as Native Secretary and Chief Land Commissioner than any other imperial official with the possible exception of his mentor, George Grey. He was Gore Browne's adviser on Waitara and Thomas Buddle's primary source of information on the King Movement. A Scotsman, who was more racially tolerant than many Englishmen, McLean was a paradox. He argued for Maori political representation in the General Assembly. Yet he consistently devised schemes to acquire all Maori "waste lands" and, not incidentally, to advance his own fortune. At his death in 1877 his estate was valued at 100,000 pounds.[1] McLean was present at three of the four most significant meetings that preceded the Land Wars: Rangiriri, Ngaruawahia, and Kohimarama. It was at Rangiriri (or Paetai),[2] where McLean

1. Alan Ward, *DNZB*, p. 257.
2. See note 10.

listened silently, that Gore Browne received the pleas of Waikato chiefs to send councils and courts to end the blood feuds over land sales.

NGARUAWAHIA AND KOHIMARAMA

On May 21, 1860, Waikato chiefs assembled at Ngaruawahia to decide whether or not they would throw their support behind Ngati Awa in the Waitara dispute. In front of some three thousand participants, Donald McLean spoke, but was unable to finish his presentation of the government's case against Kingi, after Te Heuheu interrupted him, saying, "It is night."[3] McLean waited until noon the next day to finish his address, but left after no one gathered to listen.

On July 10, 1860, the government invited 250 chiefs to assemble at Kohimarama, but only half that number came to hear McLean present the government's position on Waitara. The Kingite adherents stayed away. Kohimarama represented an attempt by McLean to undo the damage Browne had wrought with his unpopular land tenure policy and to consolidate support from the loyalist chiefs as a buffer against the Waikato separatists. He spoke for four hours to a select and friendly audience against Wiremu Kingi and the King Movement, and in favor of Browne's actions. The Kohimarama meeting raised the hopes of loyalist chiefs that they would be included in responsible rule. McLean supported them, but had already assured the General Assembly that he would complete the purchase of the North Island within eight years.[4] Despite his understanding that the Maori had a sacred attachment to their land, McLean was determined that the European settlers were entitled to any part of it not under cultivation. In return, he was willing to institute real amalgamation of the Maori by giving them full political representation in the General Assembly. However, the colonial politicians were unwilling to share power while they grabbed land, and the responsible government refused to pass legislation to enfranchise the Maori. To this day the Kohimarama conference is remembered as a Pakeha promise of *mana Maori motuhake*, "Maori sovereignty," and a positive step toward unification of purpose among the *iwi*.

The chiefs were aware of McLean's intentions to acquire the remainder of their tribal lands. The New Zealand Constitution Act of 1852

3. Buddle, *The Maori King Movement*, pp. 57–59.
4. Walker, *Ka Whawhai Tonu Motou*, p. 111.

had disenfranchised the Maori through a property qualification that most could not meet. They could not even vote for Pakeha representatives, much less serve in the General Assembly. In 1855 Tamihana had lobbied unsuccessfully for Maori representation. Aware that they were about to become a powerless minority, the chiefs turned to Article Two[5] of the Treaty of Waitangi to assert their equality with the Pakeha government under the Crown. They designated King Potatau's sacred mountain, Maungatautari, as the place where they would establish their own polity in conjoint administration with the governor, who would rule over places the Crown had already acquired. They wanted to freeze any further land sales in order to retain their hereditary *mana*.[6]

What the Kingites did not intend was war. They made a pragmatic distinction between the queen and her governors. At Ngaruawhahia Te Karamoa castigated the governor and his clients: "Who is it that has disturbed the peace? The governor has refused to listen to the million, but any ill-looking scrofulous old man, any slave that would go and offer land for sale could obtain his ear; he will listen to those who will sell their land."[7]

In response, William Naylor confessed to being the "ill-looking scrofulous old man" who had helped set the stage for the Waitara dispute by supporting Kingi's adversaries, Ihaia and Teira. Then Naylor turned to Tamihana to challenge his mandate for an inviolable Maori heartland:

Thompson hear my word, while I tell you where you have gone wrong. You are casting your net over both land and men. This is your error, cease to act thus. End your attempts to enclose the land in your net, and end your attempts to throw it over men. . . . Be admonished, take warning, lest we should turn aside into the old path that has been so long *whakatupued* (forsaken, not trodden) meaning the path of war.[8]

5. James Busby, the New Zealand Resident who drafted the Treaty for Hobson when the latter was ill, argued in 1860 that the sovereignty of the chiefs under the *tino rangatiratanga* clause was a "general" interpretation that was superseded by the "specific" provision in Article One for the Crown's sovereignty. The issue concerned who exercised ultimate authority over the land, and the 1860 conflict over *mana o te whenua* became a constitutional question of interpretation of the founding Treaty and "aboriginal rights." See Busby, "Remarks upon a Pamphlet."

6. Walker, *Ka Whawhai Tonu Matou*, pp. 98–116.

7. Buddle, *The Maori King Movement*, p. 47.

8. Ibid., p. 48 (Buddle's translation).

Naylor, "one of the Governor's firmest friends,"[9] joined with McLean to warn the Kingites that the government and its clients would actively oppose their union.

RANGIRIRI

All who heard Naylor at Ngaruawahia, recalled that he had engaged in a contest with Tamihana for the loyalty of the Waikato tribes at a *korero* in May of 1857 at Rangiriri.[10] It was on this occasion that Paora spoke in favor of setting up a king, just as Israel had done. His words, "Let us have order. So that we may grow as the Pakeha grows," expressed the view that *mana Maori* would return only with an increase in their numbers and power relative to the colonists.

At Rangiriri, Takirau's words testified to the religious foundation of the movement: "Let our Island ascend in the unity to God. . . . God made man, and so on until the Jews reached Canaan, then he gave them Saul to be king. This is why we seek for [desire] a king, and let the Queen be made one with the king."[11]

Te Heuheu of Taupo angrily called for the expulsion of the Pakeha from the country, although he had explained on the way to the meeting to Governor Browne that the separatists "would not interfere with the English in the settlements; but the laws [the Kingites] intended to make should be binding on all who chose to reside among the natives."[12]

Loyalist attendees reported the names of those who supported a king to the government and scoffed at their religious fervor.[13] In response to those who feared the queen's retaliation, Tamihana responded, "But if God is our friend who shall fight against us?"[14]

Gore Browne attended the meeting at Rangiriri, which is where the chiefs from the lower Waikato asked him to set up a structure of gov-

9. Ibid., p. 9.

10. According to Buddle the confrontation took place in May at Paetai, while according to Gorst it occurred in April at Rangiriri. The "Native Report of the Meeting at Paetai," in *AJHR*, 1860, F-No. 3, pp. 143–45, agrees with Buddle, who may have used this document as his source. In any event, both meetings took place on the Waikato River.

11. *AJHR*, 1860, p. 143.

12. Buddle, *The Maori King Movement*, p. 9, alleges that he called for expulsion, and Gorst, *The Maori King*, p. 57, reports his promise of noninterference (from Te Heuheu's conversation with Governor Browne as they traveled together to the meeting).

13. *AJHR*, 1860, p. 144; in their view the Kingites "improperly used the scriptures as an authority (foundation)."

14. *AJHR*, 1860, p. 143.

ernance that included tribal councils, a European magistrate, and civil laws. Browne gave his assent, and the assembly cheered, but when he returned to Auckland, he spoke against the election of a Maori king and neglected his promises.[15] His attempt to introduce one resident magistrate, F. D. Fenton, failed after Fenton clumsily alienated the elder chiefs.

THE BATTLE OF THE FLAGS

After Browne departed from Rangiriri, a great ceremony took place, marked by a debate between those who supported the government and those who desired to "maintain their separate nationality."[16] The assembly numbered about 2,200. On May 11, everyone feasted together, songs were song, and "the day was devoted to the reconciliation of old hostilities."[17]

The next day the Ngatihaua proceeded through the town bearing the king's flag and planted it on the *marae*. After a suitable pause, William Naylor and Waata Kukutai led a procession of their supporters from a hill to the sacred plaza, where they placed the Union Jack opposite the king's flag, while the parties to the meeting formally arranged themselves in the geometry of debate: on one side were Tamihana's faction and the king's flag, a red and white standard with two crosses and the words, "Potatau, King of New Zealand";[18] opposite them was Naylor's faction with the Union Jack; on the third side were those who were undecided, and the square was closed by the "teachers" who opened the dialogue with prayers and a "short discourse on temper and moderation."[19] In the center stood the leaders and orators. The juxtaposition of the two flags harked back to the precedent set in 1834 when the British Resident convened a meeting of twenty-five chiefs at Waitangi to hoist a flag "of their country" beside the Union Jack, "an act signifying recognition of Maori sovereignty over New Zealand."[20]

The confrontation of rivals at a *korero* is both a war of words and a battle between their tutelary spirits. *Mana*, like Roman *virtus*, is incar-

15. Gorst, *The Maori King*, pp. 58–59.
16. Ibid., p. 87.
17. Ibid., p. 90.
18. The flag indicated that they had decided upon Te Wherowhero as king, although he was not formally installed until the following year.
19. Gorst, *The Maori King*, p. 60.
20. Walker, *Ka Whawhai Tonu Matou*, p. 88.

nate in the exemplary leader. During *whaikorero* an insult can wound like a physical blow, and the victim can die from it as easily as from a war club. In his novel *The Matriarch* Witi Ihimaera reveals the sacred dimension of the contest between the matriarch, who is a *kuia tapu*, "woman of power," and Timoti, a rival who threatens to usurp the *mana* she intends to bequeath to her favorite grandchild. Ihimaera depicts power as a spider that possesses the woman and is unleashed upon her enemy in a scene which sends a *frisson* through the observers. The lethal dialogue opens with references to the mythological goddess of death, Hinenuitepo:

"My brother," the matriarch repeated.

And Timoti put a hand around her waist and began to draw her face towards his, "Homai koe ki te hongi,"[21] he hissed." *Homai koe.*"

"Yes, come to the hongi, my sister. And let me, by virtue of my descent from Tane, take back the breath of life which he gave to Hine ahuone when he fashioned her from the red earth. He gave her the breath of life, from his nostrils into hers, in the first hongi. In Tane's name, let me take the breath of life from you. Let this be your last breath, my sister."

"My brother, be warned," she began. (It was a voice which came from the depths of the earth. From the pits of hell. Like the arrival of death.)

"Be warned, lest the evil in your words and intentions be returned to you. For although Tane breathed life into Hine ahuone, and mated with her, it was their daughter, Hine titama, who became Hine nui te Po."[22]

Their contest takes place on the threshold of the meeting house, which represents the sacred horizon between Sky and Earth, the male and female deities; and it is completed at the feast in the nearby dining hall when the elder is overcome by a cascade of spiders from the rafters. The spider represents the *mana* invested in the *kuia tapu* by the female goddesses that are associated with earth, underworld, and

21. To *hongi* is to press noses in a ritual greeting.

22. Ihimaera, *The Matriarch*, p. 251. Their contest recalls the making of *Hine ahuone*, first woman, by Tane, and the transformation of woman into the power of earth, night (*te po*), and death. Timoti claims Tane's power, while the matriarch calls upon the power of Great Woman of the Night, the goddess of death.

death. The *mana* of the orators while they are speaking before an assembly comes from transcendent sources.

Thus we must look beyond Pakeha accounts[23] to understand the ritual battle at Rangiriri between rival factions over *mana o te whenua*, bearing in mind that it was waged not only by two pious *Christian* chiefs but also in a thoroughly *Maori* religious context.

Like the sacred poles of Tane that hold up the world and like the poles used to establish a claim to territory in Maori annals of canoe migrations and revered ancestors, flags and flagpoles in Maori renewal movements signify the sacred bond between a place and a people. Maori flags were emblazoned with mottoes and symbols. They were raised in front of meeting houses and carried into battle. After the wars, most of the flags were desecrated by the victors, and a few found their way into museums or private collections, where they remain as a varied and colorful testament to the struggle for *mana* over New Zealand. At Rangiriri William Naylor spoke to the chiefs with great skill and artifice to shame the Kingites claim to their "new flag."

> I am a small man and a fool. Ngatihaua, [Tamihana's tribe] be not dark [angry], Waikato listen, Taupo attend. My name has been heard of in the old day, and sometimes it is still mentioned. I am going to speak mildly, like a father. My word is this, I promised the first Governor, when he came to see me, and I promised all the rest, that I would stick to him, and be a subject of the Queen. I intend to keep my promise, for they have kept theirs; they have taken no land. Mine was the desire to sell, and they gave me the money. Why do you bring that new flag here? There is trouble in it. I am content with the old one. It is seen all over the world, and it belongs to me. I get some of its honour! What honour can I get from your flag? It is like a fountain without water. You say we are slaves. If acknowledging that flag makes me a slave, I am a slave. Let me alone.[24]

Buddle and Gorst agree in their respective reports that the assembly was stunned into silence for a half hour after Naylor's speech until that silence was broken by Tamihana, who replied, according to Gorst, "I am sorry my father has spoken so strongly. He has killed me."[25]

23. John Gorst's source for his account of the Rangiriri meeting was an article from the *Southern Cross*, June 5, 1857. Thomas Buddle, Gore Browne, and Donald McLean attended the meeting.

24. Gorst, *The Maori King*, p. 61.

25. Ibid.

Clearly, the power of Naylor's speech is lost in the translation. We can comprehend it only if we admit that the sacred dimension has been obscured. Although Tamihana called the meeting to establish the kingship, Naylor is the senior person and a man who could have been king. As Potatau's former war chief and a friend of Tamihana's father, he has earned the right to call himself a "father." Respectfully, the Kingmaker acknowledged the impact of Naylor's words. Then, turning to his charismatic ally, Rewi Maniapoto, Tamihana instructed him to pull down *the king's flag.* "Rewi stepped forward without speaking, and in anger took the king's flag, threw it at the foot of the Union-Jack, and sat down again." At this, another Kingite sprang up and rehoisted the flag, saying, "I love New Zealand. It shall not lie down in this way. Let it look at the sun and we will support it." Waata Kukutai, Naylor's ally, tried to soften the adamancy of the Kingites in a final appeal: "Let the flag stand, but wash out the writing on it. Let us not talk like children, but find out some real good for ourselves. We cannot do it by ourselves. The white men have the money, the knowledge—everything. I shall remain a subject of the Queen and look up to her flag as my flag for ever and ever." Hearing this, the assembly became increasingly agitated, and the moderator called out, "Let us pray," at which everyone fell silent and the meeting was adjourned.[26]

Tamihana honored Naylor by asking Rewi to throw down the flag, but the clever stratagem forced those present to declare themselves for one side or the other. Naylor's faction departed from the meeting having gained no new support and resigned to the Maori kingship.

The flag played a metaphorical role in the proceedings, since its treatment displayed what would happen if the assembly listened to Naylor: the people would "lie down" before the Pakeha and become "slaves," nonpersons without representation in government. The contest between Naylor and Tamihana also revealed the split between older and younger chiefs: the former largely accepted subordination in a Pakeha world, and the latter mostly refused to relinquish their *mana ariki* under responsible rule. Tamihana carried the day, and Naylor retired from the field—only to reappear with Donald McLean three years later at Ngaruawahia to speak in favor of Browne and against Kingi. The division between loyalist and dissident tribes vitiated the prewar *kotahitanga* movement and split the tribes during the bitter years of war.

26. Ibid., pp. 61–62.

In spite of their differences, both factions agreed that the they had to have a political identity in New Zealand. Loyalist chiefs lobbied Browne for a Maori assembly, while Te Heuheu argued for an assembly and a king.[27] Browne, however, "felt that the establishment of a distinct nationality in any form, would end sooner or later in collision. . . . he considered it highly important that the European population should in future be as little scattered as possible."[28] Accordingly, he instructed his commissioners to consolidate the landholdings of the Crown and to make no new purchases of lands isolated from one another in order to prevent reprisals against the settlers, but the landholdings of the Crown and the natives were already intermixed, and Gorst observed that "a clear line of demarcation between the territories of the rival nations could not be obtained without war and conquest."[29]

THE ROAD TO SELF-GOVERNANCE

G. W. Rusden chronicled the evolution of Pakeha self-governance in volume 2 of his *History of New Zealand*, which is sympathetic to the Maori. Unlike the Humanitarians in London, settler officials cast the Maori in the role of enemy, and what began as a "suppression of rebellion" at Waitara soon "degenerated into a war of extermination."[30] Grey's imperial welfare policies died under the first aggressive settler administration.[31] A generation of colonists had labored to create a home in an alien place. They bore the brunt of the wars and convinced themselves that the "rebels" had forfeited any aboriginal title to their lands that the imperial government had acknowledged. Their harsh confiscation legislation affected even those tribes that had fought on the side of the militia.[32] By the 1880s disillusioned loyalists joined their former

27. In 1867, legislation that mandated four Maori representatives (one each from the East, West, North, and South) in the Assembly finally passed; Ward, *A Show of Justice*, p. 208. This woefully inadequate provision did not alter the dissidents' perception of "enslavement."

28. Gorst, *The Maori King*, pp. 63–64.

29. Ibid. Gorst's words, not Browne's.

30. Fox, *The War in New Zealand*, p. 260. His account of the war until November 1865 constitutes an example of the majority view of the settlers and their ministers toward the Maori, see especially pp. 255–61.

31. See Ward, *A Show of Justice*, pp. 194–223.

32. Ward, *A Show of Justice*, p. 176, acknowledges the bitterness engendered by the confiscation policy, but he temporizes on its effects. Evelyn Stokes, in her study *Te Raupatu o Tauranga*, clearly demonstrates how the net of confiscation caught up nonresisters with the dissidents and how this amplified hostilities and grievances. Fox resigned from his first administration in 1862 because London successfully blocked his hard-line policy, which he renewed during his second ministry in 1863–64.

enemies in native "parliaments" and resurrected *kotahitanga* move-ments.[33] Depression struck many pastoralists and farmers, rendering the Maori economic base even more precarious. Maori population de-cline continued unabated until the end of the century.

In the 1850s the Kingite sympathizers took note of clouds on the horizon and drummed up support for their *pa* until Tamihana com-pleted the task by installing Potatau I in 1858. Kukutai and Naylor read the same signs of trouble and counseled their supporters to make peace with the Pakeha. Others have praised Tamihana as a man ahead of his time, recognizing his gift for words and his prodigious knowledge of the Bible. Despite his prowess in speech, after war erupted in Wai-kato Tamihana's leadership faltered. He could not prevent the Ngati Maniapoto, Rewi's people, from joining with Kingi against the British. The following year he brokered a shaky truce in Taranaki, but he hesi-tated while warriors clashed with Cameron's troops in the Waikato. Convinced after the shocking attack on civilians at Rangiaowhia that the British had gained the upper hand, he made a separate peace and retired from the fray. Then as Cameron approached his own settlement he prepared to do battle, but the British were deflected by a graver threat at Orakau, where a coalition of tribes[34] under Rewi's leadership gathered to stop the army's progress. Although British soldiers overran Orakau after a valiant defense, the battle is remembered for a cry of ultimate defiance, *Ka whawhai tonu ahau ki a koe, ake, ake, ake,* "I shall fight you forever, and ever, and ever."[35] After Orakau, Cameron marched east and attacked the defenders of Tauranga at Gate Pa. Rewi retreated to his homeland, refusing to surrender. The King country had been pacified but not conquered. It was only after two decades of sub-sequent land confiscations and poverty that the Waikato tribes abol-ished the *tapu* barrier between themselves and the settlers, who flowed in to found towns and industries in the verdant Waikato.

A PROPHET OF THE MIDDLE WAY

What set Tamihana apart from his contemporaries, Te Heuheu and Naylor, was his refusal to follow either the old way of war or the new way of collaboration. He sought to establish an alternative to amal-

---

33. Ward, *A Show of Justice*, p. 290.
34. The East Coast Tuhoe had joined the Waikato people in the defense of their homeland even earlier at Paterangi.
35. Walker, *Ka Whawhai Tonu Matou*, p. 126.

gamation or enslavement that would bring order and law out of the chaos of the Maori sickness. He was a quintessential prophet of the middle way during a time without precedent in the history of his people. Tamihana's charisma was evident in his craft: he fought best on the *marae*. At the very end of his life, called by Grey to Wellington to address the Assembly and hobnob with the Pakeha elite, he challenged his former enemies to a game of draughts with the Waikato as the "stake" and proceeded to defeat three Pakeha officials in turn, including Donald McLean.[36]

Because the Maori kingdom was founded upon *te aroha*, it is no surprise that it split apart under the stresses of invasion and atrocity. Nevertheless, the King Movement promised to restore Maori pride and establish self-governance, and it handed down the defiant words uttered at Orakau and the ideal of *kotahitanga* to a succession of charismatic and political movements. Tamihana was a prophet who appropriated his opponents' religion in order to judge their oppressive practices. He knew better than anyone of his generation how to craft a message with the use of symbols, and the power he embodied came, he was convinced, from God. Although he died the discredited leader of a people defeated in war, with their *mana o te whenua* substantially decreased by punitive confiscations, his ideas did not evaporate; they sought other channels. In sum, like Samuel, Wiremu Tamihana was a prophet and a judge, and under his guidance, the King Movement was a fundamentally religious renewal movement that sought to reorganize and sacralize Maori space.

A SEPARATE VISION

In the Kingite scenario the queen would bring her officers to heel and hold them accountable to fair play in the finest Humanitarian tradition. Over the unsold lands, the king would establish a system of justice based on biblical law. Instead of British magistrates, traditional chiefs and their councils would govern the *iwi*. The *mana* of the chiefs would be sheltered by the higher *mana* of the king, whose sovereignty would be respected by the queen. In such a Maori manner would the King Movement bring unity to the tribes and law and order back to their world. The chiefs thought everyone would benefit thereby. It is an ingenious vision, a powerful dream of a peaceable kingdom that vied with

36. Rickard, *Tamihana the Kingmaker*, p. 176.

Pakeha determination to build an English state out of Maori "waste lands," summed up in the words of Gore Browne, "The colonists covet the lands of the natives, and are determined to have them *'recte si possunt, si non quocunque mode* [justly if possible; if not, then, by any means].'"[37]

In 1866 William Fox countered the Kingite charge that the colonists wished to appropriate the lands of the natives for their own profit with the ultimate Pakeha vision of a domesticated wilderness:

> The colonists do desire, and very earnestly, to get possession, for colonizing purposes, of those large tracts of fertile land which lie waste and unimproved in the hands of the natives. . . . We went out to colonize; not to "grub for money," but to convert the wilderness into farms and gardens, and spot it all over with smiling villages and pleasant homesteads. Districts which, in the hands of the colonists, might maintain millions of industrious and civilized men, lie absolutely unoccupied, and put to none of the uses for which the Creator intended them. The colonists do desire to people these districts; to create out of them a flourishing country, instead of a barren uninhabited desert.[38]

Out of the void, God created the world. To the European, New Zealand was a dark land waiting for a new creation *ex nihilo.* On departing the North Island in 1835, Darwin put it starkly, "I believe we are all glad to leave New Zealand. It is not a pleasant place. Among the natives there is absent that charming simplicity which is found at Tahiti. . . . I look back but to one bright spot, and that is Waimate, with its Christian inhabitants."[39]

FINALE

It was the historic clash between the landholding movements in Taranaki and Waikato and the rising Pakeha demand for "waste lands" that led two peoples to the abyss of war. Governor Browne's capitulation to settler interests drove Wiremu Kingi, a loyalist, into the arms of his former enemy, King Potatau. Cameron's army fought its way to the Bay of Plenty, leaving a de facto Maori kingdom in place. Civil war

37. Harrop, *England and the Maori Wars*, p. 64.
38. Fox, *The War in New Zealand*, pp. 14–15.
39. Darwin, *Voyage of the Beagle*, p. 429.

broke out on the East Coast, while Titokowaru provoked a second Taranaki War in the West. The last battle of the New Zealand wars was fought in the tussock at Orakei against Te Kooti's remnant before the final curtain rang down in 1872.

Wiremu Tamihana died, probably from tuberculosis, in 1866, shortly after the Waikato hostilities ceased. In his last speech he excoriated General Cameron and Bishop Selwyn for attacking women and children at Rangiowhia.[40] Pakeha chroniclers have discounted this atrocity,[41] which weighed heavily upon Tamihana and became an enduring symbol among the Maori of Christian hypocrisy.

In 1862, during a lull in the Taranaki wars, the "good and peaceful" Pai Marire movement sprang up. Out of its defeat was born the Ringatu movement, which generated a Ringatu messiah and the Ringatu church, proving that resistance movements may be ephemeral, but their dreams persist.

---

40. Rickard, *Tamihana the Kingmaker*, p. 189.

41. The account by Cowan, *The New Zealand Wars*, 1:351–57, is the most explicit one among the general histories of the wars. Fox, *The War in New Zealand*, dismissed the event with one sentence in 1866: "From Awamutu General Cameron pushed on to Rangiaowhia [*sic*], where he surprised a considerable body of rebels, and a running fight, carried on among the huts of the village, ensued, ending in the defeat of the natives, with considerable loss." Note how Fox avoids any explicit mention of agent or cause in this euphemistic cover-up of an atrocity.

11

PAI MARIRE: A COMPLEX CREATION

History modifies, transforms, debases, or, when a really strong religious personality comes on the scene, transfigures all theophanies.

Mircea Eliade

MILLENARIANISM

Millenarian movements arise out of a context of despair, and they promise salvation through the direct intervention of a deity, who reveals to an elect community that he will create a disordered world anew. Maori millenarians combined Jewish apocalyptic expectations of an imminent transformation of the world with the Austronesian "myth of the eternal return"[1] that envisions a golden age of peace and plenty. Te Ua's movement expected the future to restore a wholeness that the children of Shem had lost when they had forgotten or forsaken Jehovah in many generations of wandering.

1. From Eliade, *Myth of the Eternal Return.*

THE PAI MARIRE / HAUHAU MOVEMENT

The appearance of Pai Marire in the early 1860s facilitated the passing of *mana* from the chiefs to the *tohunga*, ritual experts who spoke as *mangai*, or "mouthpieces," of the gods.[2] The charismatic "good and peaceful" movement[3] was "the first expression of pentecostalism, in New Zealand."[4] Te Ua Haumene, a Taranaki tribesman and native assessor[5] who lived among the Ngati Ruanui at Te Namu, was inspired by the account of Pentecost in Acts 2 and by the canonical Christian apocalypse, the Revelation of John.[6] Pai Marire was also called Hauhau, because its adherents were possessed by the *hau*, or wind-spirits. The angel Gabriel instructed Te Ua in a vision to build a tall pole from the mast, yards, and rigging of a ship and to call people to march around it chanting prayers. The unusual rite conferred on entranced disciples the power to speak in tongues, knowledge of English, and spontaneous insight into the word of Jehovah.[7]

The movement predated the "cargo cults"[8] of Melanesia, whose followers gave up their jobs and gardens in expectation that material goods would imminently arrive in ships or airplanes to transform the world into a place of wealth and peace.[9] The Fijians who initiated the Tuka Movement of 1885 (which influenced subsequent cargo cults in Fiji) had heard of the Hauhau in New Zealand.[10] In Fijian and Maori *tu* means "to stand upright." Fijian *ka* means "to stand forever, immortal." The Fijians had suffered from war, epidemics, and economic dislocation; they too were aggrieved by the cession and sale of their ancestral land. Tuka adherents believed that their ancient lands would be restored to them after a paradise was established on earth, and the chosen remnant would enjoy eternal pleasure and the renewal of youth.

2. Cowan, *The New Zealand Wars*, 2:4, remarked that "the old *tohunga* Maori, schooled in the ancient religion, were the first to accept Pai-marire."

3. Pai Marire also refers to Jehovah as the "good and peaceful god."

4. Lyndsay Head, *DNZB*, p. 513.

5. Ibid., p. 512; he was the leader of a local administrative council at Matakaha that guarded the boundary of the land under the king's *mana*.

6. Paul Clark explores the social and psychological aspects of Te Ua's religion in *Hauhau*.

7. See Stokes, *Pai Marire*, p. 38.

8. See Trompf, *Cargo Cults and Millenarian Movements*; Burridge, *New Heaven, New Earth*; and Worsley, *The Trumpet Shall Sound*.

9. There is an extensive literature on cargo cults. These localized movements in the islands of Melanesia were messianic and nativist "revitalization" phenomena.

10. Worsley, *The Trumpet Shall Sound*, p. 25, states, "The Tuka movement has been attributed by Brewster (A. B. Brewster, *The Hill Tribes of Fiji*) partly to contact with Maori sailors on whaling ships who brought stories of the millenarian Hau Hau movement in New Zealand to Fiji."

Polynesian myths are resplendent with color and light. Illustrated English Bibles of the nineteenth century with their hundreds of striking lithographs and their myths of Eden and the Apocalypse must have attracted the Maori charismatics. Te Ua and Te Kooti may have been exposed to these Bibles during their few years of instruction in Christianity, as they were the treasured possessions of the pioneering missionaries.[11]

Te Ua revealed the source of his inspiration in *Te Ua Rongopai*: "My friends, it was a thing signified by the Spirit to his angel, that salvation be revealed to this generation, as it was, likewise, to John, when it was revealed to him by the Spirit at Patmos. Indeed it was he also who revealed this name of the Christ, and all the things which he had seen."

Te Ua's words illustrate the dependence upon "Spirit" that became the hallmark of Pai Marire and its offshoots, the Ringatu and Wairua Tapu movements. These three related movements constitute a continuous Spirit tradition of hermeneutics that looked to angels to redeem Aotearoa from the Pakeha. Pai Marire adapted Christian apocalyptic to Maori experience in the mid-nineteenth century in a religious *tour de force* that was completely lost on the Pakeha, who considered Te Ua a political threat, a madman, an imbecile, but certainly not a *matakite*, a "seer."

Te Ua's baptismal name was *Horopapera*, "Zerubbabel," the one who led the Jews out of captivity in Babylon. According to Lyndsay Head, Te Ua initiated the "first organised expression of an independent Maori Christianity."[12] James Cowan compared Pai Marire to the Native American Ghost Dance movement that arose independently about thirty years later.[13] In both cases indigenous people had been dislocated by invasions of white-skinned strangers with guns, diseases, and new technologies, against which the tribes employed supernatural weapons of power and knowledge. Te Ua appropriated the traditional role of the *tohunga ariki*,[14] utilizing it to found an unorthodox movement that dispensed Spirit among all worshipers and promised that the land would soon be cleansed by angels and returned to the faithful people of Jehovah.

---

11. *Cassell's Illustrated Family Bible*, 1860–61, had over nine hundred illustrations.
12. Head, *DNZB*, p. 511.
13. Cowan, *The New Zealand Wars*, 2:19–20.
14. Simmons, *Iconography*, p. 1, defines *tohunga* as an "expert" and a *tohunga ariki* as an expert in religious matters. Te Ua was not a member of the *ariki* class by birth.

TE UA'S CALL

Te Ua formulated his complex creation during the first few months after his call from God. Although he had recently supported the land holders at Waitara,[15] he was a Christian convert who counseled peace. On September 1, 1862, the *Lord Worsley* sank off the coast near Te Namu. Tribesmen took the passengers and crew hostage while they deliberated on their punishment for crossing their *aukati.*[16] Wracked by internal conflict over his impulse to release the hostages and his commitment to maintain the sacred boundary, on September 5, 1862, Te Ua suffered a vision of the archangel Gabriel, who told him that the "last days described in the Revelation of St. John were at hand" and that God promised to reestablish the people of Israel [the Maori] in the land of Canaan [New Zealand].[17]

Te Ua admitted to being stupefied by the crisis he experienced over the *Lord Worsley* case, but he was cured by Gabriel Rura (ruler). Pai Marire scribes recorded two different versions of *Te Ua Rongopai,*[18] in which the prophet tells the story of his call.

Chapter 1
Taranaki Land of Canaan. July 8, 1864

The Casting Off of Te Ua, the first prophet. In the month of September, on the first of the days, 1862, the love of God was carried to his people, Forgetful, Standing Naked. The mind of man was not informed, and thus he was said to be "Standing Forgetful."

Those indeed were the days of dispute and mistrust within the natural man.[19] I said let the ship and its cargo be guarded, and the news be carried to the councils of King Tawhiao. However, it was not approved. Who could listen to the lowliness of the natural man who spoke?

On the fifth of the days of September there appeared to me the angel of God. He told me to fast for the sins of my people.

15. Head, "The Gospel of Te Ua Haumene," p. 9.
16. The traditional punishment for violating a *tapu* boundary was death.
17. Head, *DNZB*, p. 512; Winiata, *The Changing Role of the Leader in Maori Society,* p. 68.
18. Head, "The Gospel of Te Ua Haumene," pp. 13–14, identifies three copies of the document, one written down by an unnamed scribe in 1864, one (the one she uses) written down by Karaitiana Te Korou of Ngati Kahungunu and found in 1866 at Putahi, and a third "inferior" translation by George Grey (who held Te Ua in custody).
19. In *Te Ua Rongopai,* "natural man" was the phrase Te Ua used to refer to himself.

And I passed one great day, when I subjected myself to suffering. I was delivered into the hands of strange children, whose mouths speak vanity, and whose right hands are hands of falsehood.

Today, my friends, I have been restored to my birthright. The strangers have been banished from my table.

And my people did not perceive my circumstances; indeed, they thought I was mad. No! It was a thing willed by God, that I should be carried to the north of my people['s territory], that I might be mocked by my kinsmen.

Only my elders did not remember the example of Peter, for whom the door of the prison house was opened by the angel of the Lord, and his bonds were loosed. Three times, likewise, I was bound in chains, and three times they were loosed by the angel.

And they knew not what they did; for there they beat me, and innocent blood was shed. . . .

This is the foolish work of your younger brothers, the people who feared not God, neither regarded man, each saying within his heart, I will not be moved; for I shall never be in adversity. . . .

O friends, do not do likewise. O strangers, look upon your father Abraham, and upon Abel, from whom you sprung.

It was I who called him. THE END[20]

Although the ship's hostages were eventually released, Te Ua was imprisoned by his relatives: "And my people did not understand my situation; indeed, they thought I was mad."[21] It soon became apparent to them, however, that he was a mouthpiece through whom "Peaceable God" spoke. Like Peter in Acts 12:7, Te Ua was released from his shackles by the angel of the Lord.[22] By January 13, 1863, he had completed the prayers and rites of the *niu* cult and the organizational chapter in his gospel.[23] He developed a unique liturgical jargon that combined features of The Book of Common Prayer, Maori *karakia*, and English military orders.[24] Within a few months he established the new

20. Head, "The Gospel of Te Ua Haumene, pp. 15–17.

21. Ibid., p. 27.

22. Elsmore, *Mana from Heaven*, p. 191.

23. Chapter 2 was composed shortly after his visions, and chapter 1 was written in anticipation of the visit of King Matutaera (Tawhiao) in August 1864. Head, "The Gospel of Te Ua Haumene, pp. 17, 32.

24. Cowan, *The New Zealand Wars*, 2:10f; Head, "The Gospel of Te Ua Haumene," p. 512; Winiata, *The Changing Role of the Leader in Maori Society*, p. 68.

cult and sent out apostles to spread his gospel beyond the Ngati Ruanui tribe. From the outset, Pai Marire was a charismatic phenomenon initiated by new gods speaking through a person of "lowliness." It democratized the Maori caste system of royals, commoners, and slaves, and it contributed to the emergence and proliferation of local, charismatic *tohunga* across the North Island.

The Spirit tradition perpetuated the claim that the Maori were descended from the Jews. Te Ua identified the Pakeha as "Samaritans" in the land of "New Canaan," and he prophesied that Jehovah would banish them from New Zealand. Regarding Christian missionaries, Te Ua wrote,

> This is a word for the ministers,[25] for Whiteley, Te Kooti, and Brown, for every minister living in the island. Let them go back to the other side of the sea in Goodness and Peace, go back in Goodness and Peace, because Peaceable God has told me twice that his people, Forgetful, Standing Naked, in the Island in Two Halves will be restored, even to that which was given unto Abraham, for this is Israel.[26]

Uppermost in Te Ua's mind was God's promise of the land to the Maori, just as He had promised the land of Canaan to Abraham. Accordingly, he admonished: "Listen, O people and island, to these signs I am teaching you. Do not mock, but turn to the abiding thing, namely, the raising of the land."[27] Government informant, John White of Wanganui, reported inaccurately that Pai Marire exhorted its converts themselves to drive the Pakeha out of New Zealand. In fact, the banishment was to be carried out by divine, not human, agents.

A NEW CULT

The prophet of Peaceable God compared himself to John of Patmos.[28] He fused evangelical Christianity with Maori rites of the *niu,* "sacred

---

25. The missionaries named are the ones who baptized Te Ua into the Methodist Church, a Maori convert from Taranaki who ministered to prisoners (not the prophet, Te Kooti), and the pacifist neighbor of Thomas Gilbert, respectively; Head, "The Gospel of Te Ua Haumene," pp. 17, 34–35.

26. Stokes, *Pai Marire*, pp. 34–35.

27. Ibid., p. 21.

28. Stokes, *Pai Marire*, p. 4.

sticks,"[29] and the *tohunga* tradition. The *niu* symbolism recalls the posts of Tane that are invoked in ancient healing rituals. Although Te Ua was a worshiper of *Ihowa*, "Jehovah," the world-creating power of Tane suffused the rites and symbols of the new cult. As a *tohunga* he was associated with the shamanic legacy of secret knowledge, spirit-possession, and entrancement that marked those who approached the *atua*, whether they were local tutelary spirits or tribal gods.

Pai Marire is only one among many revitalization movements that appeal to sky/creator/lawgiver deities to repair the world by fixing divinely sanctioned boundaries[30] and establishing just laws for an orderly society.[31] Although Rangi is a celestial god, Te Ua appealed to Jehovah-Yahweh, the author of divine commandments whose word and breath fashioned the world as we know it and all that is in it. Wind, breath, and spirit express the creative power of God the Father and God the Son in the first chapter of the Gospel of John and the First Epistle of John, respectively. Te Ua took the name Haumene, which means "wind man." In first-century Galilee the "man of deed," or wonder worker, was a weather shaman who could pray down the blessing of rain.[32] Pai Marire called on many deities that shared celestial attributes—angels, birds, and winds—who transmitted the transcendent power and knowledge of a heavenly Father.

The deity of the *niu* rite was the Holy Spirit of Acts 2:1–4 and Rupe, a mythological bird who adorned the sacred pole, who like the Holy Spirit in the figure of a dove, carried divine messages from heaven to earth.[33] In a shamanic myth Rupe, "the dove," ascends to the highest heavens, the ones Tane pierced when he separated Rangi and Papa at the creation of the world of light. In Tuhoe rites a bird would be cooked and placed on the post of the sacred precinct; this bird represented both Rupe and Tane.[34] Te Ua's cult bridged the old and

29. Head, "The Gospel of Te Ua Haumene," p. 40 n. 115, de-emphasizes the conflation of *niu* sticks with the *niu* pole, but Te Ua conveys multiple meanings that bring together the pre- and postcolonial worlds. Pillar symbolism is a formal feature of both old and new Maori religions.

30. Te Ua wrote in *Te Ua Rongopai*, "Natural Man [Te Ua] made the boundary . . . in the peaceable northern districts." Te Ua had led a King Movement council that policed the *aukati*. Thus, "maintenance of boundaries and the establishment of a Maori state through supernatural intervention" were central to his message; Head, "The Gospel of Te Ua Haumene," pp. 9, 19.

31. Eliade, *Patterns in Comparative Religion*, p. 62.

32. Geza Vermes, *Jesus the Jew: A Historian's Reading of the Gospels*, pp. 70ff.

33. Stokes, *Pai Marire*, p. 54; Cowan, *The New Zealand Wars*, 2:14; on bird symbolism in Jewish and Christian traditions, see Dale Allison Jr., "The Baptism of Jesus and a New Dead Sea Scroll"; on the myth of Rupe, see Johansen, "Studies in Maori Rites and Myths," pp. 90f, 105f.

34. Johansen, "Studies in Maori Rites and Myths," p. 90.

new, the biblical and traditional, religions. Israelite prophets sought to transform a moribund orthopraxy into a reinvigorated means of salvation. A renewal movement provides a new means of salvation out of parent religions, rejecting some of their aspects and revalorizing others. Ultimately, the prophet is compelled to be a vessel through which the god(s) make a ruined world whole once again.

12

HAUHAU: THE PAKEHA VIEW

> *Vague rumours had been current for some*
> *time that a new form of religion, called*
> *"Paimarire," had been the subject of a*
> *Divine revelation made through the Angel*
> *Gabriel to a Maori prophet named*
> *Horopapera Te Ua at Taranaki, and that*
> *emissaries of his, who were spoken of as*
> *"Tiu" (or Jews), were going about the*
> *country to make the various Maori tribes*
> *acquainted with it. Te Ua was an*
> *inoffensive old man whose mental faculties*
> *were more or less deranged.*
>
> William Leonard Williams

A NATIVE REBELLION

After it spread beyond Taranaki, Hauhau became a name of opprobrium in New Zealand history because it was identified with atrocities in Taranaki and on the East Coast. The demonization of Pai Marire began with John White's official report on Pai Marire to the Colonial Secretary of the Native Department on April 29, 1864, only a few weeks after Captain Thomas Lloyd and one hundred soldiers, who were engaged in a crop-destroying raid, were attacked by a Pai Marire war party near New Plymouth. In Prime Minister Fox's words:

> The rebels drank the blood of those who fell, and cut off their
> heads, burying for a time the heads and bodies in separate places.
> A few days afterwards, according to the native account, the angel

Gabriel appeared to those who had partaken of the blood, and by
the medium of Captain Lloyd's spirit, ordered his head to be ex-
humed, cured in their own way, and taken throughout the length
and breadth of New Zealand; that from henceforth this head
should be the medium of man's communication with Jehovah.[1]

Fox's account of war in the colony was published in 1866 and became the standard by which Pai Marire was judged among the worried
settlers, who were scattered on their homesteads among a presumably
hostile populace of natives. Lloyd's head was preserved and carried by
Te Ua's emissaries to the eastern tribes.[2] John White reported that the
head "imparted" the following tenets to its listeners, and Fox repeated
his distortions in his memoir:

> The people who adopt this religion will shortly drive the whole
> European population out of New Zealand. . . .
>   Legions of angels await the bidding of the priests to aid the
> Maories in exterminating the Europeans.
>   Immediately the Europeans were destroyed and driven away
> men will be sent from heaven to teach the Maories all the arts and
> sciences now known by Europeans.[3]

White asserted that Te Ua was fomenting a Maori uprising and that
his mission was to turn the people away from Christianity to a barbaric
creed. Both White's alarm and the use of Lloyd's head as a medium
incited government fears of an island-wide rebellion by Te Ua's "fanatics" and the Kingites, who, it was rumored, were combining their
efforts to drive the Pakeha into the sea.[4] A link between the two renewal movements was forged for a brief time after Te Ua baptized (or
anointed) Potatau's son, Matutaera "Methusaleh" and renamed him
King Tawhiao, "Encircle the world," in 1864.[5] Fear that the Kingites
would ally themselves with the Hauhau also led to the persecution of
Pai Marire followers in the Bay of Plenty region,[6] at the eastern ter-

1. Fox, *The War in New Zealand*, pp. 127–28.
2. Clark, *Hauhau*, pp. 12–13.
3. Ibid., pp. 13–14.
4. Stokes, *Pai Marire*, pp. 12–15; Tamihana did not join Pai Marire, according to Clark,
Hauhau, p. 61, but Te Ua was a member of the King Movement; Head, "The Gospel of Te Ua
Haumene," p. 13. Tamihana and Te Ua shared the conviction that impermeable boundaries must
separate Maori and European settlements.
5. Clark, *Hauhau*, pp. 54–62.
6. Stokes, *Te Raupatu o Tauranga*, pp. 16–22.

minus of Cameron's Waikato campaign.[7] However, Te Ua preached reconciliation between "white" and "black," and he called upon Jehovah, not Hauhau warriors, to restore the land.

THE LAND CONFLICT

Historian James Cowan indicted the Fox-Whitaker administration for unjustly confiscating land as a means of pacifying the "rebels" and funding the New Zealand militia. On the East Coast, in Tauranga and Matawhero, soldiers settled on the confiscated territory. Frederick Whitaker, co-founder of the Bank of New Zealand, expected to acquire Waikato land for settlement. He and Fox appropriated territories where tribespeople were believed to be rebels.[8] The pressures of war and dissident movements often split Maori kinship groups into pro- and anti-government factions, but sweeping confiscation legislation impacted dissidents and loyalists alike. Governor Grey had tried to administer land disputes evenhandedly in Taranaki,[9] but he only provoked a second Taranaki War in 1864. According to Cowan, "The confiscation of land, the territory of the so-called rebels, was a prime factor in the renewal of the war."[10]

Given the intensity of the dispute over land on the West Coast, it is not surprising that Te Ua's renewal movement began in this fiercely contested region among the separatist Ngati Ruanui. Fueled by confiscation threats, Te Ua's cult spread throughout the North Island in a remarkably short time; it appealed to those who trusted in the direct intervention of Peaceable God and his angels to save the land.

TE UA'S LOSS OF CONTROL

Te Ua tried to institute a hierarchy of offices—the *pou*, "pillars," the *tuku*, "dukes," and the *porewarewa*, "teachers"—but he lost control over his emissaries. He was not a practical leader, and his influence over the movement he had founded in 1862 waned even before his

7. See Captain Gilbert Mair, *The Story of Gate Pa, April 29th, 1864*.

8. Walker, *Ka Whawhai Tonu Matou*, pp. 118, 122, concludes that "for the Government it was a war to take land by conquest."

9. As imperial governor, Grey had control over Maori affairs and the army, while the Fox-Whitaker ministry was charged with the task of administering responsible rule. Fox consistently pressured Grey to confiscate Maori land.

10. Cowan, *The New Zealand Wars*, 2:1.

death in 1866. His apostles were zealous and independent. Some of them met with rejection from other tribes, some were persecuted by the government soldiers, and some instigated violent conflict. But even Cowan conceded that "the founder of Pai Marire did not authorize murders—or, indeed, hostile acts of any kind" and offered as evidence Te Ua's pacific written instructions to his rogue apostles, Kereopa and Patara, in 1864.[11] The Maori people of Opotiki remained divided for more than a century after Kereopa hanged Reverend Carl Volkner in 1865. The killing caused King Tawhiao to renounce Te Ua's religion and to found his own instead. After Te Ua was confined on the orders of Governor Grey, he lost his *mana* as a leader and in late 1866 he died of a "nasty sepulchral cough,"[12] most likely, tuberculosis.[13]

A FEARSOME RITUAL

The most bizarre feature of Pai Marire from the European point of view was the rite of the *niu* pole that Gabriel Rura commanded Te Ua to initiate.[14]

> The *niu* was the central symbol of worship under Te Ua's dispensation. The term was the olden Maori word for the short sticks used by the *tohunga* in his mystic arts of divination, particularly before a battle. Te Ua's *niu* was a tall pole or flagmast, round which the faithful were to march in procession chanting their hymns. . . . Crossed with a yard, rigged with stays and halliards, and adorned with flags of curious design, it was the first visible emblem of the fantastic religion. Te Ua stood at the foot leading the chants, while his band of believers went round him chanting the responses in the "angel"-inspired ritual. Each tribe as it fell convert to the magic of Pai-marire set up its *niu* under the direction of Te Ua or his sub-priests. By the end of 1865 a *niu* stood in nearly every large village from Taranaki to the Bay of Plenty . . . and from the north of the Wellington district to the Waikato frontier. Some of these masts of worship were of great size, and very

11. Ibid., 2:72–73.

12. Clark, *Hauhau*, p. 26.

13. Like all Polynesian populations contacted by Europeans, the Maori suffered from foreign diseases in virulent form. The London epidemic of tuberculosis arrived in New Zealand in the early 1900s. Tamihana, Te Ua, and possibly Te Kooti contracted it.

14. Stokes, *Pai Marire*, p. 37.

decorative they were when the war-flags of many colours and many devices were displayed upon them from truck to yardarm, while below the earnest worshippers marched around the sacred pole.[15]

This unique ceremony appealed to many converts who faced the threat of government persecution.[16] The tall masts and crossbars proliferated until their colorful banners fluttered in nearly every village from Taranaki in the West to Poverty Bay on the East Coast. Te Ua could not restrain the enthusiasm of his followers once the rite had revived the *mana* of local *tohunga*. In the eyes of the civil authorities Pai Marire became more terrifying as it became more spontaneous. Most scholarly accounts of Pai Marire were not dispassionate.[17] Emotion overcame Cowan as he related the story of the "cannibal" Kereopa Te Rau. As it succeeded in uniting people under the standards of the *niu* staff, Hauhauism provoked extreme reactions.

15. Cowan, *The New Zealand Wars*, 2:6.

16. Stokes, *Te Raupatu o Tauranga*, p. 13, argues persuasively for the connection between confiscation, or the threat thereof, and the increase in converts on the East Coast.

17. See Winiata, *The Changing Role of the Leader in Maori Society*, p. 70.

13

THE SHIFT IN MAORI
LEADERSHIP

Bearers of mana . . . *are sharply
distinguished from the rest of the world:
they are self-sufficient.*

Gerardus van der Leeuw

POWER PASSES TO THE TOHUNGA

I n his study *The Changing Role of the Leader in Maori Society*
Maharia Winiata concludes that a major shift in Maori leadership
occurred during the "crises in Maori society created by direct
conflict with the European."[1] The political leadership of the King
Movement was assumed by hereditary chiefs and their councils, but
after the first Taranaki war, General Cameron's subsequent invasion,
and the battle of Orakau in April 1864, the essential task of holding
the land fell to the charismatic leaders. It was "the *tohunga*, or the
tohunga features, of the old society which were now assuming the more
aggressive direction of the tribe."[2] In Polynesia the chiefs traditionally
acted as "the means of asserting unquestionable right of possession to

1. Winiata, *The Changing Role of the Leader in Maori Society*, p. 67.
2. Ibid.

a piece of land."[3] Even though the troops were not able to occupy the King Country, substantial parts of it were confiscated and given to soldiers and their families. Potatau's successor, Tawhiao, continued to guard the sacred center.

CHARISMATIC LEADERS

In Cowan's opinion the Hauhau phenomenon would have posed a grave threat to the government only if a "Maori statesman with a brain like Wiremu Tamehana's" had been able to build upon the "common bond established by the new religion."[4] It was the waking nightmare of civil authorities in 1864 that Tamihana might join Te Ua; some asserted that he had, but their evidence was equivocal.[5]

According to Winiata, the decline of the chiefs and the rise of the charismatics signified a retreat from politics and a corresponding reliance upon religious resources:

> The crises in Maori society created by direct conflict with the European resulted in the replacement of the sober-minded judicial and political leaders of the pre-war period by the charismatic leaders of protest against the Europeans—the prophets, high priests, and religio-political leaders of the latter part of the war period. Earlier political leadership had been based on the same principles as the hereditary chiefship, but the charismatic leaders, although they were often of superior kinship background and included *ariki* and *rangatira,* emphasized the ritual aspects of traditional leadership. Some had been trained as *tohunga,* or had been educated in the mission schools and were thus versed in the newer rituals and also in European skills.[6]

In fact, the new charismatics were seldom from the same chiefly class as the *tohunga* of old. A few days after his attack on Matawhero township, Te Kooti was identified as a new kind of leader: "This chief has not derived his influence from illustrious birth, but, like all the modern school of Hauhau leaders, had gradually obtained an ascendancy over the old chiefs, and outstripped them in influence by the

3. Van der Leeuw, *Religion in Essence and Manifestation,* p. 50.
4. Cowan, *The New Zealand Wars,* 2:9.
5. Stokes, *Pai Marire,* pp. 12–13.
6. Winiata, *The Changing Role of the Leader in Maori Society,* p. 67.

mere form of superior energy and intelligence."[7] Te Ua had been a slave at Kawhia from the age of three until he returned to Taranaki as a young man; Rua Kenana held no inherited position or status. In traditional understanding, all three suffered a loss of *mana* as slaves or prisoners. Yet, under the dispensation of Christian baptism, they were called to be prophets and saviors of their dislocated people. They did not faithfully restore the old traditions, but instituted complex creations that were authentically Maori, demonstrating how religious traditions metamorphose under the heat and pressure of extraordinary historical events.

THE CONFLICT OVER TAPU

One finds the beginning of the break between *te ao tawhito* and *te ao hou* in clashes such as that recorded by William Yate in September 1829, after he and a determined crew of settlers, including a woman and her child, deliberately crossed a *tapu* barrier established by men who were preparing a fishing net. In the skirmish that ensued, the baby was temporarily taken hostage, but the Maori relented, and Yate concluded with satisfaction: "I think this will be the last time they let any of their tapus interfere with any of our proceedings. Many of them [i.e., the "tapus"] have already given way; and next to those connected with the dead, those of the nets are the most sacred."[8]

Yate noted that the people of Aotearoa set aside particular *tapu* spaces and drew boundaries to regulate every aspect of a person's life from the cradle to the grave. Those who violated *tapu* boundaries incurred divine reprisals. It is no coincidence that Maori Christians felt drawn to the Israelites, whose God strictly enforced laws governing purity and pollution.

SECULAR ANALYSIS OF CHARISMATIC MOVEMENTS

Maharaia Winiata's father was a member of the Ringatu church, but the son received a university education. Like most academics he is more comfortable describing Hauhauism as an "ideology" instead of a religion.[9] However, unlike most of his colleagues, Winiata recognized that

7. *Daily Southern Cross*, November 16, 1868.
8. Yate, *An Account of New Zealand*, p. 246.
9. Winiata, *The Changing Role of the Leader in Maori Society*, p. 68.

Pai Marire changed Maori history. Te Ua revived hope at a time when his people stood "forgotten and deserted."[10] Whereas many Pakeha dismissed Te Ua as "a low, sensual, cunning native" with "little sign of intellect or imagination,"[11] the "Maori . . . saw leadership drive and energy, insight and vision, arising . . . from the so-called abnormal and maladjusted persons [*tohunga*]."[12]

One of the problems with the scholarly analysis of the Maori prophet movements has been a rationalistic bias against the analogical and paradoxical data of religious phenomena. Paul Clark revised much of the bias he found in the pioneering work of James Cowan.[13]

APOCALYPTICISM, THE TAURANGA CASE

At Tauranga in the Bay of Plenty, Pakeha authorities reacted truculently to the rise of an apocalyptic consciousness among the resident tribes who adopted the *niu* cult, and the outcome was tragic.[14] In January 1864, the government announced that it was sending troops to Tauranga, because the local tribes were allegedly supplying food—and ammunition—to Kingite forces. The arrival of 600 soldiers stirred up fears among the Ngaiterangi and Ngati Ranginui people that their lands were about to be seized. The *Southern Cross* of April 1866 reported that Premier Whitaker intended to obtain "a fine agricultural district" for settlement. Until the troops appeared, the people of Tauranga had not been actively hostile, but in March, they prepared to defend their territory, and an intense battle broke out at Gate Pa in April 1864, where the government won a decisive victory and terminated the Waikato phase of the Land Wars.

By July the coastal Ngaiterangi tribe had surrendered their arms, but the Ngati Ranginui people retreated to their inland home and remained aloof. Governor Grey proclaimed the government's intention to confiscate no more than one-fourth of Ngaiterangi lands in punishment for rebellion. At this time, a journalist reported, "Had the troops not set foot on their lands . . . there would have been no rising amongst them . . . it was in defence of their lands which were thus unceremoniously, and . . . unnecessarily invaded, that they took up arms

10. *Te Ua Rongopai*, in Clark, *Hauhau*, p. 116.
11. Clark, *Hauhau*, p. 25.
12. Winiata, *The Changing Role of the Leader in Maori Society*, p. 70.
13. Clark, *Hauhau*, pp. *viii–ix*.
14. Stokes, *Te Raupatu o Tauranga*, passim.

against the troops, and so made, as it were, common cause with the Waikatos."[15]

The consequence of defeat at Gate Pa was *raupatu*, "land confiscation," at Tauranga, motivating numbers of people to accept the apocalyptic message of Pai Marire as an alternative to despair, as they expected Rura and Riki—the archangels Gabriel and Michael—to drive out the Pakeha with the "sword of Jehovah."[16] In December 1865 the Tauranga District was tense with expectation that Gabriel would appear, but the date set for redemption came and left without incident. Despite the failure of the prophecy, disciples continued to expect imminent divine intervention, while the government proceeded to survey far more than one-fourth of the Ngati Ranganui land. Fearful that the Hauhau would obstruct new settlement, the military instigated the Tauranga Bush Campaign in the first two months of 1867, burning crops, pursuing villagers, and killing Pai Marire leaders, including Aporo, an artist who left behind one of the few extant Pai Marire documents.[17] At no time did the dissidents take hostile action. In conformity with their apocalyptic views, they left their daily work and possessions and retreated to sacred places to wait for the angels' appearance. Gabriel and Michael are dispensers of justice in the Christian myth of the endtime. Acknowledging Hauhau as a millennial cult, Lyndsay Head observed, "As a prophet, Te Ua preached deliverance, whose corollary was the destruction of the unrighteous. In this sphere of the spirit, pacifism is an irrelevant concept."[18]

Gaining converts rapidly, the new faith lifted up downcast hearts with its angelic visions and divine promises to rid the land of Europeans and return it to Jehovah's repentant children.[19] The intense nostalgia for the lost unity of the people and their land is what marks Pai Marire as a nativist, as well as an apocalyptic, movement. Heightened concern that the Hauhau would revert to savagery led to atrocities on both sides. The appeal of Te Ua's message emptied the Anglican missions at Opotiki, Waiapu, and Tauranga in Poverty Bay, and sparked a civil war between Maori Christians and Hauhau sectarians on the volatile East Coast.

15. Quoted from the newspaper, *The New Zealander*, August 17, 1864, in Stokes, *Te Raupatu o Tauranga*, p. 10.

16. Stokes, *Te Raupatu o Tauranga*, p. 12.

17. Aporo's drawings are printed and interpreted in Stokes, *Pai Marire*, pp. 50–54.

18. Head, "The Gospel of Te Ua Haumene," p. 13.

19. Stokes, *Pai Marire*, pp. 13–17.

CHARGES OF A "RECRUDESCENCE" OF
MAORI BARBARISM

How valid was conventional wisdom in the Victorian age that the Maori were inherently bellicose, had no peacemaking traditions, and remained cannibals under their thin guise of civilized behavior? Andrew Vayda's treatise, *Maori Warfare*, characterizes them as a warlike nation, but also discusses their peacemaking customs. Warring factions often cemented a "female peace" by arranging a marriage between a high-born man and woman amid great festivity that brought the two sides together; this peace usually endured, because marriage institutes bonds of kinship. A "male peace" was sometimes arranged between enemies by envoys, but was often broken by treachery or deceit. A proverb states that "a gift connection may be severed, but not so a human link."[20]

Although the Pakeha regarded the indigenous warriors as barbarians, Maori warfare was sometimes more humane and less pragmatic than that of government troops.[21] James Belich regarded Cameron's decision to attack noncombatants at Rangiaowhia as sound military strategy.[22] In contrast, Tauranga warriors offered humane rules of engagement to the British before the battle of Gate Pa, and their compassionate treatment of Pakeha casualties testified to their genuine sense of fair play. Henare Taratoa, who sneaked past Pakeha sentries to secure water for wounded European prisoners inside Gate Pa was killed when soldiers bayoneted retreating Maori combatants, showing "no quarter." The order to show "no quarter" was also issued by Pakeha officers before the battle against Te Kooti at Ngatapa. They placed a five-pound bounty on Maori soldiers, and the *kupapa* loyalists summarily executed all male prisoners. In the East Coast civil war Pakeha officers and magistrates encouraged brutality when it served their purposes.[23]

The work of Vayda, whose major source was Sir Peter Buck,[24] created a general impression of Maori society that accorded with the Vic-

---

20. Vayda, *Maori Warfare*, pp. 119–24.

21. See the firsthand account by Gilbert, *New Zealand Settlers and Soldiers*, pp. 78–80.

22. Belich, *The New Zealand Wars*, pp. 164–65, 197.

23. Rusden, *History of New Zealand*, 2:283, 290, 298; Rickard, *Tamihana the Kingmaker*, pp. 188–89; *DNZB*, p. 503; Belich, *"I Shall Not Die,"* pp. 164–65; Major F. J. W. Gascoyne, *Soldiering in New Zealand*, pp. 66–75.

24. Buck was one of an elite class of Maori scholar-leaders in the early twentieth century who achieved distinction in the intellectual and political institutions of the West.

torians' view that before they arrived the savages suffered from a Hobbesian war of all against all.

> For centuries past, as far as we know, till the colonization of the
> country by us, the several tribes waged constant and internecine
> war with each other. . . . The habit of fighting, and disregard of
> life, had become a second nature with the Maori; . . . we need not
> be surprised that thirty years of partial peace have not eradicated
> the military propensities of the Maori.[25]

Before the fourteenth century, there is little archaeological evidence
of warfare in New Zealand.[26] During the next five hundred years a
series of migrations sparked tribal conflicts.[27] These were of low intensity compared to the most warlike era of all, which began with European commerce in the 1790s. The introduction of muskets in the 1820s
made war much deadlier and destabilized the North Island tribes. Intratribal conflicts were rare before the Pakeha government abolished
customary landholding and instituted the individual ownership of land.[28]
In sum, it was the introduction of "civilization" that exacerbated internecine conflict.

To be sure, the indigenous people did not appear particularly
friendly to visitors from abroad, such as Charles Darwin, who found
them harsh compared to the Tahitians. The Maori had migrated from
the tropics to a temperate zone, where they suffered from the cold.
Great storms and inclement winters made travel perilous and survival
more tenuous than it was in the gentler climate of Eastern Polynesia.
The sweet potato, staple of the austral Pacific peoples, could not grow
in the southernmost area of New Zealand, and the South Island remained sparsely settled. In Aotearoa eel weirs and bird snares supplemented more ancient practices of reef fishing. Native fern root also
augmented the *kumara* in their diet. William Yate lived in the Bay of
Islands where he observed a "grand annual feast" called *hahunga*,
during which the bones of the dead were reinterred at a sacred burial

25. Fox, *The War in New Zealand*, p. 6.
26. Walker, *Ka Whawhai Tonu Matou*, pp. 33–34 and 55f.; Sinclair, *History of New Zealand*, p. 15.
27. Walker, *Ka Whawhai Tonu Matou*, p. 55. These migrations originated from within New Zeal-
and as well as from outlying Pacific islands.
28. See, for example, J. A. Mackay, *Historic Poverty Bay and the East Coast, N. I., N. Z.*, pp. 72–
75, and Sidney (Hirini) Melbourne's account of Urewera region conflicts in *DNZB*, pp. 486–87.

place, and at which the *iwi* (which also means "bone") would decide political matters and make arrangements for war and hunting expeditions. Over time, this ceremony fell into desuetude and lost its central place in Maori life.[29]

It was the Pakeha who introduced the commercial practice of head-hunting: "The custom of preserving the heads of their enemies is of recent date, among the New Zealanders. They formerly used to preserve the heads of their friends, and keep them with religious strictness: and it was not till Europeans proposed to buy them, that the idea occurred to them of preparing the heads of their enemies."[30] A government order against trading in human heads met with public resistance.[31] During the Land Wars some Pakeha soldiers took the heads of their enemies, encouraged by bounties placed on the enemy by their officers.[32] Nevertheless, stories about native savagery prevailed over contrary evidence, and even those settlers sympathetic to the Maori convinced themselves that Christian converts[33] would commit atrocities under the stress of open warfare.

Cowan described the "first Hauhau campaign" in Taranaki as a "kind of holy war," a "jehad" led by "mad mullahs," and as a "recrudescence" of human sacrifice."[34] His literary excesses were based on a few instances of violence that became synonymous with "Hauhau." Winiata alleged that "the practice of using the head of a decapitated British officer as a means of communicating instructions and prophecies was widespread,"[35] Cowan reported that "the Maoris state" that Te Ua's emissary, Kereopa, took Captain Lloyd's head across the island to Opotiki in a recruitment campaign among the East Coast tribes.[36]

The attack on Captain Lloyd's detachment took place only four days after the defeat of the Kingites at Orakau, and these two events signaled the historic shift in Maori leadership from the hereditary chiefs to a new class of charismatic *tohunga*. Many *pupuri whenua* turned from their war chiefs to Rura and Riki, the gods of the *niu* pole. Pai Marire's energetic proselytizing provoked a backlash from loyalist

---

29. Yate, *An Account of New Zealand*, p. 137f.
30. Ibid., p. 131.
31. Ibid.
32. Belich, *"I Shall Not Die,"* pp. 268–69.
33. See Gilbert, *New Zealand Settlers and Soldiers*, p. 214.
34. Cowan, *The New Zealand Wars*, 2:4.
35. Winiata, *The Changing Role of the Leader in Maori Society*, p. 68.
36. Cowan, *The New Zealand Wars*, 2:17.

chiefs against those who embraced the nativist gospel.[37] Wanganui tribes defeated Pai Marire war parties and the Hawkes Bay chiefs retained the loyalty of their people. Te Ua's movement split the drive for *kotahitanga* into two recalcitrant factions, loyalists and Hauhau. As wars broke out between rebels and the government in Taranaki and Poverty Bay, the Pakeha employed Maori soldiers in bush campaigns against guerrilla leaders who aroused settler fears that the Hauhau were reverting to the former custom of cannibalism.

Two rogue followers of Ta Ua, Kereopa Te Rau and Titokowaru, consumed parts of their dead enemies. Andrew Vayda argued that war parties had traditionally eaten their prisoners because they lacked meat in their diet. In 1835 William Yate observed that cannibalism was part of the practice of *utu*, compensation for injury,[38] and more recently, J. Prytz Johansen suggested that eating one's enemy is an act of reparation.[39] But how is it that *utu* may be expressed by the quite diverse activities of eating one's adversary or repaying a feast or caressing one's lover or avenging an insult? *Utu* expresses the union of opposites within a system that regards the meeting of enemies, rivals, or even male and female lovers as the zone where the complementary polarities that define the world meet and intermingle.[40] Assurance that an insult will be requited maintains the requisite cosmic balance between male and female complements.

Mircea Eliade was repelled by cannibalism, but regarded it as an imitation of "transhuman models."

> In judging a "savage" society, we must not lose sight of the fact that even the most barbarous act and the most aberrant behavior have divine, transhuman models. To inquire why and in consequence of what degradations and misunderstandings certain religious activities deteriorate and become aberrant is an entirely different problem, into which we shall not enter here. For our purpose, what demands emphasis is the fact that religious man sought to imitate, and believed that he was imitating, his gods, even when he allowed himself to be led into acts that verged on madness, depravity, and crime.[41]

37. See Belich, *The New Zealand Wars*, p. 205.
38. Yate, *An Account of New Zealand*, p. 129.
39. Johansen, *The Maori and His Religion in Its Non-Ritualistic Aspects*, pp. 65–66.
40. Salmond, "Te Ao Tawhito."
41. Mircea Eliade, *The Sacred and the Profane: The Nature of Religion*, p. 104.

In Maori myth the human husband of the goddess Whaitiri was called Kaitangata, which can mean either "man eater" or "food of man"[42] A Taranaki story of Whaitiri and Kaitangata features the killing and offering of a slave as food; but Kaitangata does not seem to function as a general model for anthropophagy.[43] According to oral literature, gods and men have indulged in cannibalism from the beginning; it seems to have been taken for granted.[44] Allan and Louise Hanson note that Tu, the god who represents man-as-warrior, devoured his four brothers and from their bodies came the traditional foods upon which the Maori subsist.[45] This seems to be a myth about sacrifice that is associated with cannibalism. It was practiced in Aotearoa within the context of war and slavery until Christian converts renounced it with the things of Satan; however, the charge that the Hauhau revived this greatly feared custom is not sustained by the preponderance of historical evidence.

Still, Pai Marire has never fully shaken off its nefarious reputation for fanaticism. A visionary pentecostalism led by charismatic *tohunga*, it shared with the early Christian church a belief in possession by the Holy Spirit. Through participation in the *niu* pole ritual, virtually any devotee, chief or commoner, male or female, could become *porewarewa*, empowered and entranced by the wind spirits. Winiata reproved scholars who discounted the *tohunga* as "psychological aberrations" for their ethnocentric bias.[46] A charismatic's dreams, visions, and revelations connect him to divine power, and it is from this source that his authority emanates, binding his followers into a purposeful community.[47]

MANA MOTUHAKE

The New Caledonian liberationist, Jean Marie Tjibaou, could have been speaking about the Maori experience when he said: "One cannot stress too much the importance of land for any tribe. . . . Alienation of land has not only displaced tribes, but left them wholly disintegrated. A clan that has lost its land is a clan that has lost its personality."[48] The permanent separation of the people from their land leads to the

42. Johansen, "Studies in Maori Rites and Myths," pp. 101–2.
43. Ibid., p. 99.
44. Walker, *Ka Whawhai Tonu Matou*, p. 13.
45. Hanson and Hanson, *Counterpoint in Maori Culture*, p. 173.
46. Winiata, *The Changing Role of the Leader in Maori Society*, p. 70.
47. Ibid., p. 76.
48. Michael Spencer, Alan Ward, and John Connell, eds., *New Caledonia: Essays in Nationalism and Dependency*, pp. 234–35.

abyss of *aporia*. Restoring wholeness—healing the breach—is the ultimate concern of nativist prophets such as Tamihiana and Te Ua.

In New Zealand, as in New Caledonia, movements to regain the land have become increasingly political in the twentieth century. Ranginui Walker translates the contemporary political slogan of land activists, *mana Maori motuhake*, as "Maori sovereignty."[49] According to Lyndsay Head, *mana motuhake* was coined around the time the Ngati Ruanui placed a boundary around their land, and it "was institutionalised in the election of a Maori king in 1858."[50] Te Ua used the phrase, *Motu Tuu Haawhe* in the refrain that referred to his people as "forgetful, standing naked in the Island in Two Halves,"[51] to symbolize his people's separation from God and the land.[52] An 1865 report by the Assistant Native Secretary, Robert Parris, records Te Ua's vision of the angel Gabriel's "song of love to his people standing naked—*Motu Hawke*."[53] Maharaia Winiata referred to *Manamotuhake o te Iwi Maori* as "the separated *mana* of the Maori people." Today, *mana motuhake* is a catch phrase of a political movement dedicated to the return of alienated and confiscated lands.[54] By envisioning the "eternal return" of land and peace, the King Movement and Pai Marire inspired a continuous, interrelated tradition of religious and political formations.

49. Winiata, *The Changing Role of the Leader in Maori Society*, p. 68; Walker, *Ka Whawhai Tonu Matou*, pp. 186–219.

50. Head, "The Gospel of Te Ua Haumene," p. 8.

51. Ibid., p. 19.

52. Ibid., p. 18.

53. Stokes, *Pai Marire*, p. 37.

54. See review by Alan Ward of Ranginui Walker's *Nga Tau Tohetohe: Years of Anger*, in *The Contemporary Pacific* 4, no. 1 (Spring 1992): 218–20.

14

THE SYMBOLISM OF
THE CENTER

*Every people is polarized in some
particular locality, which is home, the
homeland . . . the spirit of place is a great
reality.*

D. H. Lawrence

THE AXIS MUNDI

The *axis mundi* is an expression of humanity's connection to
and communication with the realms of the gods. The Christian
cross and the British flagstaff are familiar types of this "navel
of the world."[1] The Jewish *axis mundi* is the Temple on Mt. Zion. In
Mesopotamia, it was the ziggurat—itself a constructed "mountain."
Late medieval Catholics created the Gothic cathedral, wherein the eye
was directed by vaulted ceilings to heaven, while outside, spires tow-
ered over lowly buildings in the town, overshadowing them like a
mother hen cradling her chicks. The Maori meeting house is supported
by pillars, and under the central pillar a *whatu*, "sacred stone," is
buried. In earlier times a slave may have been sacrificed and interred

1. Eliade, *The Sacred and the Profane*, pp. 33–37, 44, 52–54.

under the *manawa-pou*, "main pillar."[2] Similarly, in the ancient Near East, a human sacrifice was sometimes placed under the gate of a city wall or the cornerstone of a temple. In Pai Marire, the prophet was called *Te Pou*, "the pillar," and in the Ringatu church, the head is called the *Poutikanga*, or "pillar of righteousness," a term that resembles the Hebrew *tzaddik*, "righteous man." Thus, there are many kinds of symbolic pillars that support the world in a fundamental, mythic, social, and religious sense.

THE TREE OF LIFE

When the Anglican missionary Samuel Marsden planted the British flagstaff on the soil of Northland, he proceeded to orient himself to this "new" world in terms of English time and space. Aotearoa seemed an alien place—a chaos or void—to the members of Marsden's party, who, like Charles Darwin ten years later, yearned for the hedgerows and orchards of their native land.[3] Extended vertically, the established centerpole connects the human and divine realms—sky, earth, underworld—and thus separates the ordinary from the sacred. Whether the center is signified by a staff, a tree, a mountain, a building, or some other vertical symbolism, it is set apart in a formulaic fashion from surrounding space, the *terra incognita*. Throughout history and across cultures, the fundamentally religious act of defining, mapping, constructing, space imitates the creation of the world in the beginning. Out of a void comes order and differentiation.[4] Marking a center, setting boundaries, and delineating a social world establish the standards for judging what is pure and what is not pure, what is allowed and what is prohibited, even who is a person and who is a stranger to one's own people.

The symbol of the cosmic tree as a pillar and centerpole that connects the human and the divine realms, also marks a place where humans can communicate with divine power(s). Such sacred places are named in the creation stories (cosmogonies) of various peoples. Gene-

2. Cowan, *The New Zealand Wars*, 2:15; Johannes C. Andersen, *The Maori Tohunga and His Spirit World*, p. 38.

3. McNaughton, *Countless Signs*, pp. 5–7. Darwin's experience conforms to the shamanic paradigm: he crossed a horizon into realms beyond the quotidian world and returned with transformational and extraordinary knowledge.

4. See Binney, *Legacy of Guilt*, appendix 1, and "The Lost Drawing of Nukutawhiti," pp. 3–24; Simmons, *Iconography*.

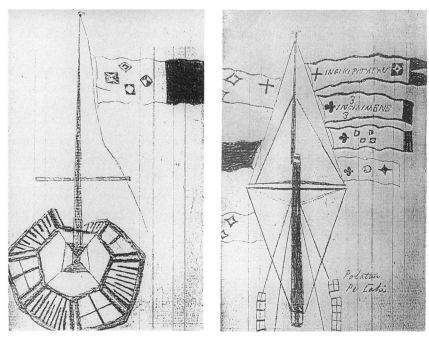

**Figs. 2a and b. Illustrations of *niu* poles from Te Ua's "gospel."
Courtesy of Auckland Public Library**

sis 2 mentions the Tree of Life several times, even though it plays no part in the account of Adam and Eve. This tree recurs as a symbol of the divine renewal of the world in Jewish and Christian scriptures together with the archaic symbol of the water of life. In Ezekiel 47:7–12, the miraculous trees associated with the sacred river flowing from beneath the Jerusalem temple which renews the Dead Sea, are givers of life. In Revelation 21:2, the "river of the water of life" and the "tree of life" recapitulate the divine act of renewal that Ezekiel foresees. The later Rabbis of diaspora Judaism regarded the Torah itself as a tree of life, and Christians equate the leaves of the Bible with the saving Word of God.

Trees of life grow from the transcendent source of all spiritual renewal. The mystic reformer, Jan van Ruysbroek, envisioned an upside-down tree, with its roots in heaven and its branches touching the earth.[5] A similar "cosmic tree" dominates a mural dedicated to the Tuhoe tribe hanging in the Urewera National Park headquarters of New Zealand. It represents Tane-mahuta. From the *totara*—the tree of Tane—

5. Jan van Ruysbroek, *The Spiritual Espousals* (Westminster: Christian Classics, 1953), p. 82.

the Tuhoe fashioned canoes and the support pillars of the *whare puni*. The tree of Tane is a Tuhoe tree of life and healing just as, to Christians, the cross signifies eternal life.

In ancient India and the Near East, an "enclosure set up round a tree" marked off a sacred place.[6] The most ancient symbolic complex associated with a place of worship is that of water/tree/stone. All three parts are still expressed, for example, in the altar (stone), crucifix (tree), and wine (water of life) in Catholic churches. Among the related Tahitian and Maori people, the *tuahu*, or "sacred precinct," consisted of an enclosed stone platform bounded by poles.[7] Any part of the ancient complex can stand for the entire pattern; hence the *pouahu*, "the pole of the mound,"[8] may signify the entire sacred precinct where god and humans communicate via rituals. Many Maori villages were depopulated in the mid-nineteenth century, but their sacred precincts remained *tapu* nonetheless.

As the *pou* symbol stood for the entire *tuahu* complex of stone and tree, so in its Pai Marire manifestation as a *niu* pole, the sacred precinct became portable. This "tree of life" established a connection with celestial deities wherever it was emplaced. Even when the land was sold or confiscated, it could be carried in the form of a pole or a meeting house to wherever the people were forced to relocate. In this manner, renewal movements maintained the life force and orientation of the people during their history of struggle.

SAVING SYMBOLS

In religions, a symbol (from the Greek, *sumballein*, "to put together") is not just a metaphor or literary conceit; it represents that which is more real than its material referent. In the Catholic mass, for example, a piece of bread is ordinary food until it is consecrated by a priest and becomes the flesh of Christ, the incarnate God who descends to the human realms. Observers from outside a religious community seldom understand that stones, rivers, trees, and artifacts are not holy in themselves. Only this *totara* tree is Tane, not all trees; only the bush that burned but did not consume itself is holy, not all bushes; only the

6. Eliade, *Patterns in Comparative Religion*, p. 270.

7. Johansen, "Studies in Maori Rites and Myths," pp. 66, 69. "The typical *tuahu* is the sacred precinct *par excellence*, the place where the gods are represented and where offerings and other important rites are performed" (p. 64). Also see Simmons, *Iconography*, passim.

8. Johansen, "Studies in Maori Rites and Myths," pp. 66, 69.

bread the priest consecrates is sacred, not all bread (and not even the very same bread prior to its transformation). Places become holy after something happens there and transforms them. For example, place and what is sacred are "put together" in the liturgical recitation of *whakapapa* when the community gathers in the meeting house.

Traditionally, a chief who set foot on unsettled land claimed it as tribal space by planting a *pou* or establishing a sacred precinct that incorporated pole symbolism.[9] When Hone Heke cut down the British flagstaff by the customs house in Korerereka four times and raised his own pole, he was following the Maori custom of asserting priority of claim to the land that Ihenga took advantage of in the following story. It is said that Ihenga tricked Tu by dismantling the sacred precinct on his own land and using its earth and partially burnt poles to construct another on the land occupied by Tu. When Tu returned and challenged Ihenga's presence on his land, Ihenga pointed to the burnt poles as proof that he had claimed the land long before it was Tu's. By this tactical deception, did Ihenga steal Tu's land.[10] Stories such as this one may symbolize prehistoric conflicts between tribes who migrated to and claimed the land.

THE FITZROY POLE

The first pole in historical time that laid claim to an inviolable territory was erected by the Ngati Awa in 1845. It marked a boundary line near New Plymouth that conformed to Governor Fitzroy's ruling, which marked off the Waitara block for Wiremu Kingi's tribe. Called the "Fitzroy Pole" by the angry settlers and *te pou tutaki*, "the pole which shuts out [the Pakeha]," by the Ngati Awa, it was described by surveyor W. H. Skinner and was sketched in detail in a painting by William Strutt, who depicted the sacred mountain, Taranaki, behind the pole.[11] According to Skinner:

The post was erected to mark the boundary beyond which the pakeha should not trespass (for the acquiring of land). . . . It was about 25 feet in height above the ground, of puriri or ironwood timber. On the pole were carved in high relief, two life-sized hu-

9. See Stokes, *Mokau*, p. 7; Johansen, "Studies in Maori Rites and Myths," pp. 73–74.
10. Edward Shortland, *Maori Religion and Mythology*, pp. 68–70.
11. See W. H. Skinner's letter and an illustration of Strutt's painting in L. S. Rickard, *Tamihana the Kingmaker*, p. 161f.

man figures, and both faced the east, or out towards the forbidden land held by the Natives. The lower of these two figures represented the cowed and beaten pakeha, with dejected countenance and limp and overawed mien, and, to demonstrate this cowed aspect in true Maori art and fashion, the membrum virile hung pendant and limp. The upper figure represented the virile, victorious Maori dancing over his beaten foe, tongue protruding, eyes glaring, hands extended, and the membrum virile erect and expanded *much* more than normal size. This latter, . . . indicating beyond anything else the strength and virility of . . . the Maori race.[12]

Skinner believed that this pole represented the first action of the "Anti-land-selling-league" Buddle warned against in 1860 that originated with the Ngati Ruanui at Taiporohenui. *Te pou takaki* was burnt down and its remains used for firewood by a Pakeha toll-bar keeper in 1877. Strutt's painting reverses the actual figures, placing the Pakeha carving above the Maori one, which, as Skinner indicated, represented the stance of the *haka* and the *mana* of the erect penis. In setting up their tall and graphic boundary marker, the relatively weak Ngati Awa set a divinely sanctioned *tapu* between British and Maori worlds.

The need to set boundaries intensified in the mid-1850s. This, you may recall, was the time that Francis Fenton first reported on the decline of the Maori population. Tribal religious experts no longer maintained sacred sites in abandoned villages. Human beings were *porewarewa*, "stupefied," by the loss of clear demarcations. They forgot where the *tapu* places were. When they inadvertently crossed an old *tapu* line, they became ill and some died. The landholding tribes in Waikato and Taranaki began to set *aukati* around their remaining lands in order to restore the life force of their people.

THE *NIU* POLE

Te Ua fell into an *urua*, a "trance," after a ship, the *Lord Worsley*, crossed the Ngati Ruanui's sacred boundary and foundered offshore on September 1, 1862, a day that became a *ra* or "holy day" in the Pai Marire sect. Te Ua was torn between recommending punishment for the ship's occupants for violating *tapu* and his desire to set them free.

12. Ibid.

Jehovah sent Gabriel to instruct Te Ua that his forsaken people could maintain the boundaries of their land by setting up *niu* poles throughout the North Island. According to the report of the Taranaki land agent who observed Te Ua acting stupefied, the angel Gabriel told him to "go back to your house and erect a niu. Horopapera [Te Ua] enquired of the Angel what a Niu was. The Angel replied 'a post.'"[13]

British symbols of the center included their flagstaffs, ship's masts, trig stations, and the Christian cross. All competed for divine approbation with the *aukati* and the pillar of Tane. The *niu* pole subsumed both Maori and British expressions of the *axis mundi*: the flagstaff as well as the *pou*, the cross, the ship's mast appearing over the line of the horizon, which marks the boundary between Earth and Sky realms in Maori cosmology, and trig stations on mountain summits. Te Ua's gospel features drawings of tribal mountains and particular *niu* poles with *tuahu*-like enclosures at their bases.[14]

The *niu* pole was a sacred precinct where devotees encountered the divine. By dancing and repeating Pai Marire prayers they entered into trance and uttered prophecies. This ceremony was called *pooti*, another name for the pole, and it could be conducted in the open under the pole or in the meeting house close by. The first *niu* pole in Taranaki was constructed from the mast of the *Lord Worsley*. "By the end of 1865, a *niu* stood in nearly every large village from Taranaki to the Bay of Plenty . . . and from the north to the Wellington district to the Waikato frontier."[15]

The ancient Maori religion was permeated with celestial symbols, such as birds, clouds, and kites. Pai Marire added Christian sky deities to the heavenly, or male, complement of Maori religion: the angels Gabriel and Michael; the Holy Spirit who descended from above to infuse worshipers with knowledge, consolation, and power, Above all, it was the divine winds, *nga wini* or the *hau* that descended from heaven to earth and breathed life into Te Ua's forsaken people. Ecstatics manifested their reception of the winds much like the disciples at Pentecost manifested the Holy Spirit—by glossolalia, speaking in tongues, which the Pakeha called "gibberish." The spiritual power obtained from heavenly sources was believed to invest adherents with mana and knowledge far superior to British technology or Christian grace.

13. Stokes, *Pai Marire*, p. 37.
14. Te Ua Haumene, *Te Ua Rongopai*.
15. See William Leonard Williams, *East Coast Historical Records*, p. 38.

Robin Winks has listed the several meanings of *hau* in the new cult. The *anahera hau* indicated heavenly messengers who descended the *niu* pole.[16] *Anahera* refers to "angels"; *hau* is a traditional word that can mean "vitality," "breath," "strike," "return gift," or "food used in rituals."[17] Te Ua coined a cultic language that seemed nonsensical to outsiders, but revelatory to practitioners. The British relied upon the wonders of science that the Maori had little access to, but the Hauhau had direct access to divine secrets through their new liturgy that the Pakeha could not share. In this manner Te Ua's religion claimed to trump Pakeha power.

Despite the popularity of the *niu* rite among its enthusiastic converts, some acculturated Maori struggled against the divine wind spirits. Heni te Kiri Karamu, an Arawa woman, described her successful contest against possession:

One night . . . the people tried to put the spirits on me—that is, to influence the Pai-marire gods to gain me as a convert. The spirits, or *nga wini* as they called them, . . . were supposed to dwell in the *niu*, but they could be invoked in the *wharepuni* [meeting house] at night . . . We were told to stand up, and then the people began their prayers and recited *karakia* after *karakia* in chorus to try and draw the *wini* down upon us, to lodge upon . . . and charm us into the new religion. . . . But I was a difficult subject; perhaps my English education made me proof against the *tohunga* powers.[18]

Heni overcame the charismata of *nga wini* with rival knowledge from her formal schooling. However, her weaker companion, Nohoroa, succumbed to a trance and uttered Hauhau incantations. Although Pakeha observers of Pai Marire rites ridiculed the cultic language,[19] Heni attests to its potency. Thus, Te Ua established a liturgy that promised to save his people from annihilation.

---

16. Cowan, *The New Zealand Wars*, 2:6; Winks, "The Doctrine of Hauhauism," pp. 201, 227.

17. Anne Salmond, "Te Ao Tawhito," p. 16.

18. Clark, *Hauhau*, pp. 13–14; also Stokes, *Pai Marire*, pp. 39–40.

19. Ibid., pp. 93–94. William Leonard Williams, *East Coast Historical Records*, p. 35, refers to Te Ua's "rambling utterances."

15

THE LANGUAGE OF PAI MARIRE

> *True millenarianism [consists of] those instances in which human beings band together and actually act on a belief in imminent and total transformation.*
>
> Michael Barkun

Prophets speak in a language that the community understands but outsiders do not. The Jesus movement devised new meanings for conventional words.[1] Te Ua learned directly from God what he proclaimed to his followers—a powerful knowledge that superseded what the Pakeha had taught. As one disciple explained, "We received our Christianity from you formerly, and now we give it back again, having found some better way, by which we may be able to keep possession of our country."[2]

---

1. See John Riches's careful study, *Jesus and the Transformation of Judaism*, especially chapter 2. Also see Robert Banks, *Paul's Idea of Community: The Early House Churches in Their Historical Setting*, for an exploration of language in a communal religious setting.

2. Clark, *Hauhau*, p. 77.

ECSTATIC CHRISTIAN INFLUENCES

The "teachers," also called *porewarewa*, that Te Ua sent out to convert other tribes exhibited the prophetic gifts that Peter announced in his quotation from the prophet Joel: "And in the last days it shall be, God declares, that I will pour out my Spirit upon all flesh, and your sons and your daughters shall prophesy, and your young men shall see visions, and your old men shall dream dreams" (Acts 2:17).

Peter's remnant expected the "day of the Lord" when there will be "wonders" and "signs" of "blood, and fire, and vapor of smoke; the sun shall be turned into darkness and the moon into blood" (Acts 2:19–20). Te Ua's followers prophesied in many tongues. Paul Clark remarks that the Pakeha "should have looked around him, at Christian pentecostal services, for example," to recognize the Hauhau teaching that "some day tongues of flame would descend from heaven and they would understand the meaning of their utterances, losing instantly their knowledge of Maori," as one contemporary writer alleged.[3]

Like the early Christians, the Hauhau were possessed by the Holy Spirit manifested as a mighty wind and tongues of flame. It is a short leap in Christian tradition from miracles of the Spirit, breathing new life into people and community, to millennialism—the expectation of God's imminent return at the end of history. Whereas Pentecost was a peaceable birth of a new faith, the Christian Apocalypse is awaited as a time of tribulation and war. Because millennial movements proclaim the total transformation of the world, they frequently provoke the militant opposition of civil authorities, especially when they set a date for the metamorphosis or disregard the norms and rules of civil society. The Pakeha must have feared the "recrudescence" of a troublesome Christian apocalypticism in Pai Marire as much as they feared its alleged "cannibalism" or charismatic "mullahs."

Te Ua regarded the missionaries as false teachers and his people as the true children of God. When he baptized King Tawhiao, he composed a "Lament" taken from Genesis 4–9, Jacob's blessings upon his twelve sons, the eponymous ancestors of the Jews—and the Maori.[4] The "Lament" grafted the sons of Israel onto the vast tree of Maori *whakapapa*. As Jews in the Promised Land, the Maori characterized the Pakeha as Samaritan interlopers. Just as Samaritans and Jews set

3. Ibid., p. 94. Clark argues that Pai Marire was not millenarian, except in Tauranga, pp. 67–68; see Stokes, *Pai Marire*, p. 15, for a contrary view.

4. Stokes, *Pai Marire*, p. 10.

up rival temples and cults of Yahweh, so Pai Marire challenged the hermeneutics and worship of Anglicans and Methodists, frightening and perplexing them despite Te Ua's familiar allusions to angels, the Holy Spirit, the Trinity, Gabriel, and Jehovah. His teachers insisted that the Day of Reckoning would be effected by "spiritual" means only and that they were committed to peace,[5] but the spread of the ecstatic cult exacerbated the split between loyalists and dissidents that had widened during the Waikato war. By proselytizing among loyal tribes, the Hauhau forced people to choose between Christian quietism and Te Ua's energetic gospel that "Peaceable God" would deliver Aotearoa to his observant children.

The earliest reference to correspondences between Maori cosmogonic myth and the Revelation of John appeared in a letter of Thomas Kendall dated July 27, 1824, almost forty years before Te Ua's visions. Kendall purported to find similar motifs in Maori and biblical traditions concerning the act of speaking and the creation of the world. The first state of the cosmogony is represented in the iconography and *whakapapa* of Northland tribes as "the First and the Last," which Kendall likens to the "Eternal Word" in John 1:

I have made use of the words *Eternal Word* in order to denote the First and Last, because in all my studying of the New Zealand Language, I cannot find any other word so suitable to express the native meaning and I have taken the above word from "St John," his writings particularly the Apocalypse having a most striking allusion to those pagan superstitions which are still preserved in New Zealand. It is remarkable that the sound of the vowel *o* from whence originates the idea the wisdom of the First and Last, exactly agrees with the revolving of the *Tongue*, or the act of *Speaking*.[6]

Judith Binney reviewed Kendall's argument in 1967 and again in 1980.[7] At first, she concluded that Kendall's analysis was tainted by Pakeha beliefs that the Maori were descended from the Egyptians (the children of Ham)[8] and that, according to Isaiah 19:24–25, the missionaries were beginning a "conquest of the Lord, who would recover

5. Stokes, *Te Raupatu o Tauranga*, p. 17.

6. Simmons, *Iconography*, p. 7.

7. Binney, "Heritage of Isaiah," pp. 124–39, and "Lost Drawing," pp. 3–24.

8. Buddle's writings in 1860 and 1873 attest to the contrary belief that the Maori were the children of Shem. A few later scholars made the case that they were Aryan in origin.

[the children of Egypt and Assyria] for his own." The theory that all peoples traced their descent from the sons of Noah was "common in the early nineteenth century" in English history texts.[9]

Kendall also directed attention to the symbolism of the Maori "First State" of pre-cosmic unity, when knowledge of the world-to-be was secret, hidden, and bound up in the "Eternal Word," the "First and Last" in the figure of a "Serpent or Reptile" who "is represented as being quiescent, having his eyes shut, and his tail closed imperceptibly in his mouth. . . . His head including his *eye* is emblematical of the First or Great or Parent word of wisdom, and his tail is emblematical of the Last, or little or son's word of Life or presence."[10]

In Genesis 2, the serpent guards a tree of knowledge before the world as we know it comes into being, and Christians teach that the Incarnation of Jesus vanquishes the serpent and restores life to humanity. In Catholic iconography the Blessed Virgin crushes the serpent with her foot. Kendall's passage describes images he had allegedly seen of the Maori First State, which is called Nuku Tawhiti.

Binney reevaluated Kendall's letter in her 1980 article,[11] after she saw a "lost drawing" of Nuku Tawhiti. She concluded that Kendall reported actual similarities between Maori and Christian myths that were independent of (now discredited) European racial and religious theories. Because both Maori and Pakeha religions include allusions to a serpent-like figure, secret knowledge, the First and the Last, and the creative power of the word[12]—it is readily conceivable that Te Ua Haumene was as aware of them as Thomas Kendall was. Scriptures such as the following may have appealed to Te Ua's distinctive religious sensibility: "And he who sat upon the throne said, 'Behold I make all things new.' Also he said, 'Write this, for these words are trustworthy and true.' And he said to me, 'It is done! I am the Alpha and the Omega, the beginning and the end'" (Revelation 21:5–6). The Greek letters, alpha and omega, were inscribed on some of the Pai Marire flags that adorned the *niu* poles. In *Te Ua Rongopai* Te Ua compared his revelation to that of St. John the Divine:

9. Binney, "Heritage of Isaiah," p. 129.

10. Simmons, *Iconography*, p. 7. Kendall's observations pertain to the myths and symbols of the northernmost tribes.

11. Binney, "Lost Drawing," pp. 3–24.

12. There is no one-to-one correspondence between the symbols of one religion and another, but there are what Eliade calls "patterns," such as the stone-tree-river microcosm, the cosmic tree, serpent symbolism, and others.

My friends, it was a thing signified by the Spirit to his angel, that salvation be revealed to this generation, as it was, likewise, to John, when it was revealed to him by the Spirit at Patmos. It was he also who revealed this name of the Christ, and all the things which he had seen. It is that same Ruler who has now appeared unto you, and brings these days to his people.[13]

In Revelation 1:1–3, St. John spoke to his followers in similar fashion:

The revelation of Jesus Christ, which God gave him to show to his servants what must soon take place; and he made it known by sending his angel to his servant John, who bore witness to the word of God and to the testimony of Jesus Christ, even to all that he saw. Blessed is he who reads aloud the words of the prophecy, and blessed are those who hear, and who keep what is written therein; for the time is near.

Te Ua proclaimed the superiority of the oral—the revealed—word and the inferiority of the Pakeha's written words. The *niu* cult dispensed salvation to its followers. This was more nourishing food for a weakened people than The Book of Common Prayer or a course in the English language.

THE MATAWHERO BIBLE

In 1990 when I visited the Matawhero church in Poverty Bay on the East Coast, I found a copy of *Cassell's Illustrated Family Bible*, which contained over nine hundred lithographs of biblical passages, lying open near the front entrance and inscribed with the following note: "This Bible was brought to New Zealand in the ship Randolph in 1850 by Mrs. Henry Long and given by her granddaughter Mrs. Florence Litchfield of Waerenga-a-hika to the Presbyterian Church, Matawhero."

Its most striking lithograph features Gabriel standing on land and sea with one hand raised in a *ringa-tu* gesture, the sacred scroll in his other hand,[14] framed by a rainbow. The passage that pertains to this illustration is Revelation 10:1–7:

13. Head, "The Gospel of Te Ua Haumene," p. 17.

14. An 1862 edition of *Cassell's Illustrated Family Bible* containing the same lithograph (or engraving) is in the possession of the Bade Institute of Biblical Archaeology, at the Pacific School of

**Fig. 3   The Angel with the Book (Revelation 10:1–6)
from *Cassell's Illustrated Family Bible***

Then I saw another mighty angel coming down from heaven,
wrapped in a cloud, with a rainbow over his head, and his face
was like the sun, and his legs like pillars of fire. He had a little

Religion in Berkeley, California. Waerenga-a-hika was the location of Bishop Williams's Mission at
Poverty Bay. Te Kooti probably received instruction in the 1850s at Williams's earlier school at
Whakato near Manutuke, according to Leo Fowler, "A New Look at Te Kooti," p. 19. It's possible that
Te Kooti saw *Cassell's Bible*, which might also have impressed Te Ua. Although Rua Kenana obtained
one, illustrated Bibles were the property of missionaries and settlers.

scroll open in his hand. And he set his right foot on the sea, and his left foot on the land, and called out with a loud voice, like a lion roaring; when he called out, the seven thunders had sounded, I was about to write, but I heard a voice from heaven saying, "Seal up what the seven thunders have said, and do not write it down." And the angel whom I saw standing on sea and land lifted up his right hand to heaven and swore by him who lives for ever and ever, who created heaven and what is in it, the earth and what is in it, and the sea and what is in it, that there should be no more delay, but that in the days of the trumpet call to be sounded by the seventh angel, the mystery of God, as he announced to his servants the prophets, should be fulfilled.

Although nothing connects Te Ua to this very Bible, it is probable he saw another like it at Kawhia, where he received his instruction in Christianity from the Methodist minister John Whiteley. I believe it is this apocalyptic Gabriel who appeared to Te Ua as Gabriel Rura, who was expected as the "angel with a sword" in Tauranga, and who inspired the upraised hand gesture in Pai Marire and Ringatu.

SECRET KNOWLEDGE

According to Thomas Kendall, the number 7 was sacred to the Nga Puhi. In their cosmogonic myth the seven principles that are bound up in the First State are loosed to govern the life of humanity in the "third state" of *te ao marama*.[15] Converts who encountered God's command in Revelation to "seal up" sacred knowledge may have found it analogous to the Maori teaching that all knowledge in the First State of the cosmogony remained tied up and hidden. A story of the archetypal shaman, Tawhaki, recounts how he ascended to the heavens to recover the baskets of knowledge and how he stored them in a fourth state, *Te Ngunga*. This knowledge is entrusted to the *tohunga ariki*, "religious expert," and the *kaitiaki*, "guardian of sacred things."[16] The visions experienced by the charismatics of the Spirit tradition, Te Ua, Te Kooti, and Rua Kenana, reflect the symbolic correspondences between Maori oral literature and the Old and New Testaments.

Pai Marire's reviled "pidgin-English" conveyed a highly prized se-

15. Simmons, *Iconography*, pp. 5, 7.
16. Ibid., p. 8.

cret knowledge; his so-called gibberish was an inspired patois of Maori and English.[17] Disciples asserted that it was a language given to them by God, and that only they could speak it. A Pai Marire *tohunga* said that he had not learned English from the missionaries, but from the celestial *hau*. Te Ua claimed that it was his Maori captors who had enabled him to read and write when he was a slave at the Kawhia, not his Pakeha teachers.[18] In asserting the precedence of sectarian language over missionary English, the Hauhau initiated a competition between their cult and Christianity over the true interpretation of God's "Eternal Word." They burned missionary texts and government documents to underscore their replacement by Te Ua's doctrines.[19]

KARAKIA

The language of Te Ua is derived in form from Maori oral liturgies. The chants that were employed in the *niu* rite and during battle resemble ancient *karakia*, such as the following (from the annual *hahunga* ceremony):

The priest places a pole in the water and recites:

> . . . *Te Po nui* [Great Night]
> *Te Po roa* [Long Night]
> *Te Po uriuri* [Dark Night]
> *Te Po tangotango* [Black Night]
> . . . *Tena toko ka tu* [This is your pole which stands]
> *ko toko o Tane-rua-nuku* [*Tane-rua-nuku*'s pole]

Another pole is erected with the words:

> . . . *Te Ao nui* [Great Day]
> *Te Ao roa* [Ever-lasting Day]
> *To Ao pouri* [Dark (sad) Day]
> *To Ao potango* [Black Day]
> . . . *Tena toko ka tu* [This pole which stands]
> *ko toko o Tane* [Tane's pole]

17. Clark, *Hauhau*, p. 93; Stokes, *Pai Marire*, p. 24; and W. L. Williams, *East Coast Historical Records*, p. 37.

18. Clark, *Hauhau*, p. 98.

19. Ibid., p. 94.

. . . *ko toko te w*[*h*]*ai Ao* [The pole which possesses (or becomes) Day]
ko toko te Ao marama [The pole, bright Day] (note: "the world of light")
. . . *Mo nga tangata ora to tenei toko* [For the saved people of this pole]"[20]

The chant identifies the *tohunga*'s pole with the cosmic pillar of Tane. Compare the *hahunga* prayer with the *niu* chant composed by Te Ua:

1–2–3–4, teihana [station or, alternatively, attention!]
Rewa, Piki Rewa, Rongo rewa, [river, big river, long river]
tone, Piki tone, teihana, [stone, big stone, station]
Rori, Piki rori, Rongo Rori . . . [road, big road, long road. . . .]
Teihana, Mautini, Piki mautini, Rongo mautini. [Station, mountain, big mountain, long mountain.]
Piki niu, Rongo niu, teihana. [Big *niu* . . . , long *niu*, station]
Hema, Hama, Pata kororia Rire Hau. [Shem, Ham, Father Glory, verily, *Hau* (Amen).[21]

The chants of Pai Marire were more than a passive reflection of a new language and Christian gods.[22] The Hauhau sect rejected Christianity in favor of its own version of Yahweh worship. Te Ua replaced Maori words with English neologisms in order to subject the language, knowledge, and power of the invader to the binding formulas of Maori *karakia*. The Hauhau chant substituted the new sacred pole, "*niu*," for the ancient sacred pole, "*pou*." Instead of Tane, the *niu* incantation invoked the sons of Noah, Shem and Ham. In place of the mythic realms of *te po* and *te ao*, Te Ua ritually called up the "river," "stone," "road," and "mountain" of the North Island. The Maori word for mountain, *maunga*, was replaced by an anglicism, *mautini*. Likewise, "stone" is rendered as *tone*, instead of *whatu*. *Rewa*, for "river," and *rori*, for "road," are also coined words. By incorporating English into his *karakia*, Te Ua symbolically appropriated the power of Pakeha

20. Johansen, "Studies in Maori Rites and Myths," pp. 26–27.
21. Clark, *Hauhau*, p. 98; cf. Cowan, *The New Zealand Wars*, 2:10.
22. According to Clark, *Hauhau*, the form of Te Ua's chants was borrowed from the Methodist prayer book, but the use of lists and repetition is also characteristic of Maori prayers. Te Ua did not need to borrow from a foreign tradition.

names and turned it against his adversaries, using sacred word to counter foreign hegemony.

The surveying and mapping of *terra incognita* signaled the eventual loss of tribal territory. In 1864 the *Taranaki Herald* reported that the word *teihana*, "attention," in the *niu* chant referred to the surveyors' "trig stations."[23] Ethnographer Elsdon Best reported that *teihana* eventually came to be understood by the Tuhoe people as "station" after "the surveyors came to erect their trig stations upon the biggest ranges and highest hills" in their ancestral territory.[24] The ultimate goal of Pai Marire followers was to hold fast to the land as it was slipping from their grasp.

DIVINE INSPIRATION

In 1865 Robert Parris reported that Gabriel had commanded Te Ua to "work for the acquirement of the languages of all races upon earth," which "the Spirit of God passing with the winds will teach you." When Te Ua asked how the winds would do this, the angel explained, "As the winds of heaven proceed to all quarters of the globe, so from the Niu proceeded all the different forms of religion upon earth."[25] Gabriel then sang to Te Ua a "song of love to his people *tukirikau, Motu Hawke.*"

Gabriel's consolation of Te Ua resembles the gifts of the Paraclete, or "comforter," alluded to in Acts 2:1–4. After Jesus' execution, his dispirited followers were gathered together in an upper room, when "suddenly a sound came from heaven like the rush of a mighty wind, and it filled all the house where they were sitting. And there appeared to them tongues as of fire, distributed and resting on each one of them. And they were all filled with the Holy Spirit and began to speak in other tongues, as the Spirit gave them utterance."

Like the Holy Spirit, the *anahera hau*, "wind angels," "came to the Maori on the winds of heaven, and . . . ascended and descended by the ropes which were left dangling from the yardarms of the sacred mast, called the *niu.*"[26] Speaking in tongues indicated the presence of the Holy Spirit at Pentecost. In the old religion, the *tohunga ariki* also

---

23. From the *Taranaki Herald* in Clark, *Hauhau,* pp. 97, 164.
24. Winks, "The Doctrine of Hauhauism," p. 216.
25. Stokes, *Pai Marire,* p. 37.
26. Cowan, *The New Zealand Wars,* 2:6.

uttered oracles when the god(s) possessed them.[27] The *niu* rite extended the charismata of the traditional priest to any entranced worshiper.

In her study of the twentieth-century Maramatanga ("enlightenment") sect Karen Sinclair notes that the old word *kura*, "sacred learning," had acquired the postcolonial meaning "angels."[28] In the text of *Ua Rongopai* the word *"KURA,"* appears above a *niu* chant. Pai Marire enlarged the semantic field of *kura* to include the spirit-induced knowledge imparted by the wind angels. Its offshoot, Maramatanga, appears to have retained this expanded meaning.

Paul Clark notes that Pai Marire offered its followers access to technology and language without the aid of the Pakeha. As a young man Te Ua studied scripture and was drawn to the phenomenon of revelation as the source of authoritative knowledge. Later, Te Ua the prophet taught that "the spirit beseeched the angel [Gabriel] that the way of the Lord be revealed to this generation as was revealed to John by the Holy Spirit at Patmos."[29]

While in bed I saw a large cloud suspended high, clouding the sun and its light. Then I heard a voice in space calling. Alas, my people appeared as stars falling from heaven, never to return again. My interpretation is that the people were being judged. . . . Understand that he [Jehovah] visits you with punishments, for it is his way of teaching. . . . Examine your reason for being saved in a time of want. . . . I believe the Day of Reckoning has come. It is right that man should form his own prayers to satisfy his own ends.[30]

Jehovah revealed to Te Ua the divine secret that a time of salvation and judgment was at hand. Te Ua's coined language proclaimed this gospel to believers in Pai Marire, who regarded the news as a harbinger of God's imminent intervention in history. Thus, Pai Marire was an apocalyptic movement, inspired by the very Christianity Te Ua rejected when "he formed his own prayers to satisfy his own ends" and adopted the "Holy Spirit" tradition of Christian pentecostalism.

The unique new cult may have preached separatism, but it was not a call to "Holy War," as Cowan charged. In his effort to revise Cowan's

27. Andersen, *The Maori Tohunga and His Spirit World*, pp. 8, 18.

28. Sinclair, *Maramatanga*, p. 232f. *Kura* also refers to the sacred feathers on the migration canoes which signified the *mana* of the voyaging ancestors.

29. Clark, *Hauhau*, p. 117.

30. Ibid., pp. 128–29.

biased view of the Hauhau, Clark emphasized Te Ua's pacifism and muted his apocalyptic interpretation of contemporaneous events. However, from its inception in Te Ua's visions, Pai Marire expected nothing less than the total transformation of the world. It bequeathed this expectation to Ringatu.

16

RINGATU: PROBLEMS
OF HISTORIOGRAPHY

Among Maori prophets, Te Kooti stands
astride them all like some colossus. Often
when we look behind myth, we find
conscious and unconscious exaggerations
of certain historical figures and the events
associated with them.

Peter Webster

The founder of the Ringatu ("upraised hand") movement, Te Kooti Arikirangi Te Turuki,[1] incited fear and loathing not only among the Pakeha but also among many of his own people. Attempts to characterize Te Kooti have often foundered on the irreconcilable opposites contained in a single, complex person. Although scholars have struggled to remain impartial, they have generally become entangled in the secrecy and schisms that often attend the birth of a new religion.

PRESENTING RINGATU

William Greenwood published his monograph on the Ringatu movement, *The Upraised Hand* (1942), under the aegis of the Polynesian

1. Te Kooti took his name from the Pakeha name, Coates. Kooti is pronounced like "coati," according to James Cowan, "The Facts about Te Kooti . . . How Injustice Made a Rebel," p. 18.

Society and their expert on Maori religion, Johannes Andersen. Andersen and his colleagues, Elsdon Best and S. Percy Smith, were biased against "tohungaism" and the Maori prophets, whom they did not
regard as the "real old" priests.[2] Greenwood encountered Ringatu at a
sensitive time when the movement needed to dissociate itself from the
Hauhau "heresy cult" in order to qualify as a licit New Zealand
church. In 1907 the New Zealand parliament had passed the Tohunga
Suppression Act, which criminalized religious prophecy and healing.
This law was not repealed until 1962.[3] Greenwood attended Ringatu
church services and was given information about the Ruatoki Meeting
of June 25–28, 1938, at which the new church drew up a constitution
and organized its hierarchy.[4] Attempting to redeem the Ringatu movement in the eyes of his fellow scholars, Greenwood subtitled his book
The Spiritual Significance of the Rise of the Ringatu Faith, while he
continued to perpetuate the demonization of Pai Marire initiated by
John White and William Fox in order to emphasize Ringatu's discontinuity with its "parent" religion[5] and to recast it as an authentically
Christian faith.

Te Ua Haumene was in earnest, but being mentally unsound, suffered from delusions when he professed that many of his messages came from the preserved head of Captain Lloyd, saying that
the Pakeha would be driven from New Zealand,[6] and that the gift
of knowledge of every science and art would fall upon the faithful.

Greenwood's hagiographic treatment of Te Kooti omitted any reference to the prophet's periodic bouts of drunkenness, his licentiousness,
or his homicidal acts.[7] Greenwood distorted Te Kooti's prophecies of a
sectarian messiah who would herald the return of the land to a faithful
remnant, by reinterpreting them as orthodox Christian predictions of
the second coming of Christ.

---

2. Andersen, *The Maori Tohunga and His Spirit World*, p. 5.

3. Malcolm Voyce, "Maori Healers in New Zealand: The Tohunga Suppression Act of 1907."

4. William Greenwood, *The Upraised Hand: The Spiritual Significance of the Rise of the Ringatu
Faith*, pp. 49–55.

5. According to Judith Binney, "Myth and Explanation in the Ringatu Tradition," p. 366, a
tradition among the Maniapoto tribe asserts that Te Kooti's *mana* descended upon him from Te Ua via
King Tawhiao. Ringatu was the successor to Pai Marire in the Spirit tradition.

6. Greenwood, *The Upraised Hand*, p. 66. This statement is not substantiated; Greenwood merely
reiterates John White's misconceptions.

7. Ibid., p. *xi*.

It must always be borne in mind that the bulk of the original
Ringatus were essentially heathen in outlook, and Te Kooti's great
task was to lead them to a knowledge of the Christian religion. . . . Just as Isaiah was speaking of the remnants of Israel,
but actually portrayed the Christ in his prophecy, so it may be
that Te Kooti in his desire to portray a great leader to succeed
him over the Ringatu people, in reality disclosed his innermost
thoughts and desires, namely that his people would find their real
leader in Christ.[8]

Few scholars would venture to guess the "innermost thoughts and
desires" of a historical figure without access to first-person accounts,
but Te Kooti's notebook had not yet been found when Greenwood began
his study.[9] Instead, Greenwood used the *kupu*, "prophecies," as if they
were Te Kooti's self-disclosures, rather than revelations from a deity to
a *matakite*, "seer." Greenwood's felicitous assumption that the prophecies referred to the second coming of Christ reflects the later desire of
the Ringatu church after Te Kooti's death to be accepted as a Christian
denomination.[10]

Since Greenwood's study, Ringatu elders have placed an embargo on
the publication of Te Kooti's prophecies. Because a sectarian movement must often struggle for the right to practice its religion without
harassment, it tries to present an acceptable face to civil authorities.
Sacred revelations (such as the *kupu*) need "to be protected with most
special care."[11] An examination of the early history of other religious
movements demonstrates that "revelations and sacred items in religious traditions have always presented themselves and guarded themselves in surprising varieties of ways."[12] The obstacles to the investigation of Ringatu history today are greater than those Greenwood faced.[13]

Te Kooti's controversial reputation among Maori and Pakeha still
constrains open inquiry. Called by God to be a new Moses, he used
violence as *utu* for the theft of Maori land in Poverty Bay. To his adher-

8. Ibid., pp. 74–75.
9. The prophet's firsthand description of his visions was inscribed in a police notebook that
disappeared from official files for a hundred years; it was rediscovered by Dr. Richard Hill in 1979.
See his article, "Te Kooti's Notebook."
10. See Binney, "Myth and Explanation," pp. 345–93, and "The Ringatu Traditions of Predictive
History," pp. 169–70.
11. Bolle, *Secrecy in Religions*, p. xv.
12. Ibid.
13. Ringatu church elders objected to Robin Winks's subsequent comparison of Ringatu with the
Latter-day Saints. See Winks, Robin, Papers, MSS and Archives, A-206 (untitled, n.d.), APL.

ents he was a miracle-worker, and to his enemies he was a demonic figure. Like Whaitiri, the goddess of *tapu* boundaries, he punished trespassers. Like Te Ua he identified the North Island as the Promised Land of the faithful Maori remnant.[14] His charisma, energy, and brutality has divided Maori inhabitants of the East Coast to the present time.[15] According to Ringatu tradition, Te Kooti was such a difficult child that even his own father tried to kill him when he was a boy by imprisoning him in the sweet potato storehouse. He stood out among his contemporaries as an *autaia*, a "troublesome fellow."[16]

FREEDOM AND ACCESS

Freedom is dependent upon access to positions of social power. In the nineteenth century Maori converts had no hope of becoming ministers in the Pakeha-dominated mission churches. Te Ua was only a Christian monitor, a low-level teacher at the Wesleyan mission where he was baptized; Rua Kenana was a "marginal man" with "more frequent contact with Pakeha than other Tuhoe," who became a faith healer among Maori daylaborers. According to Ringatu tradition, Te Kooti "had aspired to be a lay missionary teacher," but he instead was regarded as a "high-spirited man . . . with a liking for other men's women"—despite the fact that "he was always asking questions and endeavouring to acquire Pakeha skills." Sir Apirana Ngata, the foremost intellectual and political leader of the Ngati Porou, considered Te Kooti representative of "the worst side of Maori character," a man who claimed superior authority, but who was not a chief.[17]

The *iwi* did not have the freedom to mitigate the process of invasion and settlement that was taking away all that really mattered in their lives. They were not adequately represented in the political and civil institutions that formulated land policies. It is clear that they did not enjoy equality with Pakeha in the missions, the new colonial society, or government. Thus many people of the North Island turned to the new

14. Te Kooti identified the prisoners he liberated as "the remnant . . . the Chosen Few," and he named the land for the place, Havilah, outside of Eden "where there is gold." Binney, "Myth and Explanation," pp. 350, 368.

15. The recorded oral histories of first- and second-generation Ringatu adherents testify to the divisions Te Kooti created, as well as his reputation as a healer and prophet; see Judith Binney and Gillian Chaplin, *Nga Morehu, the Survivors*; Ihimaera, *The Matriarch*, pp. 133–97; and Williams, *East Coast Historical Records*, pp. 82–83.

16. Binney, "Myth and Explanation," p. 351.

17. Webster, *Rua and the Maori Millennium*, p. 156; Cowan, "The Facts about Te Kooti," p. 18.

tohunga, who taught them that the Maori were God's chosen remnant, destined to regain their land and *mana* according to Jehovah's providential plan.

Te Ua addressed the decline of his people, and Te Kooti prophesied imminent redemption. There were unmistakable continuities between Pai Marire and Ringatu. The millenarian expectation of Pai Marire found expression in Ringatu and its offshoot, Wairua Tapu. The period of Te Kooti's life after 1883 became identified in oral tradition as *te maungarongo*, "the long abiding peace."[18] Te Kooti's final *kupu*, uttered just before his death on April 12, 1893, predicted his successor and acknowledged the lingering division among his people over the land, their ultimate concern:

> In twenty-six years' time a leader shall appear for us, but if everything goes well this period will be shortened; even within three years he will appear. On the other hand, if the general administration is not sympathetic toward us, and this unsympathetic attitude is backed up with harsh treatment that will be meted out to us by leading chiefs in tribal matters, particularly in land matters, . . . then the coming shall be prolonged indefinitely.[19]

Within twenty-six years a new Ringatu leader did appear when in 1906 Rua Kenana of the Tuhoe tribe claimed to be the one Te Kooti prophesied as the "star" in the east,[20] but he was rejected by Maori intellectuals and rival chiefs, and the divine promise of Canaan's return was again delayed.

Devout Christians have lived with the delay of the *parousia* for two thousand years, while Ringatu has endured as a small, secretive religion for a little over one hundred years. Both began as movements founded by outlaws who prophesied that civil disorder would follow their deaths. They were similar in their pattern of development, which repeats itself in history whenever a messianic religion arises from a despised and outcast group. Such phenomena, no matter if they are characterized by chroniclers as barbarous, antisocial, seditious, or ri-

18. Head, "The Gospel of Te Ua Haumene," p. 9; Mikaere, *Te Maiharoa and the Promised Land*, p. 56; Binney, *Myth and Explanation*, p. 347; Fowler, "A New Look at Te Kooti," pp. 18–19; Webster, *Rua and the Maori Millennium*, pp. 156–58; and Ihimaera, *The Matriarch*, p. 196.

19. Greenwood, *The Upraised Hand*, p. 72. See Binney, *Redemption Songs*, pp. 494–95, for an updated translation.

20. Webster, *Rua and the Maori Millennium*, pp. 120–21; Judith Binney, Gillian Chaplin, and Craig Wallace, *Mihaia: The Prophet Rua Kenana and the Community at Maungapohatu*, p. 16.

diculous, can be identified as religious when they exhibit secrecy and an ultimate concern for which they incur persecution. Religion offers salvation, the most complete form of freedom. Thus, one may expect that the faithful will protect freedom's struggle by restricting access to sacred items; otherwise, their vulnerability to ridicule and oppression might jeopardize God's plan for their specific redemption. In other words, the freedom of the Ringatu church depends, in part, upon the restriction of an investigator's freedom to characterize it and its sacred data. Thus the historian is caught in the dilemma of either reporting only what is acceptable to editors, secular and sacred, or not publishing his or her findings. This is what happened to both Robin Winks of Yale, and John Rangihau, a Tuhoe academic at Waikato University. I was unable to publish an updated article on Te Kooti's Chatham Islands notebook in New Zealand. To state this openly is to contribute to New Zealand scholarship and to share with others an important aspect of the inherently controversial study of religions.

The body of existing primary material on Te Kooti and Ringatu consists of data in Maori, including a notebook of his *waiata* and *inoi* ("songs" and "prayers," most of which remain in the possession of church elders and a leading scholar), the lately rediscovered Chatham Islands notebook and its three English translations, the journal and papers of William Leonard Williams, news accounts and parliamentary documents, official correspondence between Te Kooti's military and civilian opponents, and only part of a file of contemporaneous documents in the National Museum; the other part has been stolen. There is also a first-person account by a hostage of the Matawhero attack, Maraea Morete, also known as Maria Morris. Secondary data include publications by Greenwood, James Cowan, Judith Binney, James Belich, Ormond Wilson, Peter Webster, Evelyn Stokes, Wharehuia Milroy, and Hirini Melbourne. The most recent study of the prophet is Judith Binney's *Redemption Songs* (1995), an encyclopedic biography. Te Kooti's story is told most vividly in *The Matriarch*, a novel by Witi Ihimaera, who is from Te Kooti's homeland in the Gisborne area. Te Kooti has also been the subject of a novel, *The Season of the Jew*, by Maurice Shadbolt, and a play, *The Taiaha and the Testament*, by Leo Fowler.

PRIMACY OF ORAL RECITATION

For someone who has provoked so many written accounts, it is noteworthy that Te Kooti reinstituted the Maori custom of oral history and, like

Te Ua, cautioned his followers not to accept Anglican or Methodist interpretations of the Bible. Like Te Ua, Te Kooti experienced a life-changing call to be a prophet, and the figure in his vision[21] cautioned him not to touch any book, but to heed the voice of God.[22] An oral tradition recited by selected experts can be a means of guarding sacred words from outside scrutiny, and it is as sacred as the inscribed documents of a religion. Ringatu services feature the recitation of songs, hymns, prayers, and passages edited by Te Kooti from the Bible. Some of these were written down by his secretaries.[23] Greenwood testifies to the difficult training undergone by the designated *tohunga* of the Ringatu church, who had to memorize the *panui*, "liturgical bible passages," and recite them without a single error, lest they endanger the object of their intercession with the *atua*.[24]

The danger provoked by mistakes in the performance of a ritual is a widespread phenomenon in religions. One story relates that Te Kooti declared a newly built meeting house at Te Whaiti *tapu*, "prohibited," when his horse shied from the building as he approached it, indicating there was an error in its construction. Sometimes, error is invoked to explain why an expected event did not occur.[25] In all religions certain words have efficacious power. Te Ua took great care to compose liturgies that conformed to the structure of ancient *karakia*. In Ringatu one begins the recitation of a *kupu whakaari* by speaking in tongues.[26] Maori prophets modeled their creations on an archaic oral tradition transmitted by schools of poets who faultlessly composed, memorized, and recited history and myth. Te Kooti reemphasized the oral tradition by mandating the recitation of liturgy. In the Ringatu movement the Bible is holy, but recited hymns, songs, prayers, and *kupu* are also sacred and inspired.

The birth of the Ringatu church was attended by conflict between those who adhered to the old way of Te Kooti's movement, which un-

21. Ringatu oral tradition identifies the voice/vision as Mikaere, the Archangel Michael; Binney, "Myth and Explanation," pp. 354–55, 373. Te Ua identified Michael with Riki, the god of war.

22. Binney, "Ringatu Traditions," p. 170. The voice was later named as Michael by Tawehi Wilson, a *tohunga*. "Myth and Explanation," pp. 355, 387. Te Kooti's account identifies the voice only as a messenger or manifestation of Jehovah.

23. Te Kooti had three secretaries: Hamiora Aparoa, Petera Te Rangihiroa, and Matiu Paeroa. Paeroa recorded the *kupu* of the prophet. Binney, "Myth and Explanation," p. 348. William Colenso, *Fiat Justitia*, p. 23, asserts that the book of prayers Te Kooti carried with him was written "with his own hand."

24. Greenwood, *The Upraised Hand*, pp. 56, 62, 45.

25. Ibid., p. 10. This explanation is common in instances of "cognitive dissonance," after a prophecy or prediction is disconfirmed; see Festinger, Riecken, and Schachter, *When Prophecy Fails*.

26. Binney, "Myth and Explanation," p. 369.

derstood itself paradigmatically as part of the Israelite religion, and those who wished to Christianize the movement, in order to gain its wider acceptance as a licit church.[27] The Ringatu movement tended toward schism. It had already split into "branches" by 1938 when members met at Ruatoki to form a church government.[28]

THE STRUCTURE OF RINGATU

The Ringatu church exists on at least two levels: it is simultaneously a hierarchical institutional structure that was created forty-five years after Te Kooti's death and a hermeneutical construction of the historical and spiritual experience of a prophet-led community. Greenwood refers to the former as "the polity of the church," which is nominally headed by a *poutikanga*, "righteous pillar." He (only one small branch of Ringatu allows female leaders) was elected at a biennial general assembly along with twelve (a sacred number in Judaism and Christianity) members of an executive committee that hear all grievances. In addition, a general secretary and two trustees of the church's material assets, which then included six hundred acres of land, were appointed. Local congregations had a great deal of autonomy in their appointment of ministers and the conduct of their services. The church really unified itself through its movable celebrations, which were held at a different church every month, but attended by members from all over New Zealand. Te Kooti devoted the latter part of his life to uniting his scattered followers by holding general gatherings at various locations.

On the other hand, the religio-historical structure of Ringatu is profoundly symbolic. It is on this level that the visible institution operates as a spiritual vehicle for its members. As Greenwood, Webster, and Binney have noted, the devotees attribute a miraculous or allegorical meaning to significant events in their history as a new religious movement. They speak of their history paradigmatically. Thus, the community was "born in bondage" in the Chatham Islands prison. Te Kooti, like Moses, led them out of prison to the East Coast, where they celebrated a Passover feast. Pursued and attacked by government troops, they "wandered in the wilderness" of the Urewera hinterland and "settled in the Canaan" of the King Country from 1872 until Te Kooti's pardon in 1883. In 1938, those who organized the church claimed that the movement was entering into the "fulness of the Christian religion,"

---

27. Greenwood, *The Upraised Hand*, pp. 45–46, 60.
28. Ibid., p. 50.

in accordance with the original intention of their prophet.[29] The church seal symbolizes the equivalency of the two Testaments in the phrase, "The law of God and the faith of Jesus."[30]

SACRED HISTORY

Ringatu oral tradition teaches that Te Toiroa, a Ngati Maru *matakite*, renewed the Maori Covenant with Jehovah after it had fallen into desuetude during the thousand years that had passed since the Maori's Jewish ancestors emigrated from biblical Canaan to New Zealand. He also foretold Te Kooti's birth and conducted the boy's *tohi* purification rite. The stories about Te Kooti mark him with the ambivalent sign of discord and of healing, because it was through him that the faithful remnant of Maori Jews renewed their covenant with the God of the Pakeha invaders.[31] Ringatu myth-history also presents Te Kooti as one who, like Maui, outsmarted his enemies and, like Moses, prevailed over "Pharaoh."

Oral histories are not the same as scholarly or scientific discourse. Sacred words express an ultimate truth that undergirds the quotidian world and eludes our puny understanding. One may quarrel over the election of a *poutikanga* or debate the management of church funds, but such disputations do not change the core myths and prophecies of the religio-historical structure of the movement. Black Elk, a Lakota Sioux shaman, observed that one may misinterpret a dream, but the vision itself is flawless and originates in the realm of the god(s); it is the human vessel who may apply it to the wrong events or interpret it incorrectly.[32] Hermeneutical differences are aired during contests that take place in the arena of theological interpretation, and schism is a bitter process in which contending sides each claim an exclusive knowledge of sacred matters. A *tohunga* or *matakite* receives divine knowledge, but he is human and may not fully understand his utterances. So it is said that Te Toiroa was ignorant of the full meaning of his prophecies.[33]

The process of revitalization happens when the sacred pierces the

29. Ibid., p. 60.

30. Ibid., p. 81.

31. Binney, "Myth and Explanation," pp. 351–53. There is also an alternative teaching that the first Maori canoe in New Zealand found "Io" (Jehovah) there well before the missionaries arrived.

32. Annette Aronowicz, "Musings on Teaching *The Sacred and the Profane*: The Dilemma of the Introductory Course," p. 81.

33. Binney, "Myth and Explanation, p. 353.

veil of ordinary human understanding and reveals divine knowledge to
the elect. What is conveyed is not discourse, or logic, but a spiritually
authoritative *gnosis*. A people renews itself through the memorializa-
tion and enactment of the saving miracles, visions, ceremonies, covenants, laws, and prayers given to the community by the god(s).

A HISTORY OF SACRED THINGS

Writing a history of sacred things presents one with a problem of
method. One can verify facts about an institution or a written document, but how does one regard revelation, myth-history, parables,
prophecies, miracles, symbols, and hermeneutics? Two early sources,
William L. Williams and Henry Atkinson, were able to surmount their
prejudice against Te Kooti to a limited extent. They recognized that he
was charismatic, but did not consider his message authentic. To them
he was a demonic influence upon the Maori. Most Pakeha scoffed at
his feats. No doubt, they said, he used phosphorous to make his hands
glow and to impress his fellow prisoners,[34] but even the most skeptical
investigators granted the extraordinary nature of his "miraculous" es-
capes.[35]

Judith Binney has recorded what Te Kooti's followers have to say
about his life and their experiences within Ringatu.[36] This is an effective approach, and the data Binney has published are invaluable if
only because they were inaccessible before she published them, but
analysis also requires comparison with similar and different phenomena. One should pay close attention to a diverse sampling of the reactions elicited by Te Kooti, who excited the hatred, fear, awe, disgust, or
admiration of everyone he met.

The most significant Ringatu primary document is Te Kooti's Chatham
Islands notebook; it provoked mixed responses from J. C. Richmond,
acting Minister of Native Affairs, and his brother-in-law, Henry Atkinson, editor and linguist. Maraea Morete (Maria Morris), a young Maori
woman of Patutahi who was captured by Te Kooti during the Matawhero raid, wrote an eyewitness account of his execution of Maori prisoners. The notebook's narrative of Te Kooti's visions and Morete's auto-

---

34. Cowan, *The New Zealand Wars*, 2:225–26.
35. Belich, *The New Zealand Wars*, pp. 218, 229, 234.
36. See Binney, *Redemption Songs*, and Binney and Chaplin, *Nga Morehu*.

biography present a multifaceted picture of the founder and bring us closer to the historical person.

In addition to providing diverse views from primary documents, one should strive to place a religious movement in the larger context of its broader tradition. Ringatu flared up as a new fire from the dying embers of Pai Marire. Finally, one cannot fully acknowledge the Ringatu church's case that it is "entering into the fulness of the Christian religion" without noting that this constitutes a significant paradigm shift from its counter-Christian genesis among a population of incarcerated and despairing Hauhau prisoners.

17

TE KOOTI: MAUI AND MOSES

*And the Lord your God, He shall expel
them from before you and drive them from
out of your sight; and ye shall possess their
land, as the Lord your God hath promised
you*

Te Kooti

PROPHETS

The definition of the role of "prophet" emerges from the stories that characterize a religious tradition. Since God breaks his own rules so unpredictably, one must look to the stories to determine what a prophet is. He may not be a religious expert; he may, like Moses, even be inarticulate. A prophet is set apart because he is called by God to become the mouthpiece of revelation. Prophets arise in times of grave threat to the survival and integrity of a people. The prophet's role sets him (or her) in opposition, not only to his people's enemies, but to those who have fallen away from orthopraxy within his community. He is more often than not a figure of discord in a time of disarray. He voices God's desire to save his people and set them again on the right path.

The Maori were familiar with the stories of the biblical prophets by

1866, the year Te Ua died and Te Kooti was sent to prison as an alleged spy for the Hauhau. From the time of the first Maori renewal movement in the Bay of Islands, those who were aggrieved by the behavior of the Pakeha often identified themselves with the Jews. From the Old Testament they learned the *whakapapa* of twelve tribes who resembled themselves much more than the Europeans. Jewish laws of purity and pollution, the myth of Creation, the promise of the Land to Abraham, the rainbow covenant of peace between God and Noah, a God who went before his warriors to ensure their victories, and the great men of the Israelites whose power came to them as a gift from a sky god resonated far more with Polynesian history and experience than did the gospels of the lamblike savior of the missionaries.

WARRIOR GODS

In Poverty Bay on the East Coast, the homeland of Te Kooti, the CMS mission began in 1839 with the arrival of Reverend William Williams, translator and editor of the Maori New Testament and compiler of the Maori dictionary. Reverend, later bishop, Williams worshiped "Jehovah, the jealous God, the God of wrath," vengeance, retribution, and judgment, as well as the "loving Father of the New Testament."[1] After Te Kooti had fought his way across the East Coast, Williams reported that Ringatu supplanted Christianity as the religion of the East Coast Tuhoe people. Small Christian communities remained, but it was the Old Testament stories of Jehovah, Moses, and Canaan, grafted onto Maori *whakapapa*, that energized the charismatic renewal movements. Te Kooti's *mana* attracted demoralized Hauhau prisoners to his new faith, which he initially called *nga morehu*, "the remnant," and *wairua tapu*, "Holy Spirit."

The god of warriors in Maori religion is Tu-matauenga, who thwarted the fierce onslaught of Tawhiri, the god of winds, against his brothers.[2] Another story of Tu-matauenga tells how he slew and ate the Kumara[3] people of his brother, Rongo-maraeroa. This myth was recited at the yearly harvest festival when the priest representing Tu offered him the first fruits after they had been harvested from a special field and cooked in a special oven. This ritual and its variants featured the great

1. Porter, *Turanga Journals*, p. 597.
2. Eric Schwimmer, *The World of the Maori*, p. 15.
3. The *kumara* is the Polynesian staple in the southernmost Pacific region. The white potato was introduced by the Europeans.

communal banquet called *hakari*.[4] As noted before, the word *tu* indicates an upright position. In the Maori cosmos, the direction up denotes the powerful male realm of the sky. *Turangawaewae*, "a place to stand," marks a community's divinely ordained position on native ground that binds the living and the dead together. Te Kooti's *ringa-tu* movement partakes of the symbolism of the Tu-matauenga stories, and its prophet militantly contested the displacement of the children of Shem by the children of Japhet.

THE *TOHUNGA ARIKI*

The Maori analogue of the Israelite prophet is the *tohunga ariki*, the priest of Tu at the sacred precinct, the *tuahu*,[5] where warriors gathered for purification rites after a war party[6] and where sacrifices of first fruits, or a lock of hair, or the body parts of prisoners and enemies, took place. Before a war expedition, the *tohunga* conducted a *niu* rite using two small sticks inserted into two small mounds (one representing life and the male complement and one representing death and the female complement) in order to divine victory or defeat. A *tohunga* might even manipulate one of the small sticks to turn prospective defeat into victory during a battle. The *tohunga* or an associate called a *matakite* served as the vessel through whom a deity spoke.

A CONDITION OF SINFULNESS

Every society may have its priests, prophets, and shamans, but their functions vary. Tamihana, Te Ua, and Te Kooti conflated the oracular roles of Jewish prophets and *matakite/tohunga*.[7] Te Kooti uttered prophecies, *kupu whakaari*, and Te Ua diagnosed the ills of a declining population. The visions, hopes, and ultimate concern of Maori renewal movements coalesced in one continuous, inspired Spirit tradition. The prophets divined that their people suffered from a condition of sin or

4. Johansen, "Studies in Maori Rites and Myths," pp. 180–82, 188.

5. Ibid., pp. 61–93, gives information from scattered and extant sources about this sacred place. Similar ancient platforms marked by poles or menhirs ("standing stones") have been excavated in Easter Island and eastern Polynesia.

6. Johansen, "Studies in Maori Rites and Myths," pp. 79, 81.

7. In 1854 Dr. [Edward?] Shortland reported that the *matakite* was a person who assisted the *tohunga* by diagnosing a patient's illness; *New Zealand Parliamentary Debates* (*NZPD*) July 19, 1907, p. 516. *Matakite* also denotes the seers power of foresight. Binney, "Ringatu Traditions," pp. 169–70.

loss of *mana*. In Te Ua's refrain: *ki tōna iwi Wareware, Tū Kiri Kau, ko Motu Tū Hāwhe*, "his people, Forgetful, Standing Naked in the Island in Two Halves," the plight of the people reflects the broken state of the land. They have fallen away from the Covenant of their Jewish ancestors, and the land is divided between them and the invaders. The meaning of this refrain belongs to the worshiper; we can only note its correspondences to the Bible and Maori religion. One can argue from the outside whether this phrase demonstrates an awareness of sin or the transgression of *tapu*, but the words themselves tell us that people felt literally without connections to their own past or future, intensely vulnerable, and on broken ground. In his gospel, Te Ua admonished, "To the whole body of the people: Rebelliousness is the cause of your destitution. You have altogether despised your God. You have said he is a false god. Let us not say that destitution comes from God. No it comes from disobeying the words of God. Thus we courted destitution."[8]

Te Ua accounted for the suffering of his people in Deuteronomistic terms. Their "rebelliousness" is like the murmuring of the Jews in the wilderness, who blamed their misery on Moses and fell away from Yahweh to worship a golden calf. A similar expression of the sinful condition of the people appears in a prayer Te Kooti composed while he was in prison: "O God, if our hearts arise from the land in which we now dwell as slaves, and repent and pray to Thee and confess our sins in Thy presence, then, O Jehovah, do Thou blot out the sins of Thy own people, who have sinned against Thee. Do not Thou, O God cause us to be wholly destroyed."[9]

Te Kooti adopted the language of the Psalms to extend the meaning of his exile in the Chatham Islands to the widespread condition of the Maori as exiles in their own land. He interceded for them with Jehovah, pleading that they would not be "wholly destroyed." Correspondingly, in "A Prayer for deliverance from foes" he cursed his enemies: "O Jehovah, Thou art the God who deliverest the people repenting, therefore do Thou listen hither this day to the prayer of Thy servant concerning our Enemies. Let them be destroyed and turned to flight by Thee. . . . And when Thou sendest forth Thy Angel to trample our Enemies to the earth, through Thee also shall all their bones be broken to pieces."[10]

---

8. Head, "The Gospel of Te Ua Haumene," p. 25.

9. A translation by William Colenso published in the *Hawke's Bay Herald*, April 9, 1869, and reprinted in the appendix to Colenso's apologia for Kereopa, *Fiat Justitia*, p. 19.

10. Ibid.

His reference to an avenging Angel echoes the Pai Marire devotion to Riki, the archangel Michael. However, it is the Angel, not Te Kooti, who tramples the enemy, just as in Pai Marire it was Gabriel and Michael, not Te Ua, who would cleanse the land of foreigners. This distinction is a critical one, because not all sects who embrace a violent eschatological myth believe they must enact the apocalypse.

JEHOVAH'S CALL

Like Te Ua, Te Kooti heard Jehovah's call in a series of visions and was overcome by his sense of unworthiness in his Presence. Te Ua said, "Great indeed is my own distress. I did not listen to the law [*ture*], which says, enter into life lame, or on crippled knees [i.e. , rather than sin with one's hands or feet, Matthew 15:8]."[11] Te Kooti became ill in the Chathams and was isolated in a hut expecting to die, when "the spirit of God aroused me, saying, "Arise; I am sent by God to heal you, that you may preach His name to His people who are living as captives in this land, that they may understand that it was Jehovah who drove you all here."[12] Te Kooti protested, ""My body is loathsome, my head and my bed are unclean, through the greatness of my sins. Do Thou rather turn to the great and the righteous.' I ceased speaking, and wept over the greatness of the sins within me."[13] The humility of the penitent in the face of the *mysterium tremendum et fascinans* is a mark of an authentic religious experience.

Te Kooti's enemy, J. C. Richmond, the acting Native Secretary, remarked that Te Kooti had written "some good words in a book I got at Ngatapa"[14] and that "many of the thoughts are those of the Bible. . . . But I hate cannibals and murderers of women and children and I will continue to destroy them whenever I can."[15] The book was the Chatham Islands notebook that recorded Te Kooti's visions, prompting Richmond to wrestle with the paradox of a "cannibal" who was called to be a prophet by a God they both worshiped!

Because Te Ua and Te Kooti received the call and were overcome by

11. Head, "The Gospel of Te Ua Haumene," p. 25.

12. Arthur S. Atkinson, trans., "Te Kooti," *The Monthly Review*, March 1889, p. 176.

13. Ibid.

14. Te Kooti's notebook was found by a loyalist soldier and given to the Native Secretary. I reconstructed the probable history of the notebook in "Te Kooti's Chatham Islands Notebook: The History of a Religious Document," which I submitted to the *Turnbull Library Record* in 1990.

15. Scholefield, *Richmond-Atkinson Papers*, 2:283.

a profound sense of their sinfulness, they are prophets. Accounts of their visions were written down. Each encountered God during a time of personal and community crisis, and like the biblical prophets, they felt the hand of deity upon them, lifting them up and compelling them to use divinely imparted *gnosis* to save their people from impending destruction.

God manifested himself to Te Kooti "in the likeness of a man," causing him to tremble and fall down. One vision occurred during an assembly of the prisoners, when God commanded,

> "Let all your friends be called to come here to write down the things which I say to you; you shall be a mouth-piece for me, and they shall write it down; and let there be many to search all the books; but do not you take heed of any books, for they are the work of men, and unintelligible. But I will speak to you and you to them, that they may know that I am a voice from God. If there is any saying they do not understand, do you call upon God, and I will disclose it." So these things were worked at by the people who had been summoned until they were finished.[16]

A "mouth-piece" for the god(s) utters a holy message. The Hauhau regarded speaking in tongues, the oracles of preserved heads, and Te Ua's *karakia* as oracular utterance, or *matakite*. Te Kooti continued the Spirit tradition in the prophecies and hermeneutics of his Ringatu movement.

THE RISE OF A PROPHET

Te Kooti's remarkable life began on the East Coast in Poverty Bay near present-day Gisborne, founded in 1868 on the site of Turanganui settlement. Captain Cook had first sighted land at the nearby promontory of Young Nick's Head a hundred years earlier.[17] On the southern side of this headland is Whareongaonga, the beach where Te Kooti and 297 children, women, and men disembarked on July 10, 1868, from a ship they commandeered in the Chatham Islands prison and sailed home into Poverty Bay. Ringatu tradition commemorates this "passover," or

16. Atkinson, "Te Kooti," p. 177. Despite God's command to have another write down the account, some argue that the visions narrative was inscribed in Te Kooti's own hand.

17. Cook's sighting in 1769 led to European settlement, although Abel Tasman was the first European to encounter New Zealand in 1642.

kapenga, on January 1, the Ringatu New Year. It is one of their three sacred "firsts."[18] During the 500–mile voyage the escapees' ship encountered rough weather, and a "spy," Te Kooti's uncle, was thrown overboard as a "Jonah" to pacify God's anger. Ringatu tradition celebrates the exodus from the Chathams as a miracle. At the very least, their dramatic escape established Te Kooti's reputation as a formidable strategist. He had executed a plan to overpower the prison garrison and ship's crew with almost no loss of life, and his landing struck fear into the small settlement of Europeans on the East Coast, who had, only recently, put down the Hauhau movement.

Te Kooti learned Bible at the CMS mission in Poverty Bay.[19] According to Ringatu tradition, he wanted to become a mission teacher, but Bishop Williams refused his request.[20] While he was in the Chatham Islands, Te Kooti "began speaking the words of God" on April 10, 1867, and continued until April 30th. He resumed prophesying in the "beginning of May to the 10th." His visions had occurred from February 21 through March. God's envoy gave him signs similar to Moses's serpent staff and the bush that burned but was not consumed:

> After this came the signs. I saw he had something in his hand; he held it out to me; but when I stretched out my hand to take it, lo, it was a hideous reptile. I fell to the ground, and great was my fear, for there never was a reptile like it. Afterwards he said to me, "Stretch out your hand." I did so, and, behold, there was a fire burning on my hand, and the flame was like that of a candle, but neither was my hand burnt nor any part of my clothes.[21]

During the time of his visions Te Kooti had no book in which to record them and he memorized all the "prayers and lamentations" given him by the Spirit of God. For a short while afterward, he recited them, and they may have been recorded by one of his followers. During

18. Greenwood, *The Upraised Hand,* p. 61; Binney, "Myth and Explanation," p. 360. Other designated holy days are the first fruits festival, *haumata,* on November 1 and a planting festival on June 1. Greenwood, *The Upraised Hand,* pp. 38, 59, 61.

19. Bishop Williams's mission station was founded at Turanga, but the reluctance of the Rongowhakaata tribe to provide more land for school buildings forced him to move the station inland to Waerenga-a-hika in 1857, where the resident Aitanga-a-Mahaki tribe sold the church a block of 593 acres; W. L. Williams, *East Coast Historical Records,* pp. 21–22. Cowan, *The New Zealand Wars,* 2:222, reports that Te Kooti received instruction at Waerenga-a-hika, but he was baptized at the old Whakato Mission by Williams or by Thomas Grace, who substituted for Williams in 1853–54.

20. Ihimaera, *The Matriarch,* p. 134.

21. Atkinson, "Te Kooti," p. 177.

the same period he studied the Bible intently. His notebook includes many passages from the Old Testament, but only a few from Christian scriptures. Among the notations are summaries of the biblical events Te Kooti considered significant, referenced by chapter and verse.

The notebook lists biblical genealogies that trace the *tupuna*[22] from Abraham to Christ. Also noted are significant events, the *tupuna* involved in them, and the appearances of angels to patriarchs and prophets. It appears from the Chatham Islands notebook that Te Kooti was engaged in recording a sacred history that established the descent of the Maori from the Israelites. The two New Testament notes concern Matthew 1:1, the genealogy of Christ, and Mark 1:2, the statement of John the Baptist that links the Old and New Covenants: "As it is written in the prophets behold, I send my messenger before thy face which shall prepare thy way before thee."[23] According to Ringatu oral history, Te Toiroa, the old *tohunga*, had renewed the Jewish Covenant among his people after a thousand years of their wandering from the original Canaan. It is thought that he transmitted this Covenant to Te Kooti— after the boy's escape from entombment in the *kumara* storehouse—in the traditional manner of a *tohuna ariki* training his successor, by feeding him with the stone named Tu-matauenga.[24] It is clear from the notebook and later church documents that Ringatu constituted a biblical religion with a unique origin and revelation.

Robin Winks compared Ringatu and the Church of Latter-day Saints, which has evangelized among the Maori, but the Ringatu church denies any connection between the two.[25] Their similarities arise from a general pattern that characterizes renewal movements: they are inspired by the word of the god(s), founded by a charismatic leader, regarded as threats to the civil authorities, seek refuge at a sacred place marked off by an inviolable perimeter, and often suffer persecution. The Mormon movement began with revelations of the Angel Moroni to Joseph Smith, whose successor, Brigham Young, launched an exodus across the wilderness to found a new community in Utah. The Maori Spirit tradition originated with the visions of Te Ua and was established by Te Kooti. State authorities harried both groups. Te Ua

22. Literally, "ancestors," but in this case, "patriarchs." A variant is *tipuna*.

23. G. H. Davies, "Copy of Te Kooti's Notebook."

24. Binney, "Myth and Explanation," p. 353, quoting Paul Delamere, late *poutikanga* of the Ringatu Church.

25. See margin notes on Wink's unpublished paper at Winks, Robin, Papers, UAL. Ringatu reluctance to be identified with the Mormons, as well as Pai Marire, is understandable, since both were compared and vilified by William Fox in his 1864 memoir, *The War in New Zealand*, p. 140.

and Rua Kenana, a Ringatu messiah, favored polygyny. However, Pai Marire and Ringatu were indigenous movements that expected to reoccupy confiscated land, while Mormons founded a theocracy in territory that belonged to the indigenous Americans.

Despite its adoption of biblical symbols, history, and scriptures, Ringatu remains a uniquely Maori religion. For Te Kooti and his successors, the land is paramount. God still speaks to *nga morehu* in signs and wonders; this remnant awaits an age of peace and justice during which their land will be returned to them according to their covenant with God.

Te Kooti recited a portable *whakapapa* that served a people in exile. To chronicle the experience of a people who stand upon the abyss of the loss of their past, is to restore their life. Through oral tradition and hermeneutics Jews refashioned their past in the aftermath of the wars of 70 and 134–35 C. E. that destroyed their temple and banished them from Jerusalem. When religion becomes portable, exile does not overwhelm it. Because Rabbinic Judaism sustained their tradition, Jewish exiles returned from a long diaspora to found the state of Israel. By a strange accident of history Christian missionaries transmitted Jewish paradigms to the Maori at the very time English settlement was taking away their land and their future. From Tamihana's time, the charismatic *tohunga* created an interim place to stand, first in the King Country and then on the urban *marae*, where *whakapapa* continues to be recited, people continue to be healed, and the *atua* continue to speak in the signs and events of everyday life.

TE KOOTI, THE TROUBLEMAKER

Te Kooti had a reputation as a troublemaker before he was sent to the Chathams. In Poverty Bay his enemies included Reginald Newton Biggs, who had been singled out by Prime Minister Fox as an exemplary New Zealand militia officer.[26] Biggs's energy in pursuit of Hauhau forces on the East Coast prompted Fox's story that when the lieutenant's weary men asked him "Where are we to sleep tonight?," he replied by pointing to the enemy's *pa* and commanding them to make their quarters there.[27] That this home-grown New Zealand hero was vengefully dispatched by Te Kooti at Matawhero no doubt shocked the

---

26. Fox, *The War in New Zealand*, pp. 230–36.
27. Ibid., p. 233.

close-knit European population of the time and led to a relentless pursuit of the "rebel" for the next three years.

In 1889 Te Kooti gave James Cowan an account of his life before imprisonment. He had been a supercargo on the coastal vessel, *Te Whetuki*, which brought produce from Turanga to Auckland, returning with trade goods. His entrepreneurship evidently "displeased" a local trader and storekeeper, Captain George Edward Read,[28] whose animosity is explained by Leo Fowler in his interviews of the local Pakeha families who knew Te Kooti. Read acted as a middleman for Maori farmers, but Te Kooti advised them to trade directly with Auckland and thereby "established himself in a position of some leadership among his people."[29] On the other hand, Maori land sellers resented this common upstart who was notorious for pursuing women and alcohol. The widow of Captain Ogilvie Ross, a militiaman whom Te Kooti accompanied in the battle against the Hauhau at Waerenga-a-hika, blamed Read, who operated rumshops "spread . . . like spider's webs to catch flies," for encouraging Te Kooti to drink.[30] In any event, Te Kooti was an *autaia*, a "troublemaker," and drunkard. Legends relate that he kidnapped his wife in full view of her father and that he tapped into a local publican's cask of rum from below by burrowing under the house where it was kept.

Ringatu tradition teaches that omens attending Te Kooti's birth presaged difficult times and connected the last seer of *te ao tawhito*, Te Toiroa, with the founder of Ringatu. Te Toiroa entered into a trance and spoke for the lizard deity to prophesy the Land Wars. He foresaw that through the discordant life of Te Kooti, the European's God would become the God of the Ringatu church.[31] Te Toiroa is said to have prophesied in 1866, but records show that he probably died in that year.[32] No one knows the date of Te Kooti's birth; he died in 1893. Ringatu bridges the abyss between the prehistorical and colonial eras by linking Te Toiroa and Te Kooti in a single charismatic tradition.

Te Kooti was *potiki*, the archetypal "precocious 'younger child' who contends against accepted order."[33] Like the god Maui-potiki, Te Kooti has been characterized as having "qualifications which found peculiar favor with Maoris—a restless energy, force of will, decision, and great

28. Cowan, "The Facts about Te Kooti." I am indebted to Judith Binney for giving me this article.
29. Fowler, "A New Look at Te Kooti," p. 19.
30. Ibid.
31. Binney, "Myth and Explanation," p. 353.
32. Binney, "Ringatu Traditions," p. 168.
33. Binney, "Myth and Explanation," p. 352.

ingenuity to plan, and determination to execute."[34] His miraculous ability to evade capture and use of stratagems to outwit his enemies contributed to the awesome charisma that panicked Maori and Pakeha alike.[35]

Moses and Maui are intertwined in the figure of Te Kooti, and storytellers are divided about which archetype suits him best. He is portrayed as demonic and salvific. Moses was a murderer before he was called by Yahweh to lead the Exodus. Maui is both creator and trickster in Polynesian myths. Te Kooti remains the most controversial figure in New Zealand history. An avenger and a healer, a destroyer and a founder, a guerrilla and a prophet, he was a thoroughly unamalgamated Maori man of deed.

34. *Daily Southern Cross*, November 16, 1868.

35. At Mohaka, Te Kooti gained entry to Huke Pa, which he could win only through subtle deception, pitting relative against relative; see Thomas Gudgeon, *Reminiscences of the War in New Zealand*, pp. 286–88. In his September 16, 1868, address to Parliament, Donald McLean charged that Napier and the rural districts were in a panic over Te Kooti's ability to win skirmishes and convert friendly tribes to his religion.

18

MATAWHERO

Glory to Thy Holy Name. *His name was Te Kooti Rikirangi Te Turuki and Jehovah chose him at birth to lead his Children of Israel, the Maori nation, out of the land of the Pakeha, out of slavery to Egypt. This he did so, as Moses did also, when Moses opened the Red Sea and led his people to Canaan. It was of Te Kooti that the tohunga, Toeroa [Toiroa], said to the mother of Te Kooti, "Your unborn child will be a son whose fame will reach to the four corners of the earth for good or evil." Indeed, so it has come to pass that this fame for goodness spread as foretold. But also did his fame for evil. Yet this was not of his doing, this evil, for it was the Pakeha who first themselves began the evil by denying Te Kooti his blessedness. Then, after the fall of the pa at Waerenga A Hika, during the Hauhau wars, they falsely imprisoned him and exiled him to Wharekauri. And when he escaped from Wharekauri, the Pakeha wished to hunt him down like an animal. Only then did he take up arms against Pharaoh and against all Egypt.*

Witi Ihimaera

The Land Wars resumed after the murder of Reverend Volkner at Opotiki in March 1865 by "Hau Hau fanatics."[1] This atrocity was followed on July 22 by the murder of a government interpreter, James Fulloon, at Whakatane by a "party of natives, who

---

1. Fox, *The War in New Zealand,* p. 221.

avowed themselves to have been sent by the Hau Haus."[2] The responsible government could not request more imperial troops—for Britain hoped to withdraw them from the colony as soon as it was feasible. Instead, it sent a force of 580 colonial soldiers and Maori loyalists to Volkner's town, where they were joined by another Maori contingent of 500. One discerns from this account that the East Coast Maori were engaged in a civil war, the details of which have been set down by Karen Neal in her unpublished thesis, "Maori Participation in the East Coast Wars, 1865–1872" (1976).

Neal's primary finding is that both loyalist and dissident Maori on the East Coast shared the same purpose, to preserve *mana* and territory, but they differed over how to achieve their mutual aim. Their allegiances split over their loyalty or opposition to the Kingites and Te Ua. Hauhau emissaries rekindled long-standing intertribal rivalries.[3] They were decisively defeated at the battle of Waerenga-a-hika, but after they escaped from prison, the East Coast entered into a period of unprecedented discord.[4] The loyalist tribes sought to preserve their particular families, tribes, and lands as best they could by adapting to Pakeha rule. Neal did not address the religious differences of Christian loyalists and sectarian dissidents: the Hauhau and Ringatu believed that sacred powers would return all alienated lands. The vision of God's archangels cleansing the land of the Pakeha originated with Te Ua and has probably not ended with the establishment of the Ringatu church.

Te Kooti divided his supporters and opponents into two camps: those whom God had chosen and those whom God would punish. Even though the events in the Waikato and among the Ngati Ruanui had not directly affected him, the stories of Bishop Selwyn's perfidy and Henry William's accumulation of Maori land reverberated among the North Island *iwi*.

The mission station at Waerenga-a-hika was seized by Hauhau militants after the apostles of Te Ua spread Pai Marire to the East Coast, and Te Kooti was one of only a few of his Rongowhakaata tribe who

2. Ibid., p. 226.

3. Fowler, in "A New Look at Te Kooti," p. 22, notes that Ropata Wahawaha, chief of the Ngati Porou and leader of loyalist troops who fought against Te Kooti, had been enslaved in his youth by a Rongowhakaata chief of Te Kooti's tribe. The tendency of Pacific Island peoples to take sides in colonial wars according to tribal enmities is demonstrated in an illuminating paper by Bronwyn Douglas, "Conflict and Alliance in a Colonial Context."

4. King Tawhaio sought to rally East Coast Maori to his Tariao religion in April 1866 after the Hauhau defeat at Waerenga-a-hika; see Williams, *East Coast Historical Records*, p. 51. But he feared Te Kooti's ambitions and did not allow him into the King Country after his escape from prison in July 1868, forcing Te Kooti to skirmish with Government troops outside the *aukati* for three years.

Fig. 4   The Matawhero church

sided with the government forces besieging it. During the battle Chief Paora Parau accused Te Kooti of aiding those inside the *pa*, including Te Kooti's brother. Although he was detained and released, he was rearrested on charges of spying three months later in March 1866. Major Biggs, the Resident Magistrate, and Superintendent McLean denied his request for a hearing, and he was sent to Wharekauri in the Chatham Islands with the third shipload of Hauhau prisoners. They probably acted upon the advice of Te Kooti's Pakeha enemies in Poverty Bay.[5] Among the Maori who were happy to see Te Kooti get on the boat was Paratene Turangi, who had recommended to Major Biggs that the upstart be put out of the way,[6] proving that even before his summary confinement, Te Kooti had excited strong negative feelings among some of his own people and the Poverty Bay settlers. Te Kooti believed that Captain Read and Major Biggs, in particular, had engineered his deportation.[7]

5. Judith Binney, *DNZB*, "Te Kooti Arikirangi Te Turuki," p. 463.
6. Cowan, "The Facts about Te Kooti," p. 18.
7. Fowler, "A New Look at Te Kooti," p. 20.

Two years later it was the same Magistrate Biggs who rode out to Whareongaonga, the beach where the Chatham escapees had landed and issued an ultimatum that they surrender their weapons. "Te Kooti replied that he certainly would not do so, but if he were allowed to take quiet possession of his land he would do no mischief to the Europeans; that in fact he intended to go to the Waikato & make war upon the Maori king."[8] As they retreated inland toward the King Country, the escapees were intercepted three times by hostile forces, including troops led by Biggs, on July 20 and 24 and August 8, 1868. After King Tawhiao refused to allow him into the Waikato without a fight, Te Kooti decided to return to the Turanga area and claim the "best places of the Europeans," including those that had belonged to his own family.[9]

Who can know what was in the mind of the prophet? Church tradition recorded his *kupu* of that time, and they drew largely on the Psalms, which are attributed to David, a guerrilla leader forced to flee from King Saul and seek refuge among the enemies of Israel until he could return to Jerusalem. This time between escape from government pursuit in July 1868 and asylum in the Waikato in May 1872 the Ringatu church calls "the wanderings of Israel through the desert wilderness."[10]

It began, however, with a period more akin to Joshua's entry into Canaan, as the spirit of Tu-matauenga seemed to drive the rejected *autaia* to exact *utu*, "revenge and reparation," for his enslavement. Although Biggs expected an attack, Te Kooti managed to surprise the tiny settlement at Matawhero nevertheless. In the early morning of November 10, 1868, his war party slaughtered thirty Pakeha men, women, and children, among whom were Biggs, his wife and infant child, and at least twenty-two Maori residents. Only the newly built Matawhero church was spared destruction during repeated raids on ensuing nights. Today it stands alone, a tiny, anachronistic emblem among the dairy pastures west of Gisborne.

Spreading out from Matawhero, Te Kooti's war party captured 300 Maori and executed several against whom Te Kooti had specific grievances. Among the captives was a young woman, Maraea Morete, whose husband was killed at her side. Her uncle, a Hauhau, was subsequently captured and was facing trial when she wrote her account of the attack. She later testified against the followers of Te Kooti before

8. Maria Morris, "Reminiscences," MS Papers 2296, folder. ATL, NLNZ.
9. Binney, *DNZB*, p. 464.
10. Greenwood, *The Upraised Hand*, p. 60.

the Supreme Court.[11] Morete's document is the best primary source about the attack, but it is not unbiased, since she clearly exonerated her uncle in her account and was attempting to mitigate his punishment. However, she presented a compelling, chilling picture of the dark side of Te Kooti.

Morete's account reveals that the killings on November 10 and during subsequent raids were conducted with a terrifying zeal. She quoted the prophet as saying, "'God has told me to kill women & children, now fire on them' and [she reported] about 60 guns were instantly aimed at them & fired."[12] Te Kooti was depicted as fiercely drunk, but single-mindedly aware of Jehovah's justice, while he recited Psalm 63 to his victims:

> But those who seek to destroy my life
> shall go down into the depths of the earth
> They shall be given over to the power of the sword
> they shall be prey for jackals.
> But the King shall rejoice in God;
> all who swear by him shall glory;
> for the mouths of liars will be stopped.

Later victims of Te Kooti's wrath included Paratene and Te Kooti's father-in-law. He overpowered them during a meeting he called supposedly to negotiate a "male peace." His retribution was selective, shrewdly planned and executed. After the raids, Morete witnessed the "Hauhaus" building altars on which they burned "Maori garments and greenstone ornaments . . . as a sacrifice to their God."[13] At sunrise they recited psalms and the prophet gave a sermon. Te Kooti had deliberately visited what he regarded as God's justice upon all his enemies.

Morete's account of Matawhero is damning, but a prominent Poverty Bay chief, Wi Pere, who was captured and made his escape with Morete, subsequently joined with other loyalists in partially absolving Te Kooti's actions. They testified in a letter to the government that the Chatham Island escapees intended only to return to their homes in the area, but were put on the defensive by local officials and the militia.[14] The new outbreak of war, so soon after their government had decided to

11. R. De Z. Hall, *DNZB*, p. 299.

12. Morris, "Reminiscences."

13. Binney relates that these were burned as a "deliberate rejection" of the old Maori gods. *Redemption Songs*, p. 123.

14. Fowler, "A New Look at Te Kooti," p. 21.

allow the Kingites to reside undisturbed in Waikato in the hope that hostilities would cease, angered and demoralized the settlers. For the next three years *kupapa* under the command of Pakeha officers and the Ngati Parou warrior Ropata Wahawaha pursued Te Kooti through the Urewera and Taupo regions without success. According to Leo Fowler, the prophet's action at Matawhero was a settling of scores for the stigma of imprisonment he endured at the hands of Biggs, McLean, and the loyalist leaders. Likewise, Ropata—who aided in the massacre of "some hundred or more prisoners" after the militia caught up with Te Kooti at Ngatapa—was also seeking redress; he had been enslaved by Te Kooti's tribe when he was a boy.[15] The killing of prisoners at Ngatapa was encouraged by acting Native Secretary J. C. Richmond and the Pakeha officers, who placed a bounty of five pounds on the head of each enemy soldier.[16]

Slavery, the ultimate blow to one's *mana*, cried out for retribution. The animosity between *kupapa* and dissidents predated the Land Wars. Still, Te Kooti's campaign may be regarded as a continuation of Wiremu Kingi's defense of a "place to stand" on an island broken by contention between *tangata whenua* and Pakeha settlers. It also reignited the civil war that began after Kereopa and Patara carried their gospel to the East Coast.

Te Kooti's massacre of settlers sent waves of shock and fury over the North Island. J. C. Richmond, who had just sanctioned the execution of over a hundred Ringatu partisans, railed against the "cannibal" prophet. Members of the National Assembly compared the killings at Matawhero to the Sepoy Rebellion in India and placed a bounty of one-thousand pounds on Te Kooti's head. Biggs's decision to imprison Te Kooti without trial and to pursue him after his escape from the Chathams were the retrospective subject of parliamentary debate. Even after the prophet's penitent narrative of his visions at Wharekauri was found in a hut after the Ngatapa battle in January 1869, he remained in the eyes of the Pakeha a Hauhau murderer of women and children. Little did the outraged colony foresee in the aftermath of the most notorious event in New Zealand history that the man they hounded through the Urewera forest would escape beyond the King Country *aukati* in May 1872 with his wife and seven survivors, and not only be granted asylum by his opponent, King Tawhiao, but receive a government pardon

15. Ibid., p. 22.
16. Gascoyne, *Soldiering in New Zealand*, p. 75.

ten years later. Te Kooti's reputation as a guerrilla leader may have been exaggerated; he scarcely won an engagement and his Tuhoe adherents deserted him after the militia burned their crops and villages, but he eluded his pursuers in a manner that the Ringatu faithful regard as miraculous.

The divisions he sowed among East Coast Maori continues to this day; in this he fulfilled the omen of discord at his birth. Yet no other Maori leader has captured the imagination like Te Kooti. His figure has become larger than life—one is tempted to say, even sacred—perhaps because his life conformed to mythic paradigms of the prophet and hero in Israelite tradition and Maori story. The Ringatu church has attempted to tame Te Kooti by safeguarding his reputation as a seer, healer, and founder and remaining silent about his brutality. During the last two decades of his life, Te Kooti lived in exile, building a church and embracing peace, teaching his people to live in expectation of the end of exile. Their expectation lives on in the late twentieth century.

19

RAUPATU:
LAND CONFISCATION

The most important element in Government strategy during the campaigns of the 1860s was the consolidation of military gains by establishing permanent military settlement. In July 1863 the Damett Ministry speculators . . . had already devised a scheme for military settlement on lands to be confiscated from "rebellious" tribes.

Evelyn Stokes

The 1985 *Dictionary of the Maori Language* is the latest edition of the dictionary originally compiled by Reverend William Williams (brother of Henry Williams, the peacemaker) in 1844. William Williams established the CMS Mission at Poverty Bay in 1839, and his son, William Leonard Williams, was one of the first to hear of the massacre at Matawhero. Both Bishop Williams and his son were gifted diarists. The father's writings were selectively compiled in *The Turanga Journals*, and the son's account of events during the turbulent war years were sensitively rendered in the *East Coast Historical Records*. The current Maori dictionary, edited by their descendent Herbert Williams, defines the word *raupatu* as "conquest." However, the dictionary is biased against usage that prevailed as a result of European settlement; on the East Coast in 1866 *raupatu* referred to land confiscation. As is usually the case, the Maori wordmasters intuitively touched an ultimate reality: *patu* is the word for "kill." The essential

factor in the establishing of a British commonwealth in New Zealand
was the transfer of control over the land from the chiefs to the Crown
and finally to the entrepreneurs and holders of land in fee simple. In
taking the land the Pakeha "killed" the old way, *te ao tawhito*.

Death can be symbolic as well as physical, as when Wiremu Tamihana said to William Naylor, "My father's words have killed me." His
words referred to a death of one's spirit and the loss of one's *mana*. The
identity of chief and land are symbolically intertwined, as the revered
Tuhoe leader, Te Purewa, reveals:

> In the valley of Owhakatoro there is a hill called Te Taumato-o-Te
> Purewa; below this hill is a grove of trees named after his wife,
> Hinekura. The stream Ruangarara close by was named after Te
> Purewa's tutu (a tree used for spearing birds), for at the root of the
> tree was a hollow occupied by a lizard. . . . At Waiohau there is
> "Te putaewa a Te Purewa" (Te Purewa's potato heap), indicating
> that the people there lived under his authority and protection and
> anyone attacking them would answer their lives. His village, Ar-
> opaki, is at Ohaua-te-rangi. The site of the pa, Whakaari, which
> he built during the wars against Ngati Kahungunu, is at Waikare-
> moana. Another landmark at Waikaremoana is called "Nga hina o
> Te Purewa" (Te Purewa's white hair), so named to acknowledge
> him in his later years.[1]

Geography and history are fused in *whakapapa*; place and event
amplify each other. Without place, history, which affixed itself to place,
was lost; only on the *marae* where the orators recited *whakapapa* could
place be recalled, remembered, evoked, and preserved after the land
had been taken by others. The Maori took the central feature of their
religion—sacred place—into their "diaspora" throughout the new
towns and cities of a Pakeha-dominated world and continued to recite
their history even after the land was lost.[2] Unless we can understand
the fundamental, ultimate concern for land in Maori society we cannot
understand how Tamati Ngapora, brother to King Potatau and adviser

1. Sidney Melbourne, *DNZB*, p. 486. Waikaremoana is a lake in the Urewera mountains, a
prominent feature of Tuhoe ancestral territory between Whakatane (Bay of Plenty) and Turanga (Poverty Bay).

2. The symbolic substitution of the *marae*/meeting house for ancestral territory has intensified
the value of the *marae* as a sacred place in modern New Zealand; see Walker, "Marae" and "Mana
and the Crown: A Marae at Orokei," in I. H. Kawharu, ed., *Maori and Pakeha Perspectives of the
Treaty of Waitangi*, pp. 223–24.

to King Tawhiao, could say at the conclusion of the Land Wars in 1872,
"If the blood of our people only had been spilled, and the land remained, then this trouble would have been over long ago."[3]

Maori and European differ significantly in their regard for place.
Writing of eighteenth-century England, novelist John Fowles illustrated
the British attitude toward undomesticated space: "The period had no
sympathy with unregulated or primordial nature. It was aggressive wilderness, an ugly and all-invasive reminder of the Fall, of man's eternal
exile from the Garden of Eden. . . . Even its natural sciences, remained
essentially hostile to wild nature, seeing it only as something to be
tamed, classified, utilised, exploited."[4]

James Busby would agree. The Garden of Eden would be found
again only at the end of history. Anglican missionaries attempted to
hasten the Millennium by establishing their little edens in this wilderness at the end of the earth in a symbolic enactment of their Christian
expectation of God's kingdom. As did Richard Taylor earlier, Reverend
William Williams tried mightily to bind the aboriginal people to the
Word of God and struggled to separate them from the secular pursuits
of commerce, trade, cash, and rum. He was banished from his eden by
the Hauhau who burned his East Coast mission at Waerenga-a-hika in
1865.

The rivalries between land sellers and land holders, between Pai
Marire and Christian converts in Poverty Bay, turned a rich alluvial
plain into a field of suspicion and war. The troubles began in the early
fifties when then land commissioner Donald McLean visited "beautiful
Turanga" and described Te Kooti's ancestral land of Te Arai:

> The land is rich and fertile and is intersected by three rivers,
> which strike their serpentine courses through handsome clumps
> of kahikatea and puriri forests and beside numerous wheat culti-
> vations and groves of peach and other varieties of English fruit
> trees.
>
> We reached the first settlement on the banks of the Arai River
> about sunset, when the natives were returning from reaping their
> fields, some leading horses and others driving cattle and pet pigs
> before them. They gave us the usual welcome and presented us
> with fruit and also with honey just taken from a hive.
>
> The fat cattle, the large wheat stalks of last year's growth, fine

---

3. Asher and Naulls, *Maori Land*, p. 28.
4. Quoted in James Gleick, *Chaos: Making a New Science*, p. 117.

alluvial soil and contented appearance of the natives made an impression that this was certainly anything but a land of destitution and want. Nor was this impression deranged by what I subsequently saw of the beautiful Turanga Valley, which contains about 40,000 acres of splendid land covered with rich grasses and well supplied with wood and water.[5]

Although McLean had been sent to Napier to buy as much land for the Crown as he could in Hawke's Bay, he "could not resist the temptation to put out "feelers" about buying land for a township among the Turanga chiefs, including Raharuhi, whom he came to regard as an adversary.[6] Paratene Turangi, who later conspired to send Te Kooti to the Chathams, was a land selling chief and spoke in favor of McLean's idea. As early as this visit in February 1851, the divisions between members of Te Kooti's tribe were set up, as they had been in Taranaki among the Ngati Awa, because the Crown saw, coveted, and schemed to purchase Maori land.

During the "disturbances" of the 1860s, the first military settlers under Lieutenant James Wilson (later killed at Matawhero) arrived after Hirini Te Kani, a loyalist chief, requested protection from McLean for his "comparatively few supporters" in Poverty Bay.[7] By 1869 Maori farmers had retreated to fortified *pa* near military encampments, and by 1871 the fertile Turanga plain was occupied by trader George Read's cattle and sheep.[8] According to Auckland's newspaper, "After Te Kooti's banishment to the Chatham Islands Capt. Reid [*sic*] fenced in about 30 acres of Te Kooti's land as a grazing paddock, *and it is probable that this circumstance itself had no small share in exciting revengeful feelings in the mind of Te Kooti.*"[9] By 1867 a thousand acres had been purchased for the township of Gisborne and in 1870 the first sections were sold off to Europeans.[10] By the time Te Kooti escaped from prison, military settlers had begun to occupy confiscated land to the south of Turanga at Wairoa.[11] *As a result of a compromise between the friendly chiefs and McLean in early 1868, the government took possession of the major part of the district's land, with the understanding*

5. Mackay, *Historic Poverty Bay*, p. 177 n. 774, p. 326.
6. Ibid., p. 178.
7. Williams, *East Coast Historical Records*, p. 44.
8. Porter, *Turanga Journals*, p. 603.
9. *Daily Southern Cross*, November 16, 1868, emphasis mine.
10. Williams, *East Coast Historical Records*, p. 75.
11. Ibid., p. 59, 75.

that it would later affix the boundaries between the land confiscated from ascertained rebels and the land which belonged to the friendlies. Thus did the government obtain the bulk of the land in the region, paying monetary compensation after the wars to land sellers only after a great hue and cry was raised by those who found fault with how the government had disposed of the land[12] According to William L. Williams,

> Up to the time of the disturbance very little of the land in Poverty Bay had been parted with by the natives and it had been a matter of some difficulty to induce them to give any Pakeha a lease, though there were indications in 1865 of a likelihood of this reluctance being overcome. Some of the confiscated land about Patutahi was awarded to the friendly natives who had assisted the Government in the military operations on this coast, but a compensation in money was afterwards substituted for the land, which was then made available for settlement.[13]

From 1851 to 1868 McLean had been in charge of divesting the Maori of their land in order to settle the East Coast with Europeans, and he had characteristically taken advantage of every opportunity— including the hostile Pai Marire incursions of Patara and Kereopa—to further this overarching goal. In 1865 a Pai Marire faction in Poverty Bay made threats against the settlers, who took refuge in the town of Turanganui. Some Pai Marire followers proceeded to plunder their deserted farms, unchallenged by Christian chiefs, who merely stood aside. Raharuhi, McLean's old opponent, apologized for the destruction and offered to pay whatever monetary compensation could be assessed. Wilson passed his message on to Superintendent McLean, in Napier.

The following month McLean arrived in Turanganui with a strong military show of force and on *November 10, 1865,* responded to Raharuhi's offer with the following terms: (1) that the perpetrators be surrendered to the authorities, (2) that Pai Marire be renounced and that its adherents take the government's oath of allegiance, (3) *that the Hauhau sympathizers should pay a penalty in land,* and (4) that they should give up their arms.

He received no reply from the Pai Marire contingent and subsequently ordered his troops to William Williams's mission station near

---

12. Ibid., p. 69; Mackay, *Historic Poverty Bay*, pp. 305ff.
13. Williams, *East Coast Historical Records*, p. 75.

the *pa* of Waerenga-a-hika on November 17, where from the bishop's house, they opened fire on the Hauhau in the *pa*, most of whom were members of Te Kooti's Rongowhakaata tribe.[14] Te Kooti accompanied Lieutenant Ogilvie Ross, a Pakeha friend whose in-laws leased property from Te Kooti's family,[15] to this battle with government troops, and it was here that his enemies falsely charged him with communicating with the enemy.

After the *pa* was taken, the prisoners were eventually sent to the Chatham Islands, where, two years, later they became the first members of the Ringatu movement. *And three years to the day* after McLean first threatened to confiscate their land, on *November 10, 1868*, Te Kooti led them on the "brilliant raid"[16] on Matawhero, which established his reputation as a scourge as well as a prophet. Was this only a chance coincidence of dates; or, far more likely, was it what psychoanalysts call an "anniversary reaction?"

The battle of Waerenga-a-hika ended open resistance on the East Coast, but Poverty Bay remained in a state of unease. Captain Reginald Biggs became the Resident Magistrate at Turanganui during this battle, and *it was he who eventually occupied Te Kooti's own lands at Matawhero after the prisoners were sent away.*[17]

After the Hauhau were defeated, the settlers returned to their homes, and a company of Rangers was stationed on the Te Arai River. In order to pacify the region and reverse the conversions to Te Ua's millennial religion, Sir George Grey arrived in Poverty Bay with Te Ua himself, "whom he had been taking to various places to let the people see that in spite of his fame as a prophet there was nothing awe-inspiring about him, but that on the contrary he had the appearance of an imbecile."[18] This same year Te Ua died, but his followers did not return to the Anglican fold. Anaru Matete, a dissident chief, promulgated a message from King Tawhiao urging people not to be disheartened, but instead to escape from "the Pakeha inundation" to the "high ground" of the Kingite cause.[19] They had reason to seek shelter under the um-

14. Ibid., pp. 45–47.

15. Fowler, "A New Look at Te Kooti," p. 19.

16. Belich, *The New Zealand Wars*, p. 226.

17. According to Binney, *DNZB*, p. 29, Biggs had also previously executed a "protege" of Raharuhi, an act which led to a "compact" between the Hauhau leader and Te Kooti, whereby in exchange for a weapon of wondrous power, Te Kooti killed Biggs at Matawhero.

18. Williams, *East Coast Historical Records*, p. 50.

19. Ibid., p. 51.

brella of the king, for the distant thunder of *raupatu*, like the sound of the demonic goddess, Whaitiri, was heard in the east.[20]

The imprisonment of Pai Marire dissidents in the Chathams was strategically linked to McLean's scheme to dispossess the Maori of their lands, in order to rid the new society of what Henry Sewell termed "the principle of communism" among the natives.[21] McLean's threat to punish rebels by taking their land was carried out after Parliament passed the East Coast Land Titles Investigation Act of 1866, a confiscation law that applied to people "who had been engaged in the rebellion" from East Cape in the north to Wairoa in the south.[22] At the same time, in March 1866, that Governor Grey was parading Te Ua before the population of Turanga, McLean was informing "friendly chiefs" of the government's decision *"that the prisoners should be deported to Chatham Island for a period which might not be much more than twelve months, during which arrangements might be made for the confiscation of such land as the Government should decide to take."*[23] Initially, ninety Hauhau men, women, and children were sent to prison with Te Kooti and in all about 300 from the Bay of Plenty were deported. Their twelve-month sentence became an indeterminate sentence, while their land was transformed into the new Pakeha settlement at Gisborne.

According to Judith Binney, Magistrate Biggs's "correspondence demonstrates that he expected to benefit personally from the Poverty Bay confiscation."[24] Biggs was sent north as a government representative into Ngati Porou territory to inquire into the boundaries of the lands recommended for confiscation by their friendly chiefs. He proceeded to anger his allies by demanding more land than they offered, creating a stalemate in the implementation of the policy until after his death. Likewise, in the south among the Wairoa friendlies, J. C. Richmond presided over a fractious debate concerning confiscation of land, and at least one loyal ally died shortly after excessive public pressure was applied to force him to give up his holdings.[25] All those who ob-

---

20. Whaitiri guarded the boundaries between the sacred and the ordinary world with her power to punish *tapu* transgressors with illness, death, and misfortune. Among the East Coast tribes she was symbolized by thunder from the east.

21. Asher and Naulls, *Maori Land*, p. 27.

22. Williams, *East Coast Historical Records*, p. 53. This area included all of Bishop Williams's Waiapu Diocese, where after the Hauhau evangelization, Maori Christians became a minority.

23. Ibid., p. 51.

24. Binney, *DNZB*, p. 29.

25. Williams, *East Coast Historical Records*, pp. 54–55.

jected to the government's policies were accused of siding with the enemy. The visible hand of the state confiscated the land of loyalists as well as dissidents.

It is noteworthy that the numerous legislative acts regarding the disposition of land, beginning in the 1860s, all served one interest: the conversion of customary title to individual title, after the model of the Norman Conquest and the amalgamation of the Saxon English into King William's new kingdom.[26] The replication of the Conquest paradigm is part of the Pakeha myth, as was Marsden's reference to the thousand-year-old British kingdom, and Thomas Buddle's use of the feudal analogy to dispute the natives' "manorial rights" asserted under the so-called land league. The process of amalgamation included the substitution of the conqueror's myth for that of the conquered, and the British have consistently viewed Maori history through the ethnocentric lens of their own history and experience. Pakeha paternalism included the use of the Conquest metaphor to justify and rationalize their detribalization policies. Norman Smith, a twentieth-century researcher in the Native Department, likened the 1873 Native Land Act in New Zealand to the "Domesday Book," which recorded the names of all land holders in Norman-occupied England. The Native Land Act "introduced to the Natives, a principle of ownership, theretofore unknown to them"—the "certificate of title." "The intention of this Act was to establish a system by which the Natives should be enabled . . . to have their surplus land identified and surveyed. . . . with a view to assuring to the Natives, sufficient land for their support and maintenance."[27]

Smith's words in his "objective" government document, dated 1942, reflected the bias of the Pakeha myth in land law and policy. The notions of "enabling" the Maori [paternalism], of "surplus" land [an industrial-age concept], surveying [the impetus for repeated resistance from Waitara to Pakihara], and "sufficient land" for the support of the indigenous people [a European measure applied inappropriately to a foraging people] were all extremely culture-bound, as were the commonplace characterizations of Maori society as communistic and of the King Movement as an attempt of Maori "lords" to assert their "feudal rights."

In the Chatham Islands the Hauhau prisoners were subjected to substandard treatment and accommodations.[28] In March 1867, Major J. T.

26. Norman Smith, *Native Custom and Law Affecting Native Land*, pp. 9–10, 14.
27. Ibid., p. 14.
28. Greenwood, *The Upraised Hand*, p. 22. See also the cautious account of Native Minister

Edwards of the New Zealand Militia was commissioned by the government to investigate conditions at the Wharekauri prison. His report of May 1867 indicates that a drunken guard had fired at and wounded a prisoner and that the prison doctor requested additional medicines and additional pay. The inmates reminded him of the government's promise to release them after one year, and he recommended that five be released soon, in order that the remainder would be encouraged in their good behavior.[29] A subsequent inspection by the Native Minister, W. Rolleston, and Gilbert Mair in February 1868 revealed that the doctor may have been mistreating some of the women.[30] The intent of government to keep the prisoners at Wharekauri while they confiscated land at Poverty Bay from loyalists as well as hostiles was baldly stated in the following letter of Captain Biggs to Superintendent McLean only one month before their escape:

> I have the honour to inform you that I am of the opinion that it would not be advisable to allow any of the Chatham Islands prisoners to return to Poverty Bay until the land question is settled in that district. The difficulties at present to be contended against are so great, from the combination of the loyal and rebel Natives of Poverty Bay to obstruct the fair carrying out of "The East Coast Land Titles Investigation Act, 1866," by concealing all particulars relating to the titles to land, that I fear, by allowing a portion of the prisoners to return, it might add to the perplexity of the case.[31]

The morale and condition of the prisoners, who had appealed to Major Edwards over a year earlier to be released, declined even further, and this state of affairs furnished the context within which Te Kooti fell deathly ill, received the command of Jehovah's angel to save his people, and organized the Hauhau mob into a disciplined cadre of survivors with a coherent and united purpose—to escape and return to their homeland. In the light of all the scheming to obtain Maori land at Turanga, it would not be difficult to argue that Te Kooti intended to

Rolleston's 1868 assessment of the Chatham Islands soldiers of the guard as a "public nuisance" in William Downie Stewart's biography, *William Rolleston*, p. 71.

29. *AJHR*, 1868, A-No. 15E, pp. 16–17.
30. Mackay, *Historic Poverty Bay*, p. 230.
31. *AJHR*, 1868, p. 19.

confront "Pharaoh" McLean and his allies even before he was harassed
and pursued by Biggs. Certainly, the news of the prisoners' landing
mobilized Biggs and the local *kupapa*, both of whom had ample reason
to fear the exiles whose land they had expropriated.

They also had reason to fear the leadership of the reckless "troublemaker" who was known as an admirer of King David.[32] Te Kooti's
Chatham Islands notebook records a controversial *kupu* that indicated
his proclivity for the wrath of Jehovah: *u tonu taku riri ki nga iwi nana
i whakamate toku iwi ka whakamate ahau i nga matua a tae noa ki
nga tamariki e kore e takina e ahau taku akeake,* which was hastily
rendered by the notebook's first translator as, "My wrath will alway [*sic*]
abide on those who oppress my people, I will punish the parents and
the children, it will not be removed for ever and ever."[33] Who this first
translator was has not been determined by scholars,[34] but J. C. Richmond, who was present at the site where the notebook was found and
who admitted to having received it, quoted this same *kupu* from memory during a debate about Captain Biggs in the House of Representatives on June 18, 1869, as evidence that there was "mischief in the
mind of the man" [Te Kooti] even before he escaped from prison.

> I will quote from memory a literal translation of one passage from
> it [Kooti's journal]: "My wrath against the tribe which has de-
> stroyed my tribe is unchangeable; I will destroy them, from the
> parents unto the children; I will not cease forever." That passage
> shows a spirit not altogether of a peaceable character, and I think
> that viewed in the light of subsequent events it shows that there
> was mischief in the mind of the man.[35]

The words loosely translated by Richmond[36] exemplify the wrath of
the God of Exodus. The Matawhero massacre sent a shudder throughout New Zealand at a time that everyone believed the wars had ceased
with the defeat of the Hauhau. The words of the *kupu* were uttered by

32. Mackay, *Historic Poverty Bay*, p. 299.

33. Davies, "Copy of Te Kooti's Notebook."

34. In "Te Kooti's Chatham Islands Notebook: The History of a Religious Document" (unpublished paper, 1990), I hypothesized that the earliest English translation of the visions narrative was
probably written down by J. C. Richmond. The paper's assessor, Judith Binney, disagreed at the time,
but later incorporated my thesis in her book, *Redemption Songs*, pp. 529–30.

35. *NZPD* 5 (18 June 1869): 198–99.

36. This *kupu* is a statement of Jehovah's intent to redress the balance [*utu*] between Maori and
Pakeha, because the condition of imbalance has brought misfortune upon Te Kooti's people. Richmond altered the translation of *whakamate* from "punish" and "oppress" to "destroy."

Jehovah through his "mouthpiece," Te Kooti. His "curious little book"[37] left behind in battle and delivered to Richmond was not a manual for war, but the founding document of the Ringatu movement. In attempting to defend the policies of his Native Ministry on the East Coast before Parliament, Richmond used this *kupu* cynically to absolve Biggs of any blame in his treatment of Te Kooti and to present the prophet as a man who had lied to Biggs about wanting only to proceed peacefully toward the King Country.

In fact, the *kupu*, as well as the wrathful psalm Te Kooti recited as he oversaw the execution of Maraea Morete's husband, did not indicate a premeditated plan of revenge, but constituted the Word of God in judgment on the confiscation policies of the government. A prophet is vessel of God, and the God of *nga morehu* was the warrior God of Moses, Joshua, and David.

Thus, there is ample evidence to support the case that the Hauhau were attacked, defeated, and imprisoned indefinitely by "Pharaoh" McLean[38] to facilitate a determined scheme to confiscate East Coast land for the purpose of commercial development, grazing, the creation of the European town of Gisborne, and the settlement of military veterans. All of this was part and parcel of the land legislation that was modeled after the Norman Conquest of 1066. The secular, British, parliamentary monarchy was as much motivated by its own myth-history as any tribal people it dispossessed during its centuries of imperial expansion. And the notorious return of the prophet to visit Jehovah's wrath upon the takers of the land at Matawhero was not provoked by some atavistic Maori behavior, but by the very schemes enacted by McLean, beginning with his 1851 visit to Raharuhi and Paratene on the idyllic plain of Turanga.

---

37. Richmond, *NZPD* 5 (1869): 198.

38. According to Stewart, *William Rolleston*, p. 71, the government wanted to grant an amnesty to most of the prisoners in 1868, but "Sir Donald McLean advised caution."

20

UREWERA, PEOPLE
AND FOREST

*The forests of Whirinaki are a natural
museum of a forest people.*

Native Forests Action Council

Museums are for dead people.

Tuhoe response

TUHOE SUPPORT FOR TE KOOTI

Te Kooti and Rua Kenana were connected by more than Rua's fulfillment of Te Kooti's prophecy that a Ringatu messiah would arise after his death. Rua's father had died before his birth in one of the skirmishes between New Zealand troops and the Ringatu rebels[1] in the Urewera bush, a virgin, temperate-zone rainforest between Gisborne and Whakatane on the East Coast of the North Island, where Te Kooti retreated after his lightning raids on the East Coast settlements.

In September 1868, a few months before Te Kooti's attack on Matawhero, Donald McLean called for a vote of no confidence in Prime Minister Stafford's government, squaring off against the weary execu-

1. Webster, *Rua and the Maori Millennium*, p. 155.

tive and bequeathing for posterity a lively interchange of words.
McLean asserted that a new Maori prophet had arisen just after the
government had thought it had put the "Maori question" to permanent
rest, and that he threatened to unite the "friendlies" whom McLean
had wooed with weapons and words against the Hauhau fever for the
past two years. Stafford, McLean charged, was asleep at the helm, having presided over a reduction of the guard at the Chatham Islands
prison at the moment when Te Kooti had mobilized the demoralized
inmates. Now Stafford had thrown East Coast settlers into a "panic" by
withdrawing Major Fraser's thin force of fifty-seven troops, while Te
Kooti, having beaten back his pursuers, threatened to convert the
Tuhoe tribe to his religion of vengeance.[2] McLean's claim that only he
had anticipated Maori moves throughout the Land Wars was not an
empty boast; he was the canniest student of Maori ways among the
settler politicians. Concerning Te Kooti's stunning escape, he posed the
question:

> Sir, what has been the consequence? Why, the landing on our
> shores of 160 men who had got the idea in their minds that they
> could defy us . . . in the vicinity of those mountain tribes, the
> Ureweras, who fought so bravely at Orakau, and who used those
> memorable words *"Ake, ake"*—that they never would give up,
> never yield till death. These bold mountain tribes are the very
> tribes to whom those prisoners are now looking for protection and
> shelter, and whom they wish to unite with them to carry out their
> intentions of seeking revenge for losses sustained. Why, Sir, those
> prisoners are there, making friends, spreading doubts among nu-
> merous other tribes besides the Ureweras, writing letters recount-
> ing their victories, extolling their deities for having brought them
> here in safety and granted them a series of successes. Among an
> excitable race they are propagating these ideas.[3]

Stafford's reply cited the limitations of government and the disunity
of New Zealand settlers, testifying to the struggle of the settlers to
establish their own nationality:

> We do not place so high an ideal standard before us, or arrogate
> to ourselves the power to determine when war shall cease in New

2. *NZPD* 3 (1868): 374–78.
3. Ibid., p. 375.

Zealand. We do not believe we can at once absolutely change by a rapid convulsion the minds of generations of semi-savages, nor profess to ensure that respect for law and order shall at once reign in a people some of whom have only within the last few years given over eating their own relations in order to murder and eat Europeans. . . .[4]

It is no particular pleasure to be called upon to do what is well nigh an impossibility, namely, to act as if there were a united New Zealand, when it really does not exist: when, instead of a country having a national life, national impulses, national duties, and national sympathies, we have a congeries of discontented centres, all but hating each other in some cases, jealously suspicious in all . . . I shall be delighted if others can, more effectually than my colleagues and myself, establish that nationality which has hitherto not existed.[5]

Despite McLean's attack on him in Parliament, Stafford's retirement was barely postponed when he squeaked through the test of confidence by one vote.[6] However, McLean's predictions were confirmed in Te Kooti's November raids. Rua Kenana's father, a member of Te Kooti's band, died in the government's counterattack at Ngatapa Pa. Peter Webster surmises that Rua, born a few months later, was likely to have "shared in many of the humiliations and uncertainties of the Tuhoe following the Land Wars."[7]

The Tuhoe humiliations began in what James Belich recognized as Te Kooti's feckless inability to win battles, despite his astonishing capacity to evade capture and his enduring legacy of a revitalized hope for deliverance from Pakeha hegemony. According to Belich, the difference between Te Kooti, the prophet, and Titokowaru, the West Coast Hauhau guerrilla, was that Te Kooti "made his own rules" of religion and "therefore could not break them," while "the rules of Titokowaru's religion were external to him."[8] In fact, Titokowaru was not even constrained by external rules, but simply changed his religion to accommodate his military aims.

Te Kooti's inspired leadership revived two ancient roles, that of the *matakite*, as well as that of the *tapu* chief. From a captured prisoner

4. Ibid., p. 381.
5. Ibid., p. 383.
6. Ward, *A Show of Justice*, p. 210.
7. Webster, *Rua and the Maori Millennium*, p. 155.
8. Belich, *The New Zealand Wars*, p. 288.

the military learned that Te Kooti used religious rules to regulate the behavior of his followers in the Urewera wilderness.[9] Not only did they hold services four times a day, but if Jehovah spoke to the prophet in a dream, he awakened his band and sent them out hunting for food, women, or men; and if the party returned empty-handed, its leader was confined to a dwelling without food or fire for several days. Te Kooti's *whare* (dwelling) was treated as a *tapu* area: one could not approach it without his permission. God also spoke to the prophet in traditional signs (*tohu*) of the old religion, thunder and rainbows. The Tuhoe associated thunder from the east and north (the directions of the sea) with the demonic goddess of boundaries, Whaitiri. However much Te Kooti had assimilated to a Pakeha style of living and working, he reinstated the two cornerstones of Maori religion: *mana* and *tapu*.

The Tuhoe people suffered from their decision to support the Ringatu prophet. Their cultivations were laid waste by *kupapa* raiding parties led by Pakeha officers, and starvation, an ever-present danger in the fecund but food-scarce forest, ensued. After losing warriors at Ngatapa, Te Kooti sought recruits among the Tuhoe. Fearful that Te Kooti would reassemble a fighting force in the North Island's most inaccessible area, Colonel Whitmore conceived a plan to attack the Urewera heartland from four sides: "No less than four columns were to march in this expedition, and each from a different point; three of them were, if possible, to rendezvous at Ruatahuna . . . and annihilate all opposition."[10] Two columns managed to converge at Ruatahuna on the same day, but their progress was hindered by the Tuhoe, who attacked from the bush and retreated into it, while Whitmore destroyed "all the food that might be growing or stored at the several native settlements."[11] Although the loyalists lost almost twice as many men,[12] the Tuhoe "were finally starved into 'submission' to the Government in 1872,"[13] the year the Land Wars ended. In contrast to the Bay of Plenty region, the rugged Urewera terrain was considered "worthless"[14] and not worth confiscating.[15] Survey crews did not invade Tuhoe country

    9. Cowan, *The New Zealand Wars*, 2:283–84.
    10. Gudgeon, *Reminiscences*, p. 270.
    11. Stokes, Milroy, and Melbourne, *Te Urewera*, p. 50.
    12. Gudgeon, *Reminiscences*, p. 209.
    13. Stokes, Milroy, and Melbourne, *Te Urewera*, p. 50.
    14. Ibid., p. 31.
    15. The confiscation of their lands at Opouriao pushed the Tuhoe back from more desirable coastal lands to Ruatoki, but did not affect their heartland, the Urewera mountains and forest; Stokes,

until 1895,[16] shortly before Rua Kenana's millennial movement rose up
to defend the *rohe potae*, "ancestral territory," of his people.[17]

POLITICAL *RAUPATU*

From 1894, when Prime Minister Seddon[18] and Native Minister James
Carroll (Timi Kara)[19] conducted meetings with Tuhoe elders, to 1908,
when Apirana Ngata[20] coauthored a report on Urewera lands, the Tuhoe
watched their world turn upside down. Despite their wholehearted distrust of government and canny understanding that surveying would un-
dermine the *mana* of their chiefs and herald the loss of their land, the
Tuhoe suffered a relentless political *raupatu*, proving that conquest
could proceed as well by legislative act as by military invasion. Just as
in the East Coast Wars *kupapa* troops provided the critical manpower
to quell the Hauhau "disturbance," so in the conquest of the Urewera,
James Carroll and Apirana Ngata played critical roles in the adjustment of the Maori people to a Pakeha-run state, at a time when the
decline in Maori population began to reverse itself, but the influx of
Pakeha inhabitants determined that the indigenous people would be a

---

Milroy, and Melbourne, *Te Urewera*, p. 48; Webster, *Rua and the Maori Millennium*, p. 93. Ngati Awa
and Whakatohea lands in the Bay of Plenty were taken under the New Zealand Settlements Act of
1863.

16. A survey dispute erupted in 1893 and was partially mediated by Te Kooti in the last year of
his life, but a serious dispute that caused the government to send troops to Ruatoki broke out and
threatened war in 1895. Between 1842 and 1855 the Tuhoe were tolerant and welcoming of strangers,
but the missionaries left the Ureweras in the latter year and did not return until 1917. No Pakeha
were allowed to travel in the tribal territory without permission of the chiefs until 1895.

17. The tribal territory of the Tuhoe was the object of special legislation in 1896. *Rohe potae* is
used here in a special sense to refer to the Tuhoe homeland. See Webster, *Rua and the Maori
Millennium*, p. 35.

18. Richard John Seddon headed the Liberal Government from 1892 to 1906, when he was
succeeded by J. G. Ward.

19. James Carroll was an influential Maori intellectual who played a critical role in politics at the
beginning of the twentieth century.

20. Together with Maui Pomare and James Carroll, Apirana Ngata completed the triumvirate of
highly educated and politically astute Maori statesmen who at the turn of the century, attempted to
mitigate the tide of land confiscations and sales through their sophisticated participation in the political process; see Walker, *Ka Whawhai Tonu Matou*, pp. 172–96. Ngata and Pomare graduated from Te
Aute College, a preparatory school founded by Bishop Williams. Another graduate was Peter Buck, Te
Rangi Hiroa, who later became curator of the Bishop Museum in Honolulu. These distinguished men
were the leaders of the Young Maori Party, and the one who wielded the greatest influence upon the
lives of his people was Sir Apirana Ngata of the Ngati Porou.

minority in New Zealand for years to come.[21] Although the phrase "adjustment cult" has been misapplied to the Maori renewal movements by scholars, the term "adjustment" aptly characterizes what the Maori politicians achieved for their people by participating in civil government.[22]

Peter Webster's *Rua and the Maori Millennium* chronicles the decline of Tuhoe *mana* over their land as the critical factor in the rise of the Ringatu messiah, Rua Kenana, who prophesied that King Edward VII would come to Gisborne in 1906 to ransom Tuhoe land from the Pakeha. Between 1892 and 1900, the years preceding Rua's claim to messiahship, Seddon's Liberal government alienated another three million acres[23] of the purported seven million remaining to the North Island people following the Land Wars—without firing a shot or engaging in a single battle—despite stubborn opposition from the Tuhoe.

THE UNASSIMILATED TUHOE

According to Elsdon Best, the Tuhoe numbered only about eight hundred at the turn of the century, but their reputation as a people inured to harsh living conditions and as formidable warriors, caused other tribes and the Pakeha officials to approach them with caution and a clear strategy in mind.[24] Other tribes characterized them in an aphorism, *Tuhoe moumou kai, moumou taonga, moumou tangata ki te po,* "Tuhoe, wasters of food, wasters of treasures [or heirlooms], consigners of people to the spirit world."[25]

The Tuhoe claimed descent from two peoples. The earlier group named Toi as their ancestor and intermarried with invaders who were descended from Toroa, the chief of the Mataatua canoe migration. The common ancestor of the tribe encountered by the Pakeha is Tuhoe

21. Today, the Maori constitute about 13 percent of New Zealand's population. New Zealand is also receiving an unprecedented influx of Polynesian immigrants from the Cook Islands and Western Samoa.

22. An excellent account of Ngata's shepherding of his Ngati Porou tribe during the rapacious years of the turn-of-the-century may be found in the story of Eruera Stirling, as told to Anne Salmond, in *Eruera*, pp. 139–59.

23. Webster, *Rua and the Maori Millennium*, p. 130.

24. During Whitmore's Urewera campaign in 1869, Te Arawa soldiers were reluctant to enter the Urewera fastness, and the government relied upon the Ngati Porou, neighbors and traditional enemies of the Tuhoe. The Te Arawa lived to the west of the mountains, while Ngati Parou inhabited the area between the Urewera and the eastern coastline north of Poverty Bay.

25. Translated somewhat differently by Best in Webster, *Rua and the Maori Millennium*, p. 82, and by Stokes, Milroy, and Melbourne, *Te Urewera*, p. 30.

Potiki.[26] According to tribal myth, *Te tini o toi,* "the people of Toi," sprang from the union of Hinepokuhurangi, the goddess of the mists, and the sacred mountain of Maungapohatu.[27] Their land was the great forest of Tane-mahuta, creator of the world of light. The Tuhoe have claimed the Urewera region by *ahi-ka-roa,*[28] "keeping the home fires burning," and by conquest for perhaps a thousand years. Their bond to their land is incomparably strong. Tuhoe writer, the late John Rangihau, compared mere *maoritanga,* "Maori-ness," with *tuhoetanga:*

> It seems to me there is no such thing as Maoritanga because Maoritanga is an all-inclusive term which embraces all Maoris. . . . Each tribe has its own history. And it's not a history that can be shared among others. How can I share with the history of Ngati Porou, of Te Arawa, of Waikato? Because I am not of those people. I am a Tuhoe person and all I can share in is Tuhoe history. . . . I have a faint suspicion that Maoritanga is a term coined by the Pakeha to bring the tribes together. Because if you cannot divide and rule, then for tribal people all you can do is unite them and rule. Because then they lose everything by losing their own tribal histories and traditions that give them their identity.[29]

Among the North Island people, the Tuhoe were set apart by a particular history, geographical barriers, and the fact that they were the last tribe to be subjected to the grand design of amalgamation. The earliest accounts of the Urewera region comment upon its romantic, aesthetic appeal, but one of Whitmore's officers summed up Pakeha disinterest in 1870 by pronouncing the land useless except perhaps for gold mining. By 1893 a taste for gold and the hope that it might be found in the more remote reaches of the North Island, led to severe pressure on the government to open up even the mountainous territory of the most isolationist tribe to prospecting and settlement.

OPENING UP THE *ROHE POTAE*

As Norman Smith reveals, land legislation was driven by the responsible government's policy of surveying the land, affixing the boundaries

26. Stokes, Milroy, and Melbourne, *Te Urewera,* pp. 12, 14.
27. Ibid., p. 12.
28. According to Maori custom, this is the strongest claim to land. Ibid., p. 15.
29. Rangihau, "Being Maori," pp. 232–33.

according to tribal land tenure, and converting the Maori tradition of usufruct to the European custom of individual title with the ultimate purpose of encouraging sale of land to Europeans for development of various kinds. This strategy afflicted the Tuhoe people between Prime Minister Seddon's visit in 1894 and the Report to the Minister of Lands and Native Affairs in 1921, which outlined the success of the Liberal government's land alienation scheme.

The Tuhoe anticipated the alienation of the Urewera region long before it came to pass. In 1866 the East Coast Land Titles Investigation Act, amended in 1867, prompted Captain Biggs's ill-fated journey to wheedle land from the Ngati Porou, who were enemies of the Tuhoe. This expedition resulted in the Poverty Bay confiscations carried out by Superintendent McLean while Te Kooti and his Hauhau confederates languished in prison. The town of Gisborne was founded, in part, upon trader George Read's shrewd acquisitions, which also gobbled up territory abandoned by the local tribes in the midst of civil war. In addition, the government "redistributed" 40,000 acres southeast of Lake Waikaremoana to "friendlies" and soldiers, providing the Tuhoe with a graphic example of settlement along their southern border.[30] Understandably alarmed, the Tuhoe chiefs met in 1872 to protect their *rohe potae* as one unit. Like the Ngati Ruanui in the 1850s, Tuhoe elders attempted to restrict land sales by electing a Council of Seventy to disallow any private applications to the Maori Land Court for survey, investigation of title, or alienation of lands, and also to control any local disturbance that could furnish the government with an excuse to cross their borders.

Tuhoe autonomy rested undisturbed until 1889 when the Native Minister directed a local official to arrange the opening up of the Urewera district for mineral prospecting and timber harvesting. A growing settler constituency pressured the government to acquire Maori lands by "extreme measures,"[31] if necessary, an echo of Gore Browne's famous ultimatum on the eve of the Land Wars: we will secure Maori territory "justly if possible; if not, then, by any means." In 1891 the *rohe potae* existed as an unbroken block of Tuhoe habitation, but in 1893, the government conspired with a minority of the Tuhoe to force a survey. The party was harassed by tribesmen, twenty-five people were arrested, and Te Kooti intervened to discourage more widespread vio-

---

30. Stokes, Milroy, and Melbourne, *Te Urewera*, p. 48.
31. Webster, *Rua and the Maori Millennium*, p. 126.

lence. Behind the agitation for this impenetrable district was gold fever, but the only rumor of treasure that survived the 1890s was Rua's prophecy in May 1906 that King Edward VII would bring a precious diamond to Gisborne to buy back Tuhoe land.

THE MEETING OF 1894

A sea change in the history of the Tuhoe occurred in 1894 when Premier Richard John Seddon, the Liberal Party's worthy successor to George Grey,[32] confronted the Tuhoe elders, after negotiating the first road through their country. He was accompanied by James Carroll, then one of the four Maori members of Parliament. They intended to inform the Tuhoe about the Native Land Purchase and Acquisition Act of 1893. Moreover, Seddon, by Order-in-Council, had just embarked upon the sale of 423,184 more acres of Maori territory between 1892 and 1900 in response to pressure from European settlers.[33] The 1894 Native Land Court Act, section 117, gave the Crown permission to incorporate Maori land into blocks, whose title could be investigated and converted to freehold—and subsequently partitioned and sold only to the government. This land was later sold to private purchasers.[34] Seddon sought to facilitate the conversion of all "idle" Maori land to private title that could be bought and sold for agriculture, development, or settlement. The Tuhoe were unfamiliar with paper power. They had not even signed the Treaty of Waitangi, nor were they experienced with adjudication in the postwar Land Court. *Wishing to avoid even the lengthy deliberations of the Land Court, Parliament and the governor circumvented its jurisdiction by passing "special legislation" that pertained only to the undeveloped Urewera mountains and forest.*

In March 1894 Seddon set off to contest the *mana* of the chiefs by presenting them with the stark reality of inevitable change. The Maori elders met at Ruatoki before he arrived to agree upon their own terms: no internal surveys to be conducted in the tribal territory, no gold prospecting, no land sales, no roads, no leasing of land.[35] Seddon

32. Keith Sinclair, *A History of New Zealand*, p. 177, notes the "passing of the Liberal torch" from Grey to Seddon, who consulted the aged statesman before accepting the premiership. Grey served as New Zealand premier from 1877 to 1879, some years after his last imperial governorship, 1861–68.

33. Webster, *Rua and the Maori Millennium*, p. 129.

34. Ibid., p. 130.

35. Expounded by *ariki* Numia Kereru at Ruatoki. Stokes, Milroy, and Melbourne, *Te Urewera*, p. 53.

scoffed that their opposition to surveys was "suicidal."[36] Paramount
chief Numia Kereru[37] then acceded to a survey of their external boundary only. Replied the government python to the Tuhoe mouse, we cannot "maintain you in the possession of [your] lands until we know
where those lands are situated."[38] At Te Whaiti on the eastern border of
the Urewera, Seddon warned, "Some advocate extreme measures . . .
because . . . you are taking up a negative position, and will not allow
the Government to do anything for you."[39] The "some" was a veiled
reference to Pakeha pressure on his administration. According to Peter
Webster, what the Pakeha hoped for "was that the Maori could form a
landless proletariat who could work for them, either in the countryside
or in the towns."[40] Although Seddon promised to protect their tribal
territory, he asserted that there should be one law for both peoples—
by which he meant no special status for Maori tribes. He impressed the
Tuhoe elders with the certainty that he would not tolerate any form of
Tuhoe self-government or autonomy.

The Maori had never enjoyed the same benefits as the Pakeha with
respect to land and commerce. The government advanced loans of up
to 13,000 pounds/year to Pakeha who purchased Maori land, but denied loans to Maori owners, whom they assumed were able to develop
their land without capital. Much of their land lay uncleared or unim-
proved for pasture or crops and was, therefore, subject to "acquisition"
because it was classified as "unproductive and idle."[41] In the late nineteenth century, the rural Maori were impoverished, suffered dispropor-
tionately from disease and inadequate health care, remained underedu-
cated and untrained in agricultural advances, and lacked the services
of a local bank.[42] Furthermore, they had lost access to even their most
basic traditional structures of organization, owing to conquest, wars,
and land legislation. In a word, the amalgamated tribes outside the
Urewera country lived in a state of economic and social depression,

36. Ibid.
37. Kereru later became one of Rua's opponents, charging that "collecting money is the ultimate
end of all his works"; letter to James Carroll, Native Minister, 13 December 1907, NANZ, Wellington.
38. Stokes, Milroy, and Melbourne, *Te Urewera*, p. 53.
39. Webster, *Rua and the Maori Millennium*, p. 126.
40. Ibid., p. 141.
41. Maori spending patterns often prevented the accumulation of capital, since most of their cash
went to basic necessities and the rest, in accord with a tradition of reciprocity, was sometimes spent
on relatives, friends, and good times; "They simply had a different attitude towards the use of money
from the Pakeha" (Webster, *Rua and the Maori Millennium*, pp. 138–41).
42. Ibid.

and the Tuhoe were aware of the manner in which the government had treated them.

During the time he worked in the government store at Ruatoki, Elsdon Best observed that the residents were "much lacking in energy," that they "seem to give no thought to helping themselves," that they had no latrines, and the areas surrounding their habitations was covered with human excrement.[43] Their situation was not much different from that encountered by Maori ethnologist, Peter Buck, when he visited the Ngati Ruanui some years later and found that "our ancestors had abandoned [latrines] when they left the hilltops for the flat land after European contact."[44] However, while Best regarded the situation as hopeless, Buck recited the myth of the origin of the latrine to remind the elders that it was an ancient Maori institution, not a foreign innovation, and they then readily adopted the latrines that local officials were attempting to introduce.

The absence of latrines was a significant marker of cultural decline. From time immemorial the village latrine had been a sacred place where rituals for the removal of *tapu* were performed to placate the goddess Whaitiri. Loss of these practices signified a degree of dissociation from Maori traditions that was truly alarming. By 1900 the tribes exhibited many of the socioeconomic and psychological indicators of *anomie*. In addition, they had broken with their past so completely that they had lost many of the symbolic charts and compasses of their universe, a condition I have referred to as *aporia*.

Elsdon Best was driven with curiosity about what he regarded as the ancient, pristine and disappearing "ways" of the Tuhoe. His respected mentor and informant was an elderly *tohunga*, named Tutakangahau, who spoke at the funeral of a girl who died of influenza in 1897:

> This rapid dying of our people is a new thing. In former times our people did not die so—they knew no disease; they died on the battlefield or of old age . . . These diseases which slay our people are all from the Pakeha—it was the white men who brought them among us . . . I see before me O friends, the end of the Maori people. They will not survive. We can see plainly that our people are fast going from the earth. We have discarded our laws of *tapu*

43. Ibid., p. 147.
44. Sinclair, *History of New Zealand*, p. 195.

and trampled upon our *mana* Maori . . . The Maori is passing
away and the Pakeha steps into his place.[45]

Best was an exponent of romantic anthropology that revered the allegedly pure and unadulterated ancient culture of the primitive. He
was shocked when Tutakangahau became a follower of Rua Kenana,
the charismatic leader whom Best regarded as a charlatan. Yet it was
precisely the conviction that his world was ending that led the old
tohunga to a messianic movement that prophesied a time of peace and
the return of the land. Sixty years earlier at Waitangi, Te Kemara had
foretold the loss of *mana* that afflicted the Tuhoe at the end of the
nineteenth century:

> Health to thee, O Governor! . . . I am not pleased towards thee. I
> do not wish for thee. I will not consent to thy remaining here in
> this country. . . . No, no, no; I shall never say "Yes" to your
> staying. Were all to be on an equality, then, perhaps, Te Kemara
> would say, "Yes;" but for the Governor to be up and Te Kemara
> down—Governor, high up, up, up, and Te Kemara down, low,
> small, a worm, a crawler—No, no, no. O Governor! . . . my land is
> gone, gone, all gone. The inheritances of my ancestors, fathers,
> relatives, all gone, stolen, gone with the missionaries. Yes, they
> have it all, all, all. That man there, the Busby, and that man
> there, the Williams, they have my land. The land on which we are
> now standing this day is mine . . . O Governor! I do not wish thee
> to stay. You English are not kind to us like other foreigners. You
> do not give us good things. I say, Go back, go back, Governor, we
> do not want thee here, in this country.[46]

Such was the mood of the Tuhoe elders in 1894 who were pressured
to accept the "special legislation" imposed upon them. Seddon reminded the elders that the Maori now numbered only 40,000, compared to over 600,000 Pakeha, and that the Tuhoe population had
dwindled to a mere 800.[47] The premier protested that he did not have a
"heart . . . of stone. I see a noble race, and see that they are fast
disappearing from the face of the earth."[48] He told them that their land
would be surveyed, but that they could form a council to advise the

45. Webster, *Rua and the Maori Millennium*, p. 146.
46. Colenso, *The Authentic and Genuine History*, pp. 17–18.
47. Webster, *Rua and the Maori Millennium*, pp. 82, 126, 142.
48. Ibid., p. 139.

government with respect to the administration of their lands, a crafty promise that hoped to placate Tuhoe hostility to the new laws.

Tuhoe fears were heightened in 1905 when the governor declared in his Speech from the Throne that "landless Natives . . . [would] be provided for as tenants, and that the surplus lands should be acquired . . . and the proceeds go to the Native owners."[49] Maori MPs attempted to soften the blows of increasingly harsh legislation. They objected to the unequal application of the Land for Settlements Act of 1894, complaining that "under the terms of the Act, a European settler was allowed to retain 650 acres of first class land and some 2,000 acres of second class land. However . . . the Europeans considered that if the . . . Act was applied to the Maori, 25 acres of first class land and 100 acres of second class land should suffice for each."[50] Since Maori title was usually claimed by communal or familial groups and Pakeha title by single owners, the profits of sale would benefit each individual unequally. Moreover, Pakeha land generally sold at higher prices than Maori parcels.[51] The Maori MPs recommended in a petition to Seddon in 1905 that the government assist Maori farmers, but limit the conditions under which Maori owners could sell a portion of their land in order to raise capital to improve the rest of it.[52] It was this latter provision that Rua Kenana later seized upon and exploited in his personal scheme to save the Tuhoe heartland.

THE BATTLE OVER TUHOE LAND

The confrontation between John Seddon and the Tuhoe *rangatira* in 1894 marked the closing of one era and the opening of another. The *mana* of the traditional chiefs died at Ruatoki in 1894, even though the Queen's Writ was not extended to the Urewera until after the geological survey by Alexander McKay in 1895. His party met with violent opposition, and government troops were dispatched to quell the disturbances. The Urewera Native District Reserves Act of 1896 (UNDRA) established the procedure for converting aboriginal title to freehold. Tuhoe chief Numia Kereru ended any remaining hope for Tuhoe gov-

49. Ibid., p. 132.
50. Ibid., p. 134.
51. Ibid.
52. The petition also proposed that Maori be able to apply for loans under the same conditions as applied to Pakeha applicants under the Advances to Settlers Act of 1894. Webster, *Rua and the Maori Millennium*, pp. 134–35.

ernance over the *rohe potae* in 1899 when he joined the surveyor general, a Native Land Court Judge, two cooperative Maori members, and Elsdon Best on the UNDRA Commission. After three years of contentious hearings, the Commission converted the Urewera region to individual freehold title, the first step in the process of permanent alienation.[53] In 1895 while the surveyors broke the *rohe potae* into thirty-four blocks of potentially alienable land, the Tuhoe chiefs cooled their heels in Wellington waiting for Seddon to hear their petitions against partition, but they did not have the power or the political skill to fight the Pakeha for *mana o te whenua*. In the final analysis, Seddon's strategy prevailed. While conversion of title proceeded, the Tuhoe received no loans, advice, or assistance from the government to raise their standard of living or develop their farms. Increasingly, they became seasonal laborers on Pakeha farms in order to secure cash.

Before writing this generation of leaders out of our story, however, we must credit them for their stratagems. In true Maori fashion they met Seddon argument for argument, challenging him to acknowledge a pact they had negotiated with a former administration. At another meeting in 1894, the elders invoked Sir Donald McLean and District Commissioner Locke together with the paramount chiefs, Paerua and Te Whenuanui, who in the 1870s had "arranged that this territory should be kept inviolate," that the chiefs should "reign supreme," and that "all Government matters should be excluded from this boundary." Among the "vile" things excluded were "roads, wrongful sales," and "mortgages," namely, the visible signs and transactions of the Pakeha world. "There was then a protectorate over this place, to protect these people against the advances of the Europeans," they argued.[54] If Seddon savored the irony of Tuhoe elders adopting Donald McLean as the protector of their inviolable space, he did not let on; rather, he asserted that unless the chiefs accepted his paternal authority and the Queen's Writ they would not be able to protect their lands against invasion from "the races of the world"; the only entity that could prevent such an occurrence was the New Zealand government.[55] Of course, the Tuhoe were not concerned about invasion from abroad, but only with colonialism at home.

The Tuhoe did not go gentle into the ironical good night of the secularization of their lives. Like other tribes characterized in M. P. K.

---

53. It took five more years, however, to settle 173 appeals from the Commission's findings to the Native Minister. Webster, *Rua and the Maori Millennium*, p. 141.

54. Ibid., p. 126.

55. Stokes, Milroy, and Melbourne, *Te Urewera*, p. 53.

Sorrenson's analysis of the divisiveness sown by the title procedures of the Maori Land Court, the Tuhoe battled each other bitterly over pieces of their tribal territory, refusing to concede the smallest bit. It was not until 1907 that final titles to the land were established according to the law of New Zealand. In 1908 the Stout-Ngata Native Land Commission reported to Parliament that it was time to set up the UNDRA Committees, which were empowered to sell Tuhoe parcels to the Crown. Under an amending act in 1909 special legislation circumvented the necessity for a new survey and empowered the governor to issue orders concerning Tuhoe land directly in a kind of fast-track alienation program. Between 1896 and 1907 the courts dealt with Tuhoe litigation over the conversion of their land into a commodity. Spurred by poverty and the relative starvation of the Urewera people, who suffered crop failures in 1907, incremental sales went forward. Six hundred and fifty-six thousand acres were now vulnerable to the "real power" of the government. Under UNDRA a General Committee was set up. The General Committee's powers included the "right to alienate any portion of the [Urewera] district to the Crown either absolutely . . . or by way of cession for mining purposes."[56] Extreme measures to acquire the land during the final eight years of the nineteenth century were somewhat mitigated through the combined efforts of various tribes who petitioned Parliament and Queen Victoria. In 1900 James Carroll initiated legislation that vested power over land transactions in Maori Land Councils. Yet the Maori Councils Act and the Maori Lands Administration Act only partially staunched the hemorrhage of land-selling, since the government dominated the Councils with its appointees and the Governor-in-Council still retained the right to alienate certain lands.[57]

By 1907 the old leadership was defunct and the people were dying; the land was partitioned and vulnerable to incremental sell-offs. The Tuhoe world, intact for perhaps a thousand years, faced extinction. The people lacked hope of survival as a people, or of a mediator between them and the god(s). The traditional *tohunga* were powerless to stop the engine of settlement. Beset by epidemics and periodic starvation, marginalized into seasonal work building the roads and bridges and draining the swamps for Pakeha freeholders, the Tuhoe had lost the means to protect and renew their own world. In this time of humiliation, *aporia,* and cosmic despair a messiah was born.

56. Quoted in Webster, *Rua and the Maori Millennium*, p. 129.
57. Ibid., pp. 130–31.

21

THE RINGATU MESSIAH:
RUA KENANA

*I now tell you that it is definite that a
leader will arise. There shall be a sign
when he appears. I shall be buried beneath
his feet. He may be a Pakeha, or a
Pakeha relative, or a Maori, or even one of
the Queen's grandsons. He will carry on
the faith that I have established, and I
shall rest in peace. He shall pass on the
faith to our children, and to posterity
forever.*

Te Kooti, 1879

WHY RUA?

At the outset of my research a Maori educator asked me why I chose Rua Kenana as the focus of my investigation. He would have preferred that I write about Te Whiti, a highly respected leader.[1] Rua stimulated much controversy during his lifetime; among his own Tuhoe people there are still many who despise him as a false messiah, and today the followers of his Wairua Tapu (Holy Spirit) branch of Ringatu are declining in numbers. Why, then, does this particular religious leader merit study?

Rua fits a messianic paradigm. He resembles other savior figures in history and around the world more than he does other Maori leaders of the nineteenth and twentieth centuries. At the time he identified him-

1. See Riseborough, *Days of Darkness*, for the story of Te Whiti's Parihaka movement.

self as the "star in the East" prophesied by Te Kooti, Pai Marire had been supplanted by the Ringatu movement. Te Kooti had died with his *mana* intact, bequeathing to his disciples a unique oral tradition that consoled them with promises of ultimate vindication. His body had been buried in a secret place by a few trusted elders.[2] Ringatu hermeneutics taught that the titanic struggle between Pharaoh and the Iharaira for possession of Canaan would not be resolved in Te Kooti's lifetime. The *mana* of Te Kooti would descend upon a Ringatu savior who would come from the East within twenty-six years and usher in a "long peace." Meanwhile, "the survivors," *nga morehu*, would wait.

CYCLES OF REGENERATION AND THE SAVIOR

Myths and epics tell of saviors, kings, and heroes who rise up to save their people from the cosmic dragon of chaos and despair.[3] They perform great deeds of salvation. Their coming vanquishes the privations endured by their people, and they bring with them the "green herb"[4] of regeneration that initiates an era of abundance, life, peace, and great reversal of fortunes. However, their power, which comes from beyond, is doomed to rise and set like the sun. The king must die. The savior may suffer. The hero will fight one last battle before he succumbs. The only certain thing is that the savior will return again some day.[5]

Ancient Near Eastern, Indian, and Melanesian religious traditions conceived of time and history as cyclical and unending; kingdoms rose, flourished, and fell, and other kingdoms rose up in their place. Nothing was new under the sun. Van der Leeuw called this conceptualization of time "natural-periodic." Eliade referred to it as "archaic." No matter what the actual date of one monarch's death and the accession of another was, the rite of inauguration took place at the annual New Year's

2. The four elders were Eria Raukura, Rikirangi Hohepa, Huri Te Ao, and Wi Kotu; Binney, Chaplin, and Wallace, *Mihaia*, pp. 41–42.

3. The conditions that prevail before an ordered world is created out of "the void," or "the waters," are often symbolized as a sea monster, a dragon, a serpent or reptile, which is also sometimes given a female aspect, e.g., Tiamat, who is defeated by Marduk, in the Babylonian creation myth, or the dragon Apophis whom Pharoah must conquer in his aspect as the god Re. Similarly, Daniel and Revelation allegorize the Gentile nations and Rome as fantastic beasts.

4. Eliade, *Patterns in Comparative Religion*, pp. 306–8, on the regenerating herb.

5. This pattern is distilled, in part, from van der Leeuw, *Religion in Essence and Manifestation*, pp. 106–27; Eliade, *Myth of the Eternal Return*, and also, Eliade, "'Cargo Cults' and Cosmic Regeneration," which owes much to Vittorio Lanternari and Peter Worsley.

festival[6] when the myth of creation was recited and a new cosmic era was ritually established. The New Year's festival accomplished what ordinary acts could not; by reenacting the birth of the world it "abolished," the "continual terror" that human beings are subject to, the humiliations, sufferings, defeats, and pollutions that seem to have no end. The inauguration of the king converted despair to hope that a golden age of plenitude and peace had begun.

For van der Leeuw the paramount symbol of the savior-king was spring, the ancient symbol of renewal in Europe's temperate zone: "This is because the periodic salvation of spring was probably the strongest root of belief in the saviour: in the young god's form life renews itself. His epiphany . . . is the newly awakening life. . . . his potency . . . is perpetually changing, an ascending and declining power."[7] Different symbols of renewal may conform to seasonal variations in other parts of the world. For example, the annual summer flood was associated with destruction and regeneration of the world in the Nile River valley.[8] In Egypt a "gospel" was proclaimed at the accession of Pharaoh-as-god:

"What a happy day! Heaven and earth rejoice, (for) thou art the great lord of Egypt. They that had fled have come again to their towns, and they that were hidden have again come forth. They that hungered are satisfied and happy, and they that thirsted are drunken. They that were naked are clad in fine linen, and they that were dirty have white garments. They that were in prison are set free, and he that was in bonds is full of joy" That is the good tidings as it was announced at the accession of Rameses IV: the Gospel (evangelium), as people said later on.[9]

Pharaoh's "gospel" promised a paradisal "great year" that would reverse all misfortunes. He liberated his subjects from suffering and defeat.[10] The king-savior's power was greater than the powers of this

6. The end of a specific reign was a "great year," but the king renewed his office each year at the annual festival.

7. Van der Leeuw, *Religion in Essence and Manifestation*, p. 107.

8. The "uncreation" myth of a Flood is found in many traditions. Considering that settled agriculture and cities originated in great river valleys—Nile, Tigris-Euphrates, Yellow, and Indus—the symbolism of destruction and regeneration is a "natural" one.

9. Van der Leeuw, *Religion in Essence and Manifestation*, p. 120. Compare Luke 4:16–21 and 7:22–23.

10. I am taking some liberties with van der Leeuw's data and interpreting it as a remedy for what Eliade terms "historicism."

world. It emanated from the realm of the sacred, much as the Roman *imperium* descended from the planetary spheres into the soul of the emperor.[11]

In Egypt the expectation that Pharaoh's potency would revitalize the kingdom was encoded in the Isis-Osiris-Horus myth of death, searching [waiting], and regeneration through resurrection, a metaphor of collective renewal. Elsewhere also king figures were identified with cosmic plenitude. In Scandinavia the fish harvests increased with increase in the king's power.[12] In southern Nigeria the chief was literally shut up in his house, lest his power to maintain the plenitude of his rule be dissipated or lost.[13] The king bestowed gifts as evidence of his sacred, overflowing power, and in Egypt the monarch was both "he who gives life" and "he upon whom life was bestowed."[14] In this sense, the king's position of relative potency positioned him as the archetypal mediator between god(s) and human beings.

MILLENARIAN FEATURES IN INDO-PACIFIC RELIGIONS

In New Zealand power-from-beyond, or *mana*, manifested itself in the powers of the chief and the *tohunga*. Like the African king imprisoned in his hut, the chiefs sometimes felt burdened by the *tapu* barrier. *Tapu* set apart the one who possessed *mana* from ordinary people. The head of the chief, his hair, all that he touched, was *tapu*. In Polynesian Hawaii the king could go about only at night, as gazing upon him by day was a capital offense. The ritual expert, the one who recited the *karakia*, who prophesied, who healed the sick, was the *tohunga ariki*, who also manifested power-from-beyond. Thus, as we have established, *mana* and *tapu* were indispensable expressions of Maori religion. After Christianity and European laws superseded *mana* and *tapu*, the power of chiefs and *tohunga* to mediate between the people and the gods declined. Consequently, the community suffered humiliation, illness, infertility, and death.

As the repository of power-from-beyond, kingship bestowed godlike attributes upon a mortal human; everyone knew that he was, in fact, subject to aging and death. However, it was necessary that his gift-

---

11. Van der Leeuw, *Religion in Essence and Manifestation*, p. 116.
12. Ibid. Note that this statement may also be reversed.
13. Ibid., p. 118.
14. Ibid., p. 269.

giving, healing power continue even after death, to shelter and console his people. The office endured even after the particular king died. In a few recorded cases, as in Egypt and Indonesia, the king might have been the first person who was regarded as immortal.[15]

I have deliberately mentioned only a few of many instances[16] where the archetype of the savior developed in a non-Christian, non-Jewish tradition, in order to establish that messianism/millennialism is not an exclusively post-Christian phenomenon. Although the data on Maori pre-contact religion is lamentably incomplete, we may infer that it belonged to an ancient complex (with many variations) that spread throughout the Indo-Pacific region with the Austronesian family of languages during the migrations of a far-flung people.[17] Scholarly consensus holds that the ancestors of the Polynesians dispersed from southeast Asia and Indonesia. The sweet-potato staple[18] of the Maori diet was a sacred gift, and rituals accompanied the planting of the *kumara*. Melanesians in New Caledonia treat the yam as a virtual person in its total life-cycle from birth to death.[19] The annual festival of the return of the dead and the expectation of a "Great Year" when the Ancestor(s) will return characterizes Melanesian religion. A Great Year is defined as "the complete renewal of the Cosmos through the destruction of all existing forms, a regression to Chaos, followed by a new Creation."[20] This is a type of apocalyptic myth.

The ancient rituals of *hakari*[21] and *hahunga* among the Maori, which apparently ceased to be celebrated annually sometime after 1834, may have corresponded to the Melanesian festivals of the New Year and the Return of the Ancestors. The *hahunga*—the annual exhumation of the dead,[22] the cleansing of their bones, and their reinterment in a sacred burial place—was celebrated by feasting and rituals. If it was a variant

15. Ibid., p. 121.

16. The *avataras*, "descents," of Vishnu in Indian religion constitute another major complex of soteriological myths that include myriad symbols of world destruction and re-creation; see Eliade, *Encyclopedia of Religion*, 1:87f.

17. Ibid., 13:523f.

18. Polynesians south of the line above which taro was widely cultivated, relied, like the Melanesians, on the yam or sweet potato.

19. Leenhardt, *Do Kamo*, pp. 61–64.

20. Eliade, "'Cargo Cults' and Cosmic Regeneration," p. 138.

21. Yate, *An Account of New Zealand*, p. 139. *Hakari* is referred to by Yate as a great annual feast; by Irwin, *Introduction to Maori Religion*, as a funeral feast; and by Salmond, *Hui*, as the feast at the end of the ritual of meeting. To some extent, their treatment of *hakari* indicates its historical transformation from a great festival in the ancient tradition to a part of the central ritual, *hui*, of postcolonial Maori religion.

22. Yate, *An Account of New Zealand*, p. 137f.

of the Melanesian feast of the return of the dead, then it probably
entailed the expectation of a new era, the renewal of the cosmos, the
return of a savior, and the inauguration of a time of plenitude.[23] Christian millennialism may have appealed to Pacific Islanders, in significant part because it had features in common with Indo-Pacific myths of
return. Adopting parts of the conqueror's religion that resemble one's
own may be an effective way to retain the familiar in a tolerated guise.

However, Christian apocalyptic was peculiar in that it offered an
ultimate liberation from the archaic cycles of world-destruction and
renewal in Asian myths. The biblical religions replaced archaic time
with a linear "salvation history" that was bracketed by a Genesis and
an Eschaton. Apocalyptic myth proclaimed a triumphant end to suffering in the Millennium. This was the good news appropriated by charismatics like Te Ua, Te Kooti, and Rua Kenana into their Spirit tradition
of new religious formations.

THE JEWISH INNOVATION OF "SALVATION HISTORY"

The conceptualization of time as linear "salvation history" arose among
Jewish exiles in Babylonia. Their prophets foretold the coming of the
"anointed one" who would annihilate the Dragon (Nebuchadrezzar),
who had dealt them "military defeats and political humiliations."[24] After Cyrus of Persia conquered Babylon in 539 B.C.E. and released the
Jews, some hailed him as the messiah. Around 165 B.C.E. the author of
Daniel 12:2 prophesied that "many of those who sleep in the dust of
the earth shall awake, some to everlasting life, and some to shame and
everlasting contempt." Jews under Syrian Greek domination expected
"one like a son of man" to be given "everlasting dominion" over "all
peoples, nations, and languages."[25] A new genre of apocalyptic texts
flourished over the next three centuries as Jewish renewal movements
contended with the cultural blandishments and superior power of
Greek and Roman emperors.

23. Eliade, "'Cargo Cults' and Cosmic Regeneration," passim.
24. Eliade, *Myth of the Eternal Return*, p. 37.
25. Daniel 7:13–14. This apocalyptic text refers to the Babylonian captivity, but was written at
the time of Antiochus Epiphanes.

THE PARADOX OF APOCALYPTIC

The paradox of apocalyptic is its focus upon the reign of God[26] at the end of history, on the one hand, and its myth of the messiah, on the other. Daniel's vision of the "end of the days"[27] when those who are purified will be saved, was grounded in the Jewish innovation of linear time. Conversely, the Jewish expectation of a savior-king seemed remarkably similar to archaic, cyclical myths of the return of a savior-god.[28] Similar saviors have appeared in other religious traditions, including Indo-Pacific ones. One can only surmise that Jewish apocalyptic myth transformed archaic soteriologies into a specific myth of a definitive endtime, a Day of Judgment, which became part of Christianity as well. Jewish apocalyptic has proved to be one of the most enduring and resonant gospels with colonized peoples. It is ironic that Maori prophets repeated the Jewish process, namely, they converted indigenous myths of the return of the ancestors into the unique event of the "second coming" of the messiah.[29]

Eliade and van der Leeuw emphasize that savior myths promise to requite the terror of historical events.[30] Jesus in John 1 "overcame" evil once and for all through the unique event of his Incarnation. When the "Word became flesh," time as salvation history was "fulfilled." The paradox of the king as god and the king as man was resolved in a *coincidenta oppositorum,* the reconciliation of the demonic and the benevolent aspects of the numinous. It transcends what we commonly perceive as paradoxical.[31] The doctrine of the Incarnation reconciled the human condition of sin and death with the benevolent promise of salvation by faith (thus, Paul refers to Jesus as the new Adam). Never again would the savior die; the good news was that he lived and reigned forever. In Christianity, his death was transformed into life as an eternal *numen praesens.*

26. Daniel 7:9–14. The specific reference to the length of that reign, the Millennium, is found in Revelation 20.

27. Daniel 12:13.

28. The Persian myth of Saoshyant, whose coming is associated with the resurrection of all who have died and with the restoration of all things, may have influenced Jewish apocalyptic. Van der Leeuw, *Religion in Essence and Manifestation,* pp. 112–13.

29. In Judaism "the idea of periodicity gave place to that of the end of the world" (Eliade, *Myth of the Eternal Return,* pp. 143, 148).

30. See van der Leeuw, *Religion in Essence and Manifestation,* p. 126.

31. Eliade, *Patterns in Comparative Religion,* pp. 419–23, 428.

WHY DO THE GOOD NOT PROSPER?

Had the missionaries been able to act in accordance with their expectation of the reign of God, the Maori might not have turned away from them. It was the joining of Christian evangelism with conquest, resplendently conveyed by Thomas Buddle in his hermeneutics of colonization and Christianization, that grieved the *tangata whenua*. The savior had arrived, but apparently he had no interest in saving the Maori. They did not share in the treasures of Britain's brave new world. While the Pakeha prospered, the Maori declined. Moreover, the Pakeha prospered because they took the ancestral treasures from the indigenous tribes. The queen's power was badly used by evil servants, and the justice of God—the rafters of the bicultural "house"—did not clothe the naked or feed the hungry, except through the subsidies of fickle officials, whose policies changed as the Maori were outnumbered by immigrants and pushed to the margins of a cash economy. The Pakeha were a secularized people, for whom supreme power was state power—supported, ironically, by the old mythology of monarchy and the Roman *imperium*. Their wealth, knowledge, and technology were products of scientific and industrial revolutions that had superseded the medieval synthesis of faith and reason. Secularized, rational, scientific, the nineteenth-century English viewed Maori prophets as curiosities and were ever ready to contend with them over their "stubborn and headstrong" views.[32]

HISTORICISM

Eliade's concept of "historicism" refers to the tradition that began with the idea of progress in the Enlightenment, was elaborated in the nineteenth-century theory of social evolution, and reached its apogee in the twentieth-century totalitarian philosophies of fascism and communism. Historicism may also be conceptualized as apocalyptic myth divorced from its religious context: *der Führer* as savior-king, "the withering away of the state" as Eden at the end of history.[33] Only when 'linear, historical, once-and-for-all time was divorced from its connection with

---

32. John P. Ward, who was assigned as guide and interpreter to the Parihaka prophets, Te Whiti and Tohu, from April 1882 to March 1883, frequently tried to impress them with British technology, such as steam power, "without which we Pakehas would not be nearly as strong or rich as we are." *Wanderings with the Maori Prophets, Te Whiti & Tohu*, p. 9.

33. See Karl Lowith on Marxism in *Meaning in History*.

Jewish hope and Christian faith, was historicism deified as an omnipotent force in Germany and Russia, where cults of Hitler and Stalin flourished. The residue of the modern process of demythologizing Western culture was not a truer notion of man's fate, but a more oppressive one.[34] Eliade asked, "How does the 'historicistic view' enable modern man to tolerate the increasingly powerful pressure of contemporary history?"[35] Indeed, how can one fight dragons without gods? From where does the world-creating power to initiate and sustain the kingdom emanate if it comes not from beyond, but only out of the barrel of a gun. Historicism and the terror it engenders threaten civil societies either with the specter of endless warlordism and the rise and fall of dynasties or the resolution of chaos in the secular rule of the absolutist state. Without god(s) and prophets, who has the authority to proclaim the good news that gives hope to those in hiding from the beast? I suspect that Eliade, who witnessed the "terror of history" that wracked Europe in the mid-twentieth century, felt compelled by the events of his own day to ruminate about archaic humanity's "revolt against concrete, historical time, their nostalgia for a periodical return to the mythical time of the beginning of things, the "Great Time."[36]

TUHOE DESPAIR

The turn of the century was, for the Maori, likewise a time of despair. A world was ending. The people of Ruatoki were imprisoned by the dragon of chaos and their rituals of renewal had fallen into disuse. The missionaries had been expelled from the Urewera region since 1855, just as Bishop Williams was forced to abandon his long-standing mission at Poverty Bay during the Hauhau fervor. East Coast *tohunga* had become Ringatu clergy or faith healers. *Tapu* was not observed. In Ruatoki pollution was both physical and religious. Not only were the people separated from their ancient traditions, but their leaders were impotent. The king was dead and the people were hungry. The potato crop had failed. Children were dying, and the land had been carved into pieces to be sold in the marketplace. Tuhoe men served as contract laborers who constructed fences, bridges, water projects, and

34. Eliade, *Myth of the Eternal Return*, pp. 141–62.
35. This question haunted Eliade after World War II—so much so that he considered his treatise on time, *Le Mythe de l'eternel retour* (1949), "the most significant of my books."
36. Eliade, *Myth of the Eternal Return*, p. ix.

roads for Pakeha employers. For eighteen years Rua Kenana was a member of this rural proletariat.

THE TUHOE SAVIOR AS A FIGURE OF SCORN

News accounts during Rua's life record that the government regarded Rua with contempt. The judge and prosecutors at his trial adopted a mocking tone. He was presented to the public as naive and ignorant at best, and amoral and pernicious at worst. What was a journalist to make of his claim in an interview given to the *Poverty Bay Herald* in 1908 that he had had a miraculous birth, *three years* after his father had died? How could a rational person understand why his followers abandoned their meager possessions and followed him on an arduous trek into the wilderness after his prophecies had failed? Was the report that he would rise again three days after he died the cynical invention of a local reporter or a sincere hope among his devoted followers, who only repeated a claim he made while he was still alive? Did he wish to enrich himself by selling blocks of land in order to consolidate others, or did he desire to protect the most sacred place of the Tuhoe from any future sale? Unlike Apirana Ngata, the great Ngati Porou politician whose intellectual prowess has been compared to that of his classmate, Ernest Rutherford,[37] Rua spoke broken English and was ridiculed as a simpleton. Unlike Tutakangahau, Elsdon Best's revered informant, Rua did not practice an ancient—and supposedly unadulterated—Maori religion. Rua was an upstart; he proclaimed himself King and Savior. An outcast by his own admission; how could he claim to be the paramount leader of the Mataatua people when he was neither a hereditary chief like Numia Kereru nor an educated MP like James Carroll?

Rua claimed an innovative mantle of leadership, that of the Ringatu messiah, by fulfilling the prophecies of Te Kooti's movement. I chose to study Rua Kenana, because he exemplifies messiahship in history and because, by studying Rua, we may come to better understand the savior phenomenon.

I do not intend to debunk the legend of Rua Kenana or to test the validity of his assertions, because that would not contribute to an impartial understanding of his Wairua Tapu[38] movement. However, I

37. Eruera Stirling, as told to Anne Salmond, in *Eruera*, p. 143.
38. The name Wairua Tapu, "Holy Spirit," was applied first by Te Kooti to his church. However, the Wairua Tapu branch of Ringatu refers to the Iharaira, Rua's movement.

would like to confront the occasional misperception that nativist groups that agitate for the return of their land, such as the Hawaiian Sovereigntists, or the Kanak Liberationists in New Caledonia, or the proponents of *mana motuhake* in New Zealand, have adulterated their allegedly genuine ancient practices with foreign "borrowings" from ethnologists, folklorists, or even hippies.[39] I propose that Rua was a savior and that the conditions of his time called for salvation. At the same time, Rua, like Black Elk, shaman of the Ghost Dance movement among the Lakota, was merely a man called by a power-from-beyond to save his community from the abyss of annihilation. The revelation of god(s) through symbols, dreams, visions, and signs compel the savior to make right choices and perform great deeds. As Annette Aronowicz puts it:

> The green herb, the gift of the Great Spirit, is not only an image; it is a reality concealed in the ordinary social and political events of Black Elk's world. It can only be made manifest through Black Elk's attempt to uncover it through his deeds. Symbols cannot be properly understood unless they have been incarnated in actions. This means that the religious life is tied to the concrete, historical moment, to the particular choices people make.[40]

Sometimes Rua misinterpreted his own visions and prophecies. At first, he was certain that King Edward VII would come to Gisborne in 1906, but then he realized that it was he, Rua the King, who had united his people at Gisborne.[41] His power ascended and declined, and like the legendary Arthur, Rua was to his followers "sometime king and king to be."[42] After his death, Rua's wife, Pemia, denied a news report that Rua had claimed he would rise from the dead within three days; she said he had announced that "he would come back one day, but he didn't say when."[43] As in other religions, the fine-tuning of the interpretation of the events of the savior's life continued beyond his death.

---

39. This argument may be responsible and muted, as in Hanson's "The Making of the Maori," or somewhat paternalistic, as in Keesing's "Creating the Past," but it tends to question the validity and integrity of current renewal movements as a continuation of indigenous traditions. It recalls the Polynesian Society's conviction that Maori renewal movements were a less genuine form of religion.

40. Aronowicz, "Musings on Teaching *The Sacred and the Profane*," pp. 75–89.

41. Binney, Chaplin, and Wallace, *Mihaia*, pp. 29–30.

42. Eliade, *Myth of the Eternal Return*, p. 127. Rua lost and gained adherents over his lifetime.

43. Webster, *Rua and the Maori Millennium*, p. 21.

THE SAVIOR ARCHETYPE IN HISTORY

There is a general pattern to savior phenomena throughout history, even though the specific instance may not incorporate some or may vary other details of the pattern. In general, the story of the savior is mythicized over time to conform to an archetype. Eliade explains: "The recollection of a historical event or a real personage survives in popular memory for two or three centuries at the utmost. This is because popular memory finds difficulty in retaining individual events and real figures. The structures by means of which it functions are different: categories instead of events, archetypes instead of historical personages."[44]

In the case of Te Kooti, Eliade's "two or three centuries" has been whittled down to forty years. The Ringatu legend of the healer and prophet recorded by Greenwood differs significantly from the eyewitness report of Maraea Morete that details his venality and lust.

GENERAL FEATURES OF THE SAVIOR ARCHETYPE

The usefulness of the archetype as an analytic tool becomes clear when one compares data from a particular case to that synthesized by historians from innumerable cases. Gerardus van der Leeuw compiled formal features of a "savior myth,"[45] to which particular data on Rua's life and role conform:

1. The savior's birth is miraculous, as befits his "supernatural aspect." Rua claimed to have been born three years after his father died at Ngatapa.

2. The savior appears from an unknown place. Rua lived in exile before he returned to his people and their sacred mountain, Maungapohatu.

3. He performs a "deed of salvation," which consists of a combat, wherein he overcomes powers hostile to life. Often this is symbolized as a triumph over death itself. Rua met a goddess like Whaitiri (who is associated with sickness and death) face-to-face when he climbed Maungapohatu, the Tuhoe sacred mountain.[46]

4. He returns at the end of time and "rightly orders all." Rua told

44. Eliade, *Myth of the Eternal Return*, p. 43.

45. See van der Leeuw, *Religion in Essence and Manifestation*, pp. 106–14. I have applied his basic pattern to Rua's life.

46. Rua's deed of salvation was his struggle to consolidate the land around the precious treasure of the sacred mountain; his ascent of the mountain symbolized the deed.

his community that he would return at some future time, and his followers adhere to that expectation.

5. In keeping with the archaic view of time, the savior who comes from beyond is born "when the time is fulfilled," namely, at the fateful time of salvation when the Great Year is at the end of one cycle and the beginning of a new cosmic era is inaugurated. Since he preexisted before his birth, so he "returns" at a particular time. Rua's appearance was prophesied by Te Kooti, whose own appearance had been prophesied by Te Toiroa.

6. The time of the savior is marked by signs and miracles, astral events and cataclysms. Te Kooti prophesied a "star from the west" and "a star from the east," who would contend as his successors. The future of the land would depend upon whether the good savior prevailed over the evil one.[47] Rua came from the east between the geographical coordinates specified by Te Kooti. A comet heralded his prophecy of the Tuhoe millennium.

In conforming to these formal features of savior myths, Rua's life and deeds identify him as one of a general category of messiahs who have appeared in various places and times.

INDO-PACIFIC MILLENARIANISM

Mircea Eliade developed a list of specific features of the Melanesian savior from the work of Lanternari and Worsley on cargo cults, specifically, the cults of Mansren that arose in Dutch New Guinea between 1867 and World War II. The ancient Indonesian myth of Mansren[48] promises that the demigod will return as a "miracle child" who runs down the trunk of a cosmic tree that bends from the place of Mansren to the island of Miok Wundi. The child's return will mark the beginning of an age when the old will become young, the ill will be cured, and the dead will be resurrected. This age will be one of plenitude, featuring women, food, clothes, and weapons in abundance.

Typical of renewal movements occurring after colonial settlement, the first recorded cult of Mansren in Melanesia predicted not only an age of "youth, beauty, wealth and harmony," but promised to abolish the Dutch administration, forced labor, and taxation.[49] Cargo cults transformed the precolonial myths of Mansren by adding the following

47. Webster, *Rua and the Maori Millennium*, p. 120.
48. "Mansren" means "the Lord"; see Worsley, *The Trumpet Shall Sound*, p. 129, for his other titles.
49. Worsley, *The Trumpet Shall Sound*, p. 130.

elaborations: (1) the astral sign of a comet over Miok Wundi, which signals the return of the *konor*, "miracle child"; (2) the imminent arrival of a ship full of material goods; (3) prophets who claim to be either the child or the Lord Mansren and who perform miracles; (4) a period of waiting for the savior, characterized by abandoning ordinary tasks and building a house for the Lord and preparing a feast of reception; (5) separation from and hostility toward "strangers in the land"; and (6) the prediction of a new heaven and earth when nature and society would reverse existing laws, e.g., sea creatures would become land creatures, tubers would grow on trees; the dead would be raised, the indigenous people would enjoy privileges as the "Chosen" of the Lord.[50]

The many cults of Mansren illustrate how indigenous religions may incorporate homologous features of foreign soteriologies in order to confront the upheavals of invasion and dislocation.[51] We have seen the same historical pattern develop in New Zealand, and it would be fallacious to conclude *post hoc ergo propter hoc* that Maori renewal movements sprang exclusively from the imported biblical tradition. Heroes and saviors abound also in the great oral myths of the *tangata whenua*. Maori religion, not Christianity, formed the intact core of Maori renewal movements. If we pursue the paradigm of renewal beyond the horizon of Christianization, we can discern the revival of ancient myths and practices in the Maori Spirit tradition as well as in the cults of Mansren. Cargo cults in New Guinea and Fiji arose after Pai Marire. Rua is a messiah in the Pai Marire tradition. What unites cargo cults and Maori millenarianism are the general features of Indo-Pacific myths of return, including:

1. The time of return as a time of cosmic reversals, manifested in the Indo-Pacific theme of the flattening of the earth, namely, mountains would tumble down into plains of fertile soil.[52] Rua insisted upon "one law for both peoples" in order to provide the Maori with equal access to capital and profit from development of their land.

2. The return of the Ancestors, annually reenacted in rituals that regenerate the cosmos. Rua and Eria Raukura engaged in a *hahunga* ritual in 1913 or 1915 (variously reported).

---

50. Ibid., pp. 131–45.

51. Christian elements became prominent in the movements after 1908, after thousands of Papuans had converted. Worsley, *The Trumpet Shall Sound*, p. 135.

52. See Basil F. Kirtley, *Motif Index of Traditional Polynesian Narratives* (Honolulu: University of Hawaii Press, 1971), p. 58.

3. The myth of the Great Year, namely, a "regression to Chaos," followed by a new Creation. Rua founded his "New Jerusalem" at the foot of the mountain that held the bones of Tuhoe ancestors. His followers prepared to welcome a new Tuhoe cosmos in 1906 and again in 1927.

4. A golden "age of abundance." Rua predicted that he would inaugurate "a time of peace," followed by the return of the land and the payment of reparations by the Crown.

5. The return of a god with the return of the dead.[53] Rua referred to himself as "the brother of Christ" who would return at some future date.

Indo-Pacific myths predate the arrival of missionaries in the region. Cargo cults did not debase Melanesian religion; syncretism often enriches religion as it transforms and preserves it. The symbol of salvation in Rua's movement was the sacred diamond, a treasure that was associated with the arrival of King Edward at Gisborne. The return of the diamond would inaugurate a golden age marked by the return of Canaan to the Maori. Rua expressly imitated King Solomon, the Jewish archetype of wisdom and wealth, who resembled Austronesian ancestors like Mansren. Wairua Tapu shared some features in common with Melanesian cargo cults: the return of a wondrous figure on a ship bringing treasure from abroad, the abandonment of ordinary work and cultivation in order to prepare for a total transformation of the world, and the expectation that the colonial administration would leave the land.

Rua was born in a village at the foot of the Tuhoe "mountain of stone," Maungapohatu, where the bones of the ancestors had been buried in caves from time immemorial. He was acutely conscious of the centrality of sacred place in Maori religion and the connection between the ancestors and the living community.

To charismatic Maori prophets Christianity may have appeared as one of various myths of a better world-to-come, although it was a particularly powerful and immediate one. Jehovah, the warrior-savior of Exodus, impressed Maori chiefs far more than the Jesus who extolled servanthood in the Gospels, but the Christ of the *parousia* is a "high," celestial chief who abolishes the travails of history in a heavenly reign. He is like the demigod Mansren and also like Gabriel Rura, who

53. Ibid., pp. 126–34; Eliade, "'Cargo Cults' and Cosmic Regeneration," pp. 139–41. This ancient myth was recorded by German missionaries only two years after their arrival in 1855; by 1867 the first cult based upon the return of the child, the forerunner of the redeemer, had arisen.

cleanses the earth but touches the rainbow—a sky deity. He battles Satan/Mammon in this world. The Ngati Ruanui had never allowed missionaries in their midst. Missionaries at Taupo and Awamutu in the King Country were forced out by Kingite separatists, just as the Hauhau frightened the Williams family into leaving Tauranga. Everywhere prophets looked in the Bible and found a people like themselves—enslaved, exiled, dislocated, and championed by divine beings. They recognized themselves as the children of Shem. Why shouldn't their Jewish ancestors return, Moses in the form of Te Kooti and the "brother of Jesus" in the form of Rua Kenana?

22

MAUNGAPOHATU IS THE MOUNTAIN, RUA IS THE MAN

> *Rua's intentions were separatist. . . . They
> [he and his followers] were to seek refuge
> at Maungapohatu, adapting their lives and
> their land at their own pace and under
> their own leadership.*
>
> Judith Binney

RUA KENANA, THE "SON" OF TE KOOTI

Rua Kenana Hepetipa was born in the village named for the Tuhoe's own sacred mountain, Maungapohatu. His tribe had cast its lot with the elusive guerrilla prophet, Te Kooti, in the final years of the Land Wars. His biological father died before he was born, and Rua claimed to be the "son" of Te Kooti.[1] His early life was marked by rejection. Like Te Ua he claimed that he was turned away by his own people, and lacking a father, he was cast into exile with relatives among the Ngati Kunhungunu in Hawke's Bay until he was nine years old. After his return to Maungapohatu, he lamented that he was "rejected and despised" by fellow tribesmen.[2] As a young man he became one of the first generation of Tuhoe to work as contract laborers

1. Binney, *Redemption Songs*, pp. 480, 510.
2. Binney, Chaplin, and Wallace, *Mihaia*, p. 18.

on the coastal plains. For eighteen years he lived in marginal circumstances, becoming increasingly cognizant of the root problem of his people: they were rich in land, but poor in the capital necessary to develop it in an age when competition with other food-producing colonies required a level of productivity in wool and other crops that could only be achieved by draining swamps, bridging rivers, cutting forests, and seeding pastures that needed many miles of fencing. Rua's indenturement coincided with the time of crisis for his people when their land had become the focus of Pakeha rumors that the *terra incognita* of the Urewera region was replete with fertile valleys and gold.

THE THREAT TO TUHOE LAND

Maori politician James Carroll proposed *taihoa*, a policy delaying land alienation. It was ridiculed in the newspapers of 1909 as an affront to immigrants claiming the inherent right to settle the idle lands. At the turn of the century the Tuhoe could no longer defend their tribal territory against internal land surveys. Compelled to finance the cost of a magnetic survey of their territory and to improve their lands or have them seized by the government, many tribesmen were forced to allow prospecting and to sell some portions in order to keep others. The sudden loss of autonomy over their territory constituted for the Tuhoe a fall from grace, a withdrawal of *mana,* the displacement of a tribe bound to the forest of Tane the creator. "Alienation" implies that they became strangers in their own land. In actuality, the Pakeha began to assume control over their lives, transforming them into a servant class in an industrializing state. Pharaoh had come to Canaan, created a desolation, and called it progress. For the Tuhoe, the problem was one of economic adjustment to a new European state, where land was interchangeable with cash and goods, and where an "autonomous communalism"[3] was regarded as subversive, because it could exist only in isolation from modern commercial society.

THE CALL TO MESSIAHSHIP

Living apart from his people as a self-described outcast on leased property in the confiscated lands of the Waimana Valley, Rua Kenana began to discern a divine purpose at work in his self-imposed exile. By

3. Ibid., p. 24.

1905 he was one of many local *tohunga,* or faith healers. According to his disciple, Fred Teka, one day Rua was baking bread with his wife, Pinepine, in their house at the base of Maungapohatu, when he heard a voice calling him to be a savior of his people. He responded, "If your wish is for me to save only people, I won't help, but if it is to save the land, then I shall carry out this task . . . I shall save the land, for if I save only people, there will soon be no land on which they can live."[4] Directly, Rua and Pinepine followed the command of the Holy Spirit to ascend the mountain.

His call and ascent of the mountain initiated Rua's mission as the messiah foretold by Te Kooti. The story of the ascent has many variations. According to Rua's son, his father and Pinepine were going up a narrow track when the mists came down, confounding them. A woman with long black hair appeared three times to point out their way, and on the summit, the figure of Christ appeared beside her.[5] Christ led Rua to a swamp, where he and Pinepine saw that beneath the "veil" or "shawl" placed there by Te Kooti lay a gleaming diamond, which they did not touch, but covered up again. When Rua and Pinepine returned, everyone knew that he was the one foretold by Te Kooti, and his descent from Maungapohatu was associated with the rainbow, the Ringatu sign of Noah's covenant of peace.[6] Henceforth, Pinepine was a "tapu woman" who could not be approached or touched except according to certain rules. Rua referred to the woman on the mountain as a "sister of Christ" and to himself as a "brother of Christ." The diamond was spoken of as the guardian of the mountain, and, by extension, the protector of the Tuhoe lands and people.[7]

The story of Rua's ascent has received various interpretations: Rua

4. Webster, *Rua and the Maori Millennium,* p. 158. In a slightly different version, God told Rua to "take up my work." Rua allegedly replied, "If it is the sick I will not do it. If it is the land, I will." Binney, Chaplin, and Wallace, *Mihaia,* p. 18.

5. This woman was later identified as Whaitiri, the ancestral goddess of the Tuhoe, whom Binney notes is associated with the odor of perfume and a bright light; "in Wairua Tapu narratives she is called Rua's sister" (Binney and Chaplin, *Nga Morehu,* p. 204 n. 21). Webster identifies the goddess associated with Maungapohatu as Hinepukohurangi, the Mist Maiden, who mated with Te Maunga, "the mountain," to produce the Tuhoe ancestor, Potiki I; Webster, *Rua and the Maori Millennium,* p. 84. The latter goddess is local to the mountain, while Whaitiri is the great goddess of the *tapu* boundaries.

6. Binney, Chaplin, and Wallace, *Mihaia,* pp. 19–20. Note that the picture of Gabriel in *Cassell's Illustrated Family Bible* features a rainbow behind the angel.

7. In Maori tradition a sacred place may have an appointed human guardian, *kaitiaki,* or it may be guarded by a mythical beast, the *taniwha.* Maori "treasures" or *taonga* may include precious greenstone weapons or places where food is gathered, or burial caves; whereas the European notion of treasure is typified by the fever for gold in the hills and streams that was gripping the imagination of prospectors at the turn of the century. As a symbol, the diamond expresses both ideas of treasure: it guards the existence of the people/world, and it is of great value.

Fig. 5   Maungapohatu, the sacred mountain of the Tuhoe

is compared by some to Moses on Sinai; it is said that the veiled diamond will be the means of redemption for his people in days to come.[8] However, the question remains: How would the revelation that Rua received on the mountain lead to a practical resolution of the problems facing the people of the Mataatua canoe, the Tuhoe, the Wak- atohea, and the Ngati Awa tribes of the Urewera and the Bay of Plenty?

MAUNGAPOHATU IS THE MOUNTAIN

Rua's call to messiahship was literally grounded in Maungapohatu, the "mountain of stone," a rock, a foundation of the new world. Its other name is "The Spine of Maui's Fish," which refers to the North Island, which was drawn up from the sea by the demigod Maui. Maungapohatu is the threshold between the world of light and the realm of the Sky. From its summit one looks out on the entire Tuhoe world, and near a

8. Binney, Chaplin, and Wallace, *Mihaia*, pp. 19–20.

great cleft, which Rua called "The Gates of Heaven," are *wahi tapu*, the caves where the bones of the ancestors are interred.[9]

The diamond, salvation, and the mountain formed a symbolic complex in Rua's mythology. His ascent fulfilled the prophecy of Te Kooti that "in twice seven years a man shall arise in the mountains to succeed me. He shall be the new prophet of the people."[10] By 1907, Rua had begun to construct a holy city at the foot of Maungapohatu near the site of the village where he was born.

In 1906 the Tuhoe were without a bridge to *te ao hou*. Like Tamihana, Rua was a world-builder and a lawgiver. He spoke with authority because he fulfilled Ringatu prophecy, but he also implemented a practical, economic solution to the Tuhoe land problem.[11] Simultaneously visionary and enterprising, Rua revived a system of *tapu*, proclaimed himself the messiah, defined the boundaries of the Tuhoe world, and unified the Mataatua tribes of the East Coast under his *mana*.

A TIME OF PREPARATION FOR PEACE AND PLENTY

Like other millenarian leaders, Rua revealed divine secrets by exposing the hidden meaning of *tohu*, "signs." In millennial mythology the time of the messiah is sacred time. Archetypal saviors establish new calendars, promulgate new laws, set new boundaries, and proclaim good news. One of the models Rua imitated was Solomon, who raised the temple to Yahweh and resolved the most perplexing issues.

Binney identified the succession of charismatics beginning with Toiroa and culminating with Rua Kenana Hepitipa as the *wairua* or "spirit of prophecy" tradition.[12] Rua's conviction that he was the "son of God" and the "brother of Christ" did not mean he was mentally unsound. Prophets establish new communities in an orderly fashion, an impossible task for psychotics.

Rua conceived a striking plan to save the land. He consolidated Tuhoe parcels under his *mana* by marrying twelve *rangatira* women from different *hapu*. Among them they inherited title to lands belonging to the Tuhoe subtribes. He proposed to sell one portion of land in order to amass enough capital to preserve the area surrounding Maun-

9. Webster, *Rua and the Maori Millennium*, pp. 193–94.
10. Binney, Chaplin, and Wallace, *Mihaia*, pp. 16–17.
11. Of course, this is a distinction outsiders make; to Rua and his community, the mythological and the logical were reconciled in their acts and story.
12. Binney, Chaplin, and Wallace, *Mihaia*, pp. 17–18.

gapohatu. He established *Hiruharama Hou,* "New Jerusalem," at the foot of the mountain by recruiting Tuhoe and Whakatohea people whose land had been confiscated in 1866 during the Hauhau disturbances. The Tuhoe had been charged with aiding Te Kooti and Kereopa; the Whakatohea had been accused with Kereopa of murdering Carl Volkner. They separated from the ordinary world, removed their children from school, and trekked to the sacred center, where they constructed an ordered and hygienic agricultural settlement. It was a time of great discipline and diligence, motivated by the expectation that their land would soon be returned. Like Tamihana, Rua envisioned a separate Maori world, where the people would enjoy both autonomy and peace under a Maori monarch: "Rua declared that he was the brother of Jesus Christ, the Lord of the *earth* in the same way that Christ rules in *heaven.* . . . 'There were two Jacob's ladders leading to heaven, one from the white people and one for the dark coloured people.'"[13]

THE SUPPRESSION OF TOHUNGAS

Rua's burst of energy fueled his renewal movement between 1907 and 1915, but it also drew the hostility of traditional leaders, such as his father-in-law Numia Kereru, the chief of Ruatoki. More significantly, Rua was castigated by the capable new Maori political leaders, including Apirana Ngata,[14] who worked tirelessly as a member of government to ease the transition of his people to an industrializing Pakeha world. He regarded Rua as an anachronism who exerted a retarding influence upon the Maori of the East Coast. In order to nullify Rua's growing appeal, Native Minister James Carroll introduced in Parliament the "Bill to Suppress Tohungas" in 1907, the year Rua's followers constructed their sacred center at Maungapohatu.[15] With the Wairua Tapu movement specifically in mind, the legislation accused charismatic leaders of seditious behavior:

13. Webster, *Rua and the Maori Millennium,* pp. 160–61.

14. Rua and Ngata's rivalry derived not only from their antithetical schemes to save land on the East Coast, but from their roots in tribes that were traditional enemies. Ngata was first and foremost of the Ngati Porou and a fellow tribesman of Te Kooti's enemy, Ropata Wahawaha.

15. Rua called both his dwelling and the sacred precinct inside the holy settlement *Hiruharama Hou,* New Jerusalem; the settlement and the mountain are called Maungapohatu.

The effect of these tohungas is to paralyse the industries in which the Natives are engaged. To create notoriety for themselves, they generally take a hostile attitude to the laws which are in force and which are intended for the general benefit of the community. They also, by the advice they give to their followers, endeavour to as far as possible resist the progress of our civilisation. Where these preachers of tohungaism have established themselves the result has been that many industrious hapus living in a district, families, and sections of tribes have forsaken their cultivations and ordinary avocations in life necessary for their upkeep; have withdrawn their children from the district schools. . . . I am now quoting, as a type of this class of practitioner, the notorious Rua. . . . We were in hopes that the uplifting of the Maori would materially weaken the fanatical ravings of a man like Rua . . . Fanatical Natives like Rua should be early subdued, as their mutterings, beginning with a plaintive wail, usually end with stubborn and criminal resistance. . . . when we hear of sedition being openly preached, it is about time that firm steps on the part of the authorities should be taken to quench it, or it is quite possible that history may repeat itself. We have no hesitation in saying that turbulence and sedition amongst the Natives should be suppressed with a firm hand that shows no mercy to the rebel.[16]

James Carroll's diatribe indicates the hysteria aroused by an upstart's grassroots challenge to distinguished Maori politicians. Rua was also served up as a scapegoat by the Tuhoe representative, Wi Pere. Torn between his Ringatu roots and his exalted position as a token native in the House of Representatives, Pere accused Rua of "exciting a bad spirit." He alleged that Rua "has told his followers that presently the white people will all be removed from these lands," echoing John White's misinformation about Te Ua. Wi Pere had once rashly cursed the Pakeha for threatening the confiscation of his own lands. Now, he appealed to his fellow members of the House, "I do not want honourable gentlemen to recollect anything that I said in another place, where I made a challenge to let me have four thousand soldiers of my own race and I would fight the white people and send them out of the country. . . . I do not want you to say that I am something like Rua."[17]

16. *NZPD*, July 19, 1907, pp. 510–13.
17. *AJHR*, 1907, p. 375.

Thus, the Maori Native Minister and the Ringatu MHR publicly branded Rua as a violent fanatic. In fact, he had never done or said anything to warrant such a response.

THE COMING OF THE KING, "THAT THE TUHOE MIGHT BE SHELTERED"

The parliamentary debate about "tohungaism" in July and August 1907 followed a year of extraordinary events in the history of the Wairua Tapu branch of Ringatu. In 1906 Rua announced that King Edward VII would arrive at Gisborne on June 26 to receive from Rua the diamond of Maungapohatu in exchange for the return of all Tuhoe land or, alternatively, to give Rua a diamond or £4,000,000 to buy back Tuhoe land.[18] His prophecy propelled a surge of support from all tribesmen; many left their homes and jobs to follow the messiah. Rua rode to Gisborne on a white horse accompanied by eighty-two Tuhoe chiefs, fulfilling the imperative of Paora Kingi I of Te Waimana, *kia tawharautia ai a Tuhoe*, "that the Tuhoe may be sheltered," namely, that they may be brought together in unity. This consolidation of chiefly support for one leader set alarms ringing for the government. It was as if the ghost of Tamihana had risen up and gone to Gisborne.

On the way to meet King Edward, Rua established his claim to messiahship by passing an impossible test. He entered Rongopai, the most *tapu* Ringatu meeting house, built by Te Kooti's followers in Gisborne.[19] Rua's white horse (identified by Wairua Tapu legend as Te Kooti's own steed, Te Ia) opened the locked door and entered first. Rua followed, astonishing the skeptical crowd, who acclaimed him on the spot as the one foretold by Te Kooti. Only the day before, Rua had given a speech on their *marae* to enlist support for his cause. He proclaimed himself "a second Christ" and Te Kooti as "John the Baptist," his precursor. Like Te Ua, he declared that "the people were now living in bondage," and he had come to deliver them. He compared Cain to the Pakeha and Abel to the Maori and prophesied that although the

18. Webster, *Rua and the Maori Millennium*, pp. 163, 165, 167, 169. Because each of Ringatu's several branches has its own oral history, the story varies. It is also said that King Edward was going to present to Rua a great sum of money or treasure and, in effect, convey his wealth to the Maori savior and to the mountain with which he identified his messiahship. Either version of the exchange would produce the same result: great wealth and good fortune for the Tuhoe people, a reversal of their condition through the inauguration of a king who would save them from loss and decline.

19. Te Kooti never succeeded in seeing the unique house or returning to Gisborne.

world did not know it yet, King Edward had left his throne in January to arrive at Gisborne shortly.[20] It was not his fine words and confident manner that won them over, but the astonishing sight of Rua and the white horse inside Rongopai the next day."They waited for him to die and he didn't die. But they still didn't know what he meant. They still didn't know that he was the King they were waiting for."[21]

King Edward did not arrive at Gisborne on the twenty-sixth or any of the ensuing dates set by Rua, who enhanced his standing by explaining to his hopeful followers that they had come to greet a king *and that King was he*. Te Kooti had also predicted that his successor would unify the people, "that the Tuhoe may be sheltered," something he had failed to do.[22] In fulfillment of this promise, Rua constructed a "chamber of unity," a "booth" in the Israelite manner of Succoth, near a river beyond the coastal plain a few months after the chiefs accompanied him to Gisborne.

Rua attracted the support of Te Kooti's most powerful disciples, Eria Raukura, one of the four who had reinterred the founder's bones in a secret place, and Hurinui, the paramount chief of the Mataatua tribes. Eria told Colonel T. W. Porter, a veteran of the Urewera campaign against Te Kooti, that Rua was the man Te Kooti had predicted in his *kupu*, and that his emergence as a holy person was attested by signs and portents, such as shooting stars. He testified that Rua had turned from the riotous behavior of his youth.[23]

Sometime in 1905 or 1906, Eria baptized Rua in the Waipaoa River at Pakowai. Binney suggests that the baptism of Rua as *Te Mihaia Hou*, "the new Messiah," took place after his public manifestation at Gisborne.[24] However, Rua had secured Eria's support even before he went to Gisborne. As Webster notes, "Rua did not . . . suddenly appear out of the Urewera forests . . . with a message which was immediately acclaimed." Rather, he obtained the backing of a man who "represented a living link with the glories of the past" and possessed not only the reputation as a warrior in service to Te Kooti, but "the mana of a leader of the Ringatu church."[25] In short, Rua Kenana, like Wiremu

20. Binney, Chaplin, and Wallace, *Mihaia*, pp. 28–29.

21. Ibid., p. 29, from an oral interview with Rua's daughter-in-law.

22. Binney attributes these words to Te Kooti in *Mihaia*, p. 30 (see also *Redemption Songs*, p. 480); elsewhere, she reports they were uttered by Paora Kingi I. *Nga Morehu*, p. 153.

23. Webster, *Rua and the Maori Millennium*, p. 158.

24. Binney, Chaplin, and Wallace, *Mihaia*, p. 30.

25. Webster, *Rua and the Maori Millennium*, p. 159. At that time Ringatu had not been accepted as a licit church in New Zealand, although it held the allegiance of most of the Tuhoe.

Tamihana and Te Kooti, among other Maori prophet-leaders of the colonial era, wielded the craft and power of archetypal Maori heroes. Rua was inspired and energized by the god(s), shrewd in the planning and execution of his schemes, and supremely confident of his authority. Because of his audacity, he gained the support of leaders like Eria and Hurinui, but his actions excited the opposition of powerful rivals who jealously guarded their own *mana*. The legendary Maori hero conceives a plan and implements it step by step until he succeeds or is conquered by a superhuman force. One does not choose to become a hero, a prophet, or a savior. One is chosen by the god(s).

A MAORI ZION

> *Maungapohatu has been divided up into sections and is being sold (by him) to his people.*
>
> Numia Kereru, 1907

NO POWER BUT THE GOVERNMENT

Ironically, Rua borrowed a plan to save the land from Wi Pere, who joined with two of the three other Maori representatives to petition Premier Seddon in 1905: "In the case of Maori owners of land who own large and valuable areas, or a number of large areas, let them sell a block or a portion of a block for the purpose of providing themselves with the means to work and improve their other lands instead of going in for a loan."[1]

In 1894 Seddon adopted the words of Gore Browne to the Kingites in 1857 and told the Tuhoe chiefs at Ruatahuna that "there can be no power but the Government."[2] The chiefs relinquished their age-old *mana* over Tuhoe land when they acquiesced to Seddon during later

---

1. Quoted in Webster, *Rua and the Maori Millennium*, p. 135.
2. Ibid., p. 127.

negotiations at Wellington.[3] However, Seddon had held out to them one significant hope, that they "may have people to advise the Government."[4] The chiefs' willingness to compromise recalls the petitioning of Gore Browne by both loyal and dissident chiefs for an assembly of chiefs. The advisory board, of course, never materialized, but certain provisions for Land Councils and Land Reserve Boards were set up under ensuing land legislation pertaining to the "special" Urewera Native District Reserve and to the North Island Maori in general. Numia and Te Pouwhare, among others, henceforth found themselves in a *kupapa* relationship with Seddon's—and later Premier Joseph Ward's—Liberal government. They were now bound to act on behalf of the people through legal entities and the four Maori MPs. They viewed Rua's seizure of the initiative in consolidating a sacred block of land around Maungapohatu by selling a block of land in the Waimana Valley to finance his settlement as an affront to what remained of their mantle of leadership.

SPECIAL LEGISLATION TO FACILITATE LAND ALIENATION

Wi Pere's petition was ignored in the stampede of legislation to confiscate three million acres of North Island "waste land" remaining in Maori hands. This was accomplished by a provision of the Maori Land Settlement Act of 1905 that created Maori Land Boards to wield compulsory power over land "not required or not suitable for occupation by the Maori owners."[5] Maori members were outnumbered by Pakeha two to one on the Land Boards. Sensing that the "special legislation" would not protect their interests, Tuhoe chiefs became demoralized after the governor-in-council was vested with the power over the Urewera District. In effect, Tuhoe *tino rangatiratanga* was being systematically and incrementally eradicated.

In 1906 a lawyer for the House of Representatives, T. K. Macdonald, announced that it would be a great blunder for the government to allow more than one million acres to remain in the hands of the North Island tribes. Under existing laws this proposal would reduce their per capita landholdings to approximately one-seventeenth of Pakeha holdings.[6]

3. Ibid., p. 128.
4. Ibid., p. 127.
5. Ibid., p. 136.
6. Ibid., pp. 123–43.

The permanent marginalization of the indigenous people in a moderniz-
ing economy was ensured by the "special" and the general land legislation between 1893, the year of Te Kooti's death, and 1906, the year
Rua founded New Jerusalem.

CHALLENGE AND RESPONSE

Rua's response to the government remained consistent between 1906,
when he first came to their attention, and 1916, when he was arrested,
tried, and imprisoned for resistance. He emblazoned his motto, "One
Law for Both Peoples," on his flag, refused to pay the tax on Maori
dogs, and claimed the right to sell liquor. Rua regarded the imposition
of the dog tax and the prohibition on selling liquor as a double standard, since they did not apply to the Pakeha. He assumed *mana*
through his repeated claim that he was the brother of Christ. He made
predictions that Wairua Tapu adherents deemed prophetic and miraculous. A few days after he prophesied that Hiona [Zion], the round
courthouse he built at Maungapohatu, would replace the Parliament
building in Wellington, Parliament burnt down.[7] He had indeed crossed
the *tapu* barrier at Rongopai and lived.

The rise of acculturated political leaders followed the eclipse of the
chiefs after 1894. Although Apirana Ngata eventually succeeded in
safeguarding much of the Ngati Porou[8] land, James Carroll and Wi
Pere failed to thwart or delay the sale of Urewera lands to private
interests. Rua was the only Tuhoe leader with the energy and imagination to implement a Tuhoe solution for a Tuhoe problem. The politicians charged Rua with sedition because he refused to play by Seddon's rules or allow any other Maori of rank and status to supersede his
authority over the Urewera Native Reserve District. In turn, the traditional leaders, Kereru, Akuhata, and Te Pouwhare, used the passage of
the Tohunga Suppression Act to target Rua.

Ruatoki,
13th December, 1907
    Ngata has informed us that in regard to Tohunga practises the
Parliament has handed over the authority to the Native Minister.
    The second thing he informed us was that the works or [*sic*]

7. Binney, Chaplin, and Wallace, *Mihaia*, p. 35.
8. Graham V. Butterworth, "The Politics of Adaptaton: The Career of Sir Apirana Ngata, 1874–
1928"; Stirling, as told to Anne Salmond, *Eruera*, pp. 139–60.

Rua would probably be looked into, as to whether they were transgressing the law or not.

Well, we see his works, which are transgressing the law, and leading the people into misfortune, and works of madness, works of evil, & works of falsehood.

These are his said works:—

1. (He claims that) he is The Christ, that he is a son of Jehovah.

2. That no person will die, that he can save them, if they will go to Maungapohatu (but) that those who remain (away) will die. The people who have died at Maungapohatu have nearly reached one hundred.

3. That his Pa is sacred ("tapu"); food must be eaten outside the house; the clothes are left in the sacred place; no clothing for outside, whether it freezes or rains, even in the case of invalids.

In our opinion this is the cause of the deaths.

4. The properties have been sold, and the lands;[9] the dog collars:[10] The schools which have been trampled upon are[11] [sic]

   5. Maungapohatu has been divided up into sections and is being sold (by him) to his people.[12]

5. The practises of former Prophets were:—(erecting) altars; burning sacrifices: baptizings: and remission of sins: Collecting money is the ultimate end of all his works.

We desire that this matter be searched into so that the evil works may cease.[13]

---

9. There is no explanation which properties are indicated. They may have been the holdings of those who left the lowlands to participate in the trek to Maungapohatu, although some families leased their lands to tenants.

10. The Ihairara refused to pay the tax, which created a general resistance against paying it among all Tuhoe. Let Rua pay first, they told the tax collectors.

11. Binney notes that the Waimana and Waikaremoana schools were shut down and several other were seriously affected by the withdrawal of pupils who went to the mountain. Binney, Chaplin, and Wallace, *Mihaia*, pp. 34–35.

12. Rua's economic transactions were castigated by his enemies and approved by his community. He collected monies in a variety of ways, but utilized them to purchase common stores that had to be carried over rough tracks by muleback into his settlement, where they were distributed among the people. Although he dressed well, his living quarters were not luxurious, and he did not live appreciably above the general level of his people.

13. Numia Kereru, letter to James Carroll, 13 December 1907, MA 23/9, National Archives Head Office, Wellington.

This remarkable document indicates that some of the support Rua attracted with his first prophecies of King Edward VII's arrival was short-lived. His inability to maintain allegiances with other leaders enhanced government policy of dividing and acquiring land for settlement in the Urewera District.

WAITING FOR THE MILLENNIUM

Maori separatism was stigmatized as lawlessness, but making a place sacred and renewing a world requires setting it apart from the ordinary world in space, order, and time. Rua built Maungapohatu as a holy *pa* where his community awaited in faith the justice of God. The act of separation and world-building is a hallmark of a messianic movement. Binney reports that Rua adopted the name Hepitipa, "Hephzibah," to signify that he and the land, the restored Jerusalem, were "married."[14] He brought "the Covenant," a large English Bible, to Maungapohatu and installed it in a House of the Covenant. The disciples called themselves *Iharaira*, "Israelites." They took a Nazirite vow to let their hair grow and refrain from liquor and tobacco. The community lived as if they were a purified people occupying a place close to God in the time of his expected reign. Rua predicted that celestial portents, a comet and a star in the east, as well as a volcanic eruption, earthquakes, and a flood of the low-lying areas of the Bay of Plenty would herald the approaching Millennium. Outsiders were amazed "at the speed and energy with which the land had been prepared and the buildings erected" in little more than one year.[15]

Rua named twelve apostles, *Tekau-ma-rua*, whom he called the Riwaiti, "Levites," after the Israelite priests in charge of the Temple cult. They were *tapu*, forbidden entrance to areas of food preparation, and subject to sexual restraint. All were men with organizational skills who had memorized the Ringatu liturgy and were masters of scriptural study. They were the ones who primarily conducted the daily services at seven A.M. and three P.M. and the Saturday sabbath, although in the early years Rua delivered the sermons, after which the community conducted its business. Selected Levites administered "the holy pa of the

14. Isaiah 62:4, quoted in Binney, Chaplin, and Wallace, *Mihaia*, p. 33. Actually, Hephzibah means "my delight is in her." Te Kooti had adopted Isaiah's language shortly after he escaped from prison, naming his land, "Beulah," which means "married."

15. Webster, *Rua and the Maori Millennium*, p. 197.

Lord,"[16] freeing Rua to spend his time on other initiatives, including missions to various meeting houses in the greater Urewera District, where he would sit in a small hut separated from the faithful by a *tapu* barrier marked by a rope, while he collected coins that he used to heal petitioners.[17]

In order that more time could be spent by the pilgrims in clearing the land and developing their settlement, the Iharaira dispensed with the Ringatu rituals on the twelfth of each month,[18] but kept a modified observance of the "firsts," of January and July. Rua removed the words, "Give us this day our daily bread," from the Lord's Prayer, because as messiah, he would provide for them. He also deleted a description of the people as "perplexed and in doubt" in a Ringatu prayer.[19] Rua's Council posted ordinances which maintained strict standards of hygiene and law in the community, and homes were inspected twice weekly to ensure that his rules were complied with.[20]

RUA'S BID FOR LEADERSHIP

His campaign to shelter the sacred center of the Tuhoe world manifested Rua's extraordinary shrewdness and leadership qualities. Although all the Tuhoe chiefs had rallied around Rua at Gisborne, some remained skeptical of his power. Kereru, the man who had predicted ruin for the Tuhoe if their lands were sold, joined with the government in opposing Rua's assumed authority over the land. Surveying the land, dividing it into blocks, and subjecting inhabitants to the wrenching process of title conversion opened up schisms within kin groups. The struggle for *mana* between government clients and Rua's separatists "brought the Tuhoe to the brink of civil war."[21] In 1907 and 1908 Rua proposed a bold plan to:

16. Binney, Chaplin, and Wallace, *Mihaia*, p. 45. They also acted as jury in cases tried at the courthouse.

17. Coins brewed in an infusion of tea had been used to heal since Te Kooti's time, but Rua collected donations, which he willed to his surviving elder daughters, that amounted at his death to a surplus of about 700 pounds.

18. "Twelfths" were founded by Te Kooti to commemorate significant dates in the history of the Ringatu community, but twelve was also a holy number because it signified the twelve tribes of Israel and the twelve apostles of Christ.

19. Binney, Chaplin, and Wallace, *Mihaia*, p. 54.

20. Ibid., pp. 52–55.

21. Ibid., p. 35.

1. Sell a portion of Tuhoe lands to pay accruing expenses and encumbrances and to capitalize the development of Maungapohatu.

2. Demonstrate his supreme *mana* by accomplishing what no other person could: he would persuade his followers to offer some of their land for sale to the government.

3. In exchange for the land, receive government permission to administer his own separate local government in the Urewera, thereby preserving Tuhoe autonomy under the "covenant" of the Treaty of Waitangi, Article Two.

4. Set up a gold mining company with local Pakeha, who would purchase prospecting licenses from him at a cost of 11,400 pounds apiece, and Maori landowners would retain miners' rights over their own land.

5. Permit the government to complete a stock track through the Waimana Valley to Maungapohatu, thus enabling commerce, and reducing the great effort required to supply the settlement, especially during the harsh winters in the uplands.

Rua's initiative threw a spanner into the special legislation policy of the Seddon and Ward administrations to open the Urewera to European settlement, since he was not an endorsed Maori leader,[22] but had set himself up as an independent authority with the power to make local laws for the Urewera *kainga*, "settlement."[23]

PREMIER WARD MEETS RUA AT WHAKATANE

By 1907 the troublesome internal surveys and investigations of title had been completed and the land was potentially ready for settlement; all that was needed were willing sellers.[24] To the chagrin of civil authorities, only Rua held the power to persuade most land sellers to offer their parcels, initially amounting to some 30,000 acres, to the government; however, *it was legally necessary to conduct the transaction through a General Committee with compulsory authority over all sales of Tuhoe lands.*[25] Rua's de facto *mana* over the Urewera District impeded

22. In 1909 Rua refused to be photographed on the Ruatoki marae with Kereru and the governor, Lord Plunket, in order not to be seen as a member of the "'endorsed' leadership." Binney, Chaplin, and Wallace, *Mihaia*, p. 42.

23. Webster, *Rua and the Maori Millennium*, pp. 232–33.

24. See summary of the 1896–1907 process of conversion of title from aboriginal to freehold in Stokes, Milroy, and Melbourne, *Te Urewera*, p. 60.

25. Webster, *Rua and the Maori Millennium*, p. 228.

the business of the General Committee and thwarted the purpose of the special legislation. Seddon's successor, Joseph Ward, came to Whakatane on March 23, 1908, to reconcile the differences between Chief Kereru and Rua, just before a crucial tribal gathering that would elect a General Committee to accept the proffered land sales on behalf of the Urewera District.

By coming to Rua, Ward appeared to be petitioning the Iharaira. At Whakatane, Ward thanked Kereru publicly for his support, and then met privately with Rua, after which, the *New Zealand Herald* reported that Rua had conceded to his followers that it was no longer of any use to try to oppose the government. Ward had reiterated the metaphor of *imperium*: "In New Zealand Edward is King, and is represented here by government. There can be no other Government or king. . . . there can't be two suns shining in the sky at one time."[26]

In the Spirit tradition of counter-hermeneutics, Rua interpreted their meeting as a "Ceremony of Union" that extended "a promise that they [both peoples] would enjoy the same laws as they enjoyed "the one sun that shone above our heads."[27] In 1894 Seddon had used Rua's phrase, "one law for both peoples," to justify the position later taken by Ward: "This was the real crux of the issue [stated Seddon], that there should be one law for all, *that any form of Tuhoe self-government expressed in the form of separate administration of lands was not to be tolerated by Government.*"[28] Rua, on the other hand, insisted upon equality between Maori and Pakeha in all matters, including the right to enjoy the proceeds of mining and land development. He even had the temerity to propose to Ward that his Iharaira supporters be placed in nomination on the European electoral rolls to gain seats in Parliament. Ward refused, proving that nothing had really changed since McLean's time, and that the agenda of amalgamation was very much alive under the show of a Liberal government, which only *seemed* to incorporate Maori into the power structure even as it continued to alienate their lands in a more subtle manner.

THE BATTLE IS JOINED

Nevertheless, Rua held the key to land sales in the Urewera. Consequently, the enforcement of the Tohunga Suppression Act was sus-

---

26. Binney, Chaplin, and Wallace, *Mihaia*, p. 38; Webster, *Rua and the Maori Millennium*, p. 227.

27. Binney, Chaplin, and Wallace, *Mihaia*, p. 38, from court transcripts of Rua's trial in 1816.

28. Stokes, Milroy, and Melbourne, *Te Urewera*, p. 55, italics added.

pended while he continued to play a chess game against a more powerful opponent. Within two years he realized that Maungapohatu could
not become economically self-sufficient unless he could obtain capital
improvements, most importantly, a road.[29] He recommended selling
land in order to raise capital, promising the Iharaira that the land they
sold would be given back to them "in the millennium."[30] These were
strange words from a messiah who told Jehovah he would first save the
land. Throughout, he continued to act as the "big fellow" of the
Urewera.

THE RECONCILIATION OF OPPOSITES

During the Tuhoe meeting that followed Ward's visit, Rua camped four-
teen miles away and received dispatches on the conversations between
his deputy, Te Hurinui, paramount chief of the Mataatua tribes, and
Kereru, chairman of the Maori Council, a local administrative body.
Rua placed a boundary around the *marae* of Kereru, prohibiting tobacco and compelling all who entered to purify themselves with water;
he placed a *tapu* on the meeting house itself, forbidding entry.[31] Carroll
and Ngata called upon Te Heuheu Tukino of Taupo to reconcile the
Tuhoe factions. Te Heuheu convinced the assembly to elect a General
Committee to "take decisions for all the Tuhoe country"[32] in order to
shore up support for Ngata and remove Rua as an obstacle to the
implementation of the Urewera Reserve Act. Rua's deputy agreed to
sell and lease land to the government. Native Minister Carroll offered
to meet with Rua in Wellington.

MANA OVER THE UREWERA DISTRICT

On his way to Wellington, in an interview with the *Poverty Bay Herald*,
Rua declared himself the savior of the Tuhoe.[33] Upon arriving, Rua
reminded the public that he had predicted the burning of Parliament
House in December 1907 (but he did not mention his prophecy that his
own Council house would replace it and that he would be enthroned
there as king). Rua hoped to preserve 20,000 acres of land at Maunga-

29. Webster, *Rua and the Maori Millennium*, p. 209.
30. Ibid.
31. Binney, Chaplin, and Wallace, *Mihaia*, p. 39. Purification rites arm the righteous against
spiritually incurred danger.
32. Ibid.
33. *Poverty Bay Herald*, June 1908.

pohatu[34] in exchange for selling as many as 100,000 acres in the Tauranga (Waimana River) Block. There is no record of the conversations
between James Carroll and Rua on June 25, 1908, but ostensibly, the
deal for land was struck.[35] The acreage was formally offered to the
Native Minister in November 1908. Later, the General Committee was
elected from among the appointed Local Committees under the Urewera District Native Reserve Act of 1896, in order to "deal with all
questions affecting the reserve as a whole, or affecting any portion
thereof in relation to other persons than the owners thereof," wording
that Rua must have either not read or not understood, since it revoked
his *mana o te whenua.*[36]

When it dawned upon Rua that the General Committee, which included Chief Kereru, would receive the credit for the land sale he had
brokered, he demanded, in a letter in February 1910, that Carroll
"hand back to me all of my former proposals intact." At issue was the
status as "big fellow" that Rua claimed. He did not doubt that the
General Committee *could* sell the 100,000 acres under the law, but he
objected that "the *mana* goes to others."[37] Rua had to fulfill mythological imperatives. He was called to be the Christ, to usher in an age of
restitution and equality, and to preside over the Tuhoe with a divinely
instituted authority. He could not be the Tuhoe savior and relinquish
mana o te whenua to any other constituted body.[38] Carroll sent Apirana
Ngata to salvage the agreement by empaneling Rua and four others on
the General Committee: "This led in the winter of 1910 to an arrange-
ment with the General Committee whereby lands in the Waimana or
Tauranga basin, between Waimana and Maungapohatu were authorized
to be purchased by the Crown. . . . By March, 1912, the area acquired,
all in the Waimana basin, was 40, 795 acres, at a cost of £31, 353 6s."[39]

As a member of the General Committee, Rua received the *mana* he
sought. In an unforeseen manner his prediction that the land ultimately
would be returned "in the millennium" still remains a possibility, be-

34. Webster, *Rua and the Maori Millennium*, p. 230.

35. Webster on Carroll's remarks to the press, in *Rua and the Maori Millennium*, pp. 231–32.

36. Ibid., p. 128.

37. Ibid., p. 232.

38. In 1910, Rua aligned himself and 1400 followers with the "federation" movement for
rangatiratanga under the Treaty of Waitangi. It was led by Tana Taingakawa, former premier to the
Maori king. The Iharaira began to lease part of their lands outside the jurisdiction of the General
Committee. See Binney, Chaplin, and Wallace, *Mihaia*, p. 40.

39. Stokes, Milroy, and Melbourne, *Te Urewera*, p. 61, quotation from a report to Parliament in
1921.

cause a good part of the land he sold was subsequently incorporated into the Urewera National Park and remains undeveloped.[40]

THE *PA TAPU* AT MAUNGAPOHATU

While Rua engaged in politics, he built Maungapohatu and divided it into two precincts, one more sacred than the other. A fence with two gates enclosed the *pa tapu,* which included *Hiruharama Hou,* "New Jerusalem," the house where he and his wives resided; a separate dwelling for his *tapu* wife, Pinepine; the two-tiered, round Council House, Hiona [Zion]; the House of the Covenant, which held the English Bible; and the bank. Any person over twelve years of age had to purify himself with water and change his clothes before entering through the gate to the *pa tapu.* Outside this precinct were the numerous dwellings and separate cooking houses for the remainder of the inhabitants.[41] Although the Iharaira built a meeting house on the upper slopes near the *pa tapu* in 1914, liturgical services were conducted at Rua's house.

Hiruharama Hou was constructed on the highest slopes of the settlement within the *pa tapu* and remained set apart even after Rua removed *tapu* from the rest of the settlement and the sacred places in the Waimana Valley in 1915, after he was jailed for breaking the liquor laws. Returning to Maungapohatu three months later, he ended the sect's era of isolation from the profane world and began to dwell more frequently at a house down the slope at Maai, "the place freed from tapu."[42]

The biblical model for *Hiruharama Hou* has been misinterpreted as David's pattern for the temple built by Solomon in 1 Kings 6, which was cited in an article by James Cowan.[43] Following Cowan, Binney wrote:

Hiruharama Hou was built in conscious imitation of the house built by Solomon, according to the pattern given him by his father

40. The report, *Te Urewera,* by Stokes, Milroy, and Melbourne, was commissioned by the Minister of Lands and Forests in 1983 as a study to assess the Tuhoe claim to traditional use of the public lands of the Urewera region, including the National Park.

41. For extensive descriptions of the structure and symbolism of Maungapohatu, see Binney, Chaplin, and Wallace, *Mihaia,* pp. 45–80; Webster, *Rua and the Maori Millennium,* pp. 183–220; and F. Allen Hanson, "Christian Branches, Maori Roots: The Cult of Rua."

42. Binney, Chaplin, and Wallace, *Mihaia,* p. 78.

43. James Cowan, "Rua the Prophet."

David. This visual parallel was intended to confirm Rua's lineage
as King and Messiah. From David and Solomon sprang the Son of
God.[44]

In fact, Rua's house was modeled after Solomon's palace complex
mentioned in 1 Kings 7: 2–6 that featured the central symbol of Maori
religion—pillars:

> He built the House of the Forest of Lebanon; its length was a
> hundred cubits, and its breadth fifty cubits, and its height thirty
> cubits, and it was built upon three rows of cedar pillars, with
> cedar beams upon the pillars. And it was covered with cedar
> above the chambers that were upon the forty-five pillars, fifteen
> in each row. There were window frames in three rows, and window
> opposite window in three tiers. all the doorways and windows had
> square frames, and the window was opposite window in three
> tiers. And he made the Hall of Pillars; its length was fifty cubits,
> and its breadth thirty cubits; there was a porch in front with pil-
> lars, and a canopy before them.

Pillars are absent from David's pattern for the "House of the Lord."[45]
God dwelt in the temple, while the King lived in the palace complex.
In building a house with a veranda and pillars for himself and his
wives, Rua identified his reign with that of Israel's wisest king, a polyg-
amist like himself. Rua's *tapu* wife, Pinepine, lived in a separate
house, as did Solomon's Egyptian wife. Naming *Hiruharama Hou* for
the "New Jerusalem" of Revelation indicated that Rua expected his
millennial kingdom to resemble Solomon's reign of peace, justice, and
abundance. Thus Rua subscribed to a benign type of millenarianism,
not a Christian-style apocalypse.

Like Solomon's palace, *Hiruharama Hou* was distinguished from ordinary houses by its many windows. Its veranda, extending across the
front of the building, was supported by pillars and was marked at one
end with a post that displayed in ascending order, an open sphere that
stood for the World, a circle with a cross that symbolized Te Wairua
Tapu, and a crown that proclaimed Rua's kingship over the world.[46]
This post stood at the side of *Hiruharama Hou* that symbolized the

44. Binney, Chaplin, and Wallace, *Mihaia*, p. 46.

45. Ibid. Binney, following Cowan, reports that "on the front verandah there were also pillars, in
imitation of the house which King Solomon built for the Lord."

46. See Binney's photograph and caption, in Binney, Chaplin, and Wallace, *Mihaia*, p. 46.

Tuhoe people. The other side of the double-gabled structure represented the Whakatohea tribe, whose leader, Ngakohu Pera, was one of
Rua's Twelve Apostles. Pera's daughter, Whaitiri, married Rua's second
son, Toko. Because Rua's *mana* failed to prevent her untimely death,
the Whakatohea departed from the community.[47]

The *pa tapu* represented Rua's ultimate kingship over the world of
the Tuhoe people and his fulfillment of Te Kooti's prophecy that the
land would be returned in a time of *te maungarongo*, or "long abiding
peace." This word also meant "gospel." Rua's evocative symbolism
conflated Solomon and the millennial Messiah. Rua Kenana's pillars,
like the pillars of Tane, promised to hold up the Tuhoe cosmos.

HIONA

Rua's parliament house, Hiona, was like David's three-tiered "House of
the Lord" in that it had two stories, the higher one smaller than the
lower, and an upper platform upon which Rua stood to deliver public
addresses. However, there is no model for Hiona in scripture;[48] it was
Rua's creation, just as the remarkable meeting house, Rongopai, was
an innovation by Te Kooti's followers at Poverty Bay.[49] Rongopai, the
sacred house entered by Rua's white horse, also expressed in symbolic
fashion the millennial dreams of Ringatu. Unlike the carved and woven
representations of mythical figures in traditional meeting houses, Rongopai's vivid paintings include a likeness of Wi Pere, the benefactor
who built it as a tribute to Te Kooti.

> The dream was of a new, brave, world, the new Eden where the
> kowhaiwhai was embellished with new colours, where painted spi-
> rals and floral patterns provided a panacea for war and a prayer
> for peace. . . .
> *There,* the dream, painted on the pillars of puketea wood, and
> the rafters and in the decorations. *There,* the healing powers of
> the house, symbolised in the profusion of elaborate trees and
> vines, twining and climbing in a painted landscape as Eden must
> indeed have looked like; reds and purples, brilliant flowers and

47. Cited by Binney as one of the internal crises that marked the sect, in Binney, Chaplin, and
Wallace, *Mihaia,* p. 73.

48. A Gisborne policeman reported that Rua told him that Hiona represented the Tower of Babel,
whence the Maori language originated. Binney, Chaplin, and Wallace, p. 49.

49. See Ihimaera, *The Matriarch,* pp. 183–95.

pods popping out from large Victorian vases; oranges and yellows, sunbursting fruits defying botanical reality; the glorious purple of the Scotch thistle, the personal symbol of the prophet; the greens and creams of seeds winging their ways through the poutama and the roimata; the fabulous Tree of Life, with its twelve separate herbal flowers sprouting from the central trunk.[50]

The creative wellspring of a new religion brings forth forms of expression that combine with old symbols to reorder a world that, in Ihimaera's words, seems "out of kilter, spinning off its axis and out of its own orbit around the sun that Maui had tamed, ripping other galaxies apart and, in the process, severely damaging its own."[51]

Rua's Hiona expressed the Iharaira dream of a sacred and orderly kingdom of peace.

> Outside, Hiona was brightly painted, the background white, with diamonds of yellow, and clubs of blue. . . . Playing card emblems were used in the nineteenth century as mnemonics to the Scriptures by those who could not read. Te Turuki had devised such a system for the Ringatu, and Rua followed his example on the walls of Hiona. The club was the emblem to stand for the King of Clubs. He is the King who is yet to come: the last King in the line of David. . . . The Kings in the other suits have been "played," but the King of Clubs is "the Coming King": Rua, the Messiah. He is the King with the power to command, the last King, who will bring everlasting peace, "maungarongo." Rua claimed to be the "mystic fourth" in a line of Maori prophets: Te Whiti, Titokowaru, and Te Turuki.[52] Three had fallen, as prophesied, but the fourth would stand; the King of Clubs.[53]

According to Binney's oral sources, the yellow diamond symbol on Hiona represented both the saving diamond of the mountain and the Holy Ghost. The diamond was seen as Rua's stone; and "Rua is the diamond of Maungapohatu." The colors of Hiona, white, blue, and yellow derived from scripture; the former two were the hues of the royal

50. Ibid., p. 191.

51. In the Maui myths, the demiurge lassoed the sun and divided time into orderly periods of day and night.

52. Each of these leaders founded movements inspired by Pai Marire. Te Turuki is one of Te Kooti's names.

53. Binney, Chaplin, and Wallace, *Mihaia*, pp. 48–49.

vestments of Israel, "with a crown of gold" worn by Mordecai and Zerubbabel, who came from Babylon to rebuild Jerusalem. It was Zerubbabel "from whom Te Ua, the founder-prophet of the Pai Marire religion in Taranaki, had taken his identity."[54] Binney also notes that the Tuhoe regard blue as the color of life.

The wealth of consciously innovative and symbolic expression in both branches of Ringatu attest to an active Pai Marire tradition. Rua's kingship is still being interpreted by his family and followers, some of whom are still alive, not by scholars, who merely assemble the data and record them. Often, the history of a religion is hidden in the remoteness of its origins and embedded below layers of the hermeneutical tradition that springs from a living, practicing community of faith. In the Pai Marire tradition, we can trace the process of the transformation and renewal of Maori religion.

RUA'S IMPRISONMENT AND DEATH

Rua exemplified the savior who redeems his people and promises to return. Still, like the archetypal king, Rua was human and destined to die. In 1915, he was convicted of "sly-grogging," selling liquor in his Waimana settlement.

On a Sunday morning in 1916, three columns of police converged in a surprise assault on Maungapohatu to arrest Rua for refusing to show up in court (after he had sent a message to the magistrate that he could not leave the critical grass seed harvest) to face renewed charges of breaking the liquor laws. As armed constables grabbed the prophet and forced him into a humiliating "frog-march," a shot rang out; "it is not known by whom" it was fired.[55] His son, Toko, was killed in the ensuing gun battle. Rua's trial was a celebrated case, the longest in New Zealand history up to that time. Although the jury acquitted him on most of the charges, the judge sentenced him to the harshest penalty allowed under the law, two years and six months in jail. He was released in April of 1918 after serving a partial sentence.

Despite the grave blows dealt to his *mana*, Rua remained the undisputed leader of the Iharaira until his death from tuberculosis and kidney failure in 1937. His followers staged a vigil for three days at his crypt, awaiting his resurrection. His wife, Pemia, questioned the rumor that

54. Ibid., p. 49
55. Gerald J. Maloney and William Neil, "The Rua Expedition," p. 67.

Rua had said he would rise from the tomb, but a Presbyterian missionary who was present at his deathbed maintained that Rua had talked about Ezekiel's vision of the valley of dry bones and about the reign of God, saying that, like Jesus, he would rise from the dead in three days.[56]

The documents pertaining to Rua's trial are still inaccessible. The judge ordered all court transcripts destroyed. Copies of the transcripts held by the defense attorney have been reviewed by Judith Binney, who would not release them. There may be within those papers more material on the religious and mythological phenomena of Rua's messianic movement that mainstream society would consider ridiculous and/ or scandalous. The only accessible account of the trial may be found in contemporary news articles.[57] The data we do have on the Iharaira support the conclusion that Rua revived the system of *tapu* and the institution of *runanga*, the ancient "council of elders," whose eradication by missionaries and civil authorities had contributed to the disorganization of Maori society described by Elsdon Best at the turn of the century. Moreover, in declaring himself and his first wife, Pinepine, *tapu* by virtue of their encounter on the sacred mountain with Whaitiri and the "brother of Christ," Rua established himself as a traditional *rangatira*, as well as a messiah. The "myth of the eternal return" was a pre-Christian phenomenon in the South Pacific, as were annual New Year festivals and reburial of the dead. Pai Marire and Ringatu religion suggest that there are tantalizing continuities between Maori prophet movements and a preexistent Austronesian millenarianism that differs significantly from the horrific visions of Revelation and from the militant strategy of missionaries and colonists to reestablish a new Albion—the kingdom of a thousand years—in Aotearoa.

RESURRECTION/RETURN

The most intriguing evidence of a continuity between the "myth of the eternal return" and the renewal movements derives from two rather sketchy sources: the report of a celebration of a *hahunga* in the Waimana Valley in 1915 by James Cowan[58] and the report of police constable Gerald Maloney[59] of an episode in 1913 involving Eria Raukura, Rua, and the digging up of bones of victims of a typhoid epidemic. It is

---

56. Binney, Chaplin, and Wallace, *Mihaia*, p. 174.
57. I am indebted to Peter Webster for sharing his newspaper clippings with me.
58. Binney, Chaplin, and Wallace, *Mihaia*, p. 193 n. 107.
59. Maloney and Neil, "The Rua Expedition," pp. 62–68.

not clear whether or not the digging up and transfer of the bones to Maungapohatu in 1913 and the Waimana *hahunga* of 1915 reported by Cowan were related events or the same event.

Maungapohatu is where the bones of Tuhoe ancestors have been reinterred through the rite of *hahunga* for, perhaps, a thousand years. It is also the locus of Rua's epiphany and Te Kooti's marvelous diamond. It is possible that the bones Eria brought in his portmanteau to Rua were reinterred on Maungapohatu in 1913, and it is also possible that the *hahunga* Cowan reported took place in 1913, not 1915. Rua's discussion on his deathbed of Ezekiel 37 may have indicated his expectation of a communal resurrection that would involve the ancestors, as well as himself. The Maori prophets from Wiremu Tamihana to Rua Kenana succeeded in grafting biblical tradition and genealogy onto the Maori tree of life, whose roots stretch more deeply into the past than our records reach.

Collectively, Kereru, Rua, and Ngata, the principal leaders of the East Coast Maori during the time of relentless attack on their ancestral lands, shepherded their people into the twentieth century. In my view each stands for a type of Maori leadership that has developed under the pressure of colonization: Kereru, the *rangatira* who compromised with European civil powers; Ngata, the assimilated achiever, who used political power to assist his people in adapting to the status quo; Rua, the visionary who reinterpreted historic events and reorganized Maori traditions in the wake of European occupation. Rua's sacred center has been largely set aside as a National Park, and the Urewera Forest of Tane still stands as one of the last virgin rainforests in New Zealand. Ngata's policy of cooperation with the political establishment resulted in his salvaging as much land under Maori management as was possible under the European rules of land title and sale. Kereru envisioned the bleak future of his people in 1894, when he predicted that they would become as impoverished as the other tribes had after surveyors had broken the ancestral territory into blocks. However, only Rua preserved the religious integrity of Tuhoe life, which had been consigned by government policies to the margins of an industrializing state until, as the Ringatu messiah, he brilliantly revived his followers' expectations of an eternal return of the land and the ancestors in the prophesied time of the long peace.

BIBLIOGRAPHY

ABBREVIATIONS

APL	Auckland (City) Public Library
AJHR	*Appendices to the Journal of the House of Representatives*
ATL	Alexander Turnbull Library (NLNZ)
BAR	*Biblical Archeological Review*
DNZB	*Dictionary of New Zealand Biography*
JPH	*Journal of Pacific History*
JPS	*Journal of the Polynesian Society*
NLNZ	National Library of New Zealand
NZJH	*New Zealand Journal of History*
NANZ	National Archives of New Zealand
NZPD	*New Zealand Parliamentary Debates*
UAL	University of Auckland Library
UWL	University of Waikato Library

SOURCES CITED

Aberle, David. "A Note on Relative Deprivation Theory As Applied to Millenarian and Other Cult Movements." In Thrupp, ed., *Millennial Dreams in Action.*

Agent for General Government, Hawke's Bay. Inwards Correspondence Series 1/2. Paper Relating to Te Kooti, 7/3. NANZ.

Allison, Jr., Dale C. "The Baptism of Jesus and a New Dead Sea Scroll." *BAR* 18, no. 2 (March/April 1992): 58–60.

Andersen, Johannes C. "Maori Religion." *JPS* 49, no. 4. (December 1940): 513–55.

———. *The Maori Tohunga and His Spirit World.* New Plymouth: Thomas Avery & Sons, 1948.

Appendices to the Journal of the House of Representatives (AJHR). 1860, F-3; 1862, E-9; 1864, A-No. 8B, E-No. 4, E-No. 5, E-No. 8, F-No. 1; 1865; 1868, A-No. 15E; 1870, A-No. 8A, A-No. 8B, A-No. 24, A-No. 24A; 1871, F-No. 1; 1890, G-2.

Aronowicz, Annette. "Musings on Teaching *The Sacred and the Profane*: The Dilemma of the Introductory Course." *Epoche: The UCLA Journal for the History of Religions* 15 (1987): 75–91.

Asher, George, and David Naulls. *Maori Land.* New Zealand Planning Council Planning Paper No. 29. Wellington: Government Printers, 1987.

Atkinson, Arthur S. *See* Polynesian Society Papers.

Atkinson, Arthur S., trans. "Te Kooti." (Visions narrative from the Chatham Islands note-book.) *The Monthly Review* 1, no. 5 (March 1889): 175–77.

————. "Te Kooti." (Visions narrative from the Chatham Islands notebook.) *Nelson Examiner*, May 5, 1869.

Bagnall, A. G. "No Known Copy? T. S. Grace's Suppressed Circular, W264." *Turnbull Library Record* 15, no. 2 (October 1982): 77–92.

Banks, Robert. *Paul's Idea of Community: The Early House Churches in Their Historical Setting*. Grand Rapids, Mich.: William B. Eerdmans, 1980.

Barkun, Michael. *Disaster and the Millennium*. New Haven: Yale University Press, 1974.

————. *Religion and the Racist Right: The Origins of the Christian Identity Movement*. Chapel Hill: University of North Carolina Press, 1994.

————, ed. *Millennialism and Violence*. London: Frank Cass, 1996.

Begg, Alison. "Early Maori Religious Movements: A Study of the Reactions of the Maoris to the Christian Gospel Up Until 1860." Master's thesis in history, University of Otago, Dunedin, New Zealand, 1974.

Belich, James. *"I Shall Not Die": Titokowaru's War, New Zealand, 1868–9*. Wellington: Allen & Unwin / Port Nicholson Press, 1989.

————. *The New Zealand Wars and the Victorian Interpretation of Racial Conflict*. Auckland: Auckland University Press, 1986.

Bell, F. D., F. Whitaker, and T. G. Browne. *Notes on Sir William Martin's Pamphlet Entitled "The Taranaki Question."* New Zealand Government, January 1861; Dunedin: Hocken Library Facsimile No. 8, 1968.

Best, Elsdon. "Christian and Maori Mythology: Notes on the Clash of Cultures (An Address Before the Free Discussions Club, Victoria University College)." Wellington: "New Zealand Worker" Printing and Publishing, 1924.

————. *The Maori As He Was*. Wellington: Government Printer, 1974.

————. *Spiritual and Mental Concepts of the Maori*. Dominion Museum Monographs, No. 2. Wellington: Government Printer, 1954.

————. *Tuhoe: Children of the Mist*. Vol. 1. New Plymouth: Thomas Avery & Sons, 1925.

Binney, Judith. "Christianity and the Maoris to 1840: A Comment." *NZJH* 3, no. 2 (October 1969): 143–65.

————. "The Heritage of Isaiah: Thomas Kendall and Maori Religion." *NZJH* 1, no. 2 (October 1967): 124–39.

————. *The Legacy of Guilt: A Life of Thomas Kendall*. Auckland: Oxford University Press, 1968.

————. "The Lost Drawing of Nukutawhiti." *NZJH* 14, no. 1 (April 1980): 3–24.

————. "Myth and Explanation in the Ringatu Tradition." *JPS* 93, no. 4 (December 1984): 345–93.

————. *Redemption Songs: A Life of Te Kooti Arikirangi Te Turuki*. Auckland: Auckland University Press, 1995.

————. "The Ringatu Traditions of Predictive History." *JPH* 23, no. 2 (October 1988): 167–74.

————. "Te Kooti Arikirangi Te Turuki." *DNZB* 1:462.

Binney, Judith, and Gillian Chaplin. *Nga Morehu: The Survivors*. Auckland: Oxford University Press, 1986.

Binney, Judith, Gillian Chaplin, and Craig Wallace. *Mihaia: The Prophet Rua Kenana and the Community at Maungapohatu*. Wellington: Oxford University Press, 1979.

Bolle, Kees W. *The Freedom of Man in Myth*. Nashville: Vanderbilt University Press, 1968.

————. "The Great Goddess." Paper presented at the UCLA Conference on the Male and Female in Religion, May 1992.

————, ed. *Secrecy in Religions.* Leiden: E. J. Brill, 1987.

Brittan, S. J., et al., eds. *A Pioneer Missionary Among the Maoris, 1850–1879 (Being Letters and Journals of Thomas Samuel Grace).* Wellington: A. H. & A. W. Reed, 1984.

Buddle, Thomas. "Christianity and Colonisation among the Maoris." *Supplement to the "Nelson Evening Mail."* August 23 and 30, 1873.

————. *The Maori King Movement in New Zealand.* 1860. New York: AMS Press, 1979.

Buller, Walter L. "Observations on Some Peculiar Maori Remains, with Remarks on the Ancient Institution of Tapu." *Transactions & Proceedings of the Royal Society of New Zealand* 27 (1894): 148–54.

Burridge, Kenelm. *New Heaven, New Earth.* Oxford: Blackwell, 1969.

Busby, James. "Remarks upon a Pamphlet Entitled 'The Taranaki Question,' by Sir William Martin, D.C.L., Late Chief Justice of New Zealand." Auckland: Philip Kunst, The *Southern Cross* Office, 1860.

Butler, Samuel. *Erewhon.* (first published 1872) New York: Viking Penguin, 1985.

Butterworth, Graham V. "The Politics of Adaptation: The Career of Sir Apirana Ngata, 1874–1928." Master's thesis in history, Victoria University, Wellington, 1969.

Campbell, G. "Rua 'Myth Dream' and History." *New Zealand Listener,* November 24, 1979, pp. 66–71.

Caselberg, John, ed. *Maori Is My Name: Historical Maori Writings in Translation.* Dunedin: John McIndoe Press, 1975.

Cassells Illustrated Family Bible from the Authorised Version, Holy Bible. Vol. 1, from Genesis to I Samuel. London and New York: Cassell, Petter & Galpen, 1860–61.

Castaneda, Carlos. *The Teachings of Don Juan: A Yaqui Way of Knowledge.* New York: Ballantine Books, 1968.

Clark, Paul. *"Hauhau.": The Pai Marire Search for Identity.* Auckland: Auckland University Press, 1975.

Clarke, George, Esq. *Pamphlet in Answer to Mr. James Busby's "On The Taranaki Question and the Treaty of Waitangi."* Auckland: A. F. McDonnell, 1923.

Clarke, George, Jr. *Notes on Early Life in New Zealand.* Hobart: J. Walch & Sons, 1903.

Colenso, William. *The Authentic and Genuine History of the Signing of the Treaty of Waitangi.* Wellington: George Didsbury, Government Printer, 1890.

————. "Contributions Toward a Better Knowledge of the Maori Race." *Transactions and Proceedings of the Royal Society of New Zealand* 12 (1879): 108.

————. *Fiat Justicia.* Napier: Dinwiddie, Morrison, 1871.

————. *Fifty Years Ago in New Zealand.* Honolulu: Hamilton Library, Rare Books Collection, 1888.

Cowan, James. *The Adventures of Kimble Bent.* London: Whitcombe & Tombs, 1911.

————. "The Facts about Te Kooti . . . How Injustice Made a Rebel." *New Zealand Railways Magazine,* December 1, 1938, pp. 17–18.

————. "Maori War-flags." 1892. MS 580. ATL, NLNZ.

————. *The New Zealand Wars.* Vols. 1 and 2. 1922. Wellington: Government Printer, 1983.

————. "Rua the Prophet." *Wide World Magazine* 38 (1916): 229–37.

————. *Sir Donald Maclean.* Wellington: A. H. and A. W. Reed, 1940.

Craig, E. W. G. *Man of the Mist: A Biography of Elsdon Best.* Wellington: A. H. & A. W. Reed, 1964.

da Cunha, Euclides. *Os Sertoes (Rebellion in the Backlands).* Chicago: University of Chicago Press, 1944.

Darwin, Charles. *Voyage of the Beagle.* Edited by Leonard Engel. Garden City, N.Y.: Anchor Books / Doubleday, 1962.

Davidson, Allan K., and Peter J. Lineham, eds. *Transplanted Christianity*. Auckland: College Communications, 1987.

Davies, G. H. "Copy of Te Kooti's Notebook." MS Maori Manuscripts, vol. 3, folder 670. ATL, NLNZ.

Davis, Frank. *Te Kooti Rikirangi Te Turuki*. Hamilton: Waikato Museum Publication, 1971.

Douglas, Bronwyn. "Conflict and Alliance in a Colonial Context." *JPH* 15, pt. 1 (January 1980): 21–51.

Douglas, Edward M. K., ed. "Land and Maori Identity in Contemporary New Zealand." In *Waiora, Wai Maori, Waikino, Waimate, Waitai: Maori Perspectives of Water and the Environment*. Occasional Paper No. 27. Centre for Maori Studies and Research, University of Waikato, Hamilton, November 1984.

Douglas, Mary. *Natural Symbols: Explorations in Cosmology*. New York: Pantheon Books, 1982.

———. *Purity and Danger: An Analysis of the Concepts of Pollution and Taboo*. London: Routledge & Kegan Paul, 1966.

Dudley, Michael Kioni. *Man, Gods and Nature*. Honolulu: Na kane o ka Malo Press, 1990.

Easdale, Nora. *Kaiuri, The Measurer of Land*. Highgate: Price Milburn, 1988.

Eliade, Mircea. "'Cargo Cults' and Cosmic Regeneration." In Thrupp, *Millennial Dreams in Action*.

———. *A History of Religious Ideas*. Vol. 1, *From the Stone Age to the Eleusinian Mysteries*. Chicago: University of Chicago Press, 1978.

———. *Myth and Reality*. New York: Harper & Row, 1966.

———. *The Myth of the Eternal Return, or Cosmos and History*. Princeton: Princeton University Press, 1954.

———. *Patterns in Comparative Religion*. New York: Meridian, 1958.

———. *The Sacred and the Profane: The Nature of Religion*. San Diego: Harcourt Brace Jovanovich, 1959.

———. *Shamanism: Archaic Techniques of Ecstasy*. Princeton: Princeton University Press, 1964.

———, ed. *The Encyclopedia of Religion*. New York: Macmillan, 1987.

Elsmore, Bronwyn. *Like Them That Dream: The Maori and the Old Testament*. Tauranga: Tauranga Moana Press, 1985.

———. *Mana from Heaven: A Century of Maori Prophets in New Zealand*. Tauranga: Moana Press, 1989.

Featon, John. *The Waikato War (Together with Some Account of Te Kooti Rikirangi)*. 1911. Auckland: Brett Printing and Publishing, 1923.

Fenton, F. D. "Minute by Mr. Fenton in Reference to Native Affairs." 13 October 1856. *AJHR* 1860. F-3 Appendix B, No. 1, pp. 133–40.

———. *Observations on the State of the Aboriginal Inhabitants of New Zealand*. Auckland: W. C. Wilson for the New Zealand Government, 1859.

Festinger, Leon, Henry W. Riecken, and Stanley Schachter. *When Prophecy Fails*. New York: Harper & Row, 1964.

Firth, J. C. "Letters." MS Papers 3803, folder 2. ATL, NZNL.

———. Correspondence re January 1870 Meeting with Te Kooti. MS Papers 1491, folder 1. ATL, NLNZ.

Firth, Raymond. "The Analysis of Mana: An Empirical Approach." *JPS* 49, no. 4 (December 1940): 483–510.

Fitzroy, Robert. *Remarks on New Zealand*. 1846. Dunedin: Hocken Library Facsimile No. 10, 1969.

Fowler, Leo. "A New Look at Te Kooti." *Te Ao Hou* 21, no. 6 (December 1957): 18–22.

———. *The Taiaha and the Testament*. Gisborne: Gisborne Herald, n.d.

Fox, William. *The War in New Zealand*. London: Smith, Elder, 1866.

Freire, Paolo. *Pedagogy of the Oppressed*. New York: Penguin, 1972.

Friesen, Steven. "Ephesus, Key to a Vision in Revelation." *BAR* 19, no. 3 (May/June 1993): 24–37.

Gager, John G. *Kingdom and Community: The Social World of Early Christianity*. Englewood Cliffs, N.J.: Prentice-Hall, 1975.

Gascoyne, Major F.J.W. *Soldiering in New Zealand: Being the Reminiscences of a Veteran*. London: Guilford, 1916.

Gibson, Ann Judith. "Religious Organization Among the Maoris After 1860." Ph.D. diss., University of California, Berkeley, 1964. Microfilm Thesis No. 1016. UAL.

Gilbert, Thomas. *New Zealand Settlers and Soldiers or, The War in Taranaki; Being Incidents in the Life of a Settler*. London: A. W. Bennett, 1861.

Gleick, James. *Chaos: Making a New Science*. New York: Penguin Books, 1987.

Godber, A. P. "Papers on Ringatu Religion and the Ratana Church." MS Papers 78, folder 43. ATL, NLNZ.

Gordon, W. F. Collection of Maori Flags. MSS and Archives 89/17. UAL.

Gorst, John Eldon. *The Maori King*. 1864. London: Oxford University Press, 1959.

Grace, Morgan S. *A Sketch of the New Zealand War*. London: Horace Marshall & Son, 1899.

Grace, Thomas S. "Some Questions to the Maori People About the Selling of Land." 1854. In Bagnall, "No Known Copy?"

Greenwood, William. *The Upraised Hand: The Spiritual Significance of the Rise of the Ringatu Faith*. 1942. 3d ed. Wellington: The Polynesian Society Memoir No. 21, 1980.

Grey, Sir George. *Polynesian Mythology and Ancient Traditional History of the Maoris as Told by Their Priests and Chiefs*. (Original edition in Maori, 1854.) Christchurch: Whitcombe & Tombs, 1956.

Gudgeon, Thomas W. *The History and Doings of the Maoris, From the Year 1820 to the Signing of the Treaty of Waitangi in 1840*. Auckland: H. Brett, 1885.

———. *Reminiscences of the War in New Zealand*. London: Sampson Low, Marston, Searle, & Remington, 1879.

Hackshaw, Frederika. "Nineteenth Century Notions of Aboriginal Title and Their Influence on the Interpretation of the Treaty of Waitangi." In Kawharu, *Waitangi*.

Hallie, Phillip. *Lest Innocent Blood Be Shed*. New York: Harper & Row, 1979.

Hanson, F. Allan. "Christian Branches, Maori Roots: The Cult of Rua." *History of Religions* 30 (November 1990): 154–78.

———. "The Making of the Maori: Culture Invention and Its Logic." *American Anthropologist* 91, no. 4 (December 1989): 890–902.

Hanson, F. Allan, and Louise Hanson. *Counterpoint in Maori Culture*. London: Routledge & Kegan Paul, 1983.

Harrop, Angus. *England and the Maori Wars*. 1937. Freeport, N.Y: Books for Libraries Press, 1971.

Hawthorne, James. *A Dark Chapter From New Zealand History*. Napier, Hawke's Bay: James Wood Publisher, 1869.

Head, Lyndsay. "The Gospel of Te Ua Haumene." *JPS* 101, no. 1 (March 1992): 7–44.

———. "Te Ua." In *DNZB*, vol. 1.

Hill, Richard. "Te Kooti's Notebook." *Archifacts*, no. 13 (March 1980): 283–85.

Hobson, Captain William. "Instructions from the Colonial Office to Captain Hobson Regarding Land in New Zealand." 1839. In J. Ward, *Information Relative to New Zealand*.

Horsley, Richard A., and John S. Hanson. *Bandits, Prophets, and Messiahs: Popular Movements at the Time of Jesus*. Minneapolis: Winston Press, 1985.

Ihimaera, Witi. *The Matriarch*. Wellington: Heinemann, 1986.

Irwin, James. *An Introduction to Maori Religion*. Special Studies in Religions, Number 4. Bedford Park, South Australia: Australian Association for the Study of Religions, 1984.

Johansen, J. Prytz. *The Maori and His Religion in Its Non-Ritualistic Aspects*. Copenhagen: Ejnar Munksgaard, 1954.

———. "Studies in Maori Rites and Myths." *Historisk-filosofiske Meddelelser* 37, no. 4 (1958): 66–102.

Kawharu, I. H. *Conflict and Compromise: Essays on the Maori Since Colonisation*. Wellington: A. H. & A. W. Reed, 1975.

———. "Kotahitanga: Visions of Unity." *JPS* 101, no. 3 (September 1992): 221–40.

———. "Urban Immigrants and Tangata Whenua." In Schwimmer, *The Maori People in the Nineteen Sixties*.

———, ed. *Waitangi: Maori & Pakeha Perspectives of the Treaty of Waitangi*. Auckland: Oxford University Press, 1989.

Keesing, Roger. "Creating the Past: Custom and Identity in the Contemporary Pacific." *The Contemporary Pacific* 1, nos. 1 and 2 (Spring and Fall 1989): 19–42.

Kereru, Numia. "Letter to James Carroll, 13 December 1907." MA 23/9. National Archives Head Office, Wellington.

Kerry-Nicholls, J. H. *The King Country, or, Explorations in New Zealand*. London: Sampson Low, Marston, Searle & Rivington, 1884.

King, Michael. *Te Puea: A Biography*. Auckland: Hodder & Stoughton, 1977.

———, ed. *Te Ao Hurihuri, The World Moves On*. Wellington: Hicks Smith, 1975.

———, ed. *Tihe Mauri Ora: Aspects of Maoritanga*. Wellington: Methuen, 1978.

Kirtley, Bacil F. *Motif Index of Traditional Polynesian Narratives*. Honolulu: University of Hawaii Press, 1971.

Lacey, Roderic. "Journeys of Transformation: The Discovery and Disclosure of Cosmic Secrets in Melanesia." In Trompf, *Cargo Cults and Melanesian Movements*.

Lambert, Thomas. *The Story of Old Wairoa and the East Coast District, North Island, New Zealand*. Dunedin: Coulls Somerville Wilkie, 1925.

Lanternari, Vittorio. *The Religions of the Oppressed: A Study of Modern Messianic Cults*. London: MacGibbon & Kee, 1963.

Laughton, Rev. J. G. "Letter to A. P. Godber, 13 November 1939." In Godber, "Papers."

———. "Ringatuism." In Godber, "Papers."

Lawrence, Peter. "The Fugitive Years: Cosmic Space and Time in Melanesian Cargoism and Mediaeval European Chiliasm." In Wallis, *Millennialism and Charisma*.

Leenhardt, Maurice. *Do Kamo: Person and Myth in the Melanesian World*. 1947. Chicago: University of Chicago Press, 1978.

Lennard, L. M. "The Trial of Rua Kenana." *Whakatane Historical Review* 11, no. 2 (June 1963): 55–61.

Lowith, Karl. *Meaning in History*. Chicago: University of Chicago Press, 1949.

Mackay, James. *Historic Poverty Bay and the East Coast, N.I., N.Z.* Gisborne: J. A. Mackay, 1949.

Mair, Captain Gilbert. *The Story of Gate Pa., April 29, 1864*. Supplemented by extracts from Official Records and other matter and illustrations gathered and compiled from various sources by W. H. Gifford, ed., *Bay of Plenty Times*. Tauranga: Bay of Plenty Times, 1937.

————, and G. A. Preece. "Te Kooti Expeditions." In Featon, *The Waikato War*.

Mair, Gilbert. Letterbook MS, 1871–1874. Telegrams. MS 1871–1875. UAL.

Maloney, Gerald, and W. M. Neil. "The Rua Expedition." *Whakatane Historical Review* 11, no. 2 (June 1963): 62–68.

Maning, F. E. *Old New Zealand: A Tale of the Good Old Times*. London: MacMillan, 1900.

Maori Affairs Department. Maori Political and Tribal Matters. MA Series 23. National Archives Head Office, Wellington.

Maori Affairs Department. Maori Political and Tribal Matters: Te Kooti Papers, 1873–91. 23/8a. NANZ, Wellington.

Maori Land Court. Whakatane Minute Book 5, 1897. Microfilm. UAL.

Maori Land Courts Report of the Royal Commission of Inquiry. Wellington: Government Printer, 1980.

Maraenui Maori School. "Te Kooti Returns from the Dead." *Te Ao Hou*, 20:19–20. Quoted in Binney, "Myth and Explanation in the Ringatu Tradition," p. 345.

Marsden, J. B. *Life and Work of Samuel Marsden*. Christchurch: Whitcombe and Tombs Ltd., 1913.

Martin, Sir William. *The Taranaki Question*. 1860. Dunedin: Hocken Library Facsimile No. 3, 1967.

Maungapohatu Notebook. Manuscript of notebook pertaining to Rua Kenana, 1881–1916. UAL.

"Maori Titles to Land and Native Land Courts." *Monthly Review* (1889): 489–92. UWL.

McDonnell, Thomas. *Maori Titles to Land and Native Land Courts*. Monthly Review, 1889.

McGinn, Bernard, trans. *Apocalyptic Spirituality: Treatises and Letters of Lactantius, Adso of Montier-en-Der, Joachim of Fiore, the Spiritual Franciscans, Savonarola*. New York: Paulist Press, 1979.

McKenzie, D. F. *Oral Culture, Literacy, and Print in Early New Zealand: The Treaty of Waitangi*. Wellington: Victoria University Press, 1985.

McNaughton, Trudie. *Countless Signs: The New Zealand Landscape in Literature*. Auckland: Reed Methuen, 1986.

Meade, Herbert. *A Ride Through the Disturbed Districts of New Zealand*. 1870. Christchurch: Capper Press, 1984.

Mikaere, Buddy. *Te Maiharoa and the Promised Land*. Auckland: Heinemann, 1988.

Misur, Gilda. "From Prophet Cult to Established Church: The Case of the Ringatu Movement." In Kawharu, *Conflict and Compromise*.

Mol, Hans. *The Fixed and the Fickle: Religion and Identity in New Zealand*. Waterloo, Ont.: Wilfrid Laurier University Press, 1982.

Morris, Maria. "Reminiscences." MS Papers 2296. ATL, NLNZ.

Neal, Karen S. "Maori Participation in the East Coast Wars, 1865–72." Master's thesis, University of Auckland, 1976.

Neusner, Jacob. *From Politics to Piety: The Emergence of Pharisaic Judaism*. Englewood Cliffs, N.J.: Prentice Hall, 1973.

New Zealand General Assembly. *Paper Relative to Surrender of Rebel Natives and Expeditions In Search of Te Kooti: Presented to both houses of the General Assembly by command of His Excellency*. Wellington: Government Printing Office, 1871.

New Zealand Parliamentary Debates. Vol. 3 (1868); vol. 5 (1869); vol. 104 (1907). ATL. NLNZ.

New Zealand Planning Council. *Pakeha Perspectives on the Treaty. Proceedings from a Planning Council Seminar.* Wellington, 1988.

New Zealand Statutes. Native Lands Act No. 42, 1862. "An Act for the Suppression of Rebellion" No. 7, September 15, 1863. New Zealand Settlements Act No. 8, December 3, 1863. Urewera District Native Reserve Act, December 1896. East Coast Native Trust Lands Act, 1902. Tohunga Suppression Act, No. 13, 1907. Auckland: New Zealand Government Printers.

Nihoniho, Tuta. *A Narrative of the Fighting on the East Coast, 1865–71.* Wellington: John Mackay, Government Printer, 1913.

O'Regan, Tipene. "Old Myths and New Politics." *NZJH* 26, no. 1 (April 1992): 5–27.

Oliver, W. H., and Claudia Orange, eds. *Dictionary of New Zealand Biography.* Vol. 1. Wellington: Allen & Unwin and Dept. of Internal Affairs, 1990.

Oliver, W. H., and B. R. Williams, eds. *The Oxford History of New Zealand.* Wellington: The Clarendon Press, 1981.

Orange, Claudia. *The Treaty of Waitangi.* Wellington: Allen & Unwin / Port Nicholson Press, 1987.

Otto, Rudolf. *The Idea of the Holy.* London: Oxford University Press, 1923.

Owens, J.M.R. "Christianity and the Maoris to 1840." *NZJH* 2, no. 1 (April 1968): 18–40.

Park, Geoff. "Understanding and Conserving the Natural Landscape." In Phillips, *Te Whenua, Te Iwi.*

Parsonson, Ann S. "The Pursuit of Mana." In Oliver and Williams, *Oxford History of New Zealand.*

Perdue, Theda. "Native American Revitalization Movements in the Early Nineteenth Century." In Phillips, *New Worlds?* pp. 59–76.

Pettazzoni, Raffaele. *Essays on the History of Religions.* Leiden: E. J. Brill, 1954.

Phillips, Jock, ed. *New Worlds? The Comparative History of New Zealand and the U.S.* Wellington: Wright & Carman, Platform Publications, 1989.

———, ed. *Te Whenua, Te Iwi: The Land and the People.* Wellington: Allen & Unwin / Port Nicholson Press, 1987.

Polynesian Society Papers. "Copy of a Portion of a Book Belonging to Te Kooti Found at Te Karetu, December, 1868." Maori manuscript by Arthur S. Atkinson Manuscript papers. February 21, 1869. MS Papers 1187, folder 12. ATL, NLNZ.

Porter, Francis, ed. *The Turanga Journals, 1840–1850: Letters and Journals of William and Jane Williams, Missionaries to Poverty Bay.* Wellington: Victoria University Press, 1974.

Rakena, Ruawai D. *The Maori Response to the Gospel: A Study of Maori-Pakeha Relations in the Methodist Maori Mission from Its Beginnings to the Present Day.* Auckland: The Institute Press, 1971.

Rangihau, John. "Being Maori." In King, *Te Ao Hurihuri, the World Moves On.*

———. "I Am a Product of All That My People Transmit to Me." *New Zealand Listener,* July 20, 1974.

Riches, John. *Jesus and the Transformation of Judaism.* New York: The Seabury Press, 1982.

Rickard, L. S. *Tamihana the Kingmaker.* Wellington: A.H. & A.W. Reed, 1963.

"A Ringatu Meeting at Ruatoki." *Te Ao Hou,* no. 42 (March 1963): 38–41.

Rosenfeld, Jean E. "Pai Marire: Peace and Violence in a New Zealand Millenarian Tradition." In Barkun, *Millennialism and Violence,* pp. 83–103.

Rusden, G. W. *History of New Zealand.* 3 vols. Melbourne: Melville, Mullen & Slade, 1895.

Rutherford, James. *Hone Heke's Rebellion, 1844–1846; An Episode in the Establishment of British Rule in New Zealand.* Bayley Memorial Lecture, 1946. Auckland, 1947.

Salmond, Anne. *Hui, a Study of Maori Ceremonial Gatherings.* Wellington: Reed, 1975.

———. "'Te Ao Tawhito': A Semantic Approach to the Traditional Maori Cosmos." *JPS* 87, no. 1 (March 1978): 5–28.

Salmond, Anne. *See* Eruera Stirling.

Sanders, James A. *Torah and Canon.* Philadelphia: Fortress Press, 1972.

Scholefield, Guy H., ed. *The Richmond-Atkinson Papers.* Wellington: R. E. Owen, Government Printer, 1960.

Schwimmer, Eric. *The World of the Maori.* Wellington: A. H. & A. W. Reed, 1966.

———, ed. *The Maori People in the Nineteen Sixties: A Symposium.* Auckland: Blackwood and Janet Paul, 1969.

Sewell, Henry. *The New Zealand Native Rebellion: Letter to Lord Lyttelton.* Auckland, 1864. Reprint. Dunedin. Hocken Library Facsimile No. 14, 1974.

Shirres, Michael P.W. "An Introduction to Karakia." Ph.D. diss. in anthropology, University of Auckland, 1987. UAL.

Shkilnyk, Anastasia M. *A Poison Stronger Than Love: The Destruction of an Ojibwa Community.* New Haven: Yale University Press, 1985.

Shortland, Edward. *Maori Religion and Mythology.* London: Longmans, Green, 1882.

Simmons, D. R. *The Great New Zealand Myth.* Wellington: A. H. & A. W. Reed, 1976.

———. *Iconography of New Zealand Maori Religion.* Leiden: E. J. Brill, 1986.

Simpson, Tony. *Te Riri Pakeha. The White Man's Anger.* Waiura, Martinborough: Alister Taylor, 1979.

Sinclair, Karen. *Maramatanga: Ideology and Social Process Among the Maori of New Zealand.* Ann Arbor: University Microfilms International, 1980.

Sinclair, Keith. *A Destiny Apart: New Zealand's Search for National Identity.* Wellington: Allen & Unwin / Port Nicholson Press, 1986.

———. *A History of New Zealand.* Auckland: Penguin Books, 1988.

———. *The Origins of the Maori Wars.* Wellington: New Zealand University Press, 1957.

Smith, Norman. *Native Custom and Law Affecting Native Land.* Wellington. Maori Purposes Fund Board, 1942.

Smith, S. Percy. *The Lore of the Whare-wananga.* 1913. New York: AMS Press, 1978.

Sorrenson, M. P. K. "Land Purchase Methods and their Effect on Maori Population, 1865–1901." *JPS* 65, no. 3 (1956): 183–99.

———. *Maori Origins and Migrations: The Genesis of Some Pakeha Myths and Legends.* Auckland: Oxford University Press, 1979.

Spencer, Michael, Alan Ward, and John Connell, eds. *New Caledonia: Essays in Nationalism and Dependency.* New York: University of Queensland Press, 1988.

Sperber, Dan. *Rethinking Symbolism.* Cambridge: Cambridge University Press, 1974.

Staal, Frits. "The Meaninglessness of Ritual." *Numen* 26 (1979): 2–22.

Stirling, Eruera (as told to Anne Salmond). *Eruera: The Teachings of a Maori Elder.* Auckland: Oxford University Press, 1980.

Stokes, Evelyn. *Mokau: Maori Cultural and Historical Perspectives.* Hamilton: University of Waikato, 1988.

———. *Pai Marire and the Niu at Kuranui.* Occasional Paper No. 6, Centre for Maori Studies and Research. Hamilton: University of Waikato, 1980.

———. *Te Raupatu o Tauranga: Land Transactions and Race Relations at Tauranga, 1864–1866.* Hamilton: University of Waikato, 1978.

Stokes, Evelyn, J. Wharehuia Milroy, and Hirini Melbourne. *Te Urewera Nga Iwi Te*

Whenua Te Ngahere: People, Land and Forests of Te Urewera. Hamilton: University of Waikato, 1986.

Sundkler, Bengt. *Zulu Zion and Some Swazi Zionists.* London: Oxford University Press, 1976.

Swan, James A., ed. *The Power of Place.* Wheaton, Ill.: Quest Books, 1991.

Tane-nui-a-rangi, the Symbolism of the Meeting House. Auckland: University of Auckland, 1988.

Tarei, Wi. "A Church Called Ringatu." In King, *Tihe Maori Ora.*

Taylor, Richard. *The Past and Present of New Zealand; With its Prospects for the Future.* London. Wm. Macintosh, 1868.

———. *Te Ika a Maui, or New Zealand and Its Inhabitants.* London: Wertheim & MacIntosh, 1855.

Te Kooti Rikirangi. Affidavit, Justice Dept., September 8, 1889. J 1 90/407. NANZ.

Te Kooti Te Turuki, Te Kooti Rikirangi. Notebook. English translation (n.d.). (Special collection) ATL, NLNZ .

Te Kooti. Copy of Te Kooti's Notebook. *See* G. H. Davies.

Te Kooti. Letter to Native Minister Ballance, 30 December, 1886. MA 23/8a. NANZ.

Te Ua Haumene. Te Ua Rongopai (Gospel According to Te Ua). January 1863. Grey Collection. Maori MSS: GNZ, MMSS1. Auckland Public Library.

Thrupp, Sylvia, ed. *Millennial Dreams in Action.* New York: Schocken Books, 1970.

Tillich, Paul. *Dynamics of Faith.* New York: Harper & Row, 1957.

Trask, Haunani-Kay. "Natives and Anthropologists: The Colonial Struggle." *The Contemporary Pacific* 3, no. 1 (Spring 1991): 157–67.

Tregear, Edward. *The Maori Race.* Wanganui: A. D. Wallis, 1926.

Trompf, G. W., ed. *Cargo Cults and Millenarian Movements: Transoceanic Comparisons of New Religious Movements.* Berlin and New York: Mouton de Gruyter, 1990.

Turner, Harold W. *From Temple to Meeting House: The Phenomenology and Theology of Places of Worship.* New York: Mouton, 1979.

Van der Leeuw, Gerardus. *Religion in Essence and Manifestation.* Princeton: Princeton University Press, 1986.

Vayda, Andrew Peter. *Maori Warfare.* Wellington: Polynesian Society Maori Monographs, No. 2, 1970.

Vermes, Geza. *Jesus the Jew: A Historian's Reading of the Gospels.* Philadelphia: Fortress Press, 1973.

Voyce, Malcolm. "Maori Healers in New Zealand: The Tohunga Suppression Act of 1907." *Oceania* 60, no. 2 (December 1980): 99–123.

Wach, Joachim. *Sociology of Religion.* Chicago: University of Chicago Press, 1944.

———. *Types of Religious Experience: Christian and Non-Christian.* Chicago: University of Chicago Press, 1951.

Walker, Ranginui. "The Genesis of Maori Activism." *JPS* 93, no. 3 (September 1984): 267.

———. *Ka Whawhai Tonu Matou: Struggle Without End.* Auckland: Penguin Books, 1990.

———. "Maori Myth, Traditions and Philosophic Beliefs." In Philips, *Te Whenua, Te Iwi.*

———. "Marae: A Place to Stand." In King, *Te Ao Hurihuri.*

———. *Nga Tau Tohetohe: Years of Anger.* Auckland: Penguin Books, 1987.

———. "The Politics of Voluntary Association." In Kawharu, *Conflict and Compromise.*

———. "The Relevance of Maori Myth and Tradition." In King, *Tihe Mauri Ora.*

———. "The Treaty of Waitangi: As the Focus of Maori Protest," in I. H. Kawharu, *Waitangi: Maori & Pakeha Perspectives of the Treaty of Waitangi.*

Wallace, A.F.C. "Revitalization Movements." *American Anthropologist* 58, no. 2 (April 1956): 264–81.

Wallis, Roy, ed. *Millennialism and Charisma.* Belfast: The Queen's University, 1982.

Ward, Alan. "Alienation Rights in Traditional Maori Society: A Comment." *JPS* 95, no. 2 (June 1986): 259–65.

———. "Documenting Maori History: The Arrest of Te Kooti, 1889." *NZJH* 14, no. 1 (April 1980): 25–44.

———. "Origins of the Anglo-Maori Wars: A Reconsideration." *NZJH* 1, no. 2 (October 1967): 148–70.

———. *A Show of Justice: Racial "Amalgamation" in Nineteenth-Century New Zealand.* Canberra: Australian National University Press, 1974.

———. "The Treaty and the Purchase of Maori Land." *NZJH* 21 (1987): 169–74.

———. Review of Miles Fairburn's *The Ideal Society and Its Enemies. NZJH* 24, no. 1 (April 1990): 74–76.

Ward, John P. *Wanderings with the Maori Prophets, Te Whiti and Tohu.* 1883. Special Collections. UCLA.

Ward, John, Esq. *Information Relative to New Zealand (compiled for the use of colonists).* 1840. Christchurch: Capper Press, 1975.

Wards, Ian. *The Shadow of the Land: A Study of British Policy and Racial Conflict in New Zealand, 1832–1852.* Wellington: Historical Publications Branch, Dept. of Internal Affairs, 1968.

Webster, Peter. *Rua and the Maori Millennium.* Wellington: Victoria University Press, 1979.

Williams Family Papers. MS Papers 69. Letters 74a. ATL, NLNZ.

Williams, Herbert W. *Dictionary of the Maori Language.* Wellington: Government Printing Office, 1985.

Williams, John. *Politics of the New Zealand Maori: Protest and Cooperation, 1891–1909.* Auckland: Oxford University Press, 1969.

Williams, William. *Christianity Among the New Zealanders.* Edinburgh: The Banner of Truth Trust, 1989.

———. *See* Porter, ed., *The Turanga Journals.*

Williams, William L. *East Coast Historical Records.* (N.d.) Reprinted from the Poverty Bay Herald. Gisborne, New Zealand.

———. Journal, vol. 1, July 12, 1865, pp. 115–17. MS WIL 2468. ATL, NLNZ.

———. Journal, vol. 3, January 22, 1869, pp. 306–7. MS Papers 1865–75. ATL, NLNZ.

———. "Notes on the Ringa-Tū Religion." MS Papers 134U. ATL, NLNZ. Compiled from his journal, 1865–1893.

Wilson, Ormond. *War in the Tussock: Te Kooti and the Battle at Te Porere.* Wellington: National Historic Places Trust, 1961.

Winiata, Maharaia. *The Changing Role of the Leader in Maori Society.* Auckland: Blackwood and Janet Paul, 1967.

Winks, Robin. "The Doctrine of Hauhauism." *JPS* 62 (1953): 199–236.

———. Typescript of article on Ringatu, annotated by Ringatu elders. MSS A-206. UAL.

Worsley, Peter. *The Trumpet Shall Sound: A Study of "Cargo Cults" in Melanesia.* New York: Schocken Books, 1968.

Yarwood, A. T. *Samuel Marsden.* Carlton, Victoria: Melbourne University Press, 1977.

Yate, William. *An Account of New Zealand and of the Formation and Progress of the Church Missionary Society's Mission.* London: R. B. Seeley & W. Burnside, 1835.

INDEX